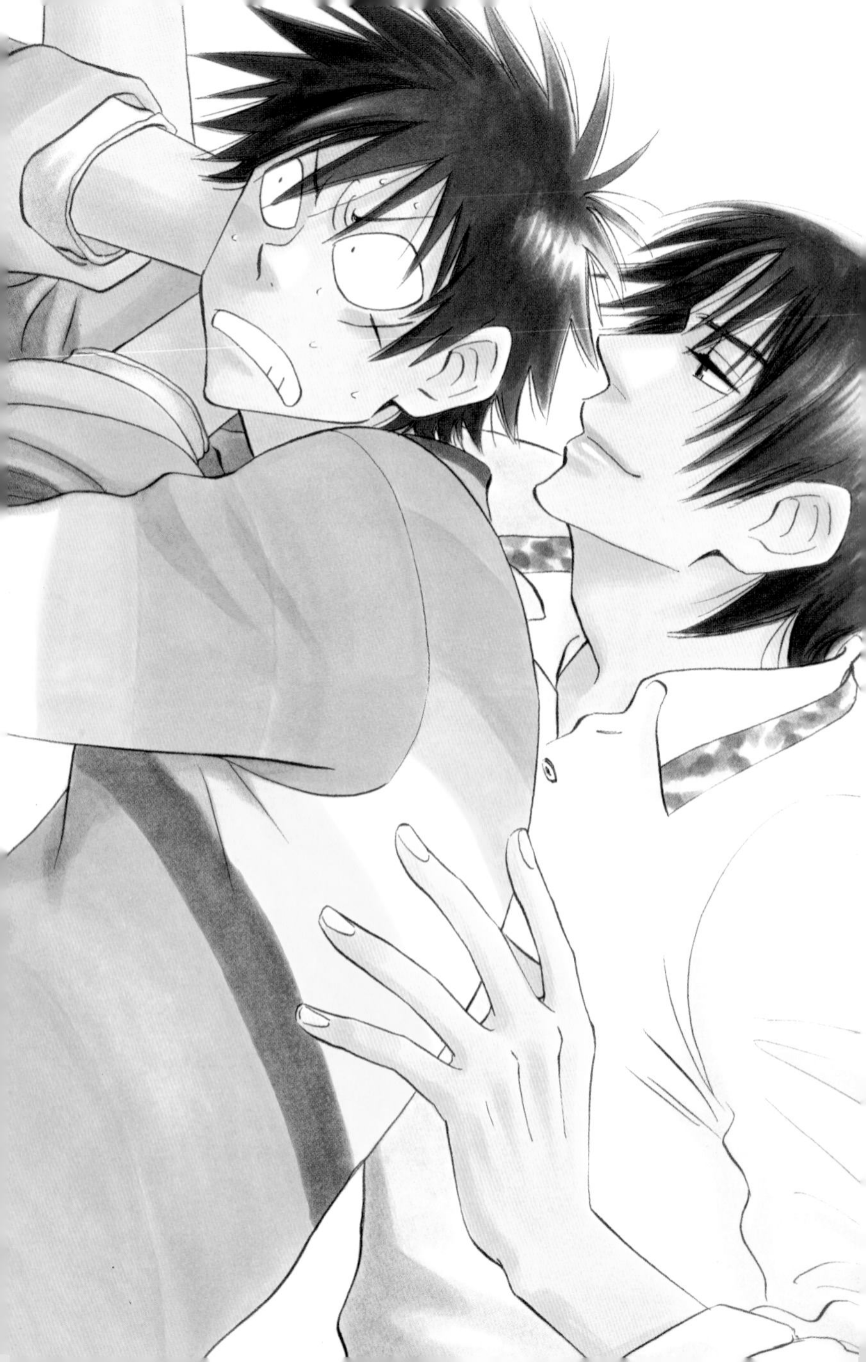

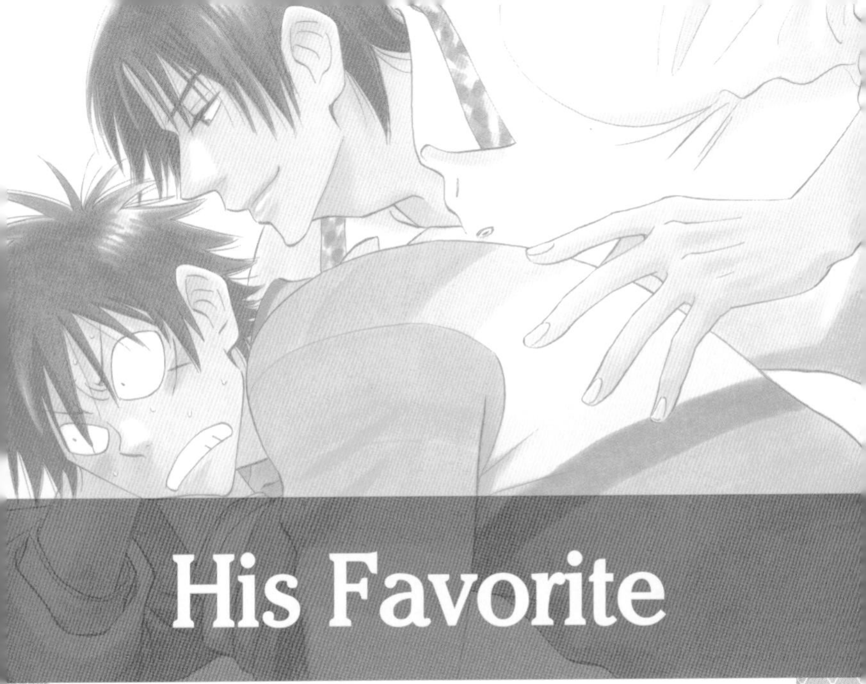

His Favorite

Story and Art by Suzuki Tanaka volume 7

CONTENTS

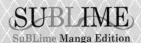

SUBLIME

SuBLime Manga Edition

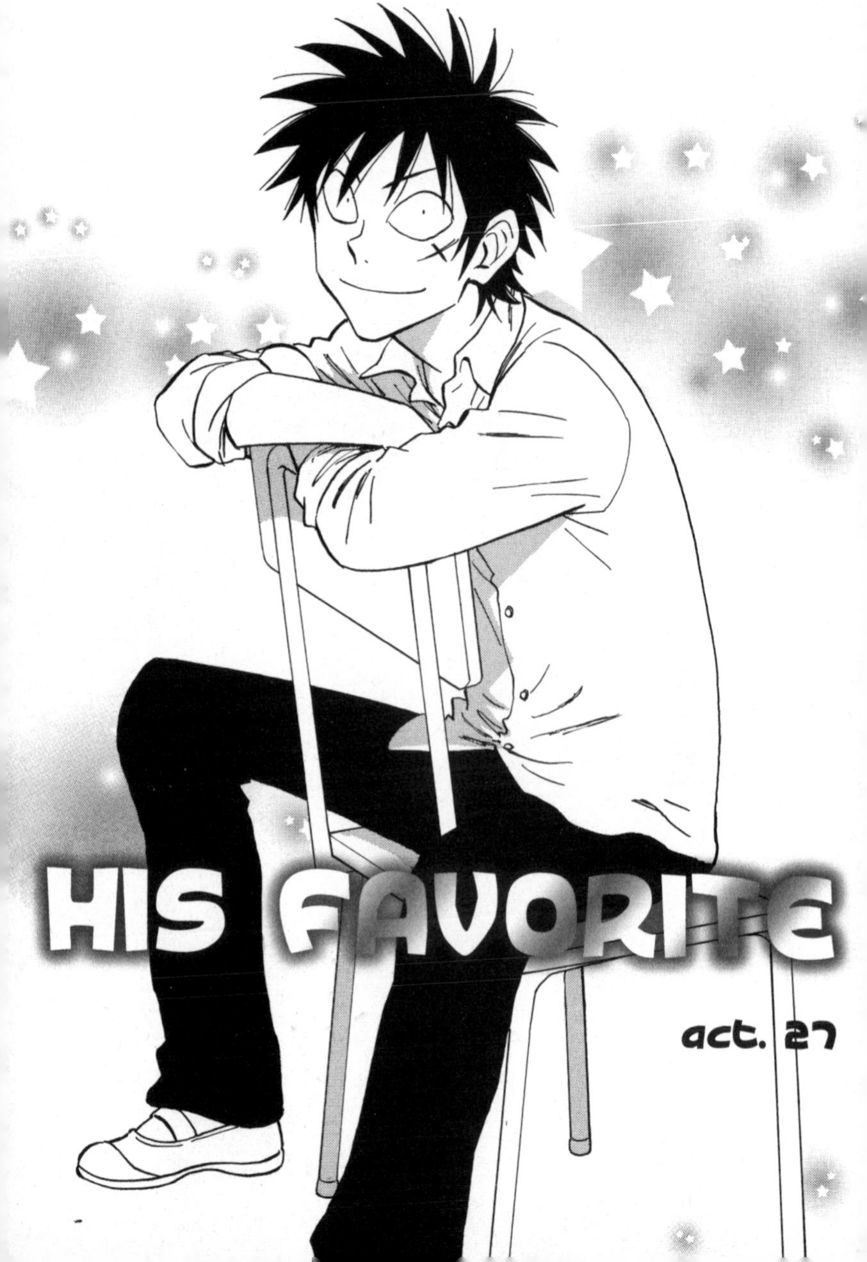
HIS FAVORITE
act. 27

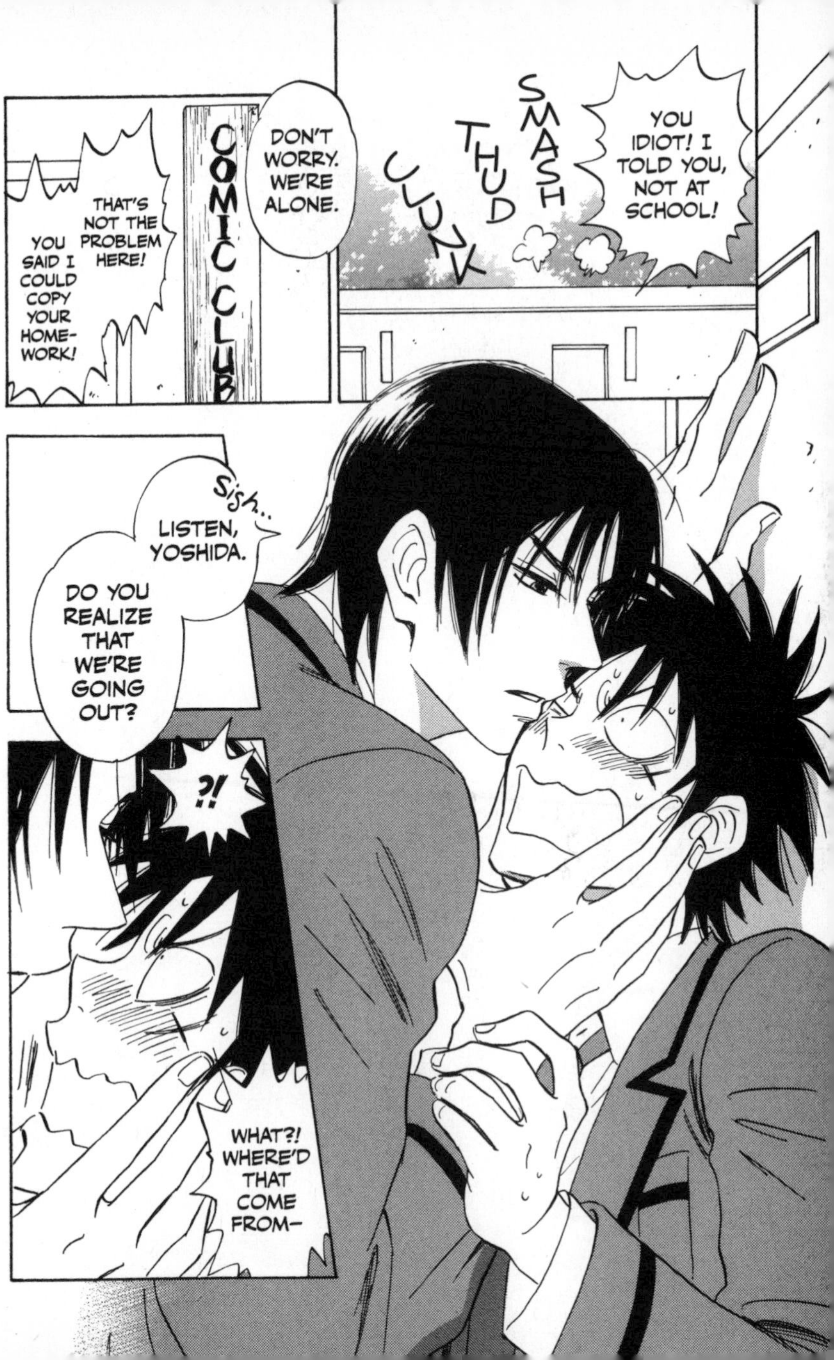
YOU IDIOT! I TOLD YOU, NOT AT SCHOOL!
SMASH
THUD
CLUNK
COMIC CLUB
DON'T WORRY. WE'RE ALONE.
THAT'S NOT THE PROBLEM HERE!
YOU SAID I COULD COPY YOUR HOME-WORK!
Sish...
LISTEN, YOSHIDA.
DO YOU REALIZE THAT WE'RE GOING OUT?
?!
WHAT?! WHERE'D THAT COME FROM-

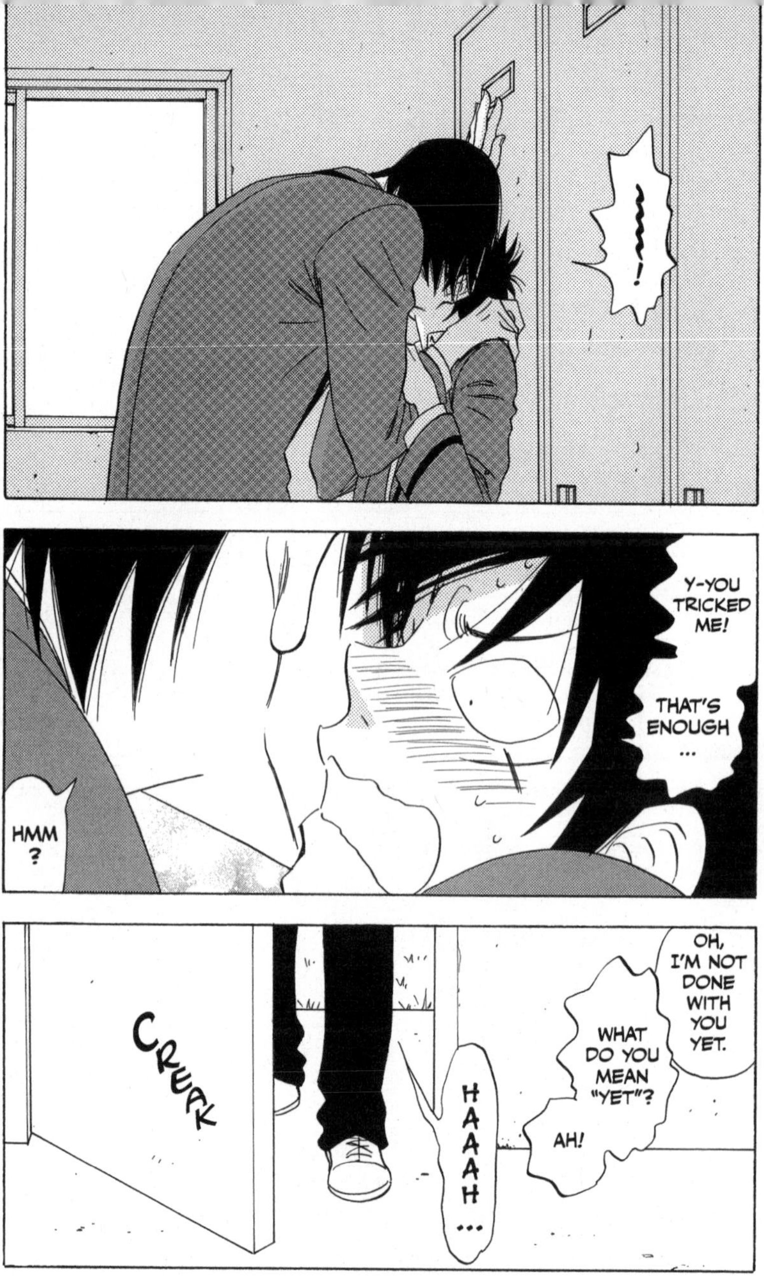

Y-YOU TRICKED ME!
THAT'S ENOUGH ...
HMM?
OH, I'M NOT DONE WITH YOU YET.
WHAT DO YOU MEAN "YET"?
AH!
HAAAAH ...
CREAK

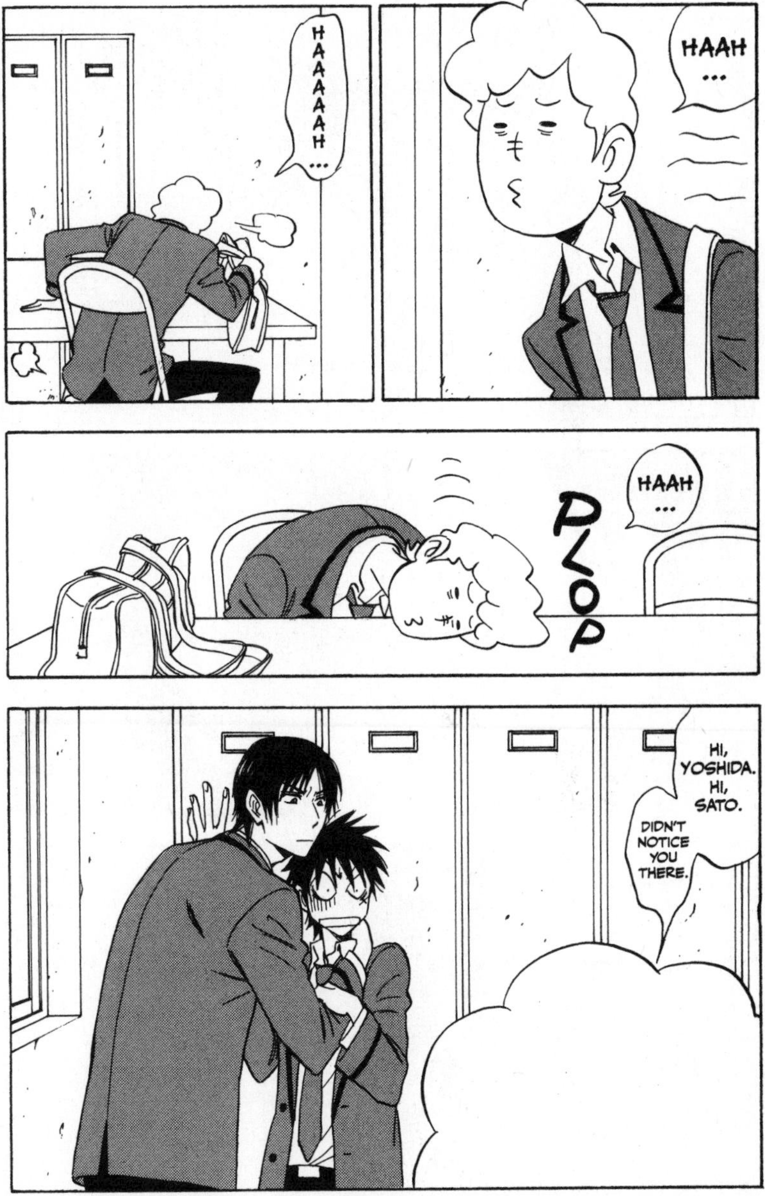
HAAH ...
HAAAAAAH ...
HAAH ...
PLOP
HI, YOSHIDA. HI, SATO.
DIDN'T NOTICE YOU THERE.

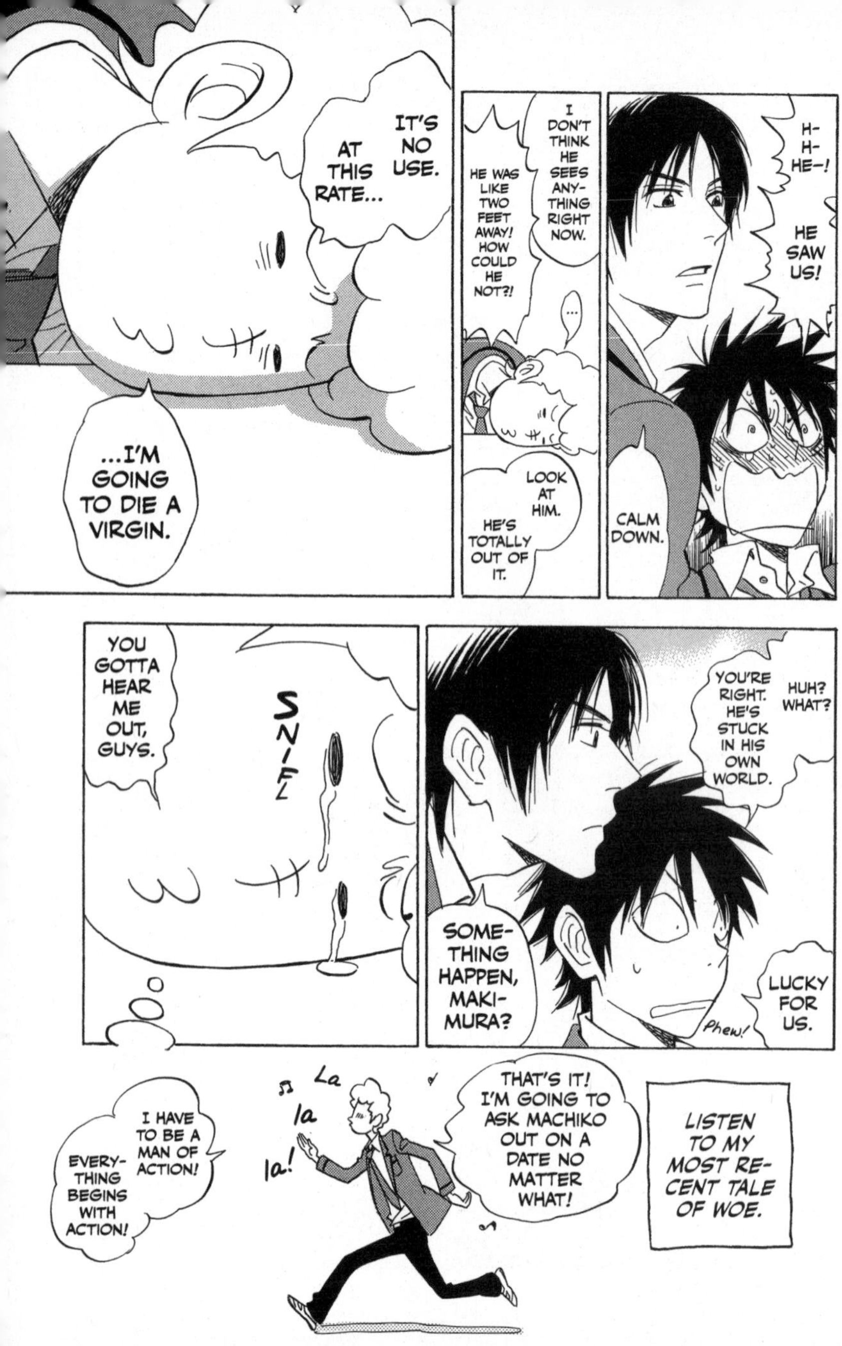
H-H-HE—!
HE SAW US!
CALM DOWN.
I DON'T THINK HE SEES ANYTHING RIGHT NOW.
HE WAS LIKE TWO FEET AWAY! HOW COULD HE NOT?!
...
LOOK AT HIM.
HE'S TOTALLY OUT OF IT.
IT'S NO USE.
AT THIS RATE...
...I'M GOING TO DIE A VIRGIN.
HUH? WHAT?
YOU'RE RIGHT. HE'S STUCK IN HIS OWN WORLD.
LUCKY FOR US.
Phew!
SOME-THING HAPPEN, MAKI-MURA?
YOU GOTTA HEAR ME OUT, GUYS.
SNIFL
LISTEN TO MY MOST RE-CENT TALE OF WOE.
THAT'S IT! I'M GOING TO ASK MACHIKO OUT ON A DATE NO MATTER WHAT!
La la la!
I HAVE TO BE A MAN OF ACTION!
EVERY-THING BEGINS WITH ACTION!

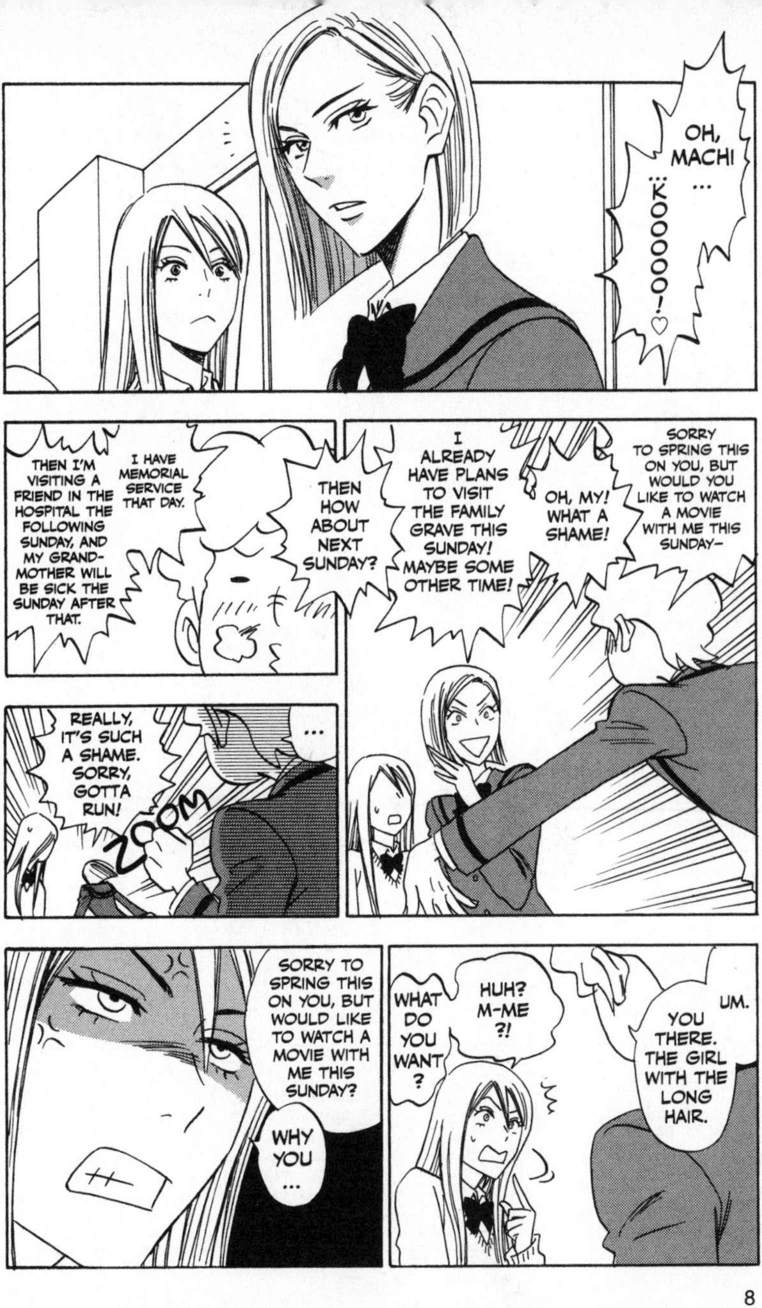
OH, MACHI ... ...KOOOOO!♡
SORRY TO SPRING THIS ON YOU, BUT WOULD YOU LIKE TO WATCH A MOVIE WITH ME THIS SUNDAY–
OH, MY! WHAT A SHAME!
I ALREADY HAVE PLANS TO VISIT THE FAMILY GRAVE THIS SUNDAY! MAYBE SOME OTHER TIME!
THEN HOW ABOUT NEXT SUNDAY?
I HAVE MEMORIAL SERVICE THAT DAY.
THEN I'M VISITING A FRIEND IN THE HOSPITAL THE FOLLOWING SUNDAY, AND MY GRANDMOTHER WILL BE SICK THE SUNDAY AFTER THAT.
...
REALLY, IT'S SUCH A SHAME. SORRY, GOTTA RUN!
ZOOM
UM.
YOU THERE. THE GIRL WITH THE LONG HAIR.
HUH? M-ME ?!
WHAT DO YOU WANT ?
SORRY TO SPRING THIS ON YOU, BUT WOULD LIKE TO WATCH A MOVIE WITH ME THIS SUNDAY?
WHY YOU ...

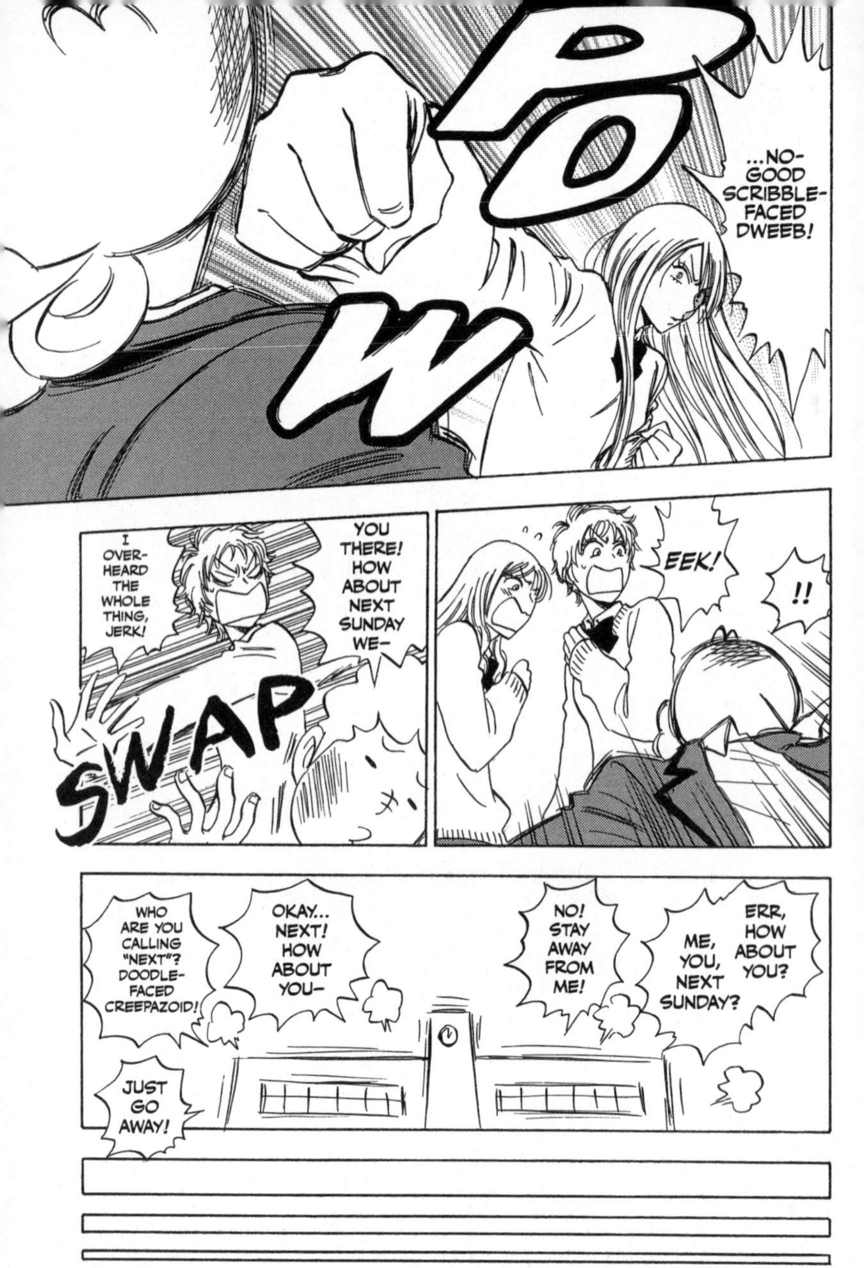
POW
...NO-GOOD SCRIBBLE-FACED DWEEB!
EEK!
!!
YOU THERE! HOW ABOUT NEXT SUNDAY WE-
I OVERHEARD THE WHOLE THING, JERK!
SWAP
ERR, HOW ABOUT YOU?
ME, YOU, NEXT SUNDAY?
NO! STAY AWAY FROM ME!
OKAY... NEXT! HOW ABOUT YOU-
WHO ARE YOU CALLING "NEXT"? DOODLE-FACED CREEPAZOID!
JUST GO AWAY!

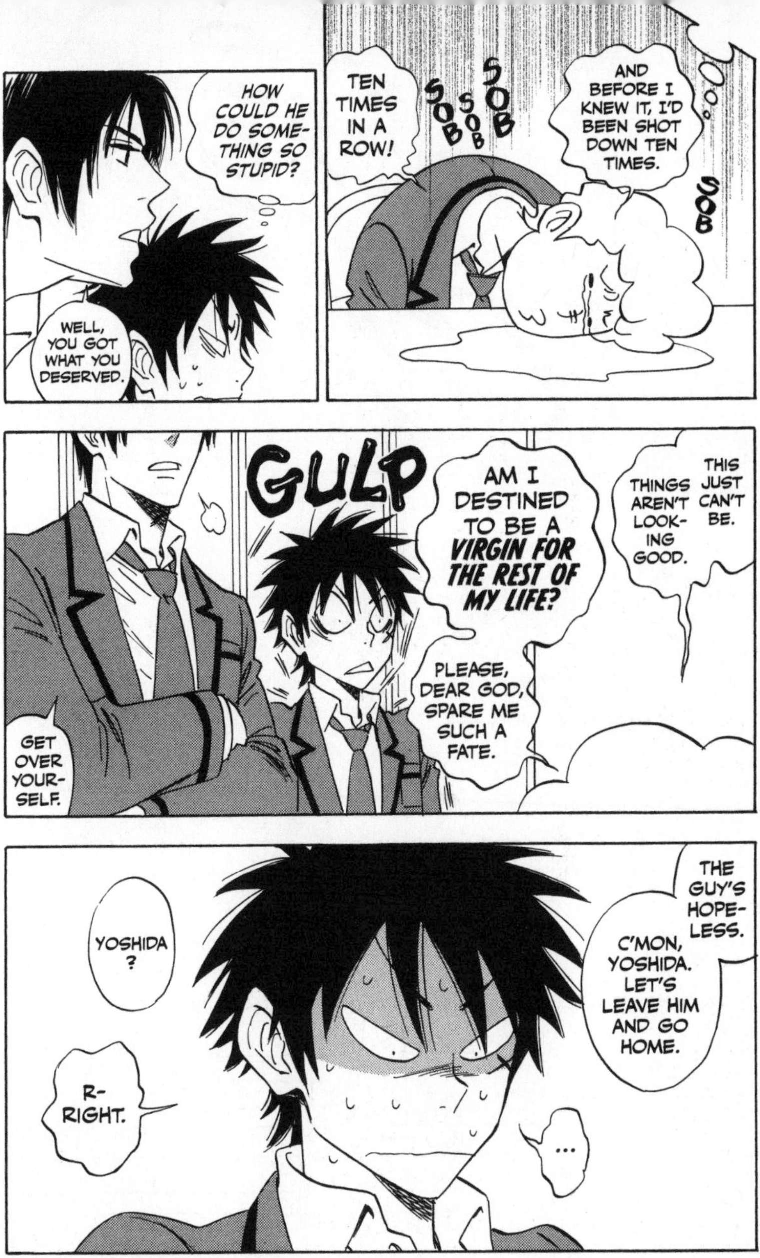
AND BEFORE I KNEW IT, I'D BEEN SHOT DOWN TEN TIMES.
SOB
SOB SOB SOB
TEN TIMES IN A ROW!
HOW COULD HE DO SOMETHING SO STUPID?
WELL, YOU GOT WHAT YOU DESERVED.
THIS JUST CAN'T BE.
THINGS AREN'T LOOKING GOOD.
AM I DESTINED TO BE A *VIRGIN FOR THE REST OF MY LIFE?*
GULP
PLEASE, DEAR GOD, SPARE ME SUCH A FATE.
GET OVER YOURSELF.
THE GUY'S HOPELESS.
C'MON, YOSHIDA. LET'S LEAVE HIM AND GO HOME.
...
YOSHIDA?
R-RIGHT.

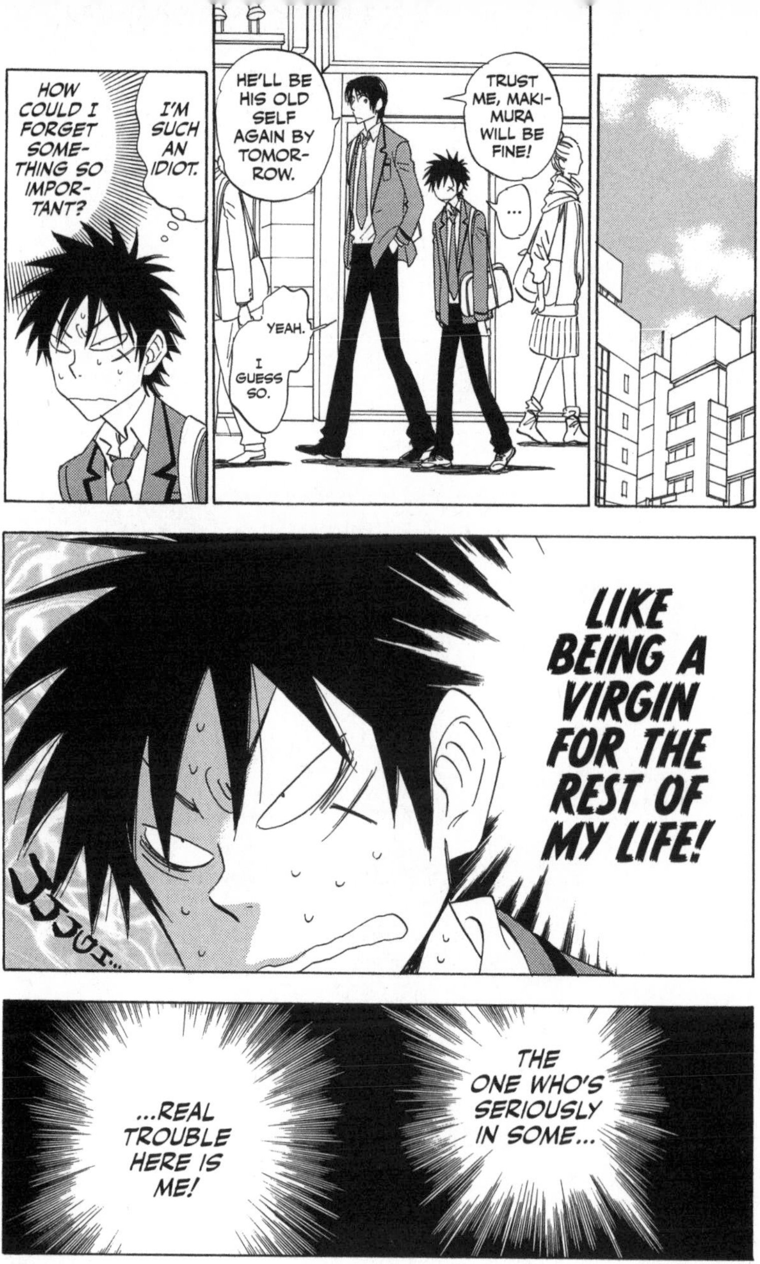
TRUST ME, MAKIMURA WILL BE FINE!
...
HE'LL BE HIS OLD SELF AGAIN BY TOMORROW.
YEAH. I GUESS SO.
I'M SUCH AN IDIOT.
HOW COULD I FORGET SOMETHING SO IMPORTANT?
LIKE BEING A VIRGIN FOR THE REST OF MY LIFE!
THE ONE WHO'S SERIOUSLY IN SOME...
...REAL TROUBLE HERE IS ME!

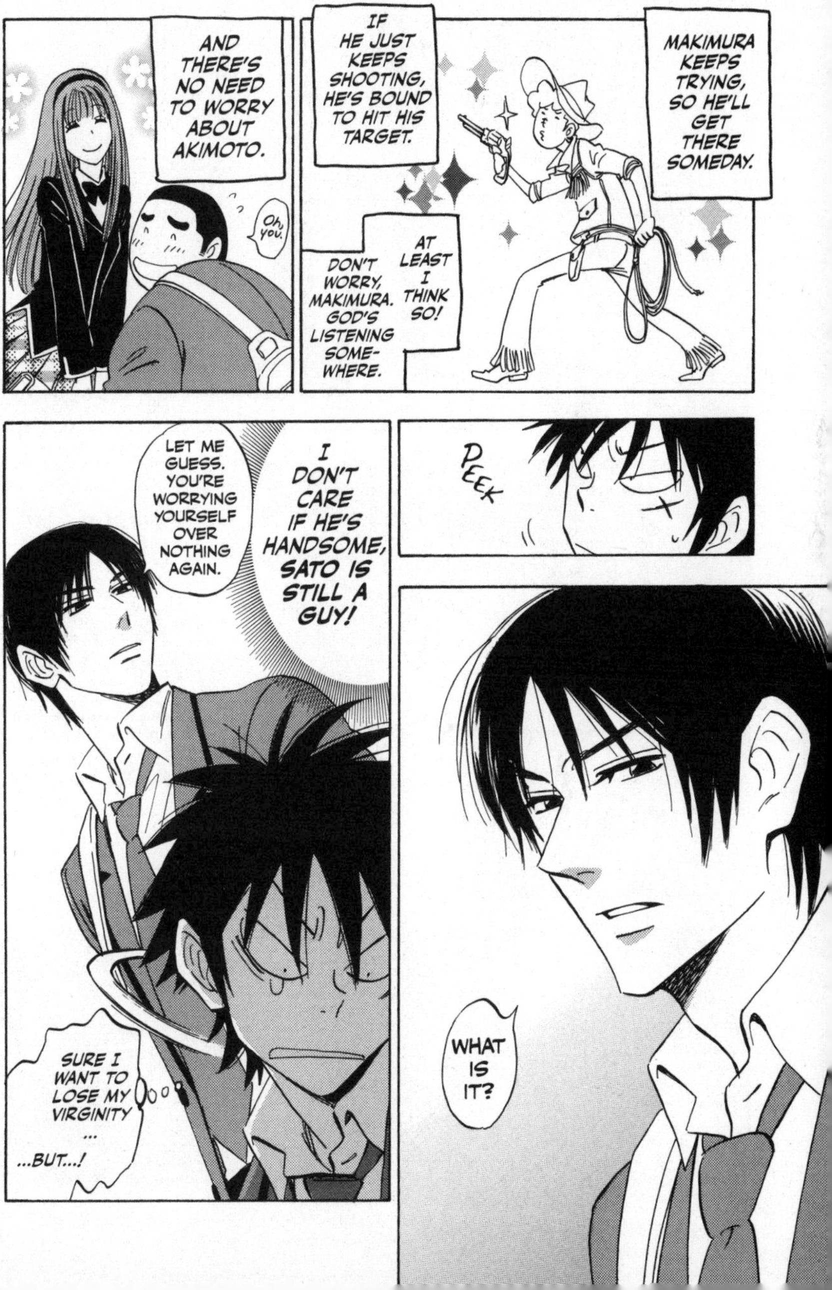
MAKIMURA KEEPS TRYING, SO HE'LL GET THERE SOMEDAY.
IF HE JUST KEEPS SHOOTING, HE'S BOUND TO HIT HIS TARGET.
AT LEAST I THINK SO!
DON'T WORRY, MAKIMURA. GOD'S LISTENING SOME-WHERE.
AND THERE'S NO NEED TO WORRY ABOUT AKIMOTO.
Oh, you.
PEEK
WHAT IS IT?
I DON'T CARE IF HE'S HANDSOME, SATO IS STILL A GUY!
LET ME GUESS. YOU'RE WORRYING YOURSELF OVER NOTHING AGAIN.
SURE I WANT TO LOSE MY VIRGINITY ...
...BUT...!

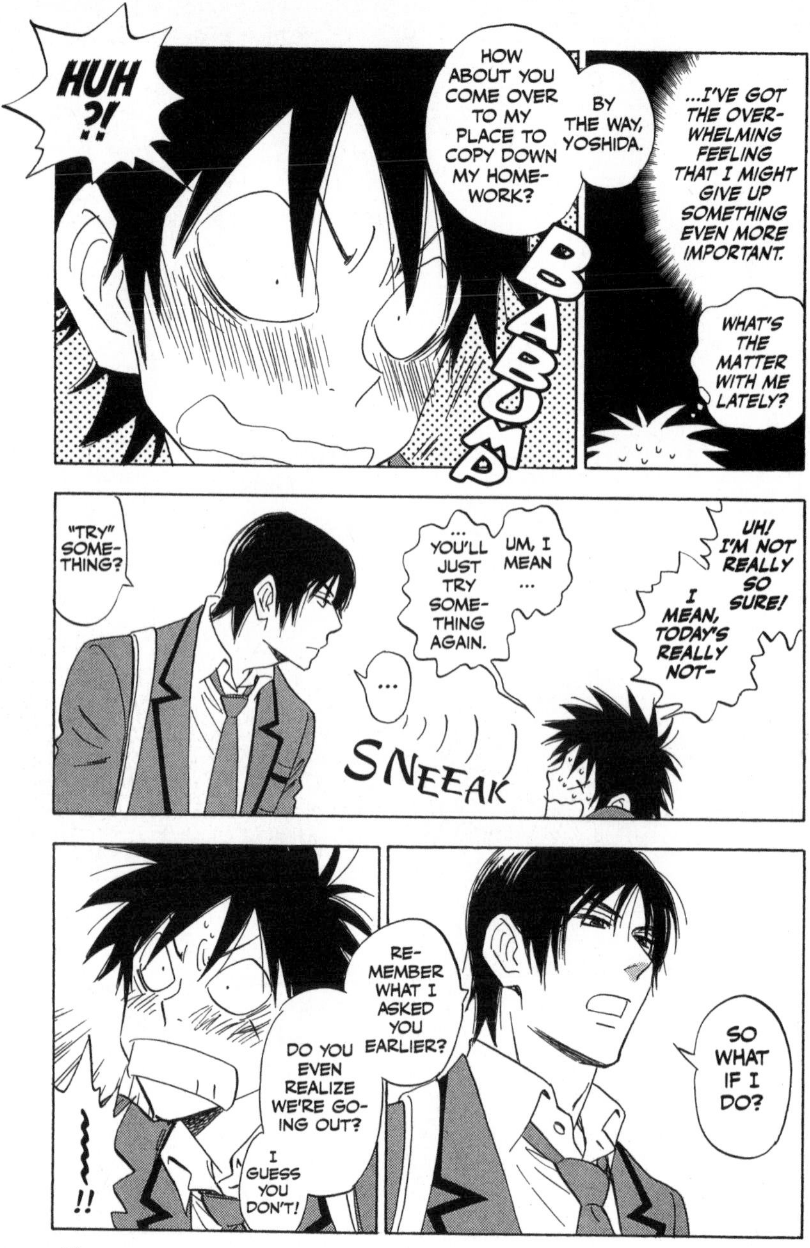
...I'VE GOT THE OVER-WHELMING FEELING THAT I MIGHT GIVE UP SOMETHING EVEN MORE IMPORTANT.
WHAT'S THE MATTER WITH ME LATELY?
BY THE WAY, YOSHIDA.
HOW ABOUT YOU COME OVER TO MY PLACE TO COPY DOWN MY HOME-WORK?
BABUMP
HUH ?!
UH! I'M NOT REALLY SO SURE!
I MEAN, TODAY'S REALLY NOT-
SNEEAK
...
UM, I MEAN ...
... YOU'LL JUST TRY SOME-THING AGAIN.
"TRY" SOME-THING?
SO WHAT IF I DO?
RE-MEMBER WHAT I ASKED YOU EARLIER?
DO YOU EVEN REALIZE WE'RE GO-ING OUT?
I GUESS YOU DON'T!
~~~!!
~~~

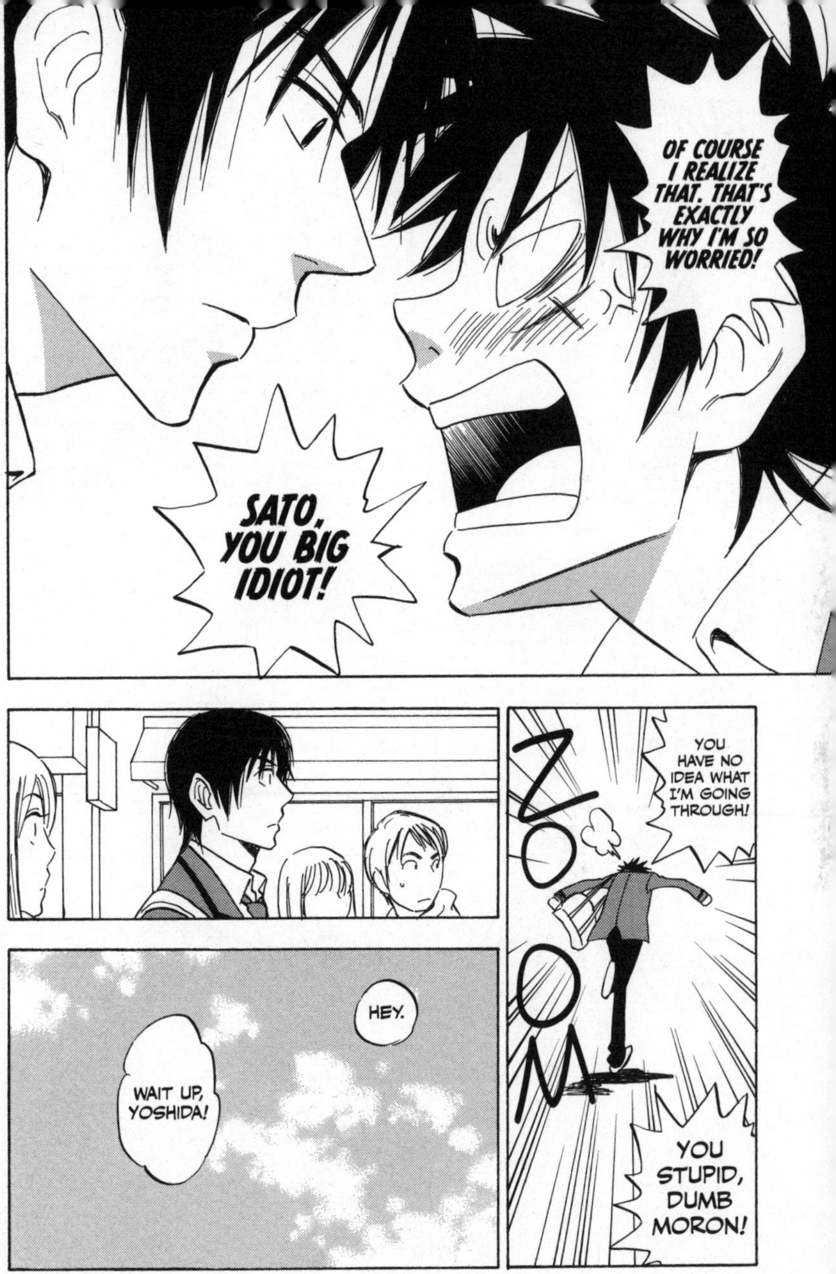
OF COURSE I REALIZE THAT. THAT'S EXACTLY WHY I'M SO WORRIED!
SATO, YOU BIG IDIOT!
ZOOM
YOU HAVE NO IDEA WHAT I'M GOING THROUGH!
YOU STUPID, DUMB MORON!
HEY.
WAIT UP, YOSHIDA!

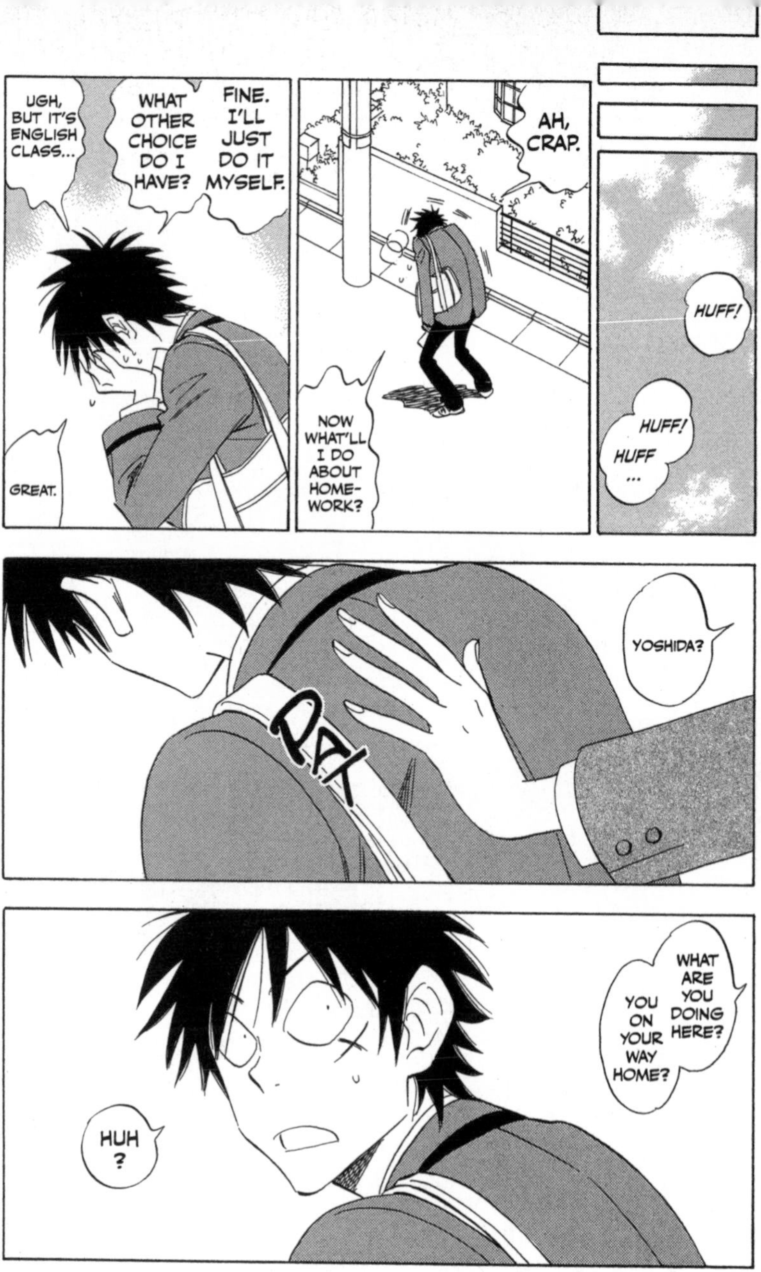
HUFF!
HUFF!
HUFF ...
AH, CRAP.
NOW WHAT'LL I DO ABOUT HOME-WORK?
FINE. I'LL JUST DO IT MYSELF.
WHAT OTHER CHOICE DO I HAVE?
UGH, BUT IT'S ENGLISH CLASS...
GREAT.
YOSHIDA?
PAT
WHAT ARE YOU DOING HERE?
YOU ON YOUR WAY HOME?
HUH ?

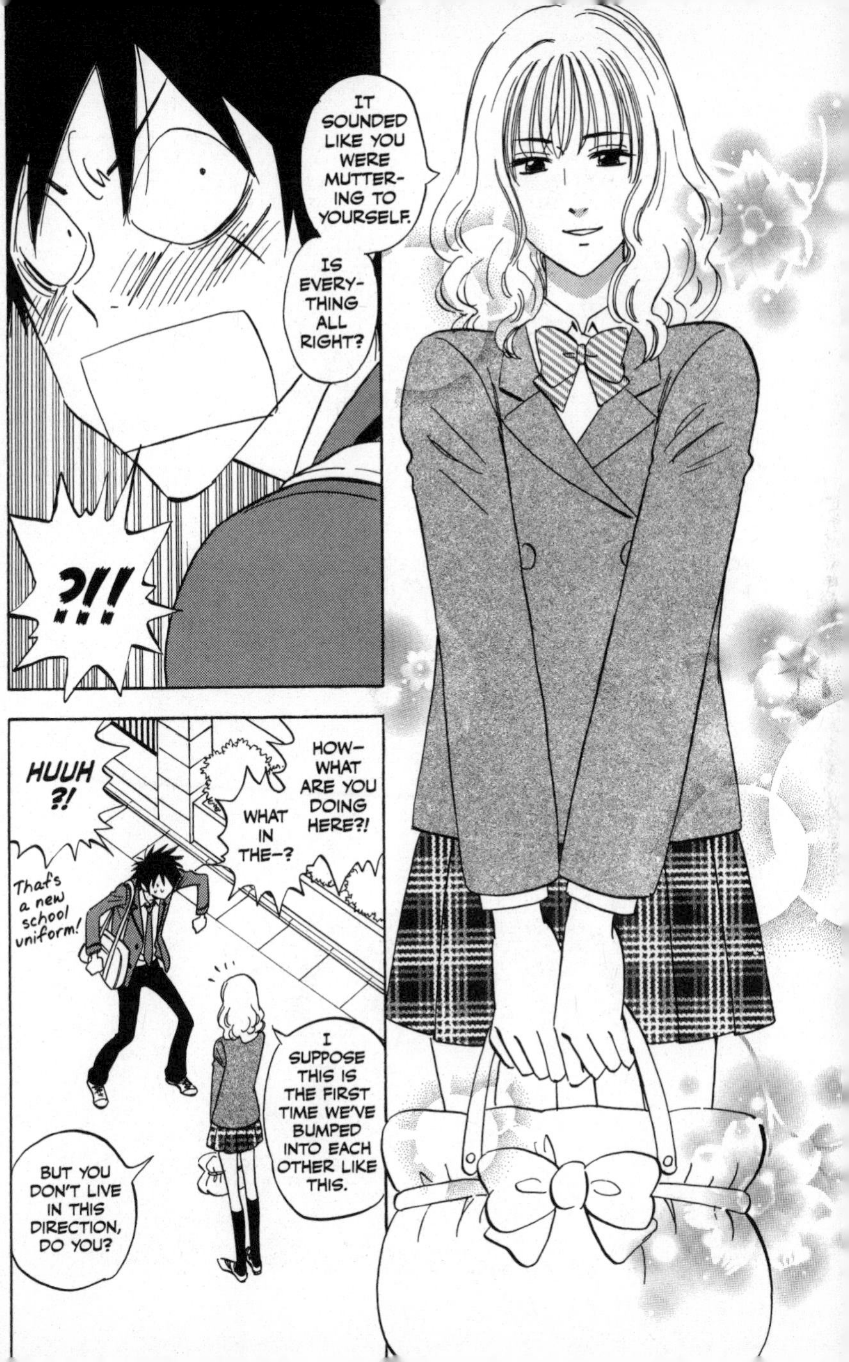
IT SOUNDED LIKE YOU WERE MUTTER-ING TO YOURSELF.
IS EVERY-THING ALL RIGHT?
?!!
HOW— WHAT ARE YOU DOING HERE?!
WHAT IN THE—?
HUUH ?!
That's a new school uniform!
I SUPPOSE THIS IS THE FIRST TIME WE'VE BUMPED INTO EACH OTHER LIKE THIS.
BUT YOU DON'T LIVE IN THIS DIRECTION, DO YOU?

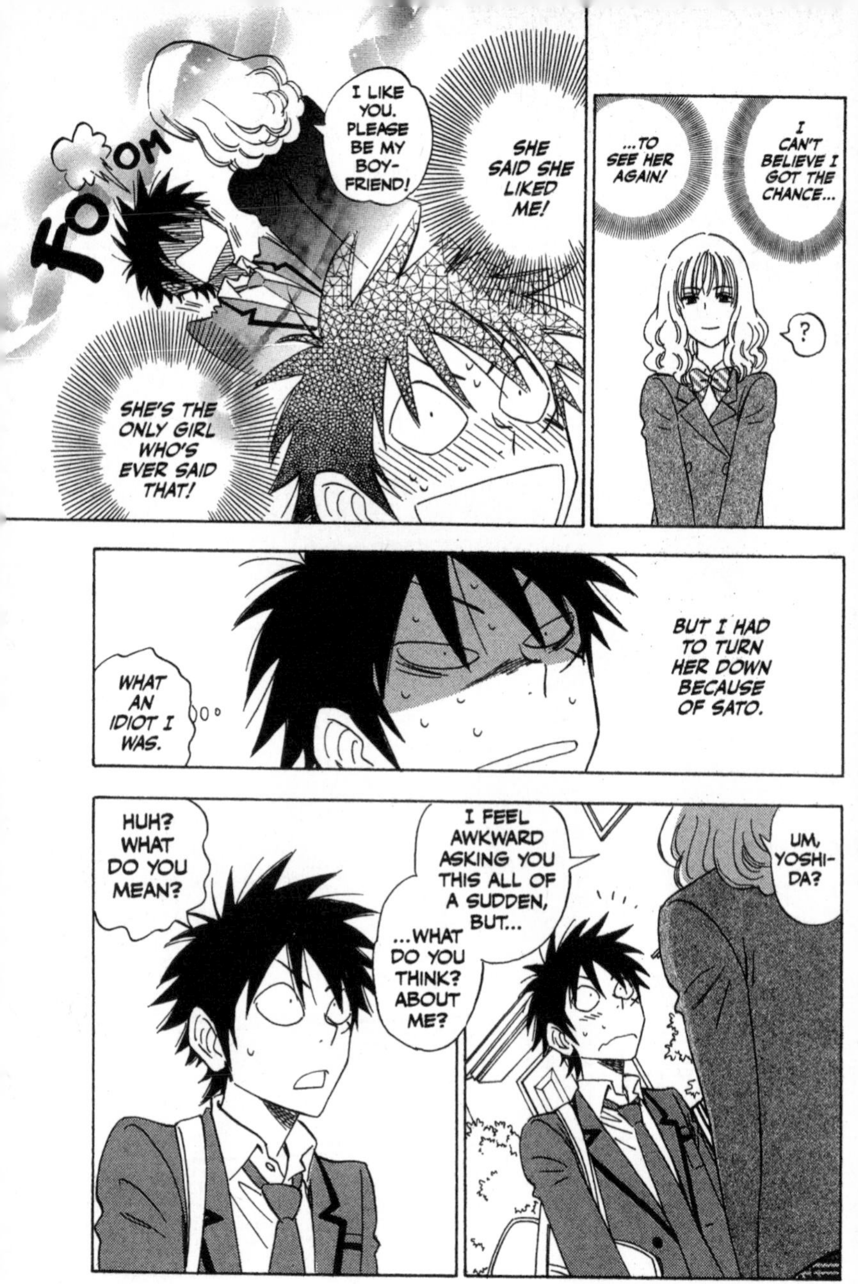
I CAN'T BELIEVE I GOT THE CHANCE...
...TO SEE HER AGAIN!
?
FOOM
I LIKE YOU. PLEASE BE MY BOY-FRIEND!
SHE SAID SHE LIKED ME!
SHE'S THE ONLY GIRL WHO'S EVER SAID THAT!
BUT I HAD TO TURN HER DOWN BECAUSE OF SATO.
WHAT AN IDIOT I WAS.
UM, YOSHI-DA?
I FEEL AWKWARD ASKING YOU THIS ALL OF A SUDDEN, BUT...
...WHAT DO YOU THINK? ABOUT ME?
HUH? WHAT DO YOU MEAN?

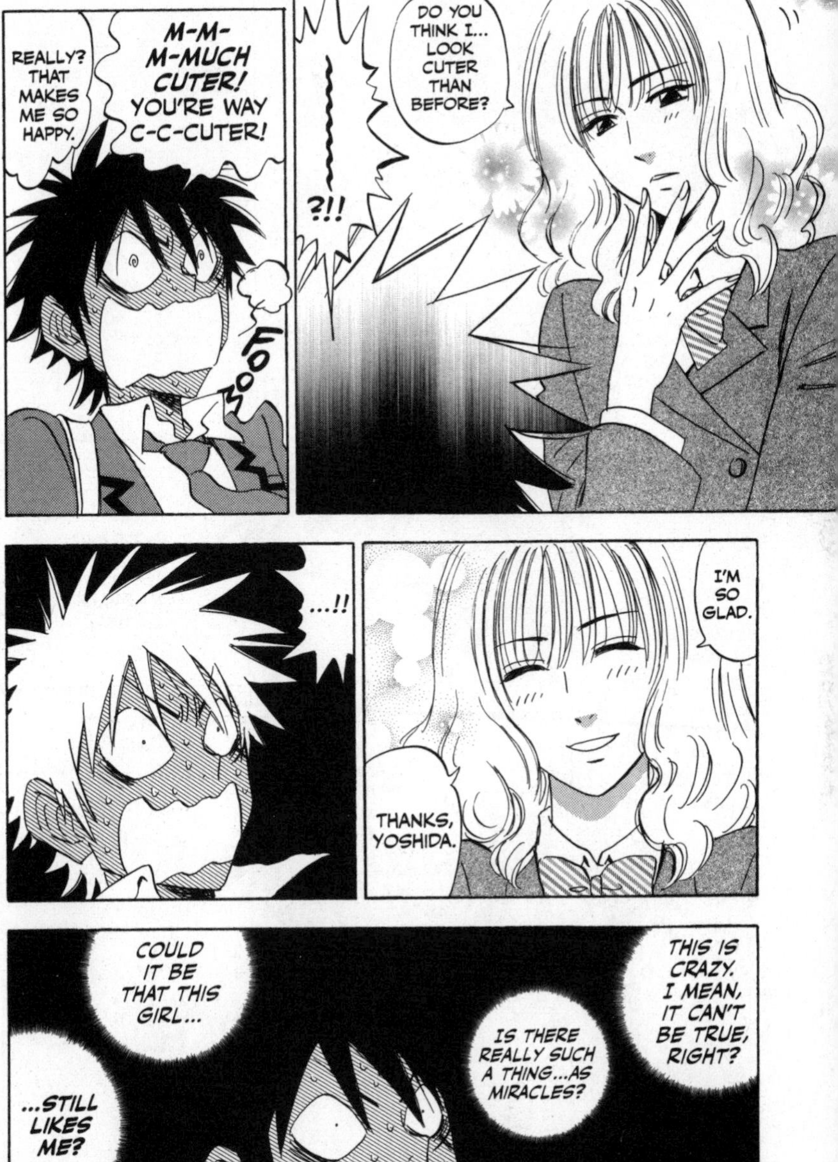
DO YOU THINK I... LOOK CUTER THAN BEFORE?
?!!
M-M-M-MUCH CUTER! YOU'RE WAY C-C-CUTER!
REALLY? THAT MAKES ME SO HAPPY.
FOOM
I'M SO GLAD.
THANKS, YOSHIDA.
...!!
THIS IS CRAZY. I MEAN, IT CAN'T BE TRUE, RIGHT?
IS THERE REALLY SUCH A THING...AS MIRACLES?
COULD IT BE THAT THIS GIRL...
...STILL LIKES ME?

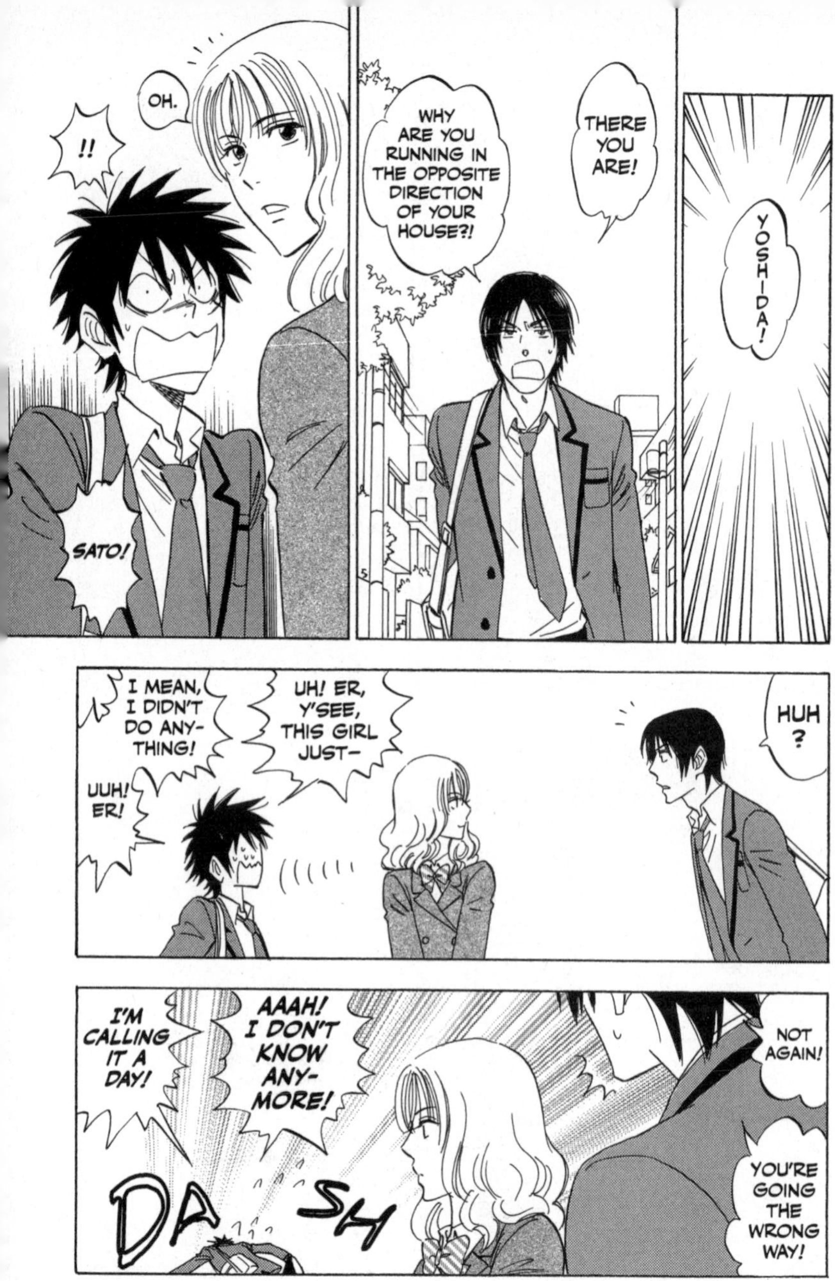
YOSHIDA!
THERE YOU ARE!
WHY ARE YOU RUNNING IN THE OPPOSITE DIRECTION OF YOUR HOUSE?!
OH.
!!
SATO!
HUH?
UH! ER, Y'SEE, THIS GIRL JUST-
I MEAN, I DIDN'T DO ANY-THING!
UUH! ER!
NOT AGAIN!
YOU'RE GOING THE WRONG WAY!
AAAH! I DON'T KNOW ANY-MORE!
I'M CALLING IT A DAY!
DASH

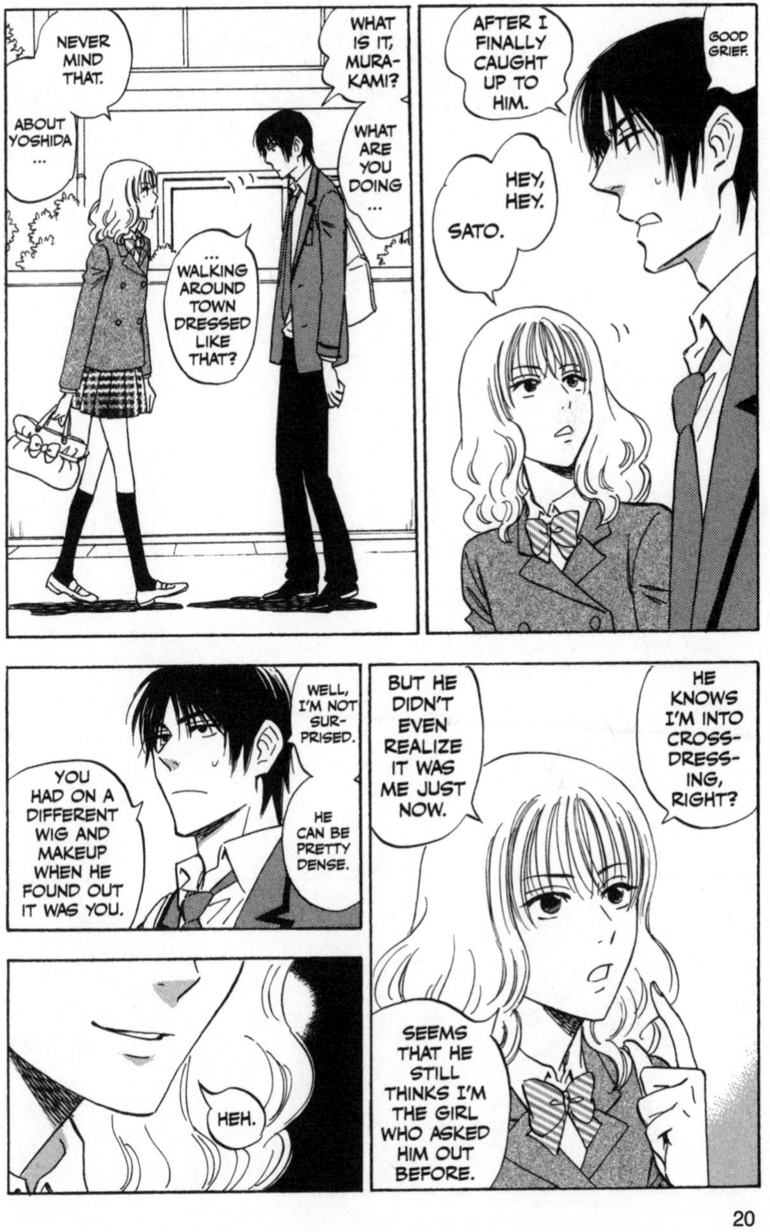
GOOD GRIEF.
AFTER I FINALLY CAUGHT UP TO HIM.
HEY, HEY.
SATO.
WHAT IS IT, MURA-KAMI?
WHAT ARE YOU DOING ...
... WALKING AROUND TOWN DRESSED LIKE THAT?
NEVER MIND THAT.
ABOUT YOSHIDA ...
HE KNOWS I'M INTO CROSS-DRESS-ING, RIGHT?
BUT HE DIDN'T EVEN REALIZE IT WAS ME JUST NOW.
WELL, I'M NOT SUR-PRISED.
HE CAN BE PRETTY DENSE.
YOU HAD ON A DIFFERENT WIG AND MAKEUP WHEN HE FOUND OUT IT WAS YOU.
SEEMS THAT HE STILL THINKS I'M THE GIRL WHO ASKED HIM OUT BEFORE.
HEH.

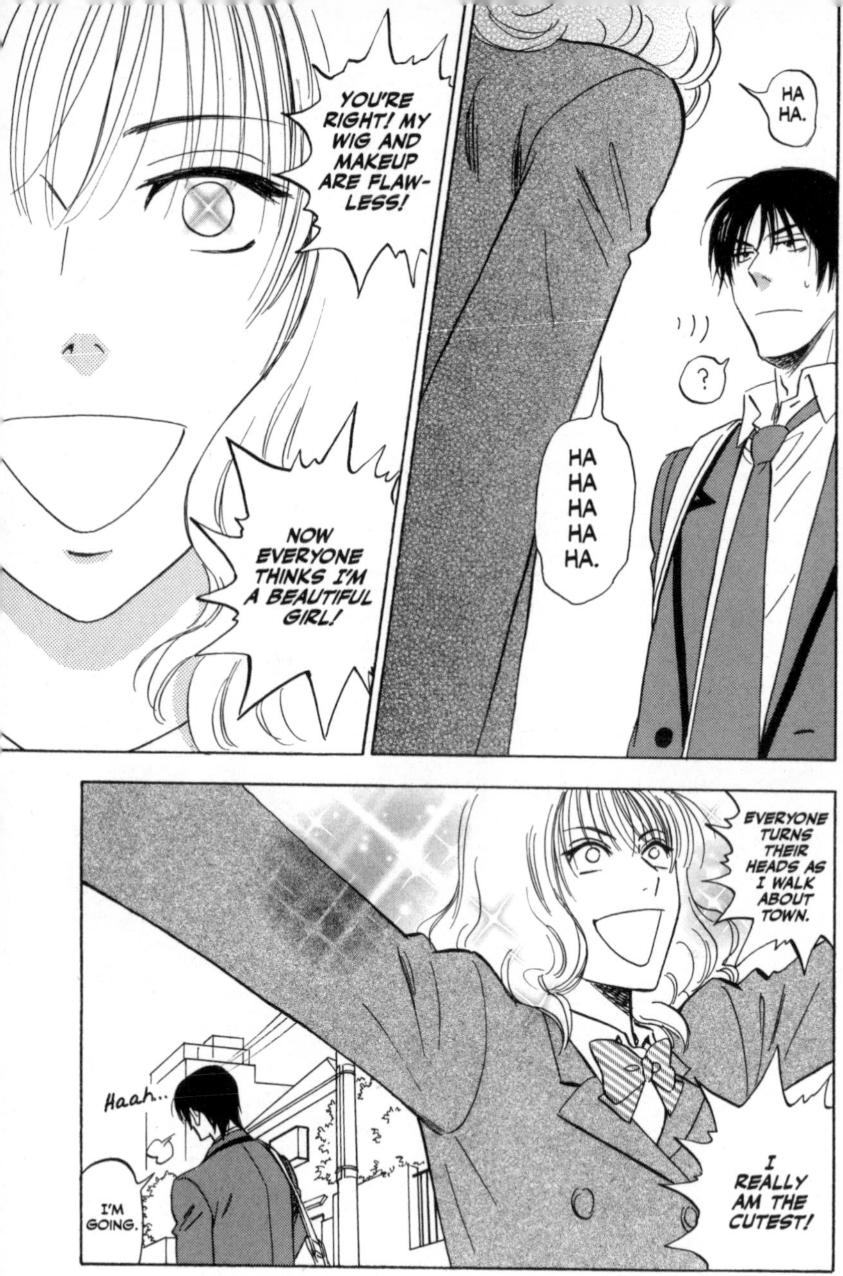
HA HA.
?
HA HA HA HA HA.
YOU'RE RIGHT! MY WIG AND MAKEUP ARE FLAWLESS!
NOW EVERYONE THINKS I'M A BEAUTIFUL GIRL!
EVERYONE TURNS THEIR HEADS AS I WALK ABOUT TOWN.
I REALLY AM THE CUTEST!
Haah..
I'M GOING.

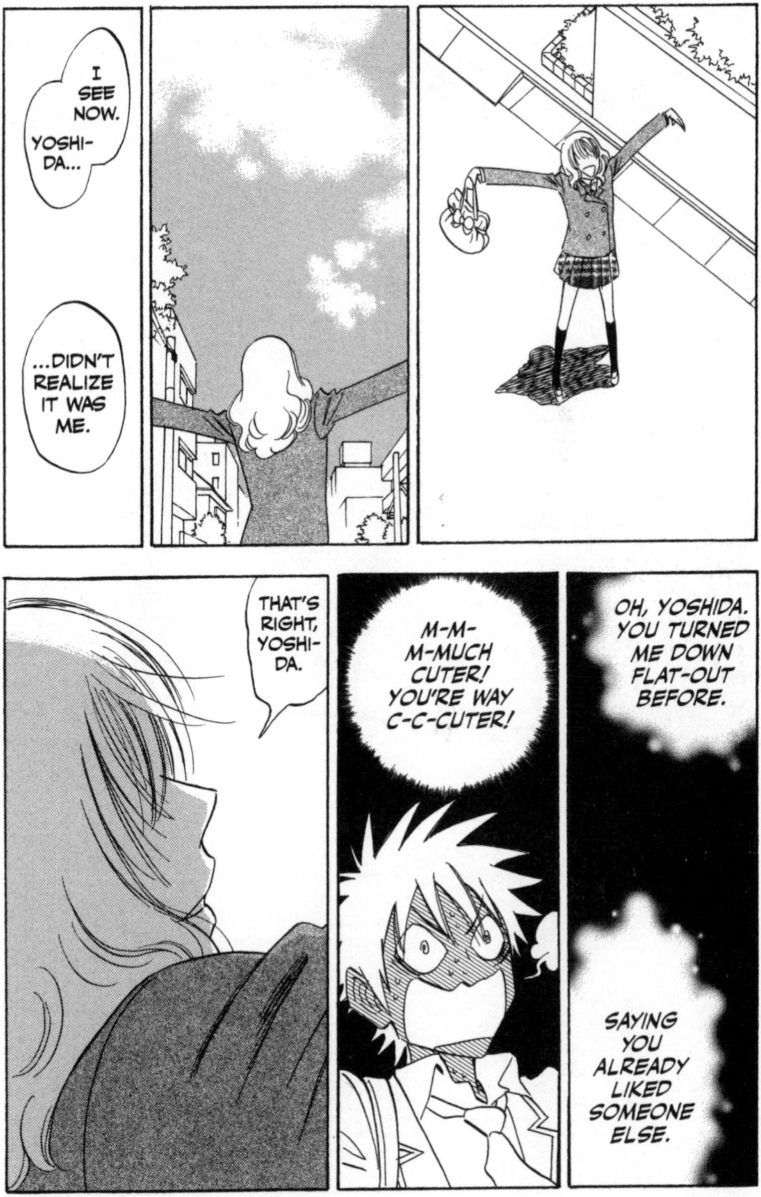
I SEE NOW. YOSHIDA...
...DIDN'T REALIZE IT WAS ME.
OH, YOSHIDA. YOU TURNED ME DOWN FLAT-OUT BEFORE.
SAYING YOU ALREADY LIKED SOMEONE ELSE.
M-M-M-MUCH CUTER! YOU'RE WAY C-C-CUTER!
THAT'S RIGHT, YOSHIDA.

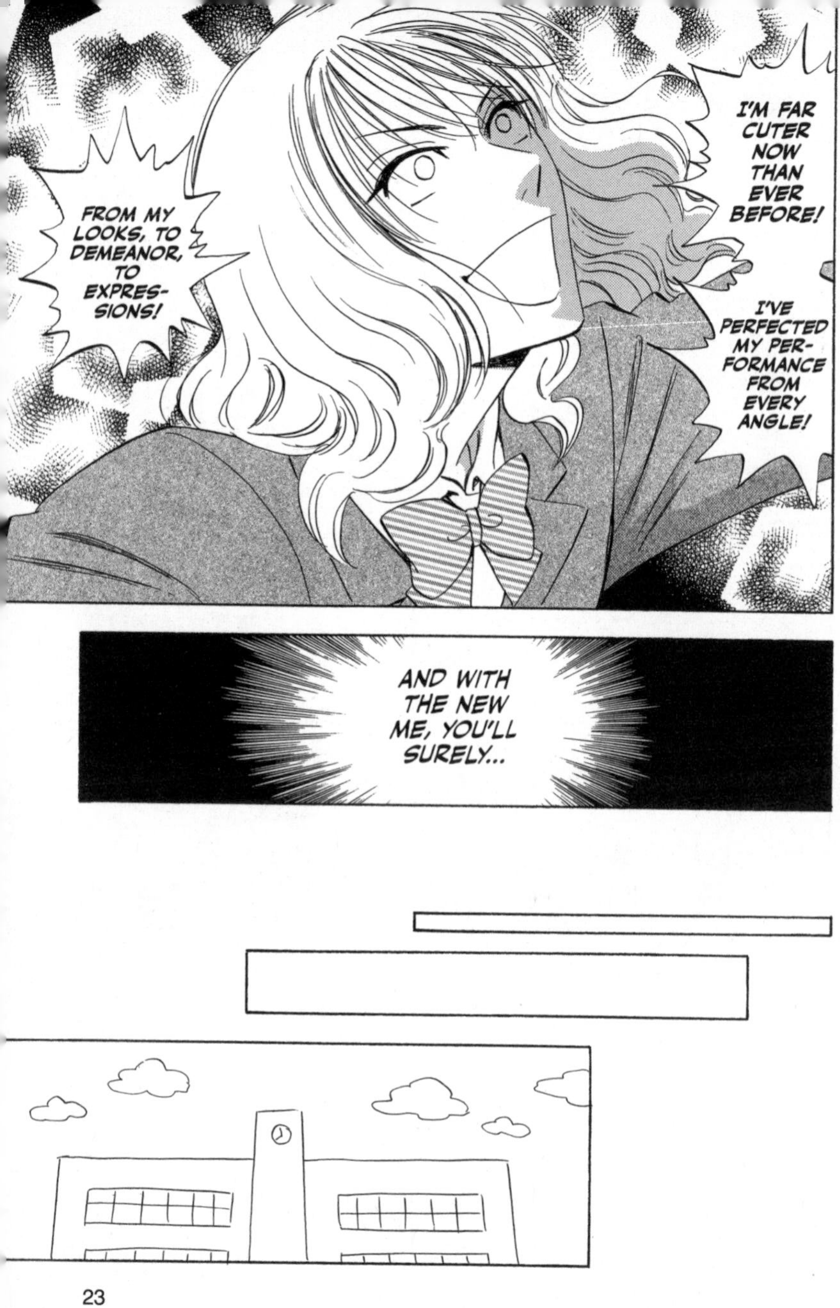
I'M FAR CUTER NOW THAN EVER BEFORE!
I'VE PERFECTED MY PERFORMANCE FROM EVERY ANGLE!
FROM MY LOOKS, TO DEMEANOR, TO EXPRESSIONS!
AND WITH THE NEW ME, YOU'LL SURELY...

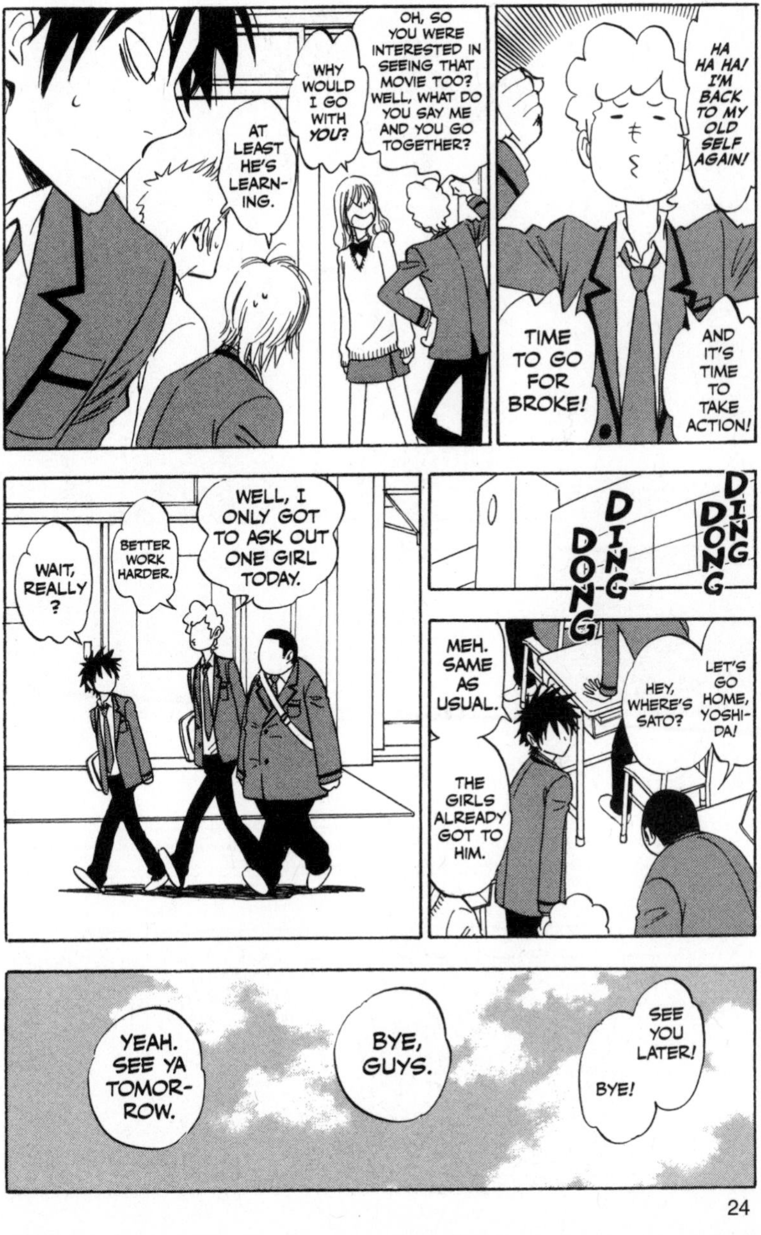
HA HA HA! I'M BACK TO MY OLD SELF AGAIN!
AND IT'S TIME TO TAKE ACTION!
TIME TO GO FOR BROKE!
OH, SO YOU WERE INTERESTED IN SEEING THAT MOVIE TOO? WELL, WHAT DO YOU SAY ME AND YOU GO TOGETHER?
WHY WOULD I GO WITH *YOU*?
AT LEAST HE'S LEARNING.
DING DONG
DING DONG
LET'S GO HOME, YOSHIDA!
HEY, WHERE'S SATO?
MEH. SAME AS USUAL.
THE GIRLS ALREADY GOT TO HIM.
WELL, I ONLY GOT TO ASK OUT ONE GIRL TODAY.
BETTER WORK HARDER.
WAIT, REALLY?
SEE YOU LATER!
BYE!
BYE, GUYS.
YEAH. SEE YA TOMORROW.

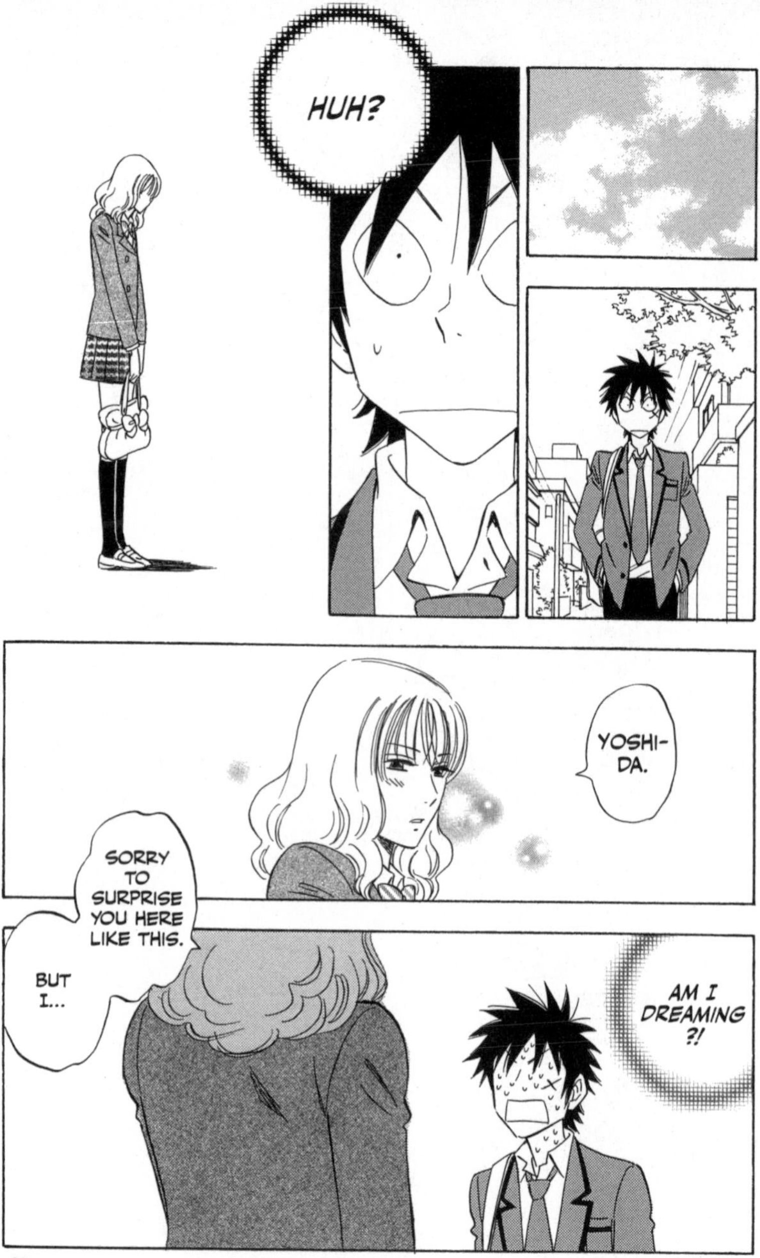
HUH?
YOSHI-DA.
SORRY TO SURPRISE YOU HERE LIKE THIS.
AM I DREAMING?!
BUT I...

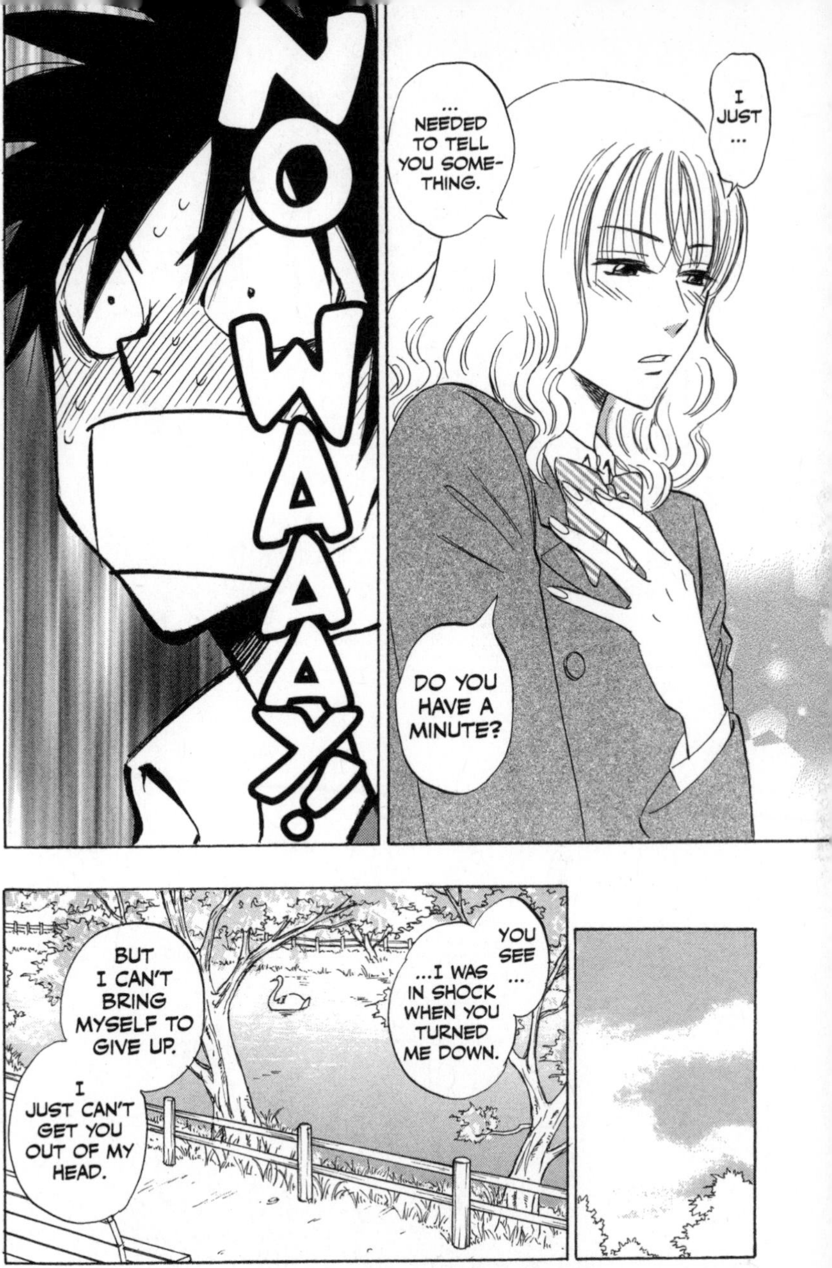
I JUST ...
... NEEDED TO TELL YOU SOMETHING.
DO YOU HAVE A MINUTE?
NOWWAAAY!
YOU SEE ...
...I WAS IN SHOCK WHEN YOU TURNED ME DOWN.
BUT I CAN'T BRING MYSELF TO GIVE UP.
I JUST CAN'T GET YOU OUT OF MY HEAD.

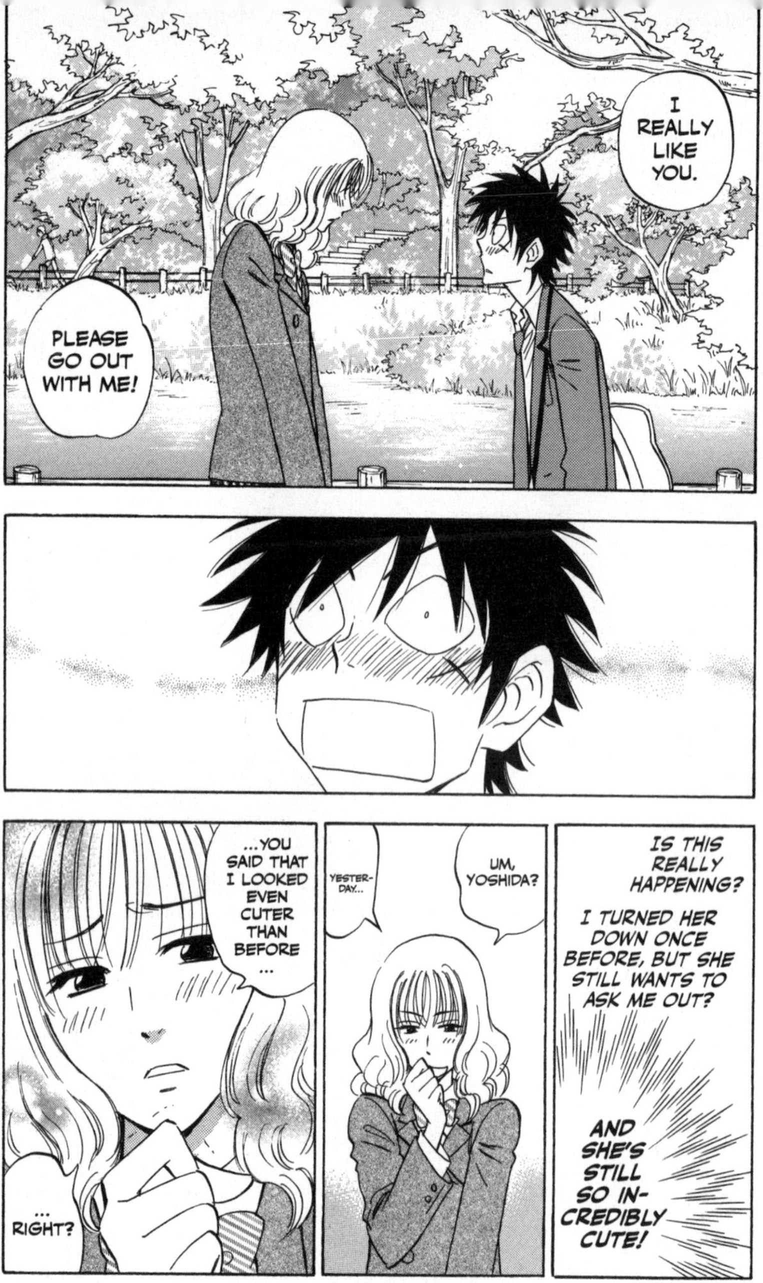
I REALLY LIKE YOU.
PLEASE GO OUT WITH ME!
IS THIS REALLY HAPPENING?
I TURNED HER DOWN ONCE BEFORE, BUT SHE STILL WANTS TO ASK ME OUT?
AND SHE'S STILL SO IN-CREDIBLY CUTE!
UM, YOSHIDA?
YESTER-DAY...
...YOU SAID THAT I LOOKED EVEN CUTER THAN BEFORE ...
... RIGHT?

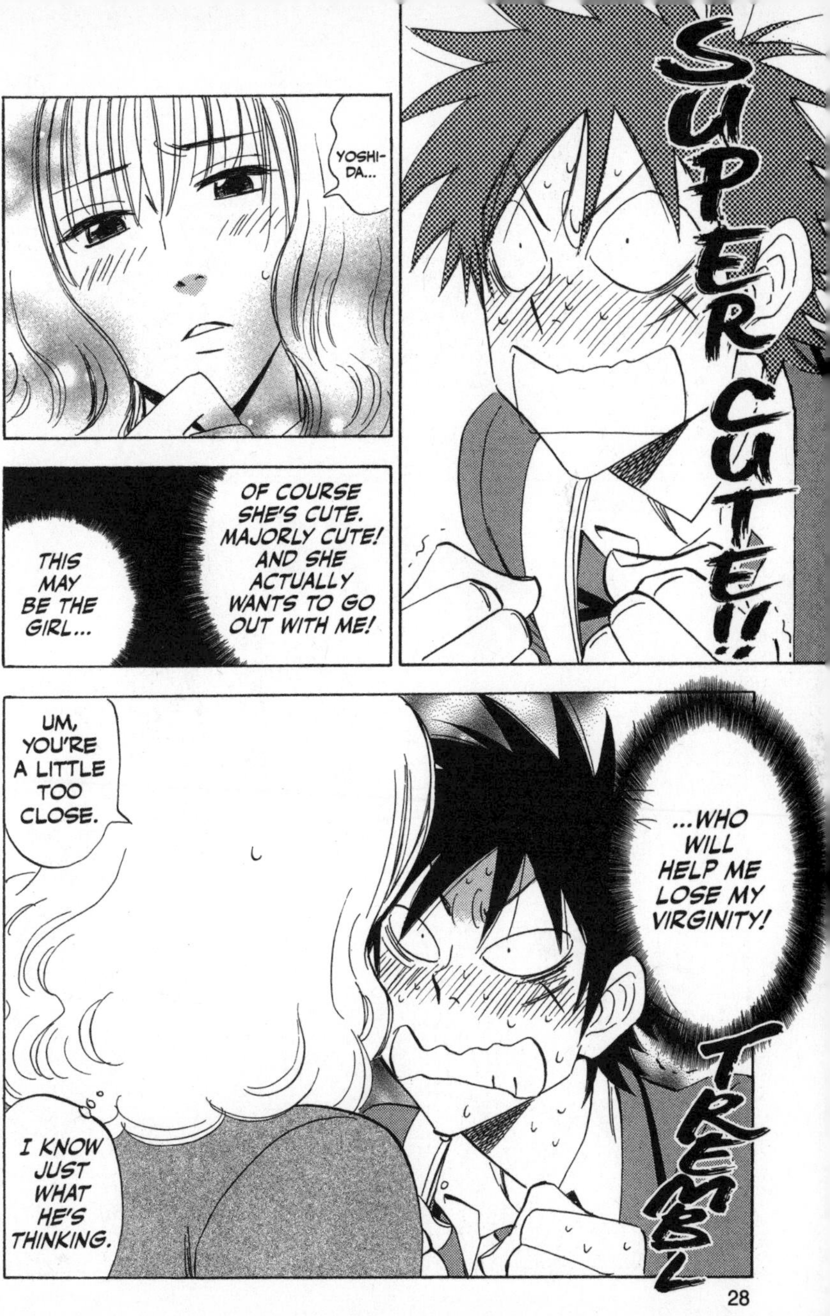
SUPER CUTE!!
YOSHIDA...
OF COURSE SHE'S CUTE. MAJORLY CUTE! AND SHE ACTUALLY WANTS TO GO OUT WITH ME!
THIS MAY BE THE GIRL...
...WHO WILL HELP ME LOSE MY VIRGINITY!
TREMBL
UM, YOU'RE A LITTLE TOO CLOSE.
I KNOW JUST WHAT HE'S THINKING.

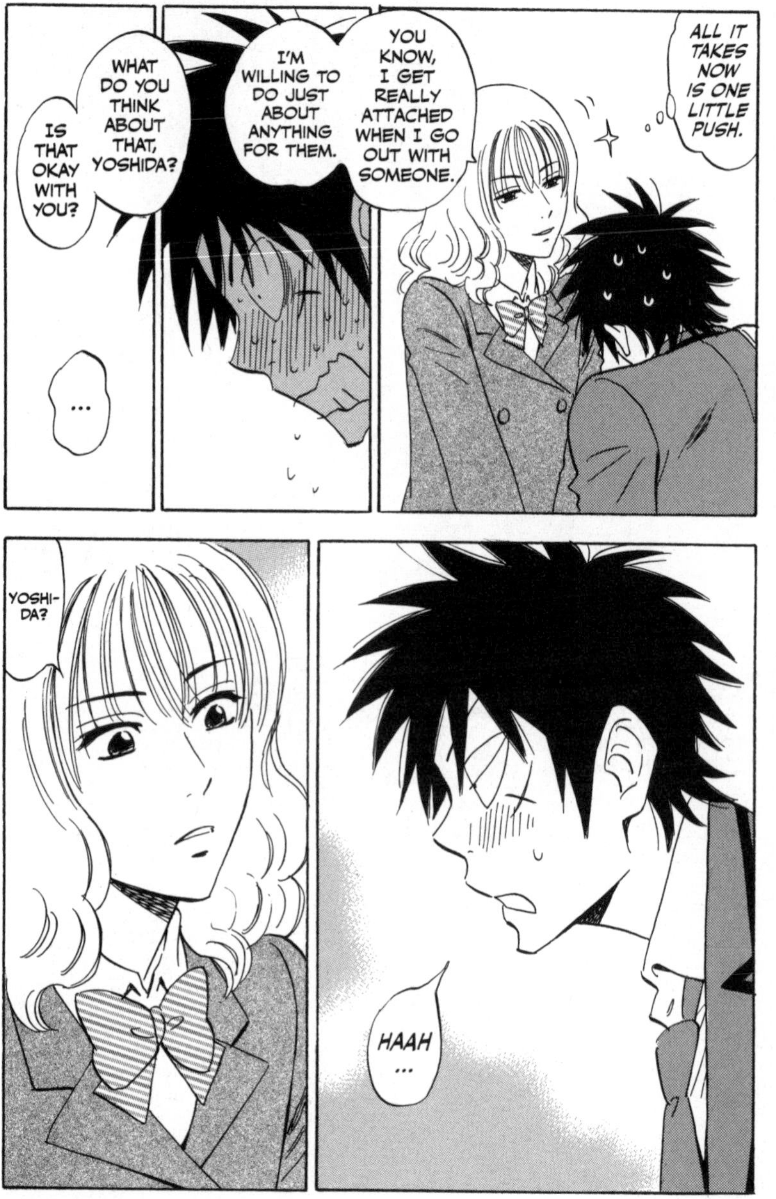
ALL IT TAKES NOW IS ONE LITTLE PUSH.
YOU KNOW, I GET REALLY ATTACHED WHEN I GO OUT WITH SOMEONE.
I'M WILLING TO DO JUST ABOUT ANYTHING FOR THEM.
WHAT DO YOU THINK ABOUT THAT, YOSHIDA?
IS THAT OKAY WITH YOU?
...
HAAH ...
YOSHI-DA?

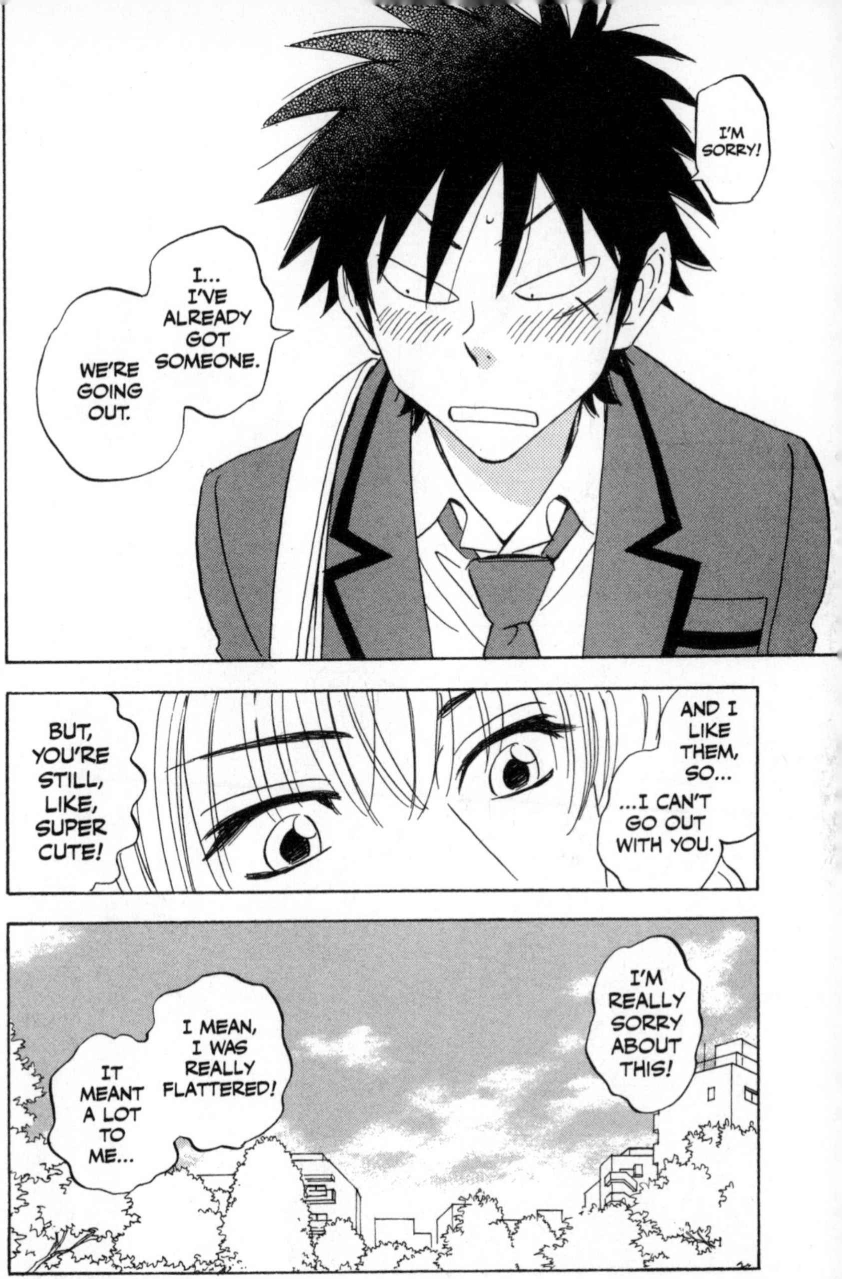
I'M SORRY!
I... I'VE ALREADY GOT SOMEONE. WE'RE GOING OUT.
AND I LIKE THEM, SO... ...I CAN'T GO OUT WITH YOU.
BUT, YOU'RE STILL, LIKE, SUPER CUTE!
I'M REALLY SORRY ABOUT THIS!
I MEAN, I WAS REALLY FLATTERED! IT MEANT A LOT TO ME...

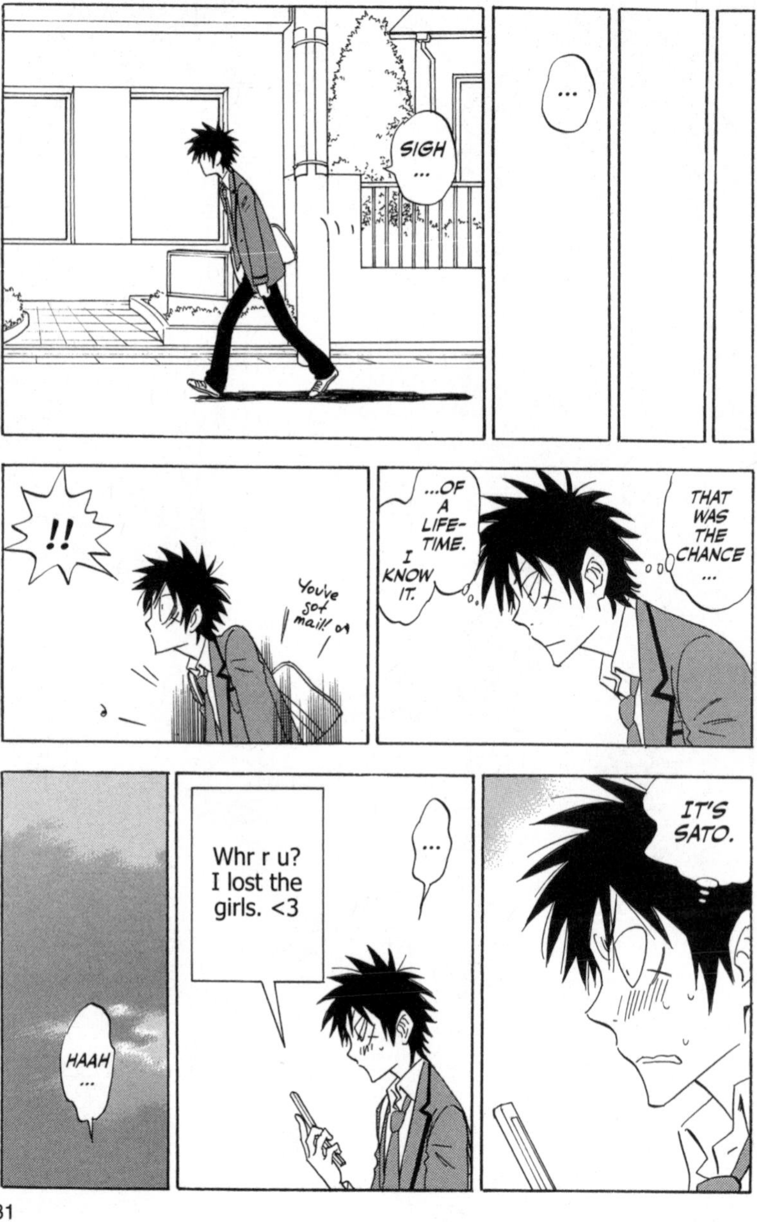
...
SIGH ...
THAT WAS THE CHANCE ...
...OF A LIFE-TIME. I KNOW IT.
!!
You've got mail!
IT'S SATO.
Whr r u? I lost the girls. <3
...
HAAH ...

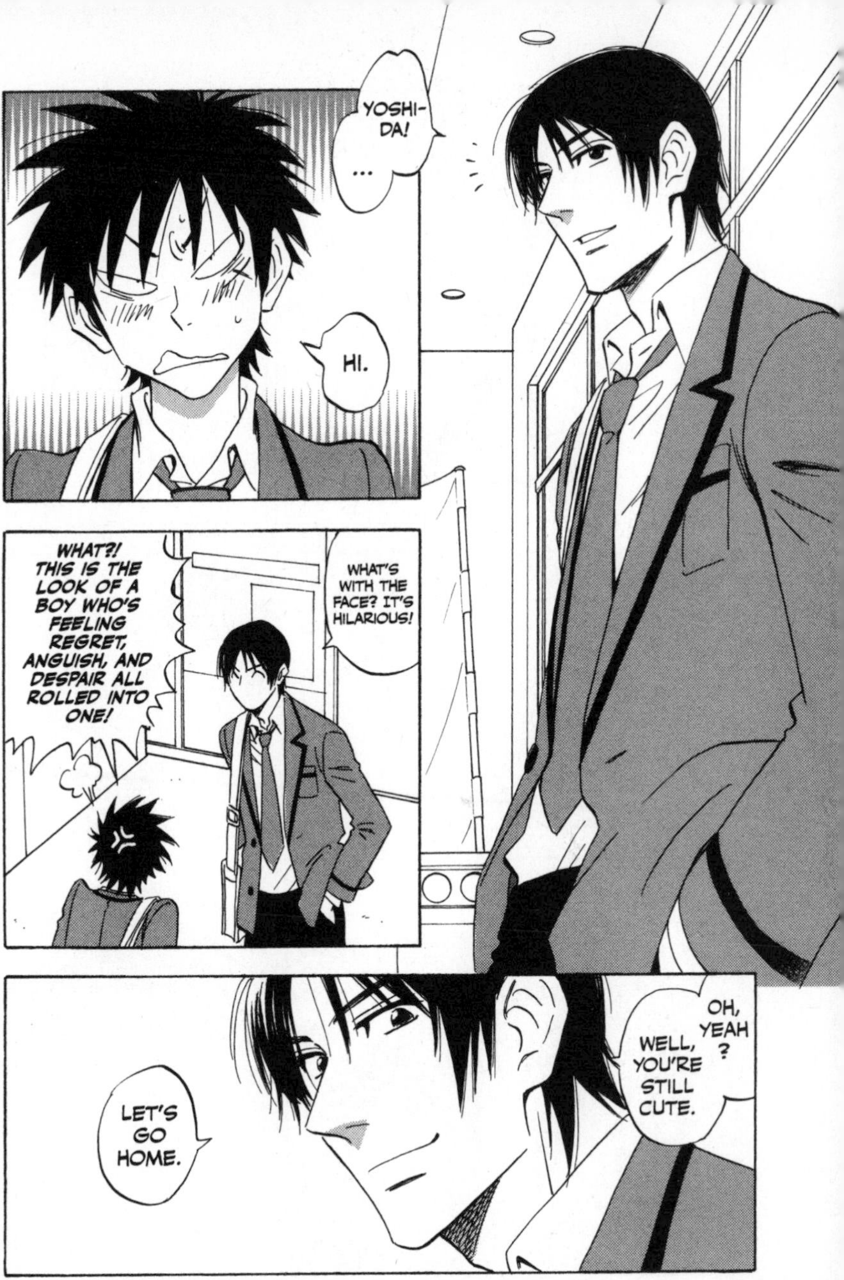
YOSHI-DA!
...
HI.
WHAT'S WITH THE FACE? IT'S HILARIOUS!
WHAT?! THIS IS THE LOOK OF A BOY WHO'S FEELING REGRET, ANGUISH, AND DESPAIR ALL ROLLED INTO ONE!
OH, YEAH?
WELL, YOU'RE STILL CUTE.
LET'S GO HOME.

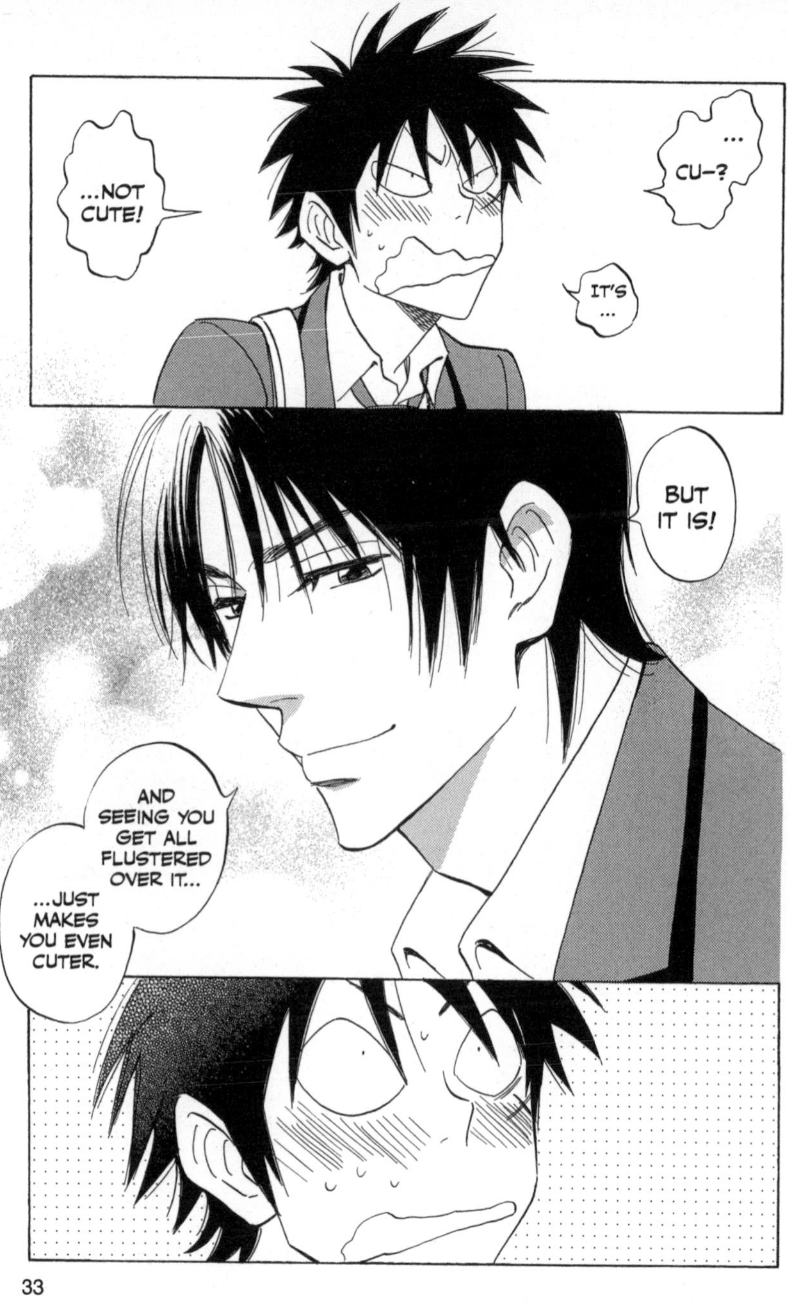
... CU-?
IT'S ...
...NOT CUTE!
BUT IT IS!
AND SEEING YOU GET ALL FLUSTERED OVER IT...
...JUST MAKES YOU EVEN CUTER.

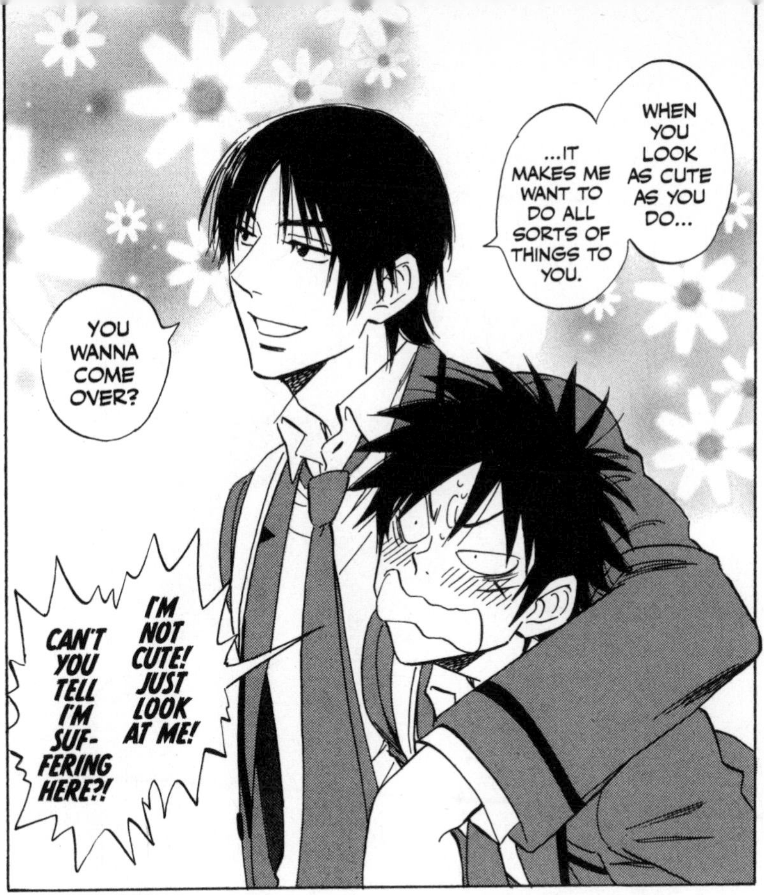
WHEN YOU LOOK AS CUTE AS YOU DO...
...IT MAKES ME WANT TO DO ALL SORTS OF THINGS TO YOU.
YOU WANNA COME OVER?
I'M NOT CUTE! JUST LOOK AT ME!
CAN'T YOU TELL I'M SUF-FERING HERE?!

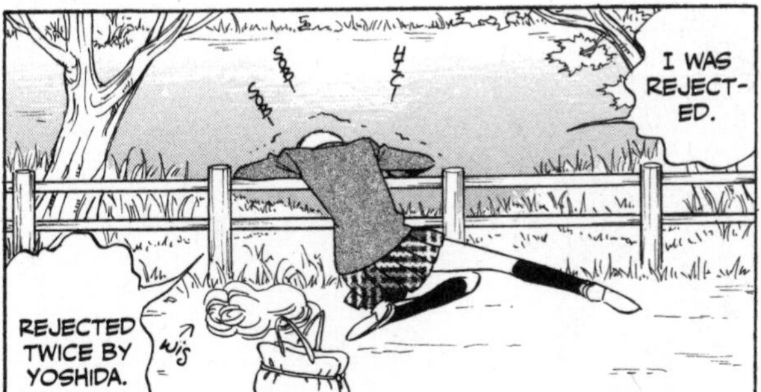
I WAS REJECT-ED.
HIC
REJECTED TWICE BY YOSHIDA.

ACT. 27 / END

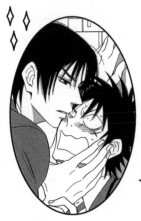

SATO & YOSHIDA

HIS FAVORITE

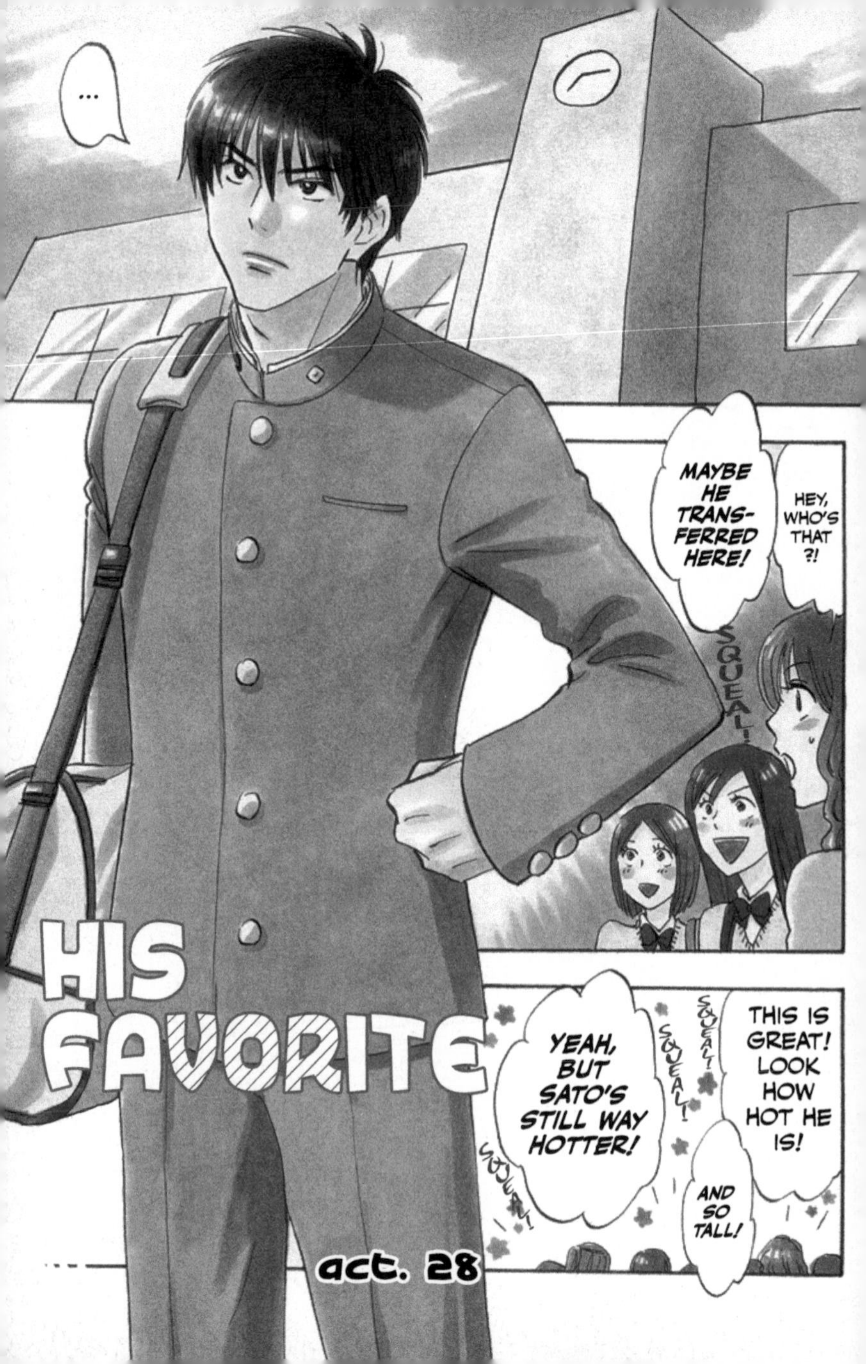
...
HEY, WHO'S THAT ?!
MAYBE HE TRANS-FERRED HERE!
SQUEAL!
THIS IS GREAT! LOOK HOW HOT HE IS!
AND SO TALL!
SQUEAL!
SQUEAL!
YEAH, BUT SATO'S STILL WAY HOTTER!
SQUEAL!
HIS FAVORITE
act. 28

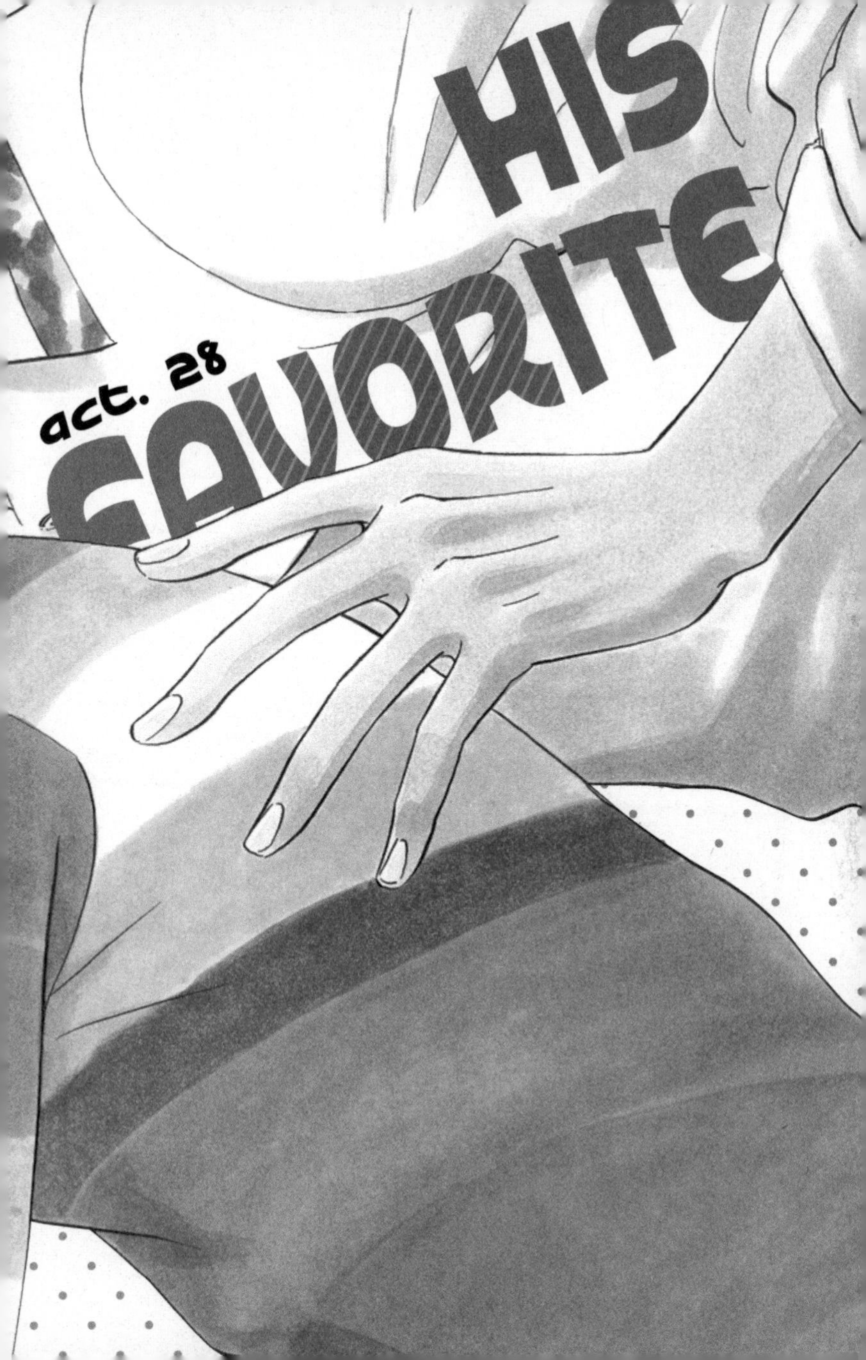
HIS
act. 28
FAVORITE

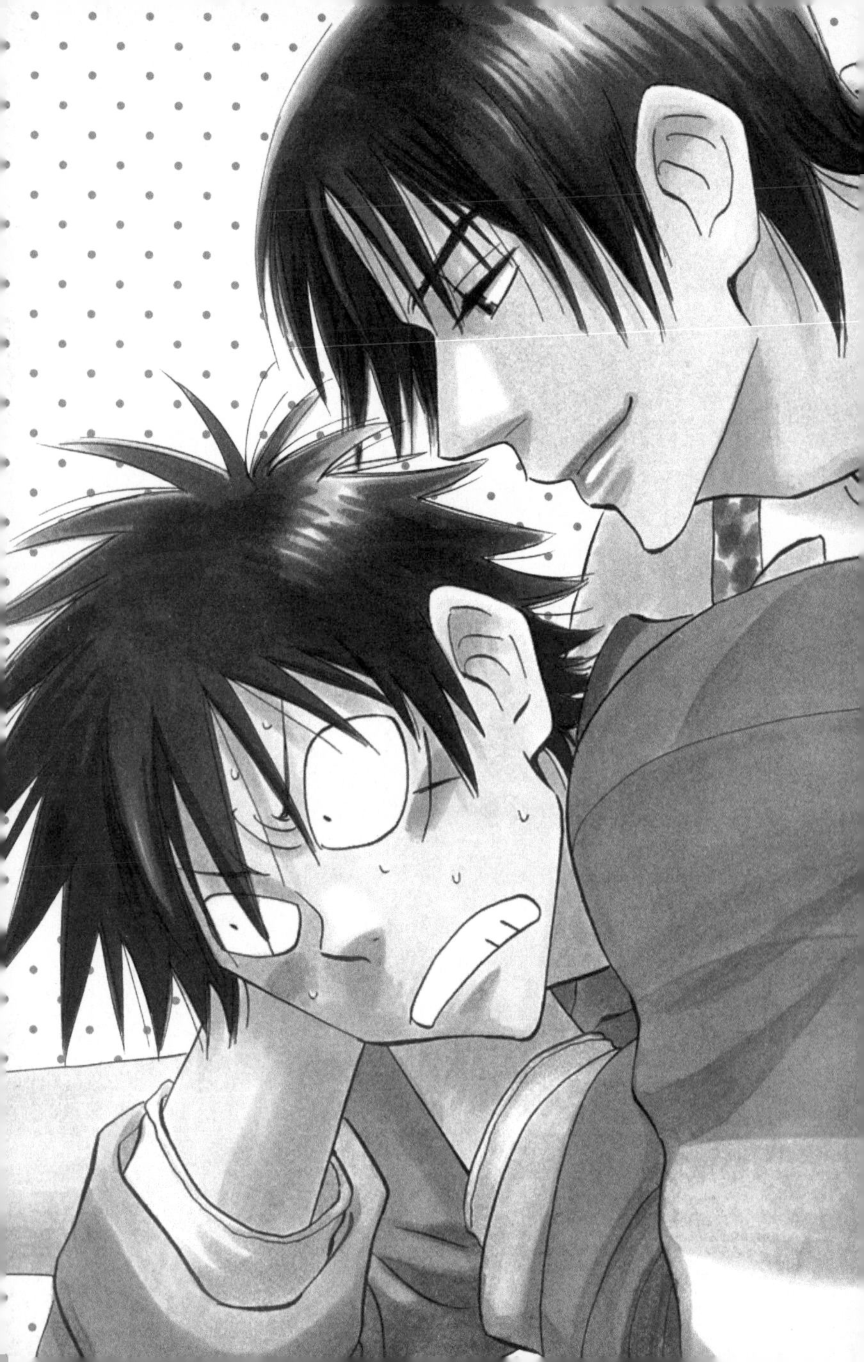

HIS FAVORITE

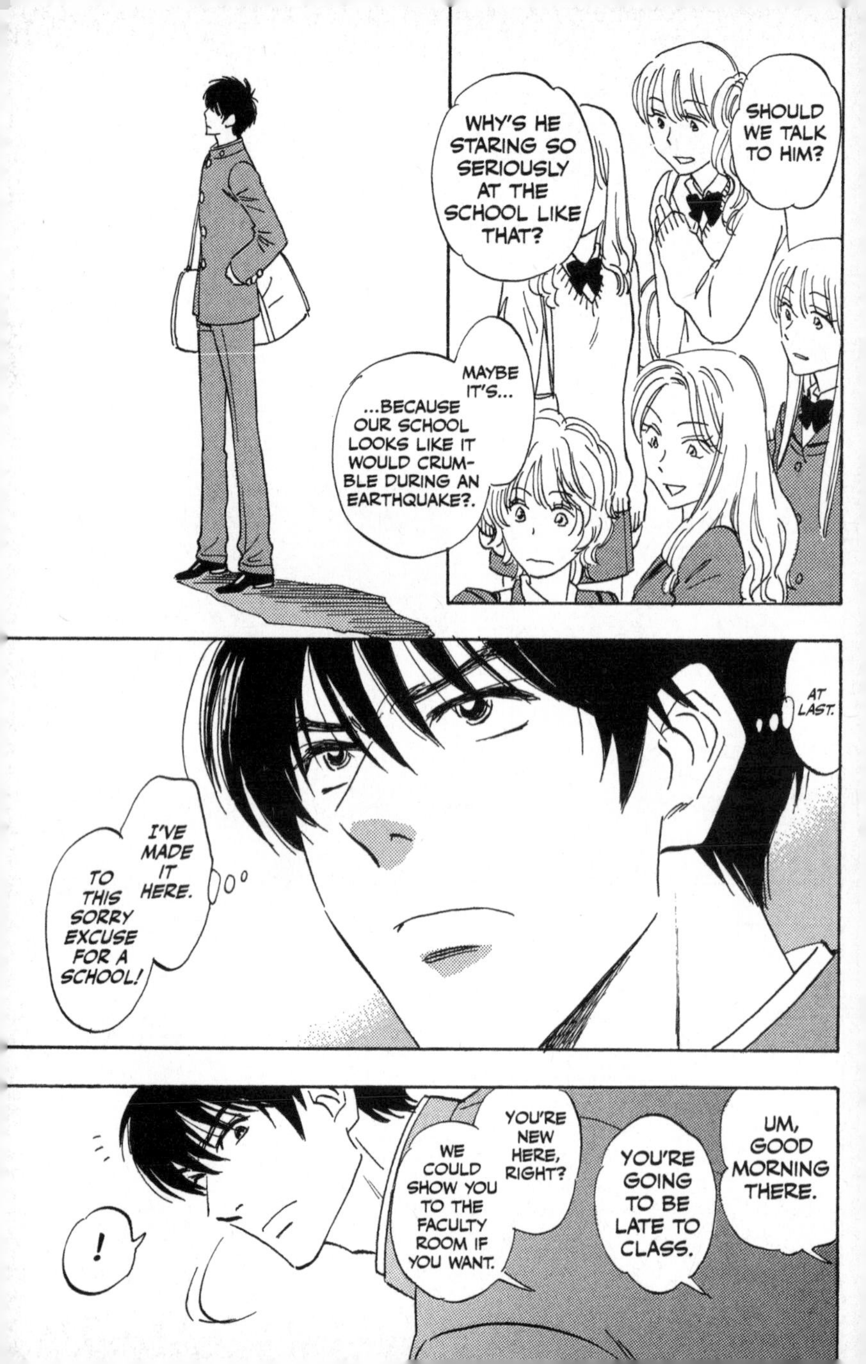
SHOULD WE TALK TO HIM?
WHY'S HE STARING SO SERIOUSLY AT THE SCHOOL LIKE THAT?
MAYBE IT'S...
...BECAUSE OUR SCHOOL LOOKS LIKE IT WOULD CRUMBLE DURING AN EARTHQUAKE?.
AT LAST.
I'VE MADE IT HERE.
TO THIS SORRY EXCUSE FOR A SCHOOL!
UM, GOOD MORNING THERE.
YOU'RE GOING TO BE LATE TO CLASS.
YOU'RE NEW HERE, RIGHT?
WE COULD SHOW YOU TO THE FACULTY ROOM IF YOU WANT.
!

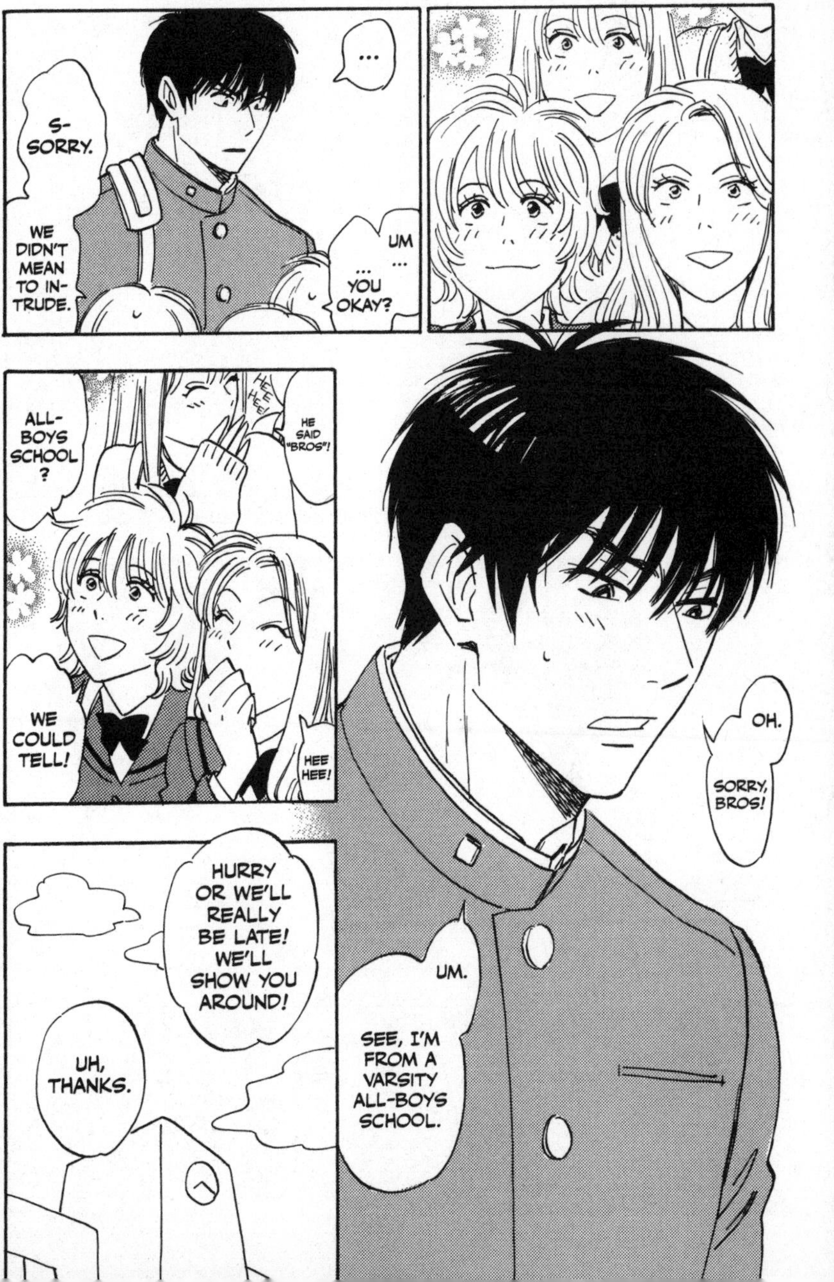
...
S-SORRY.
WE DIDN'T MEAN TO INTRUDE.
UM ... ... YOU OKAY?
OH.
SORRY, BROS!
UM.
SEE, I'M FROM A VARSITY ALL-BOYS SCHOOL.
HE SAID "BROS"!
HEE HEE!
ALL-BOYS SCHOOL?
HEE HEE!
WE COULD TELL!
HURRY OR WE'LL REALLY BE LATE! WE'LL SHOW YOU AROUND!
UH, THANKS.

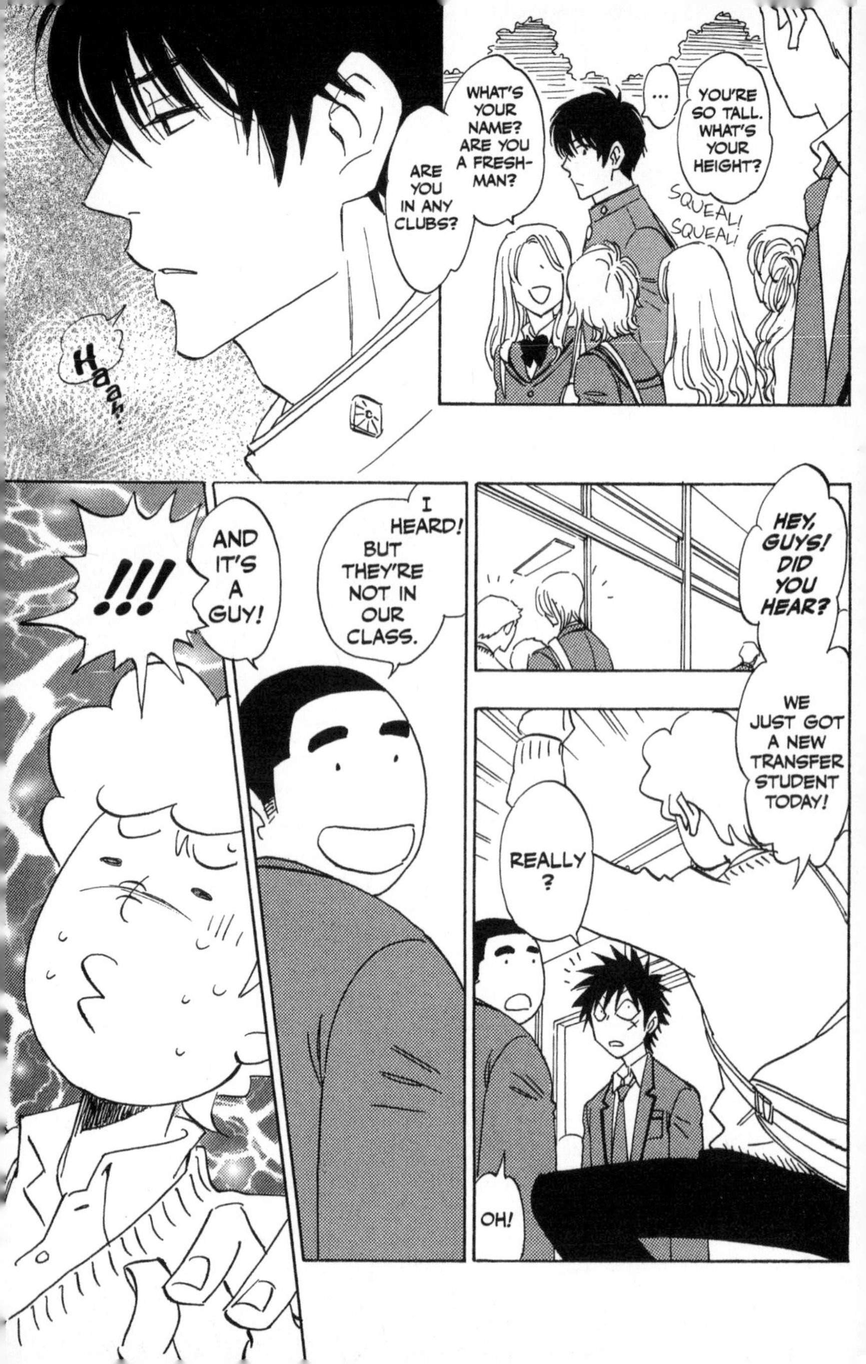
YOU'RE SO TALL. WHAT'S YOUR HEIGHT?
...
WHAT'S YOUR NAME? ARE YOU A FRESH-MAN?
ARE YOU IN ANY CLUBS?
SQUEAL! SQUEAL!
Haah...
HEY, GUYS! DID YOU HEAR?
WE JUST GOT A NEW TRANSFER STUDENT TODAY!
REALLY?
OH!
I HEARD! BUT THEY'RE NOT IN OUR CLASS.
AND IT'S A GUY!
!!!

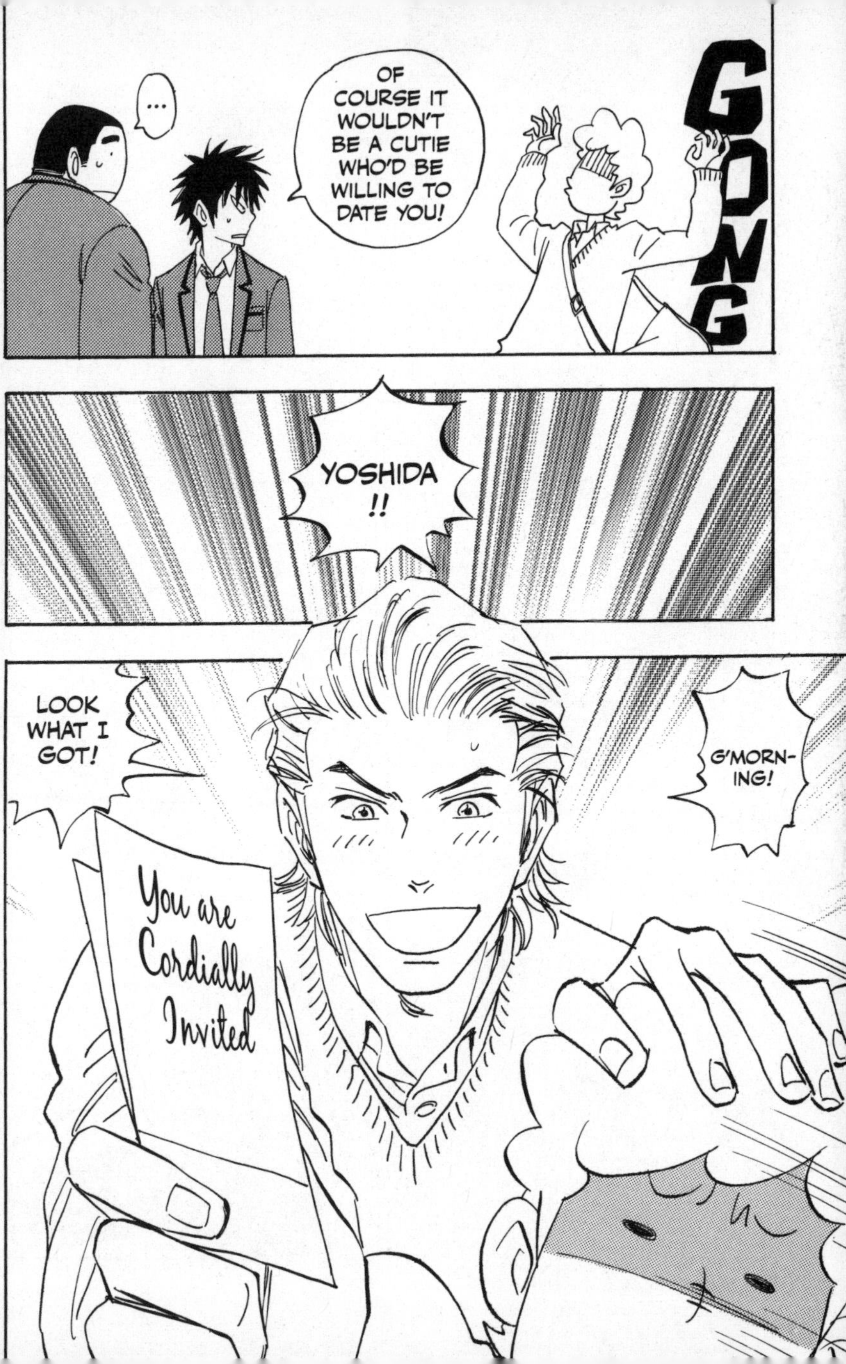
GONG
OF COURSE IT WOULDN'T BE A CUTIE WHO'D BE WILLING TO DATE YOU!
...
YOSHIDA !!
G'MORNING!
LOOK WHAT I GOT!
You are Cordially Invited

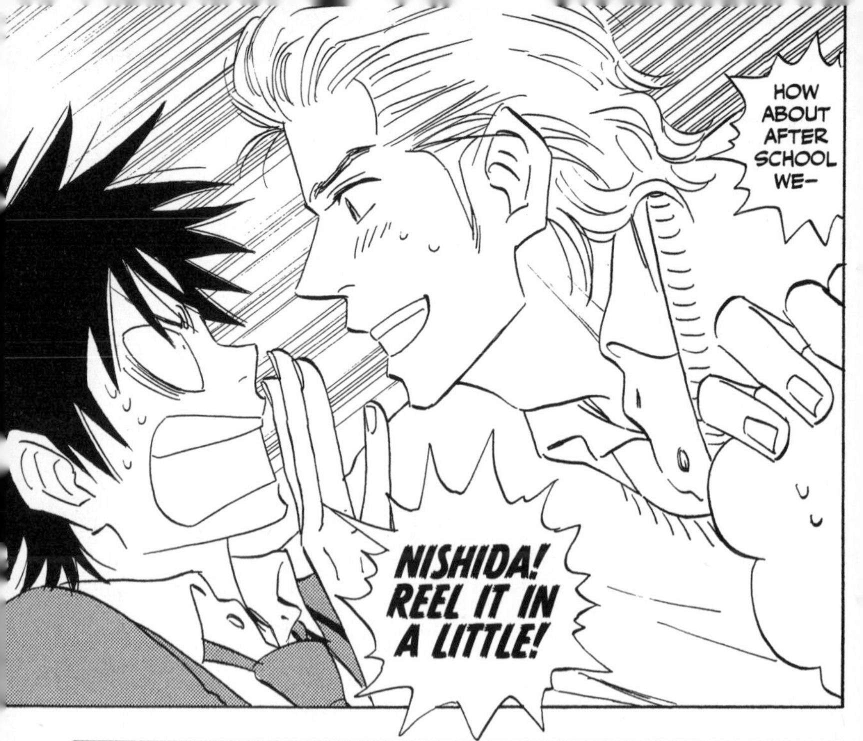
HOW ABOUT AFTER SCHOOL WE–
NISHIDA! REEL IT IN A LITTLE!

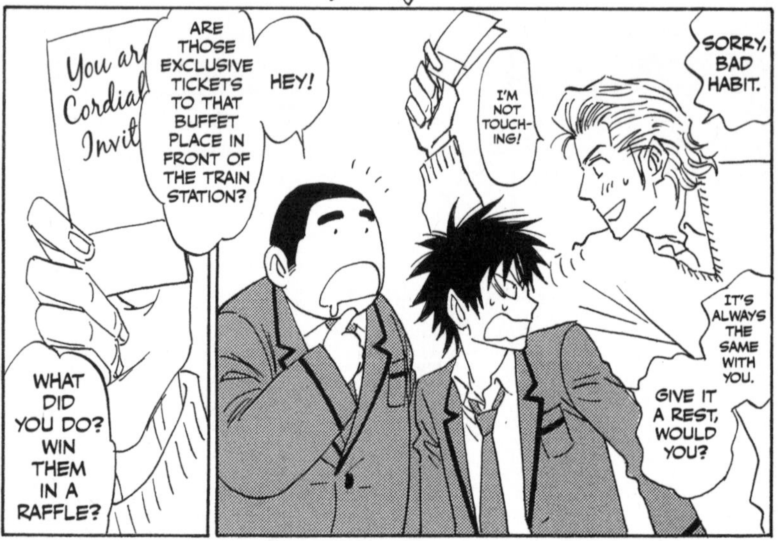
SORRY, BAD HABIT.
IT'S ALWAYS THE SAME WITH YOU.
GIVE IT A REST, WOULD YOU?
I'M NOT TOUCHING!
HEY!
ARE THOSE EXCLUSIVE TICKETS TO THAT BUFFET PLACE IN FRONT OF THE TRAIN STATION?
You ar
Cordial
Invit
WHAT DID YOU DO? WIN THEM IN A RAFFLE?

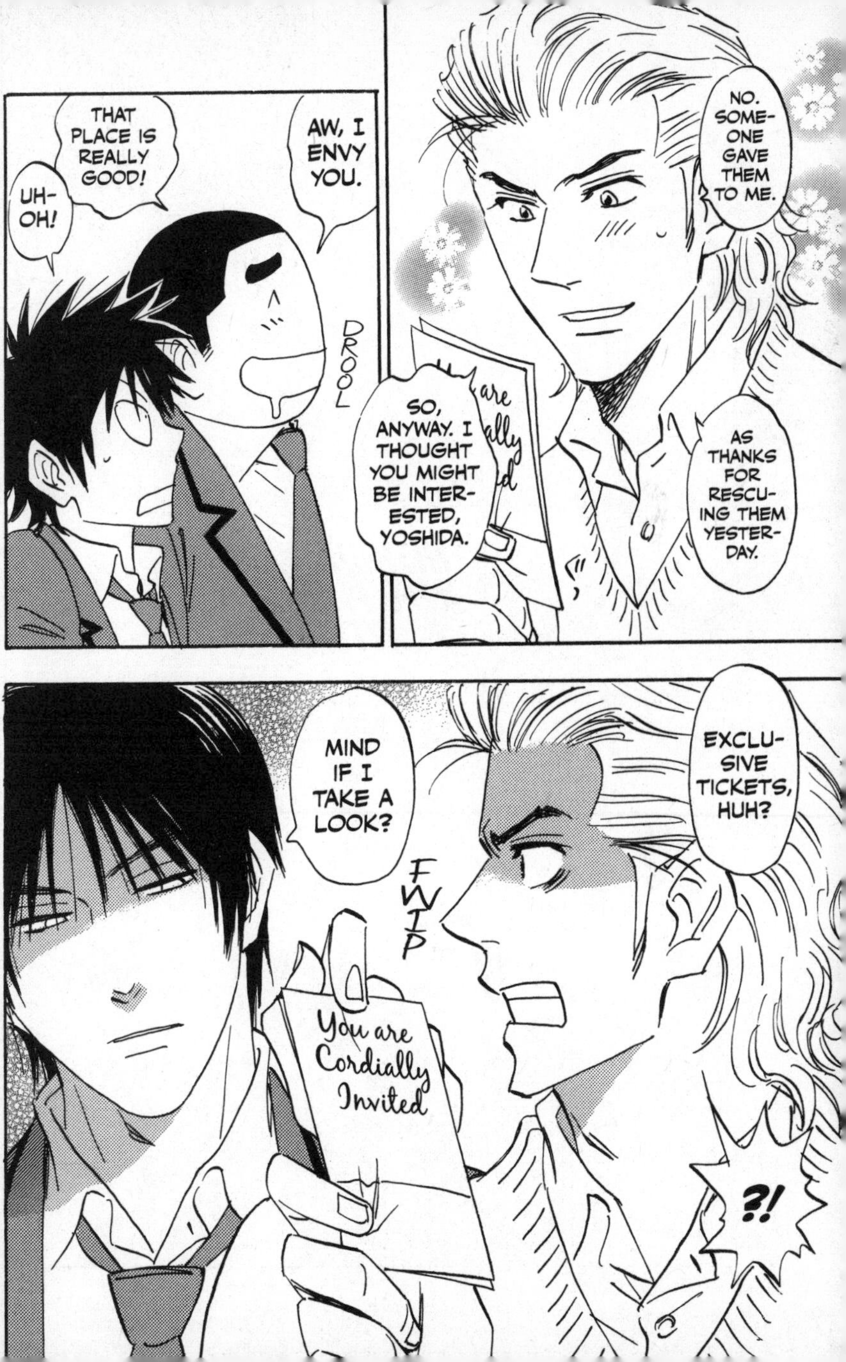
NO. SOME-ONE GAVE THEM TO ME.
AS THANKS FOR RESCU-ING THEM YESTER-DAY.
AW, I ENVY YOU.
THAT PLACE IS REALLY GOOD!
UH-OH!
DROOL
SO, ANYWAY. I THOUGHT YOU MIGHT BE INTER-ESTED, YOSHIDA.
EXCLU-SIVE TICKETS, HUH?
MIND IF I TAKE A LOOK?
FWIP
You are Cordially Invited
?!

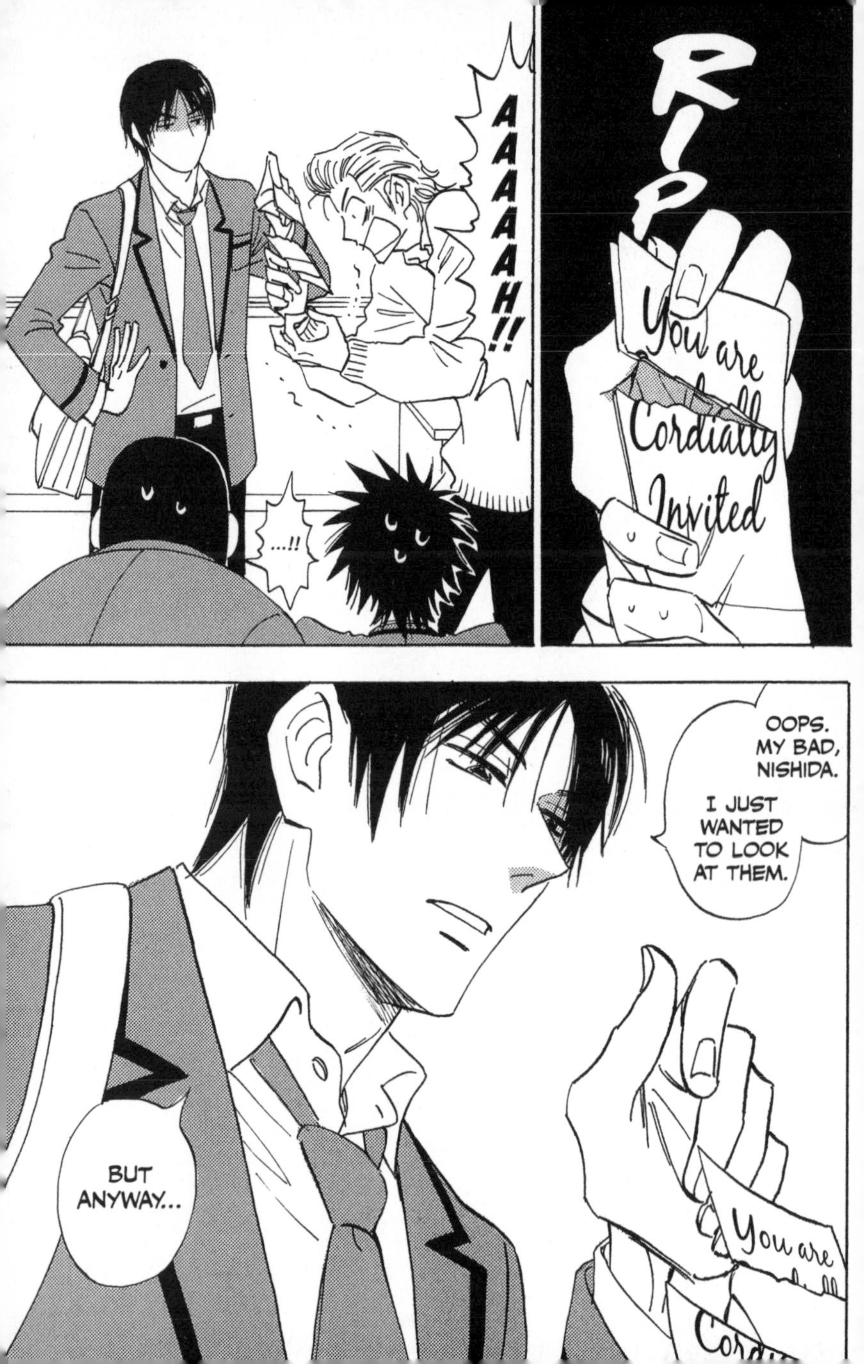
RIP
You are Cordially Invited
AAAAAAH!!
...!!
OOPS. MY BAD, NISHIDA.
I JUST WANTED TO LOOK AT THEM.
BUT ANYWAY...
You are

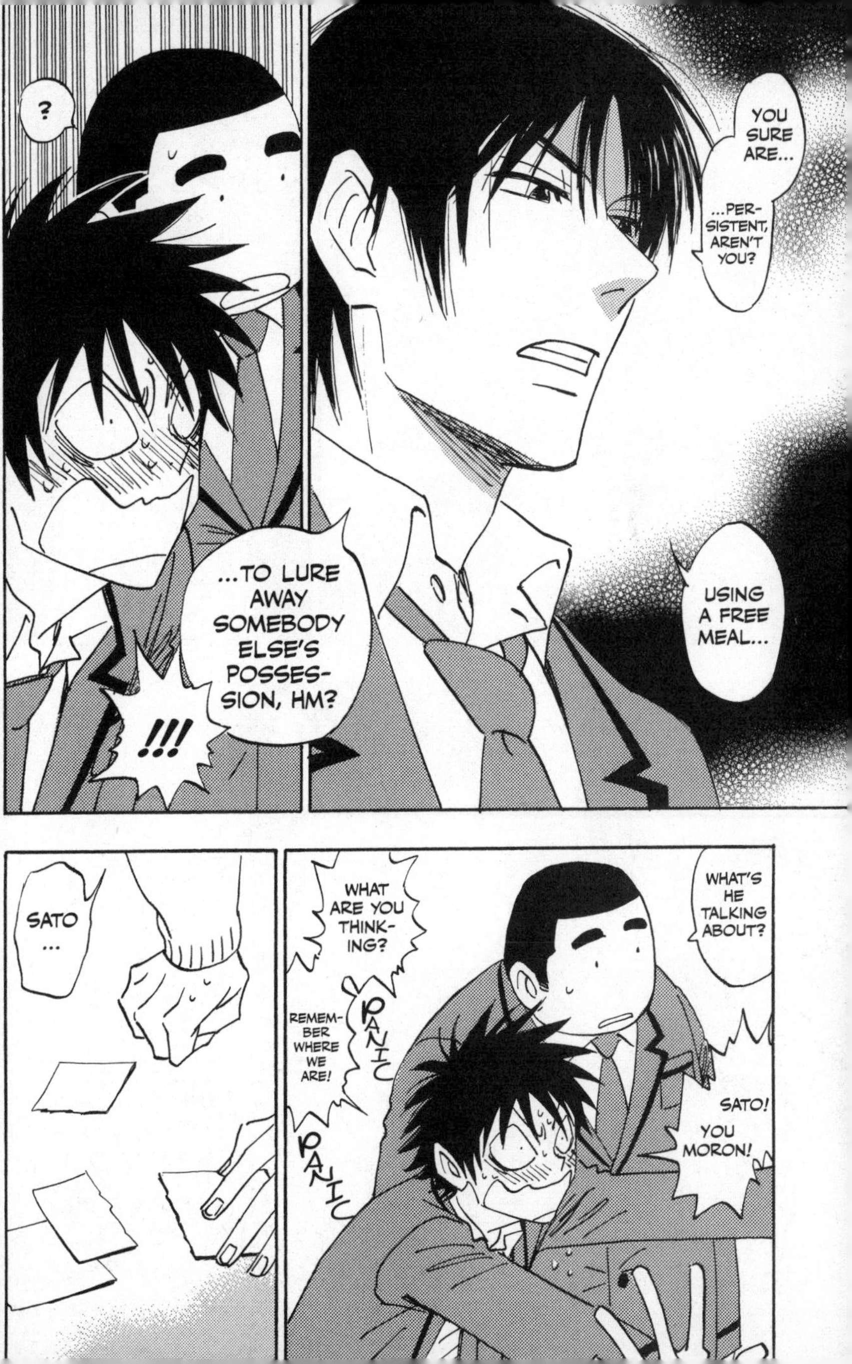
YOU SURE ARE...
...PER-SISTENT, AREN'T YOU?
USING A FREE MEAL...
...TO LURE AWAY SOMEBODY ELSE'S POSSES-SION, HM?
?
!!!
WHAT'S HE TALKING ABOUT?
SATO! YOU MORON!
WHAT ARE YOU THINK-ING?
REMEM-BER WHERE WE ARE!
PANIC
PANIC
SATO ...

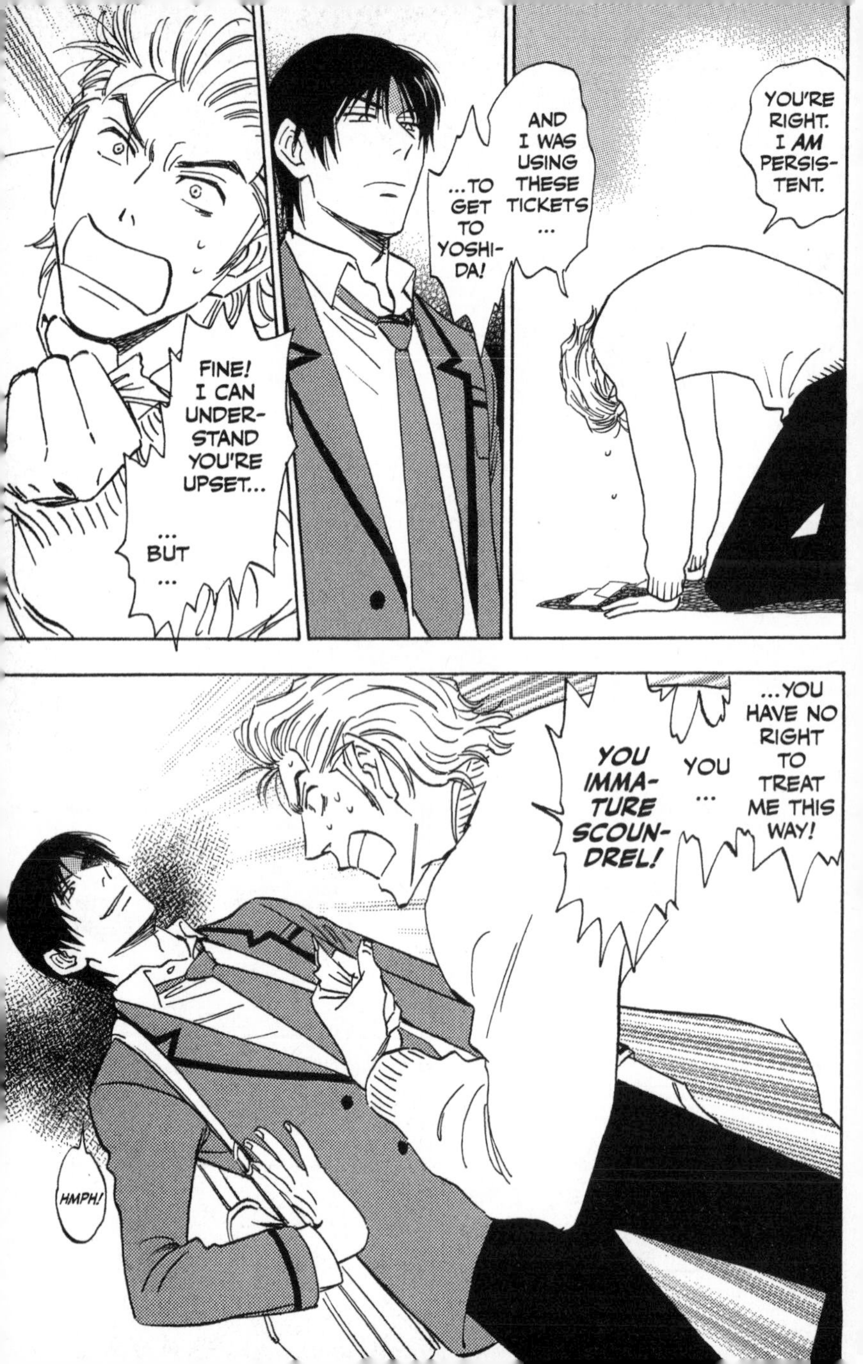
YOU'RE RIGHT. I *AM* PERSISTENT.
AND I WAS USING THESE TICKETS...
...TO GET TO YOSHIDA!
FINE! I CAN UNDERSTAND YOU'RE UPSET...
...BUT...
...YOU HAVE NO RIGHT TO TREAT ME THIS WAY!
YOU...
YOU IMMATURE SCOUNDREL!
HMPH!

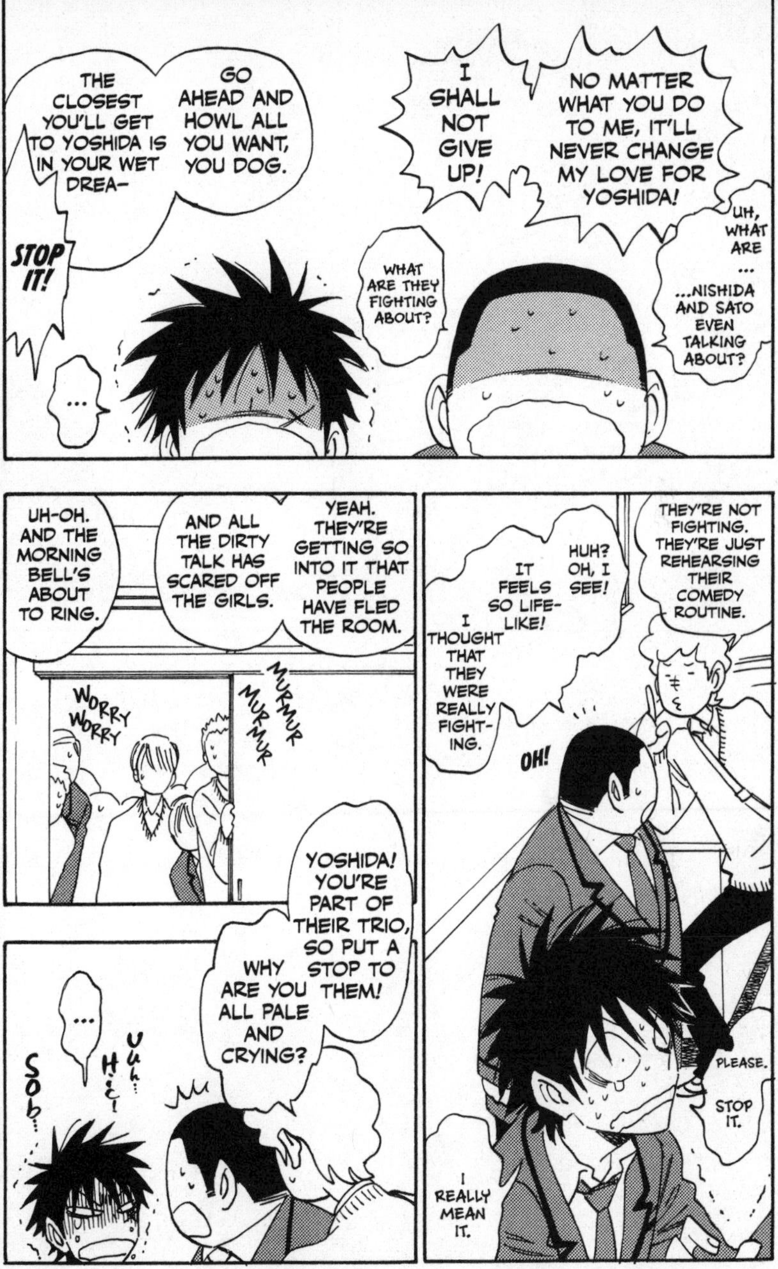
NO MATTER WHAT YOU DO TO ME, IT'LL NEVER CHANGE MY LOVE FOR YOSHIDA!
I SHALL NOT GIVE UP!
UH, WHAT ARE ... ...NISHIDA AND SATO EVEN TALKING ABOUT?
WHAT ARE THEY FIGHTING ABOUT?
GO AHEAD AND HOWL ALL YOU WANT, YOU DOG.
THE CLOSEST YOU'LL GET TO YOSHIDA IS IN YOUR WET DREA-
STOP IT!
...
THEY'RE NOT FIGHTING. THEY'RE JUST REHEARSING THEIR COMEDY ROUTINE.
HUH? OH, I SEE!
IT FEELS SO LIFE-LIKE!
I THOUGHT THAT THEY WERE REALLY FIGHT-ING.
OH!
PLEASE.
STOP IT.
I REALLY MEAN IT.
YEAH. THEY'RE GETTING SO INTO IT THAT PEOPLE HAVE FLED THE ROOM.
AND ALL THE DIRTY TALK HAS SCARED OFF THE GIRLS.
UH-OH. AND THE MORNING BELL'S ABOUT TO RING.
MURMUR MURMUR
WORRY WORRY
YOSHIDA! YOU'RE PART OF THEIR TRIO, SO PUT A STOP TO THEM!
WHY ARE YOU ALL PALE AND CRYING?
...
Uuh...
Hic!
Sob...

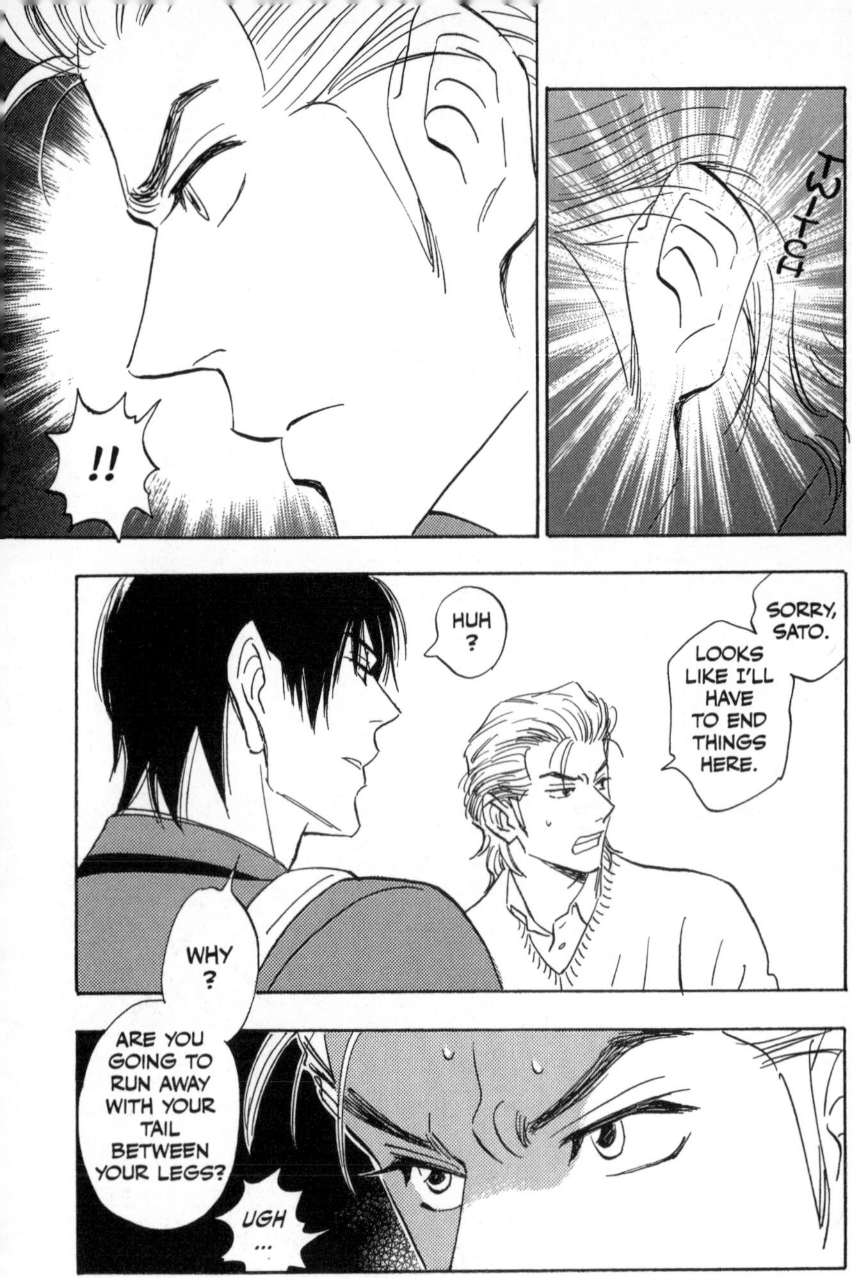
TWITCH
!!
SORRY, SATO.
LOOKS LIKE I'LL HAVE TO END THINGS HERE.
HUH?
WHY?
ARE YOU GOING TO RUN AWAY WITH YOUR TAIL BETWEEN YOUR LEGS?
UGH...

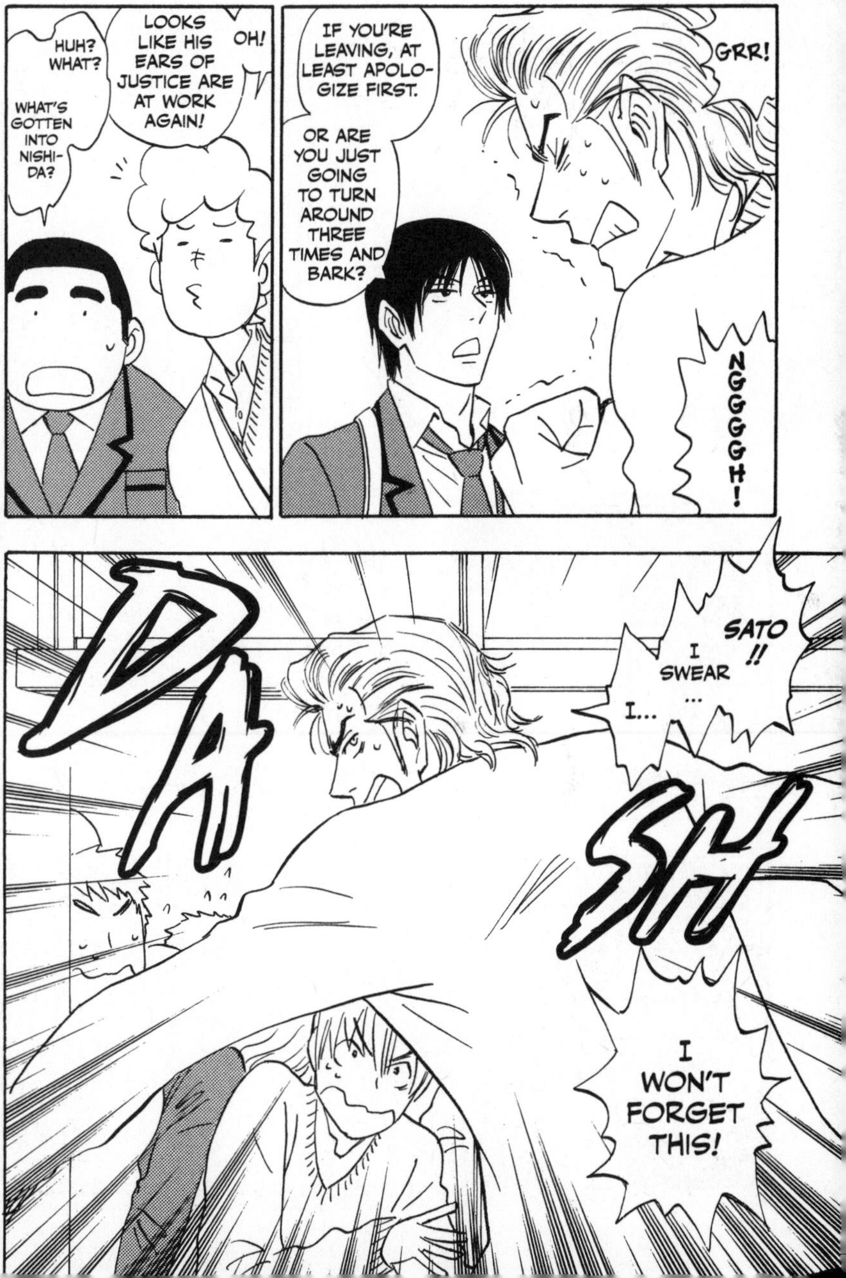
GRR!
IF YOU'RE LEAVING, AT LEAST APOLOGIZE FIRST.
OR ARE YOU JUST GOING TO TURN AROUND THREE TIMES AND BARK?
NGGGGGH!
OH!
LOOKS LIKE HIS EARS OF JUSTICE ARE AT WORK AGAIN!
HUH? WHAT?
WHAT'S GOTTEN INTO NISHIDA?
DASH
SATO!! I SWEAR... I...
I WON'T FORGET THIS!

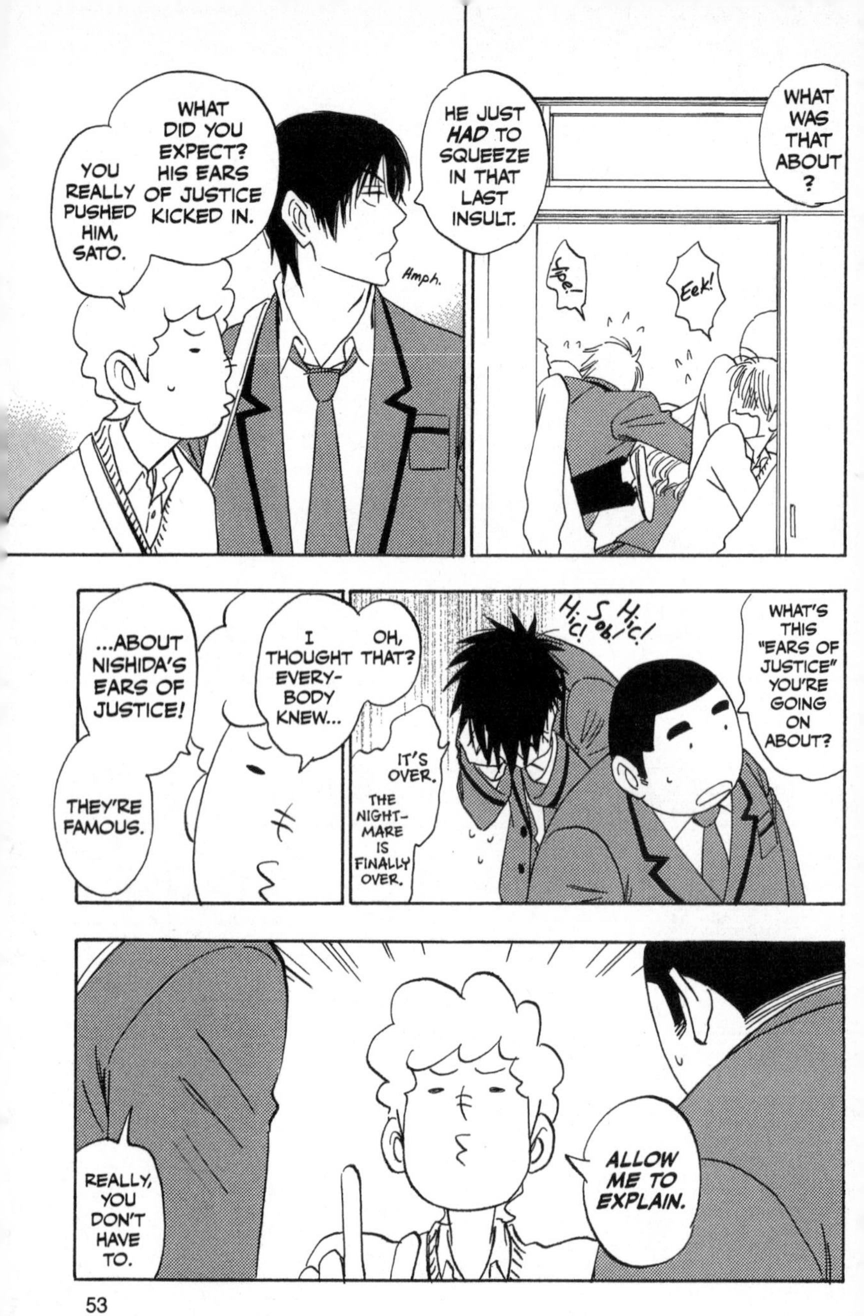
WHAT WAS THAT ABOUT?
Eek!
HE JUST HAD TO SQUEEZE IN THAT LAST INSULT.
Hmph.
WHAT DID YOU EXPECT? HIS EARS OF JUSTICE KICKED IN.
YOU REALLY PUSHED HIM, SATO.
WHAT'S THIS "EARS OF JUSTICE" YOU'RE GOING ON ABOUT?
Hic! Sob! Hic!
IT'S OVER.
THE NIGHTMARE IS FINALLY OVER.
OH, THAT?
I THOUGHT EVERYBODY KNEW...
...ABOUT NISHIDA'S EARS OF JUSTICE!
THEY'RE FAMOUS.
ALLOW ME TO EXPLAIN.
REALLY, YOU DON'T HAVE TO.

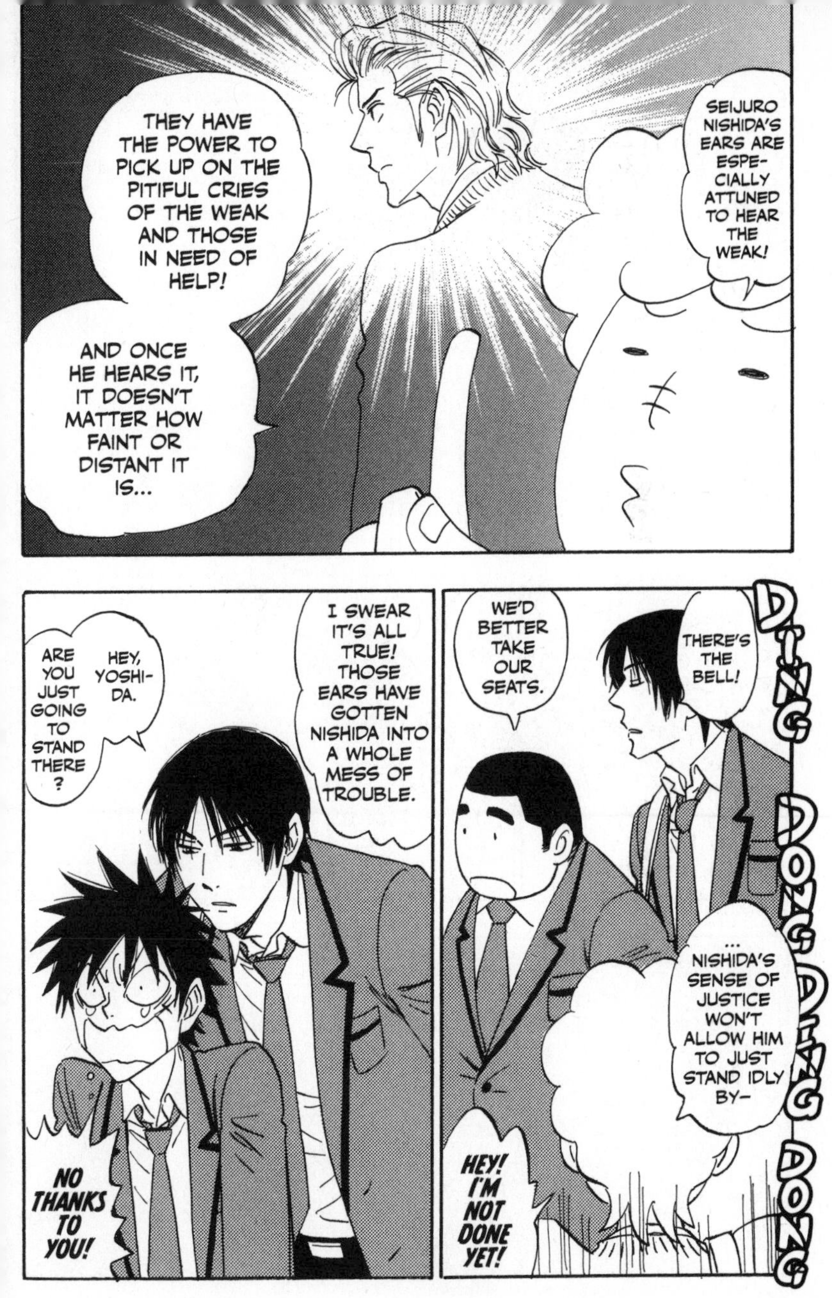
SEIJURO NISHIDA'S EARS ARE ESPE-CIALLY ATTUNED TO HEAR THE WEAK!
THEY HAVE THE POWER TO PICK UP ON THE PITIFUL CRIES OF THE WEAK AND THOSE IN NEED OF HELP!
AND ONCE HE HEARS IT, IT DOESN'T MATTER HOW FAINT OR DISTANT IT IS...
DING DONG DING DONG
THERE'S THE BELL!
WE'D BETTER TAKE OUR SEATS.
...NISHIDA'S SENSE OF JUSTICE WON'T ALLOW HIM TO JUST STAND IDLY BY–
HEY! I'M NOT DONE YET!
I SWEAR IT'S ALL TRUE! THOSE EARS HAVE GOTTEN NISHIDA INTO A WHOLE MESS OF TROUBLE.
HEY, YOSHI-DA.
ARE YOU JUST GOING TO STAND THERE?
NO THANKS TO YOU!

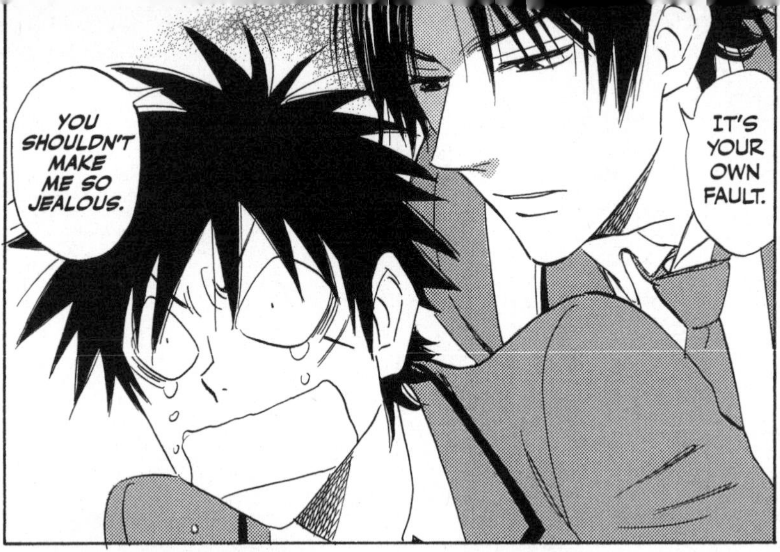
IT'S YOUR OWN FAULT.
YOU SHOULDN'T MAKE ME SO JEALOUS.

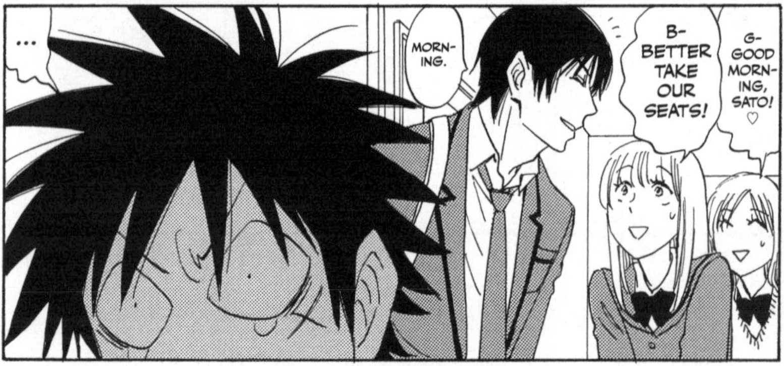
G-GOOD MORNING, SATO! ♡
B-BETTER TAKE OUR SEATS!
MORNING.
...

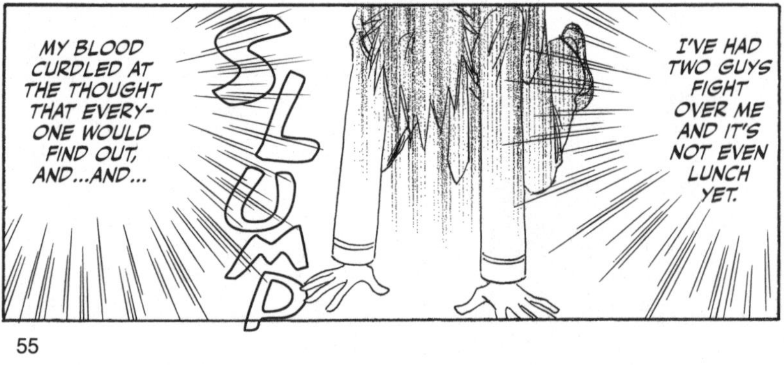
I'VE HAD TWO GUYS FIGHT OVER ME AND IT'S NOT EVEN LUNCH YET.
SLUMP
MY BLOOD CURDLED AT THE THOUGHT THAT EVERYONE WOULD FIND OUT, AND...AND...

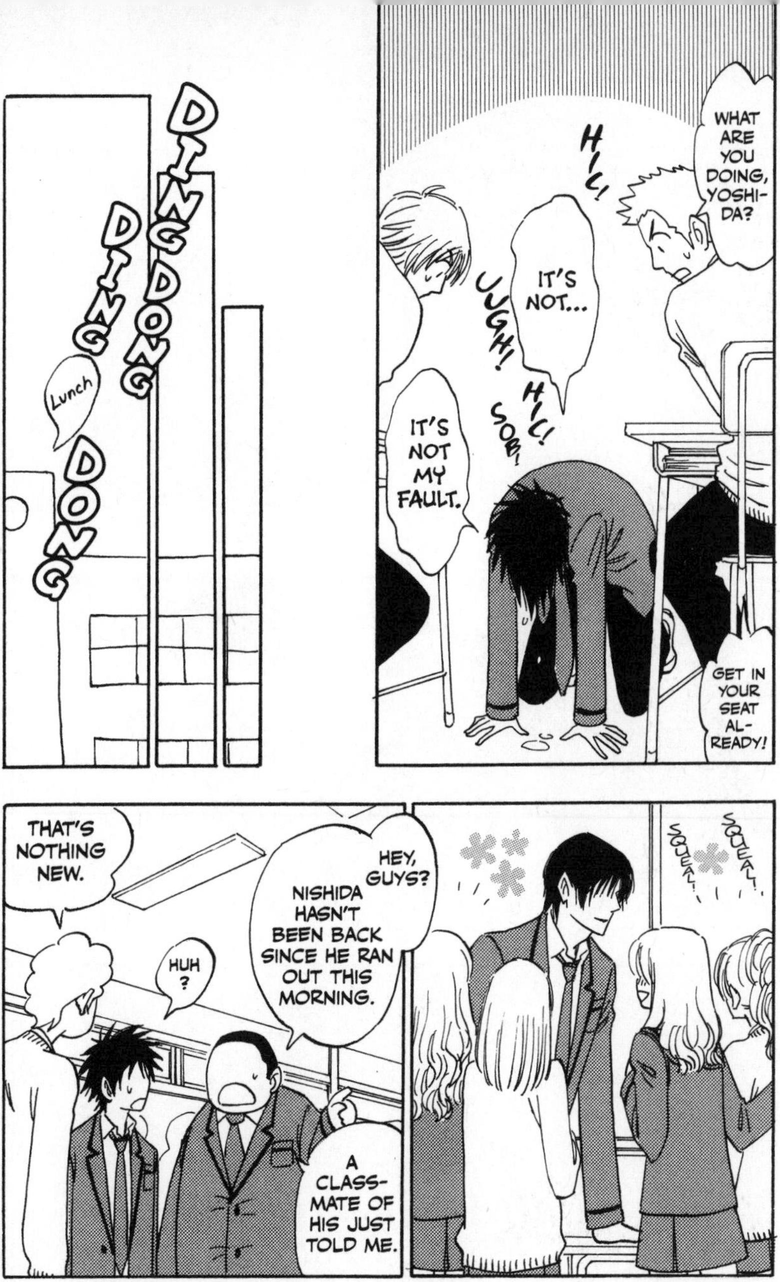
WHAT ARE YOU DOING, YOSHIDA?
HIC!
IT'S NOT...
UGH!
HIC!
SOB!
IT'S NOT MY FAULT.
GET IN YOUR SEAT ALREADY!
DING DONG
DING DONG
Lunch
SQUEAL!
SQUEAL!
HEY, GUYS? NISHIDA HASN'T BEEN BACK SINCE HE RAN OUT THIS MORNING.
A CLASSMATE OF HIS JUST TOLD ME.
HUH?
THAT'S NOTHING NEW.

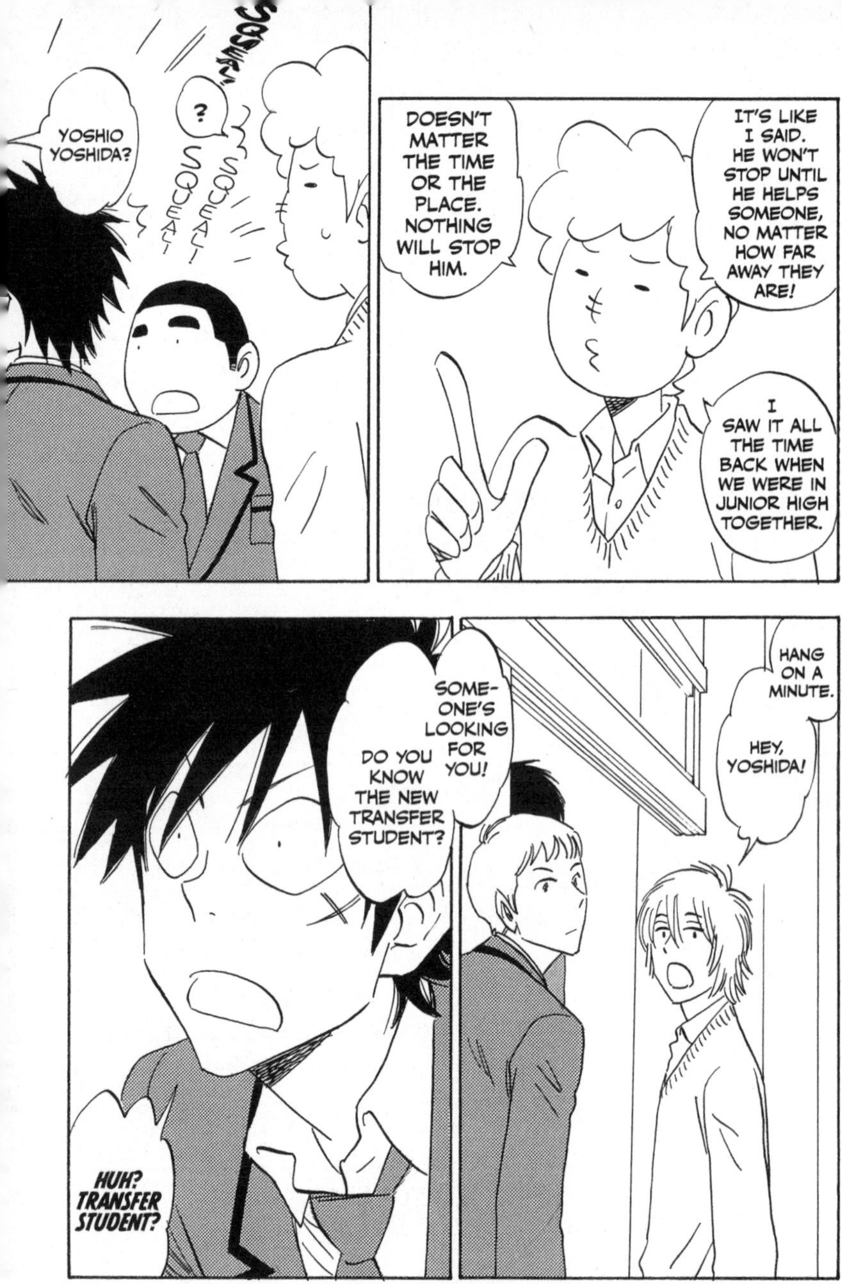
IT'S LIKE I SAID. HE WON'T STOP UNTIL HE HELPS SOMEONE, NO MATTER HOW FAR AWAY THEY ARE!
DOESN'T MATTER THE TIME OR THE PLACE. NOTHING WILL STOP HIM.
I SAW IT ALL THE TIME BACK WHEN WE WERE IN JUNIOR HIGH TOGETHER.
SQUEAK!
SQUEAK!
SQUEAK!
?
YOSHIO YOSHIDA?
HANG ON A MINUTE.
HEY, YOSHIDA!
SOME-ONE'S LOOKING FOR YOU!
DO YOU KNOW THE NEW TRANSFER STUDENT?
HUH? TRANSFER STUDENT?

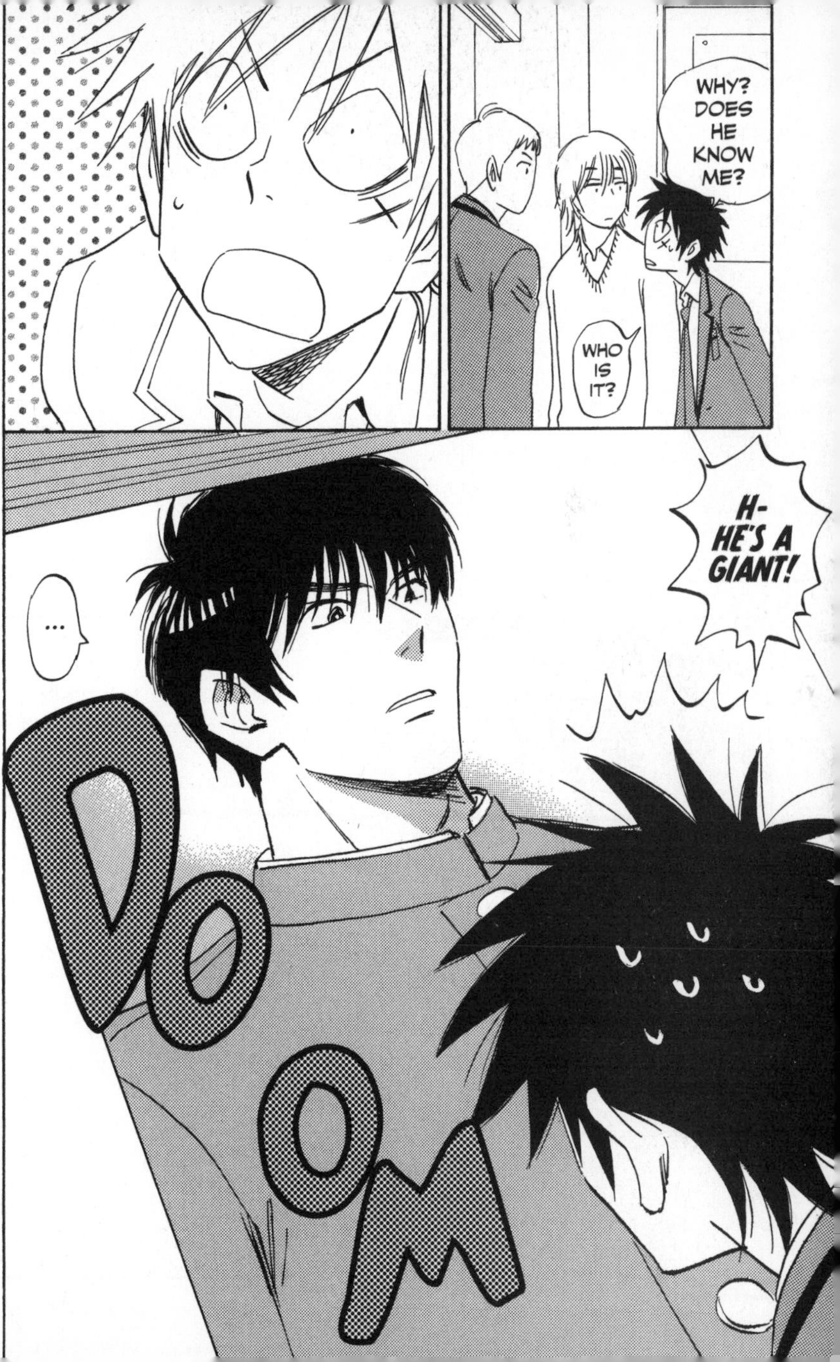
WHY? DOES HE KNOW ME?
WHO IS IT?
H-HE'S A GIANT!
...
DOOOM

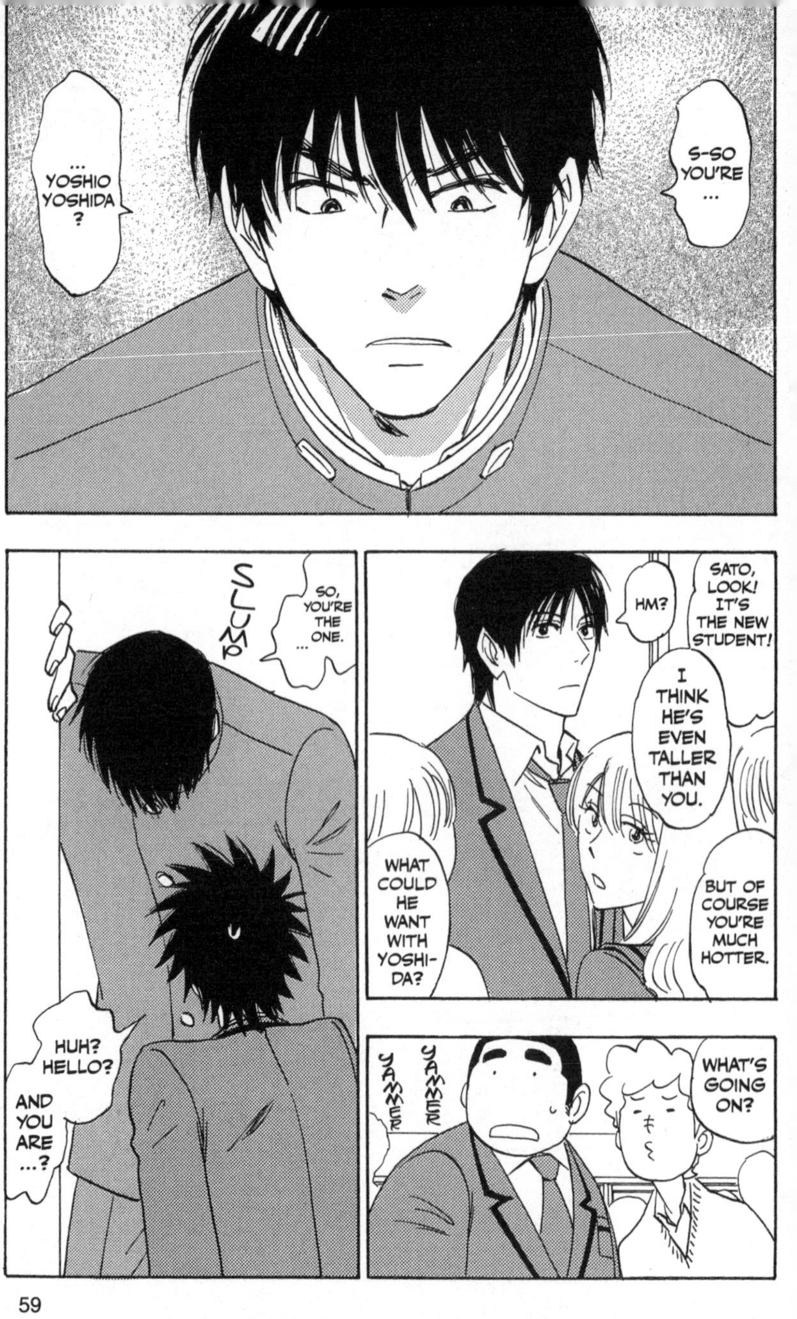
S-SO YOU'RE ...
... YOSHIO YOSHIDA ?
SATO, LOOK! IT'S THE NEW STUDENT!
HM?
I THINK HE'S EVEN TALLER THAN YOU.
BUT OF COURSE YOU'RE MUCH HOTTER.
WHAT COULD HE WANT WITH YOSHI-DA?
WHAT'S GOING ON?
YAMMER
YAMMER
SLUMP
SO, YOU'RE THE ONE. ...
HUH? HELLO?
AND YOU ARE ...?

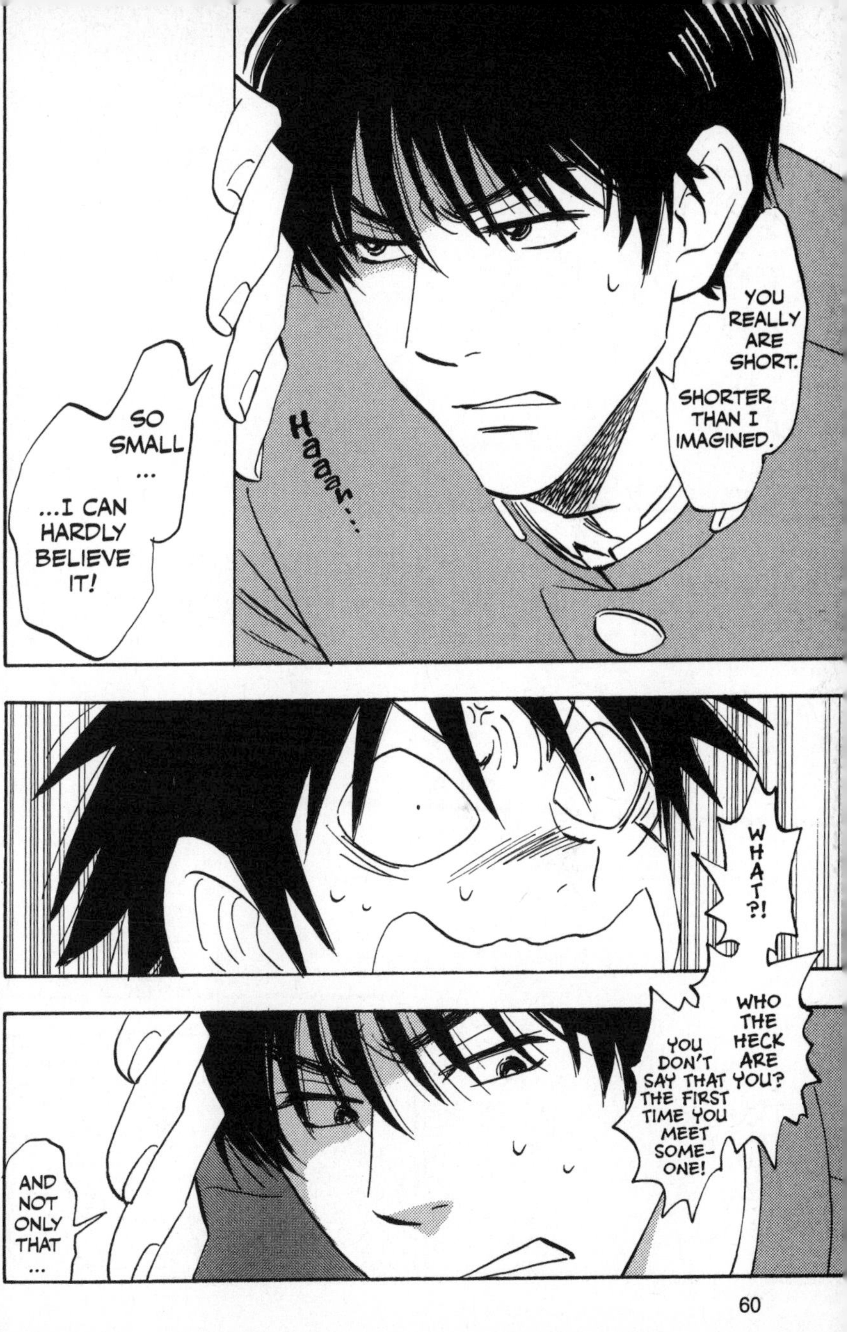
YOU REALLY ARE SHORT.
SHORTER THAN I IMAGINED.
Haaaar...
SO SMALL...
...I CAN HARDLY BELIEVE IT!
WHAT?!
WHO THE HECK ARE YOU?
YOU DON'T SAY THAT THE FIRST TIME YOU MEET SOME-ONE!
AND NOT ONLY THAT...

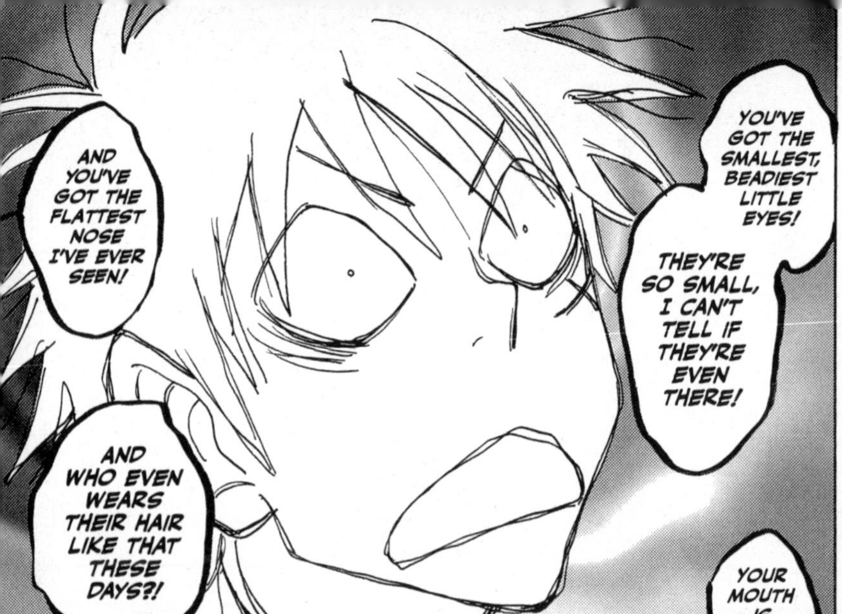
YOU'VE GOT THE SMALLEST, BEADIEST LITTLE EYES!
THEY'RE SO SMALL, I CAN'T TELL IF THEY'RE EVEN THERE!
AND YOU'VE GOT THE FLATTEST NOSE I'VE EVER SEEN!
YOUR MOUTH IS SHAPED WEIRD.
AND WHO EVEN WEARS THEIR HAIR LIKE THAT THESE DAYS?!
IT'S DISGUSTING!

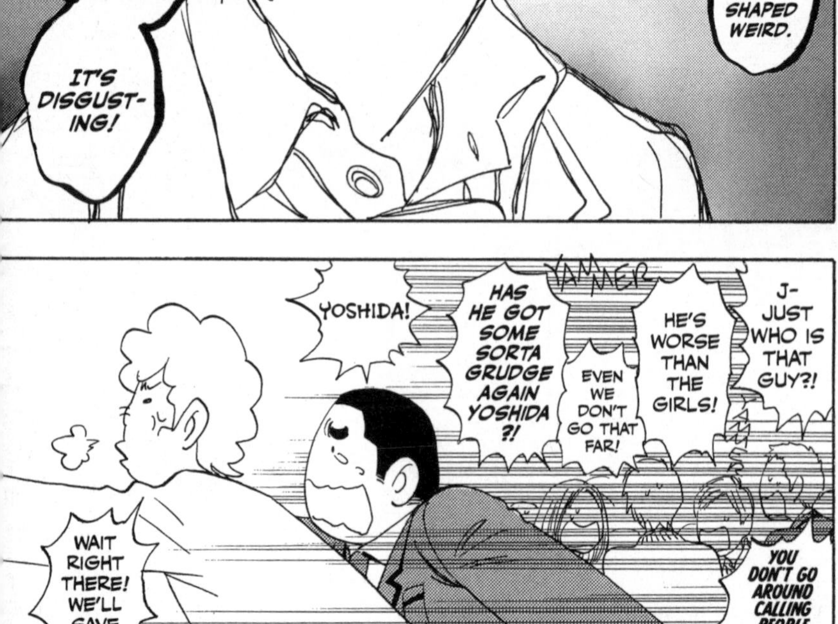
YAMMER
J-JUST WHO IS THAT GUY?!
HE'S WORSE THAN THE GIRLS!
EVEN WE DON'T GO THAT FAR!
HAS HE GOT SOME SORTA GRUDGE AGAIN YOSHIDA?!
YOSHIDA!
YOU DON'T GO AROUND CALLING PEOPLE DISGUSTING!
WAIT RIGHT THERE! WE'LL SAVE YOU–!

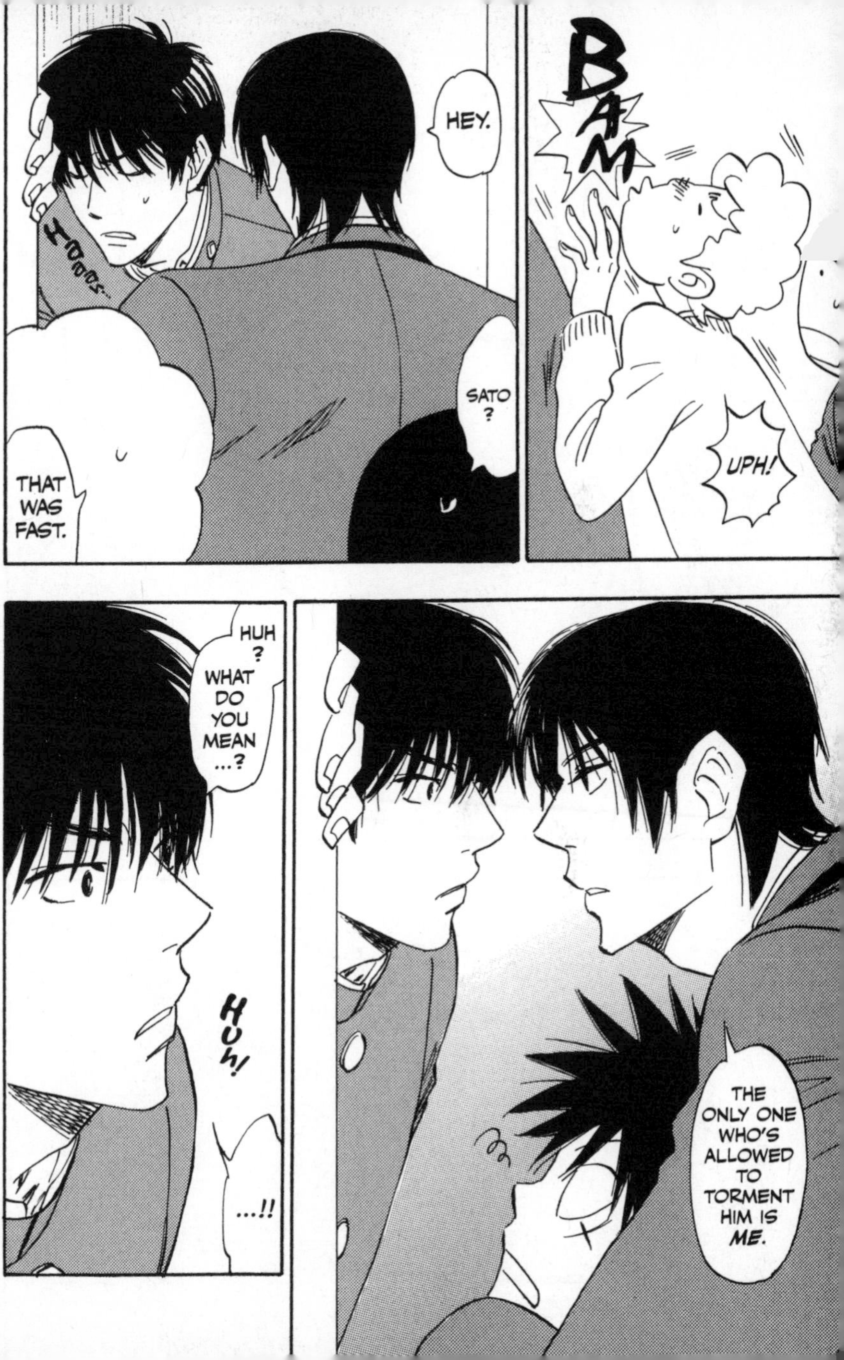
BAM
UPH!
HEY.
SATO?
THAT WAS FAST.
THE ONLY ONE WHO'S ALLOWED TO TORMENT HIM IS *ME*.
HUH? WHAT DO YOU MEAN...?
HUH!
...!!

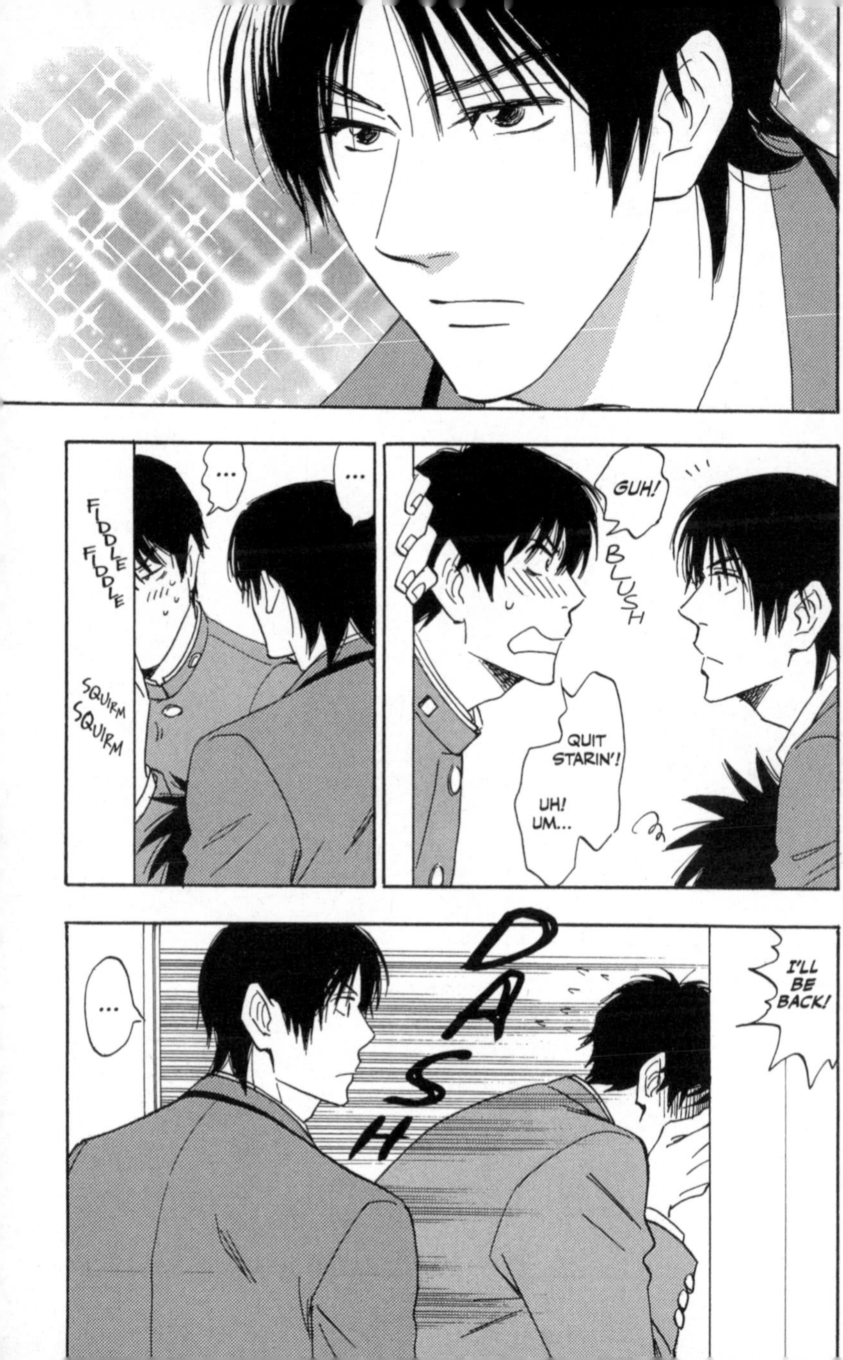
GUH!
BLUSH
QUIT STARIN'!
UH! UM...
...
...
FIDDLE FIDDLE
SQUIRM SQUIRM
I'LL BE BACK!
DASH
...

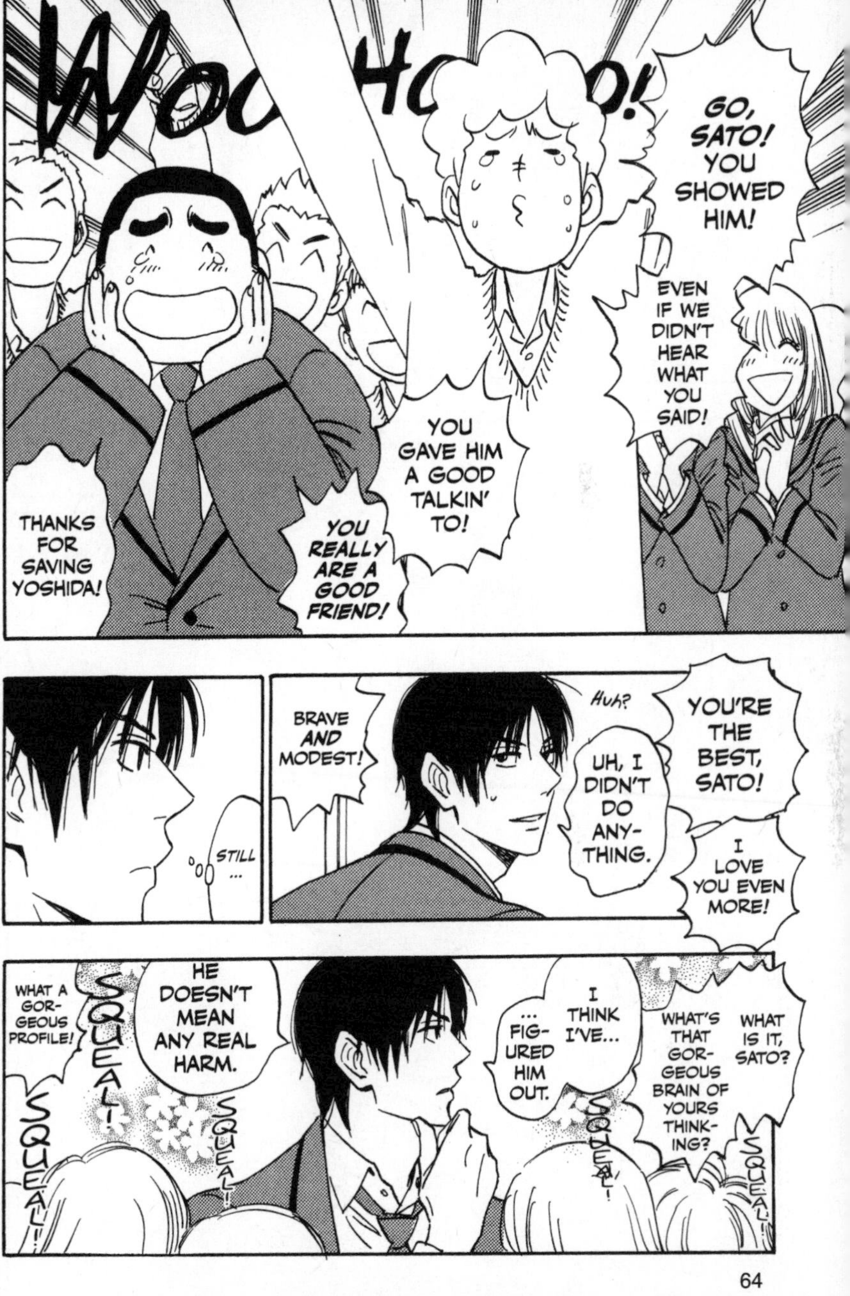
WOO HOO!
GO, SATO! YOU SHOWED HIM!
EVEN IF WE DIDN'T HEAR WHAT YOU SAID!
YOU GAVE HIM A GOOD TALKIN' TO!
YOU REALLY ARE A GOOD FRIEND!
THANKS FOR SAVING YOSHIDA!
YOU'RE THE BEST, SATO!
Huh?
I LOVE YOU EVEN MORE!
UH, I DIDN'T DO ANYTHING.
BRAVE AND MODEST!
STILL ...
WHAT IS IT, SATO?
WHAT'S THAT GORGEOUS BRAIN OF YOURS THINKING?
SQUEAL!
SQUEAL!
I THINK I'VE...
...FIGURED HIM OUT.
HE DOESN'T MEAN ANY REAL HARM.
SQUEAL!
SQUEAL!
WHAT A GORGEOUS PROFILE!
SQUEAL!

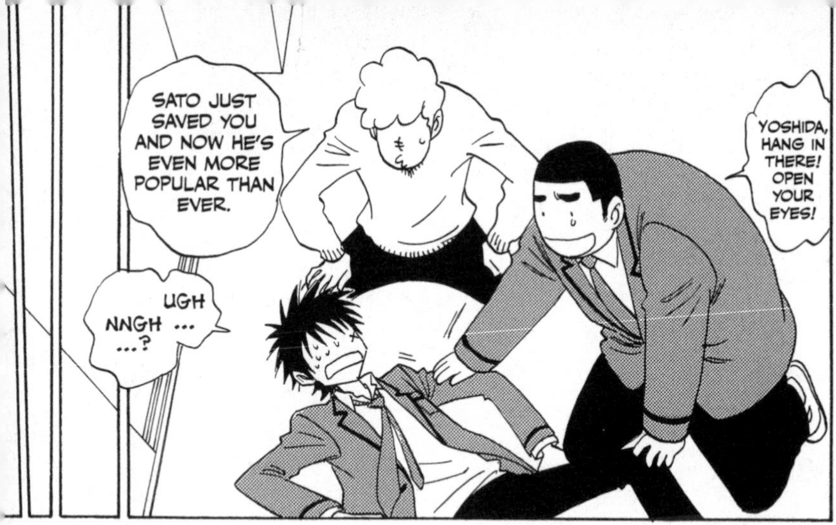
YOSHIDA, HANG IN THERE! OPEN YOUR EYES!
SATO JUST SAVED YOU AND NOW HE'S EVEN MORE POPULAR THAN EVER.
UGH NNGH ... ...?

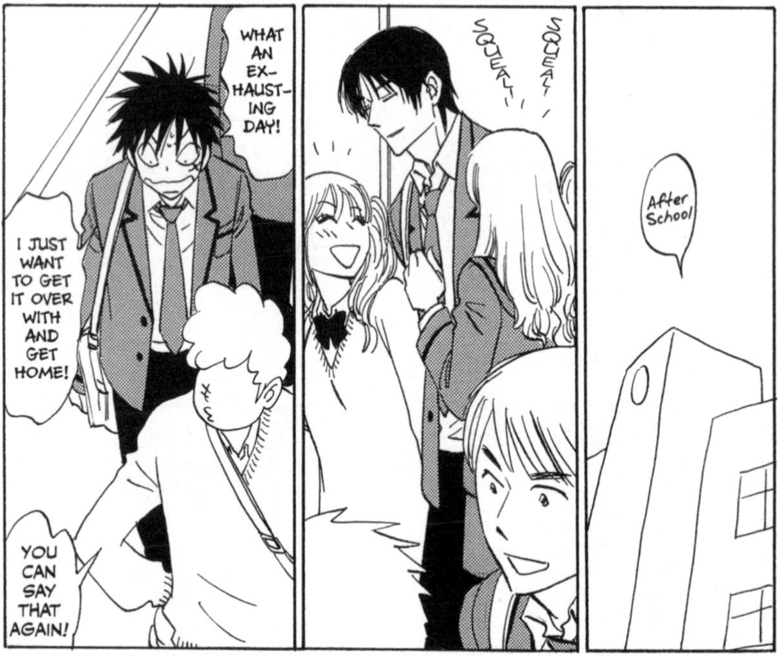
After School
SQUEAL!
SQUEAL!
WHAT AN EX-HAUSTING DAY!
I JUST WANT TO GET IT OVER WITH AND GET HOME!
YOU CAN SAY THAT AGAIN!

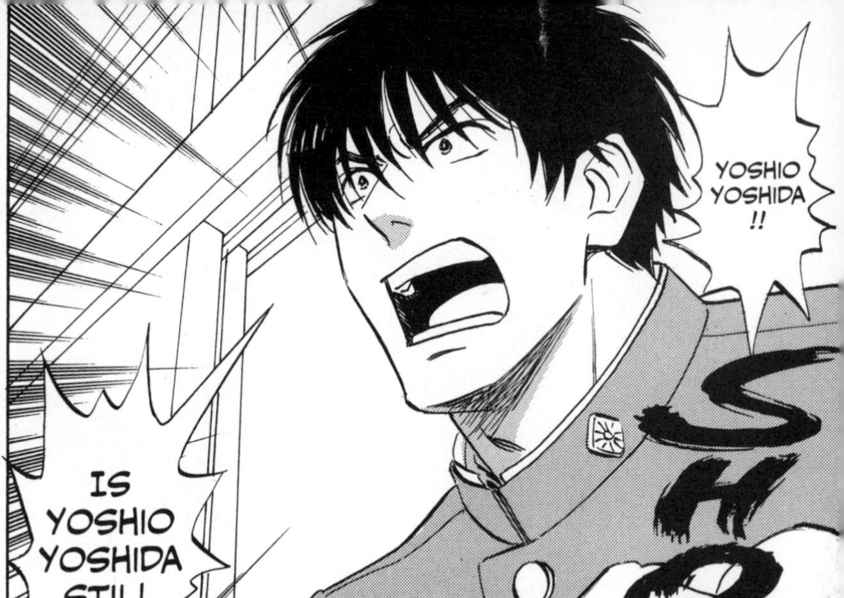
YOSHIO YOSHIDA !!
SHOVE
IS YOSHIO YOSHIDA STILL HERE?!
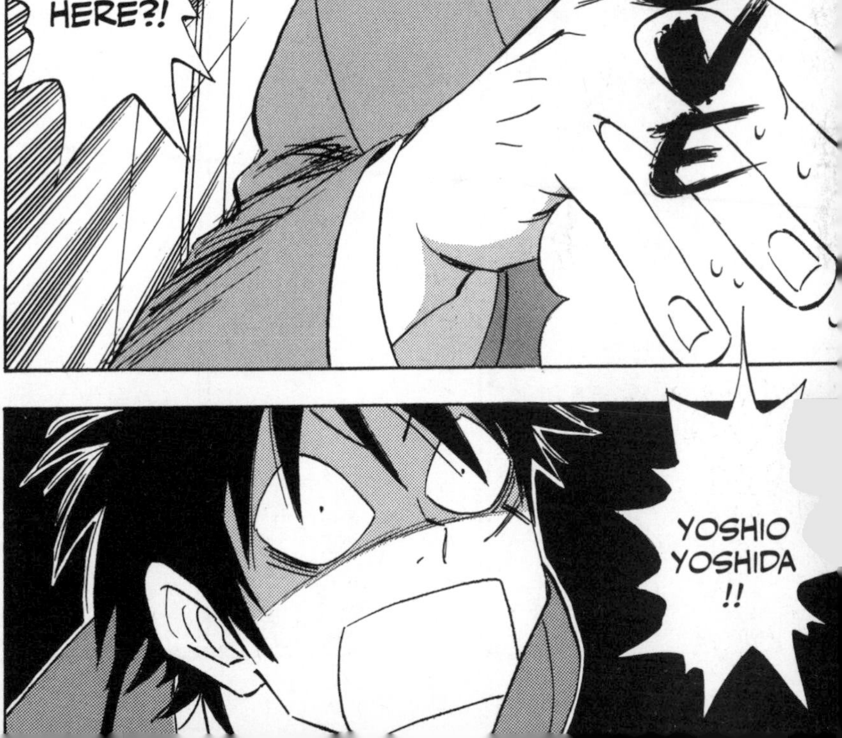
YOSHIO YOSHIDA !!

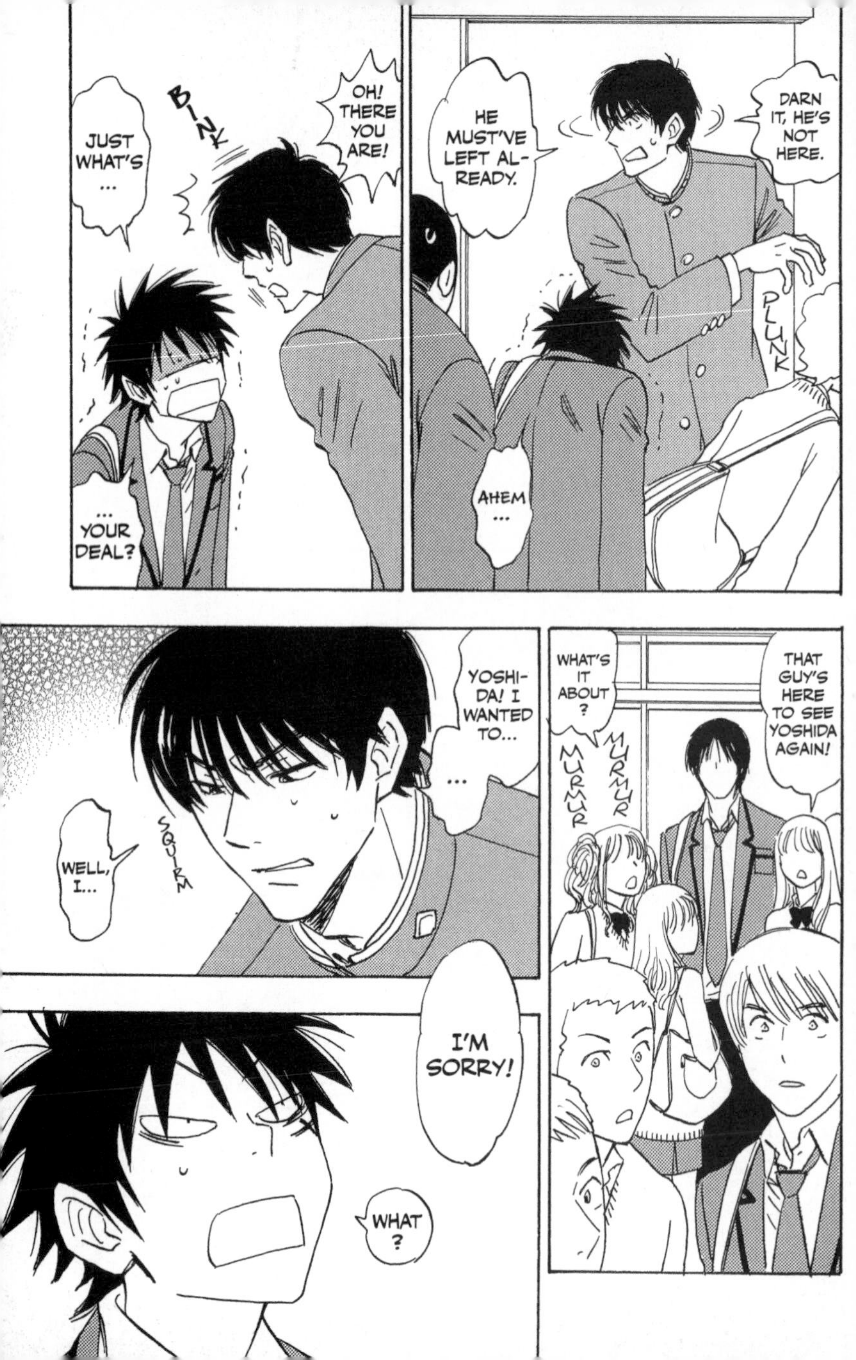
DARN IT, HE'S NOT HERE.
HE MUST'VE LEFT AL-READY.
PLUNK
AHEM ...
OH! THERE YOU ARE!
BINK
JUST WHAT'S ...
... YOUR DEAL?
THAT GUY'S HERE TO SEE YOSHIDA AGAIN!
WHAT'S IT ABOUT?
MURMUR
MURMUR
YOSHI-DA! I WANTED TO...
...
SQUIRM
WELL, I...
I'M SORRY!
WHAT?

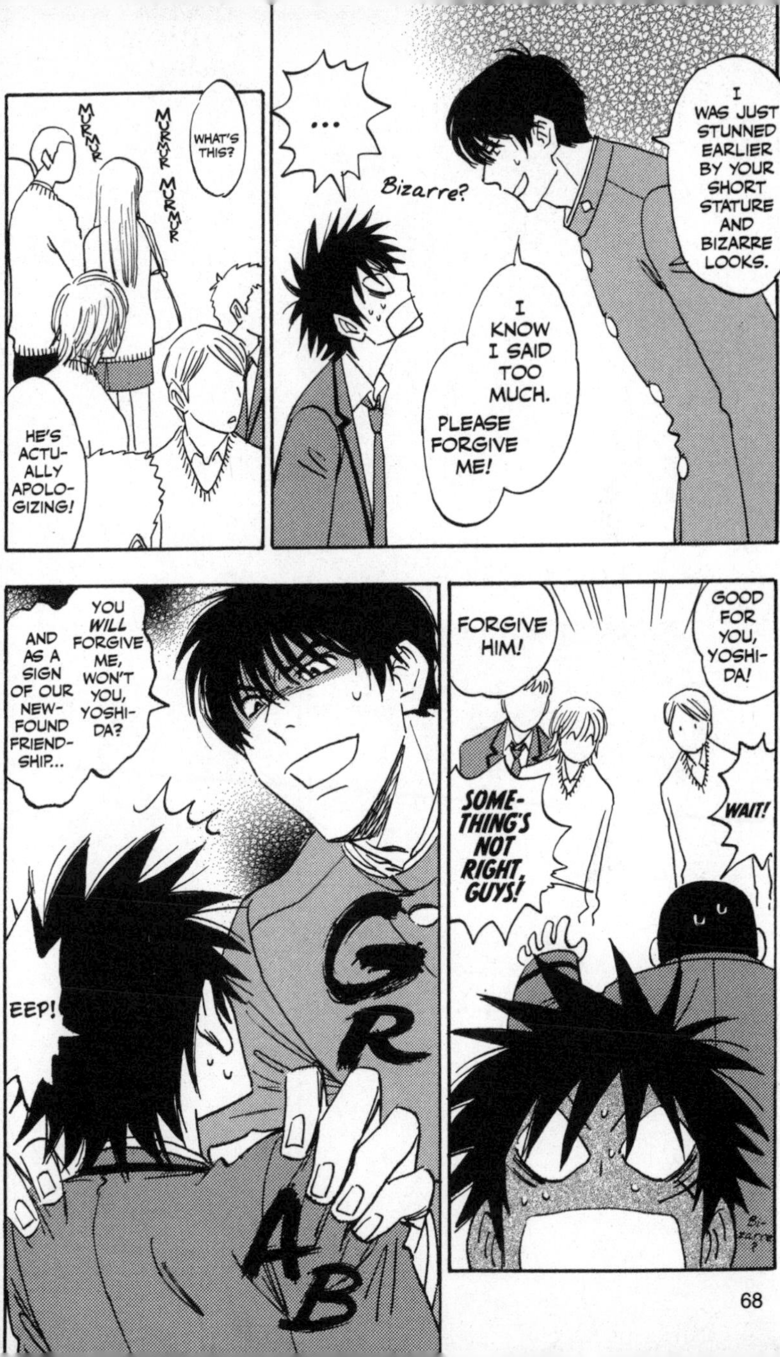
I WAS JUST STUNNED EARLIER BY YOUR SHORT STATURE AND BIZARRE LOOKS.
...
Bizarre?
I KNOW I SAID TOO MUCH.
PLEASE FORGIVE ME!
WHAT'S THIS?
MURMUR MURMUR
MURMUR
HE'S ACTUALLY APOLOGIZING!
GOOD FOR YOU, YOSHIDA!
FORGIVE HIM!
WAIT!
SOMETHING'S NOT RIGHT, GUYS!
Bizarre?
YOU *WILL* FORGIVE ME, WON'T YOU, YOSHIDA?
AND AS A SIGN OF OUR NEWFOUND FRIENDSHIP...
EEP!
GRAB

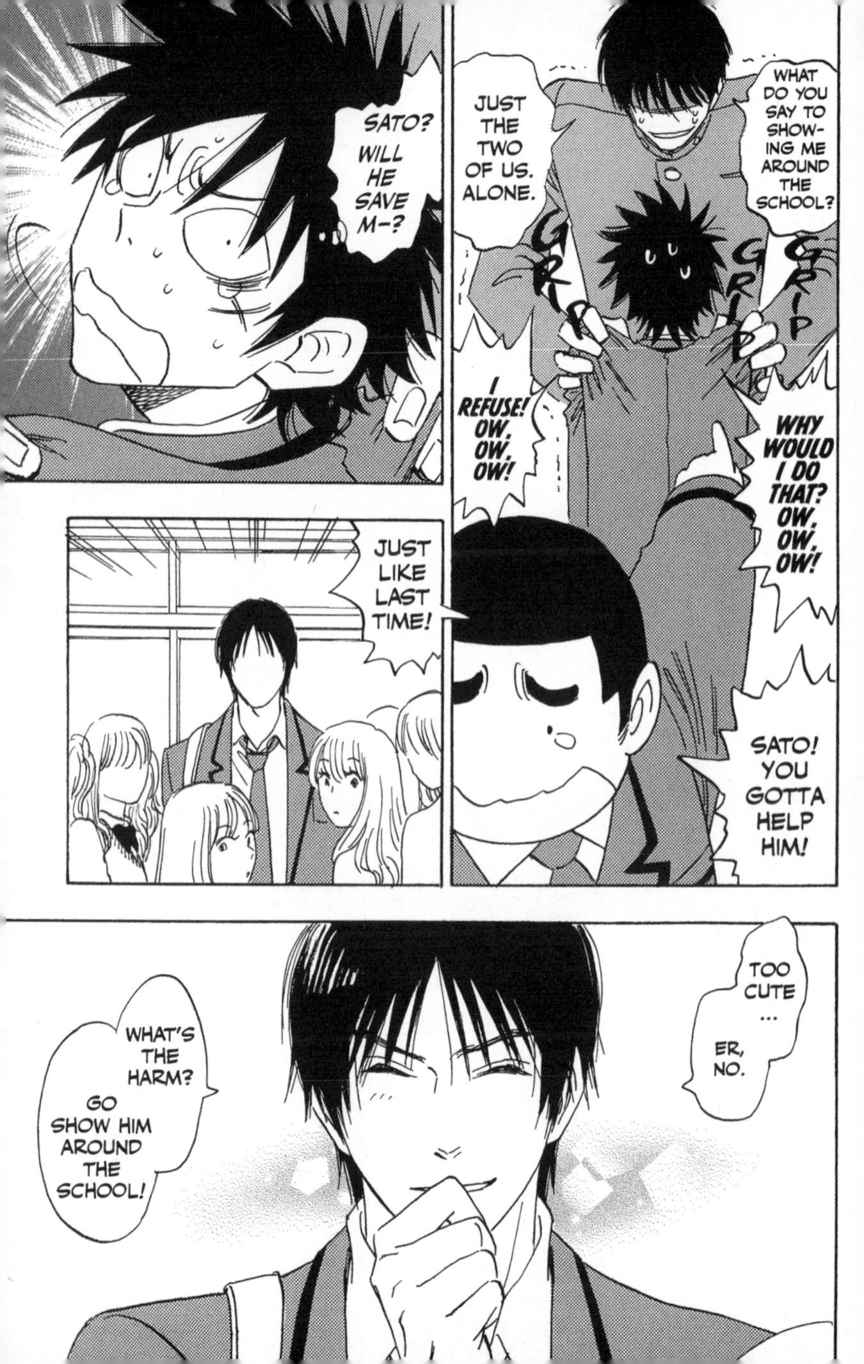
WHAT DO YOU SAY TO SHOWING ME AROUND THE SCHOOL?
JUST THE TWO OF US. ALONE.
GRIP
GRIP
GRIP
WHY WOULD I DO THAT? OW, OW, OW!
I REFUSE! OW, OW, OW!
SATO? WILL HE SAVE M-?
SATO! YOU GOTTA HELP HIM!
JUST LIKE LAST TIME!
TOO CUTE ... ER, NO.
WHAT'S THE HARM? GO SHOW HIM AROUND THE SCHOOL!

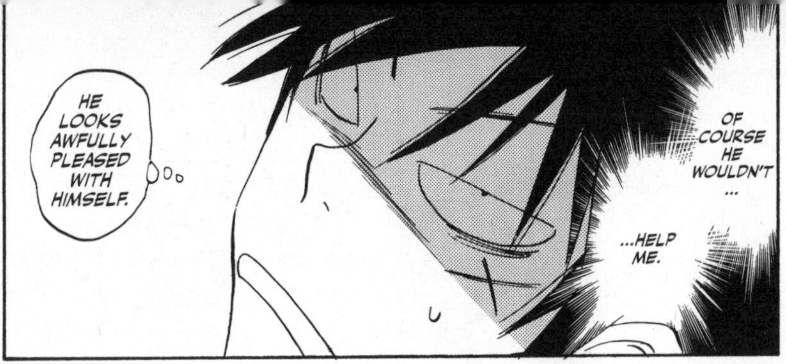
OF COURSE HE WOULDN'T ...
...HELP ME.
HE LOOKS AWFULLY PLEASED WITH HIMSELF.

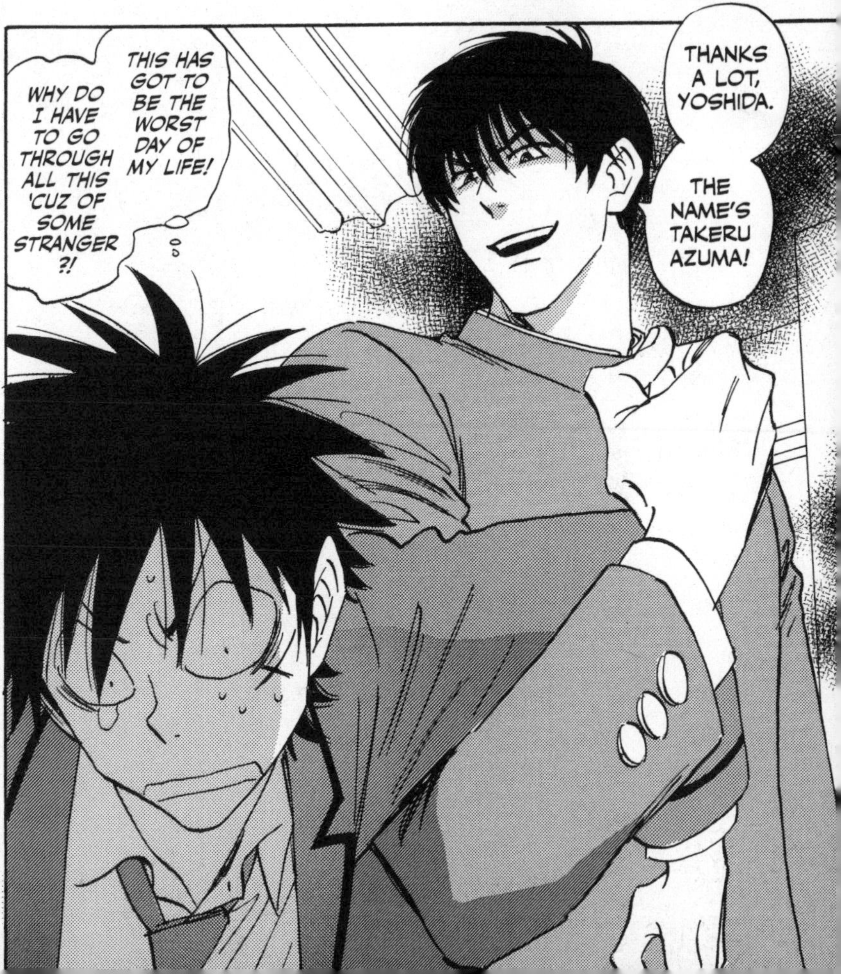
THANKS A LOT, YOSHIDA.
THE NAME'S TAKERU AZUMA!
THIS HAS GOT TO BE THE WORST DAY OF MY LIFE!
WHY DO I HAVE TO GO THROUGH ALL THIS 'CUZ OF SOME STRANGER?!

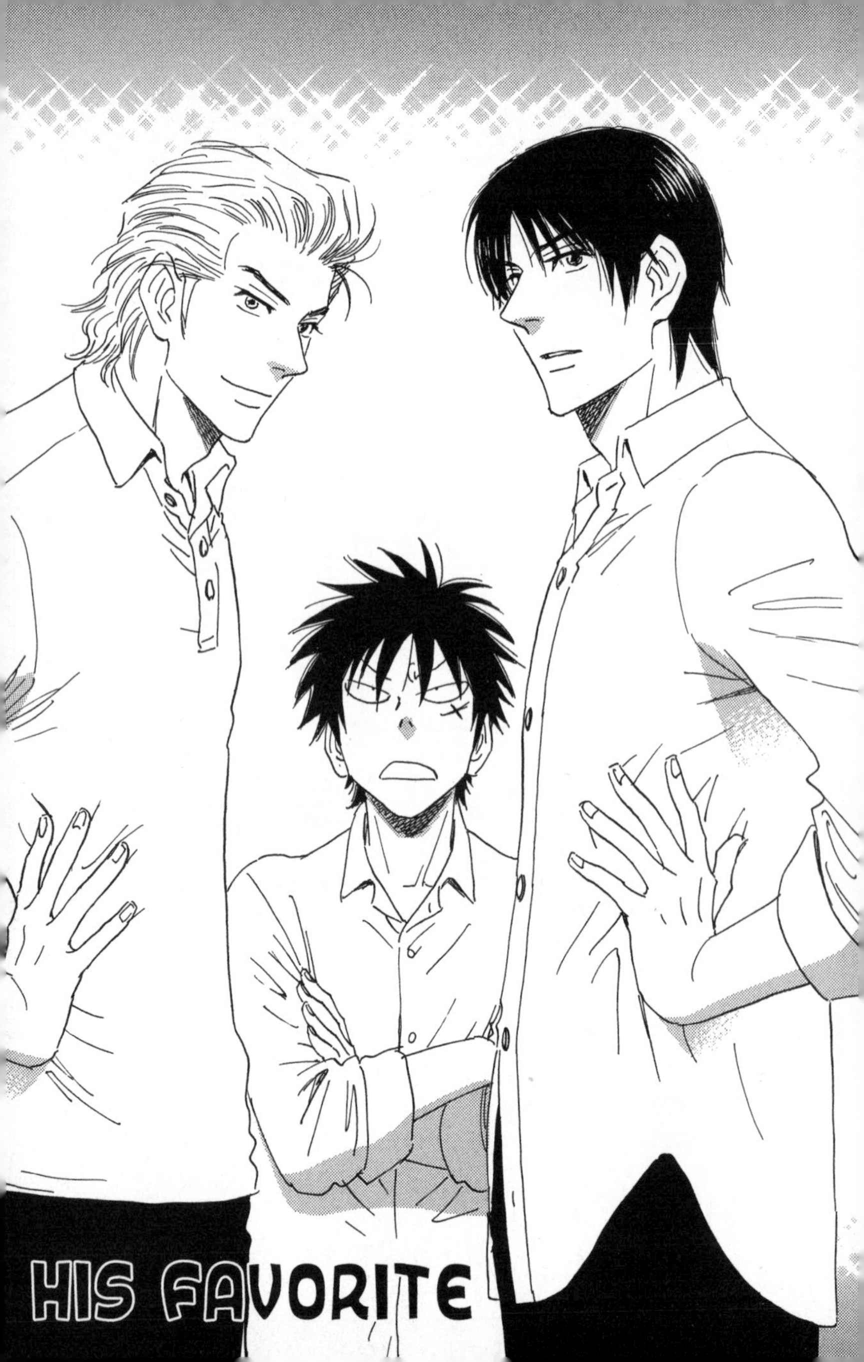
HIS FAVORITE

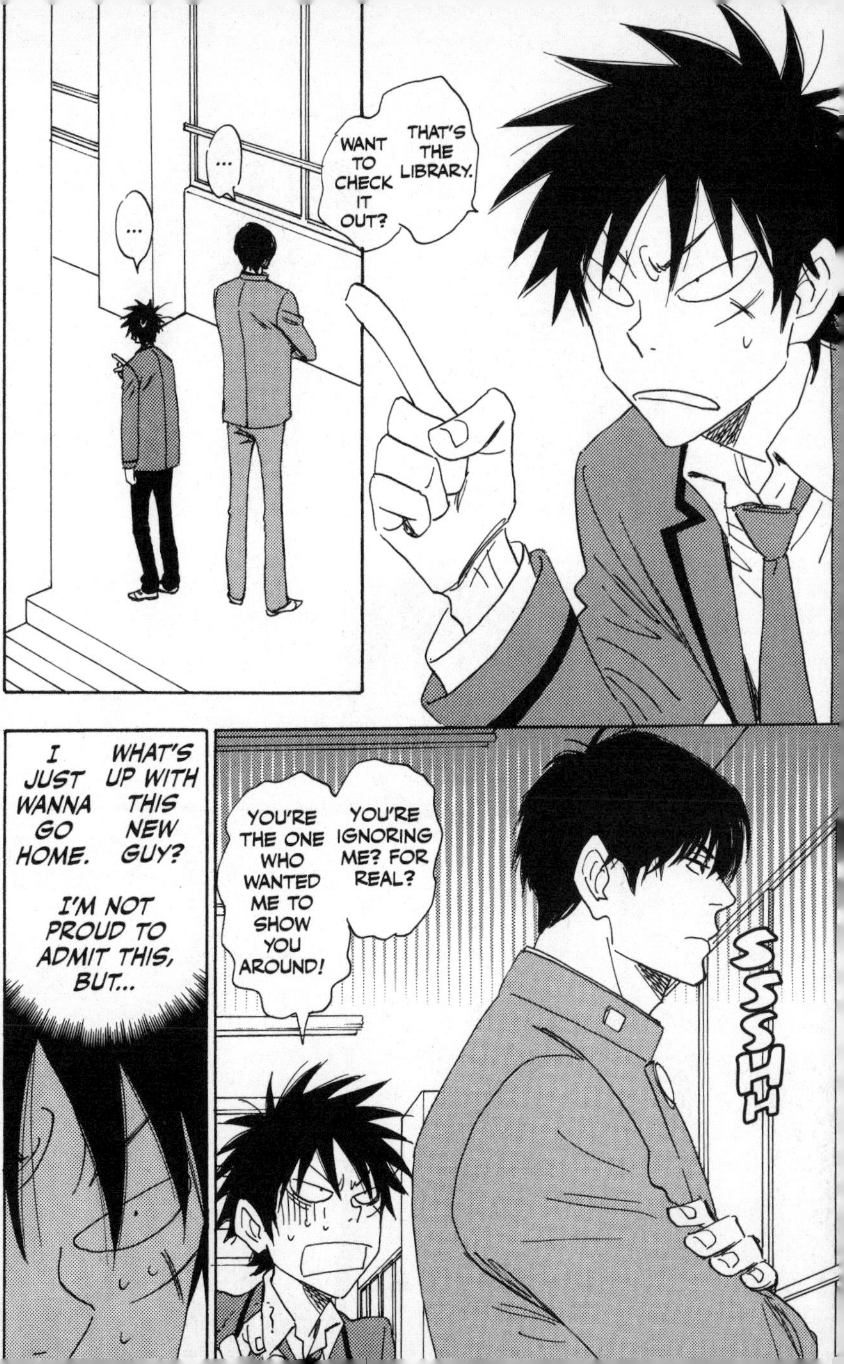
THAT'S THE LIBRARY.
WANT TO CHECK IT OUT?
...
...
YOU'RE IGNORING ME? FOR REAL?
YOU'RE THE ONE WHO WANTED ME TO SHOW YOU AROUND!
SSSHH
WHAT'S UP WITH THIS NEW GUY?
I JUST WANNA GO HOME.
I'M NOT PROUD TO ADMIT THIS, BUT...

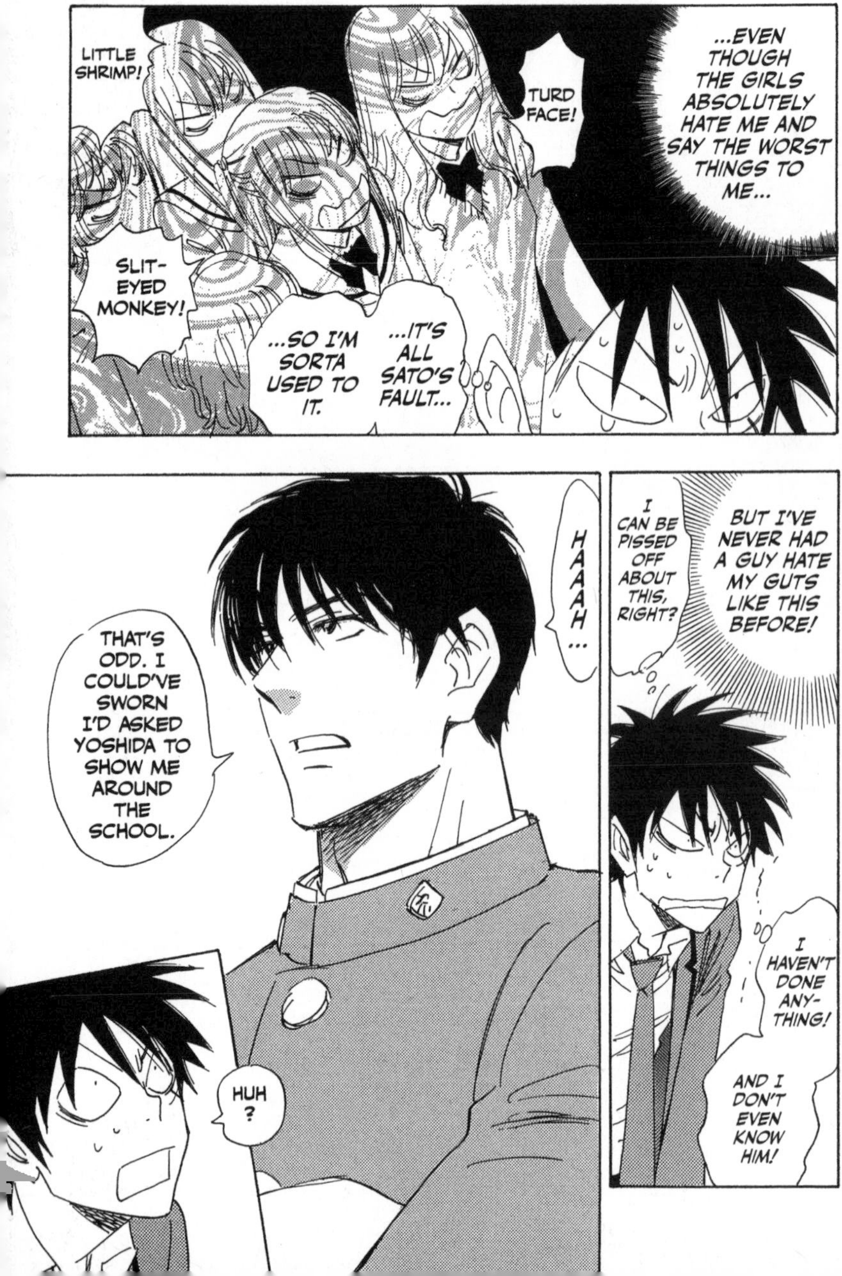

...EVEN THOUGH THE GIRLS ABSOLUTELY HATE ME AND SAY THE WORST THINGS TO ME...
TURD FACE!
LITTLE SHRIMP!
SLIT-EYED MONKEY!
...IT'S ALL SATO'S FAULT...
...SO I'M SORTA USED TO IT.
BUT I'VE NEVER HAD A GUY HATE MY GUTS LIKE THIS BEFORE!
I CAN BE PISSED OFF ABOUT THIS, RIGHT?
I HAVEN'T DONE ANY-THING!
AND I DON'T EVEN KNOW HIM!
HAAAAH...
THAT'S ODD. I COULD'VE SWORN I'D ASKED YOSHIDA TO SHOW ME AROUND THE SCHOOL.
HUH?

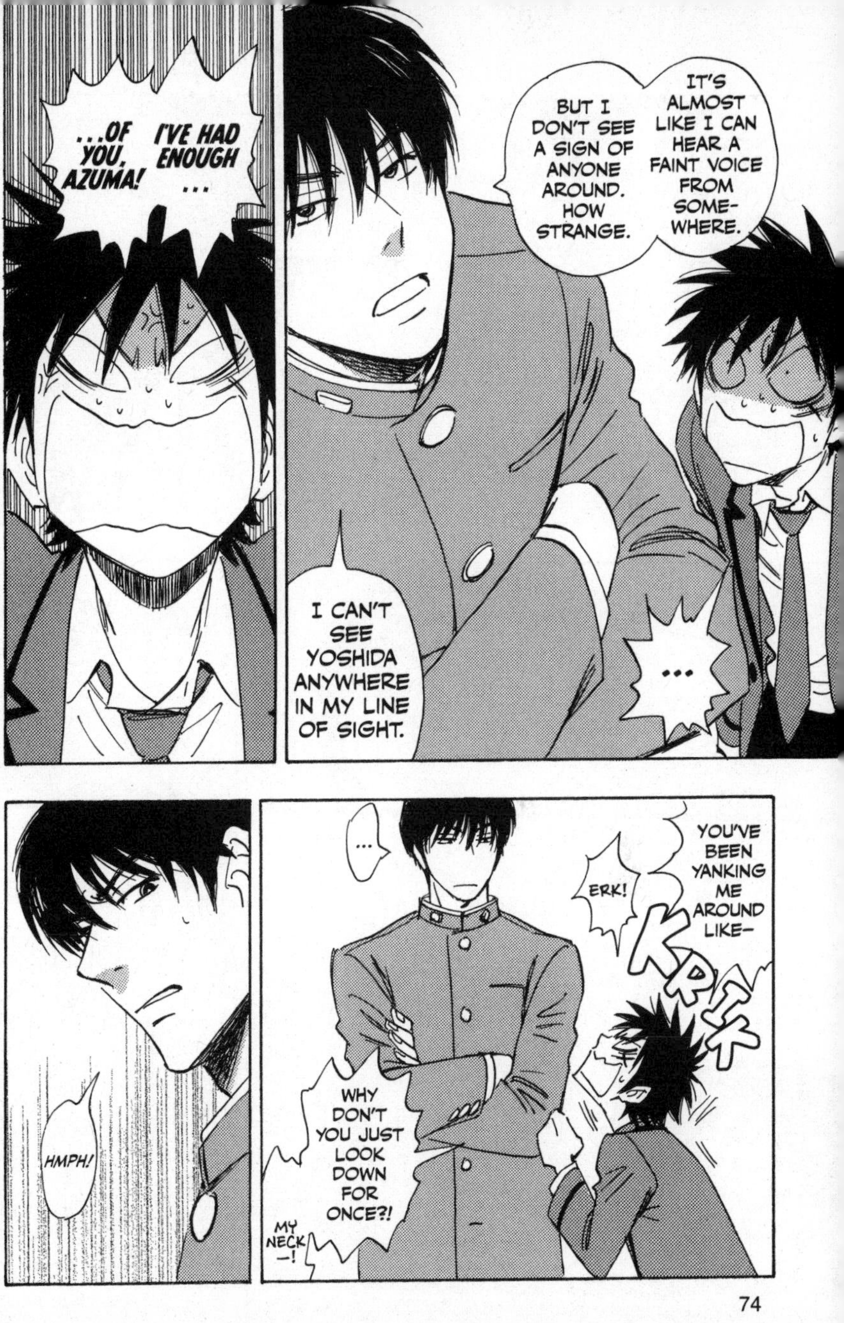
IT'S ALMOST LIKE I CAN HEAR A FAINT VOICE FROM SOME-WHERE.
BUT I DON'T SEE A SIGN OF ANYONE AROUND. HOW STRANGE.
I CAN'T SEE YOSHIDA ANYWHERE IN MY LINE OF SIGHT.
...
I'VE HAD ENOUGH ...
...OF YOU, AZUMA!
YOU'VE BEEN YANKING ME AROUND LIKE-
KRIK
ERK!
...
WHY DON'T YOU JUST LOOK DOWN FOR ONCE?!
MY NECK —!
HMPH!

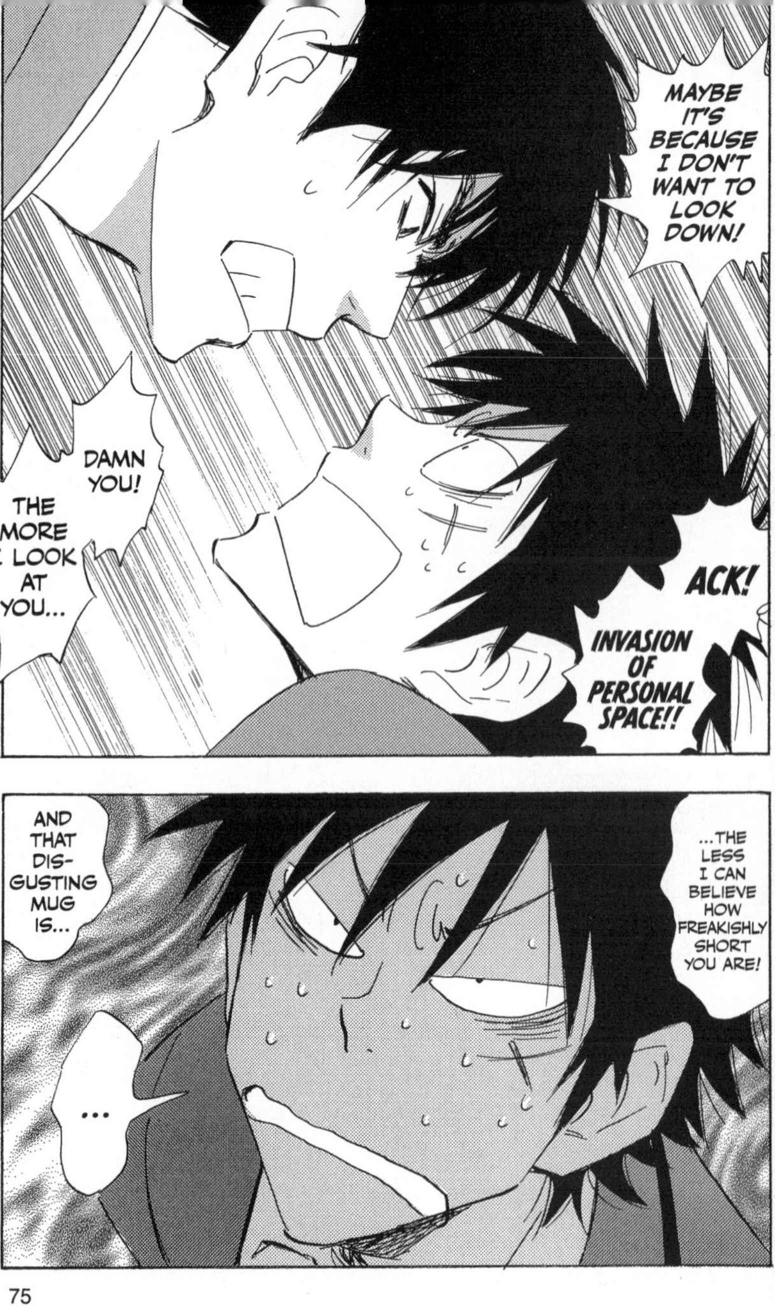
MAYBE IT'S BECAUSE I DON'T WANT TO LOOK DOWN!
ACK!
INVASION OF PERSONAL SPACE!!
DAMN YOU!
THE MORE I LOOK AT YOU...
...THE LESS I CAN BELIEVE HOW FREAKISHLY SHORT YOU ARE!
AND THAT DIS-GUSTING MUG IS...
...

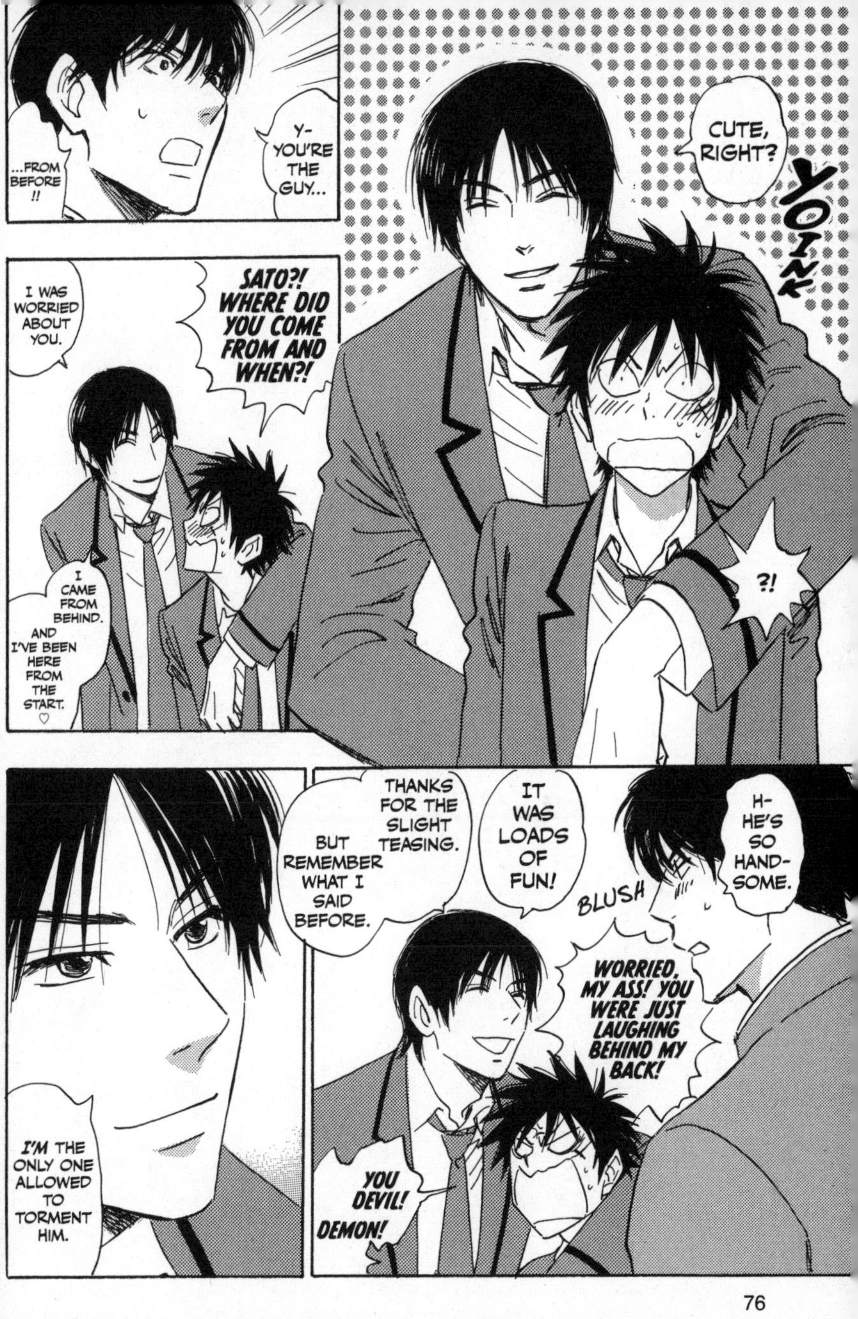
CUTE, RIGHT?
YOINK
?!
Y- YOU'RE THE GUY...
...FROM BEFORE !!
SATO?! WHERE DID YOU COME FROM AND WHEN?!
I WAS WORRIED ABOUT YOU.
I CAME FROM BEHIND. AND I'VE BEEN HERE FROM THE START. ♡
H- HE'S SO HAND- SOME.
BLUSH
IT WAS LOADS OF FUN!
THANKS FOR THE SLIGHT TEASING. BUT REMEMBER WHAT I SAID BEFORE.
WORRIED, MY ASS! YOU WERE JUST LAUGHING BEHIND MY BACK!
YOU DEVIL!
DEMON!
I'M THE ONLY ONE ALLOWED TO TORMENT HIM.

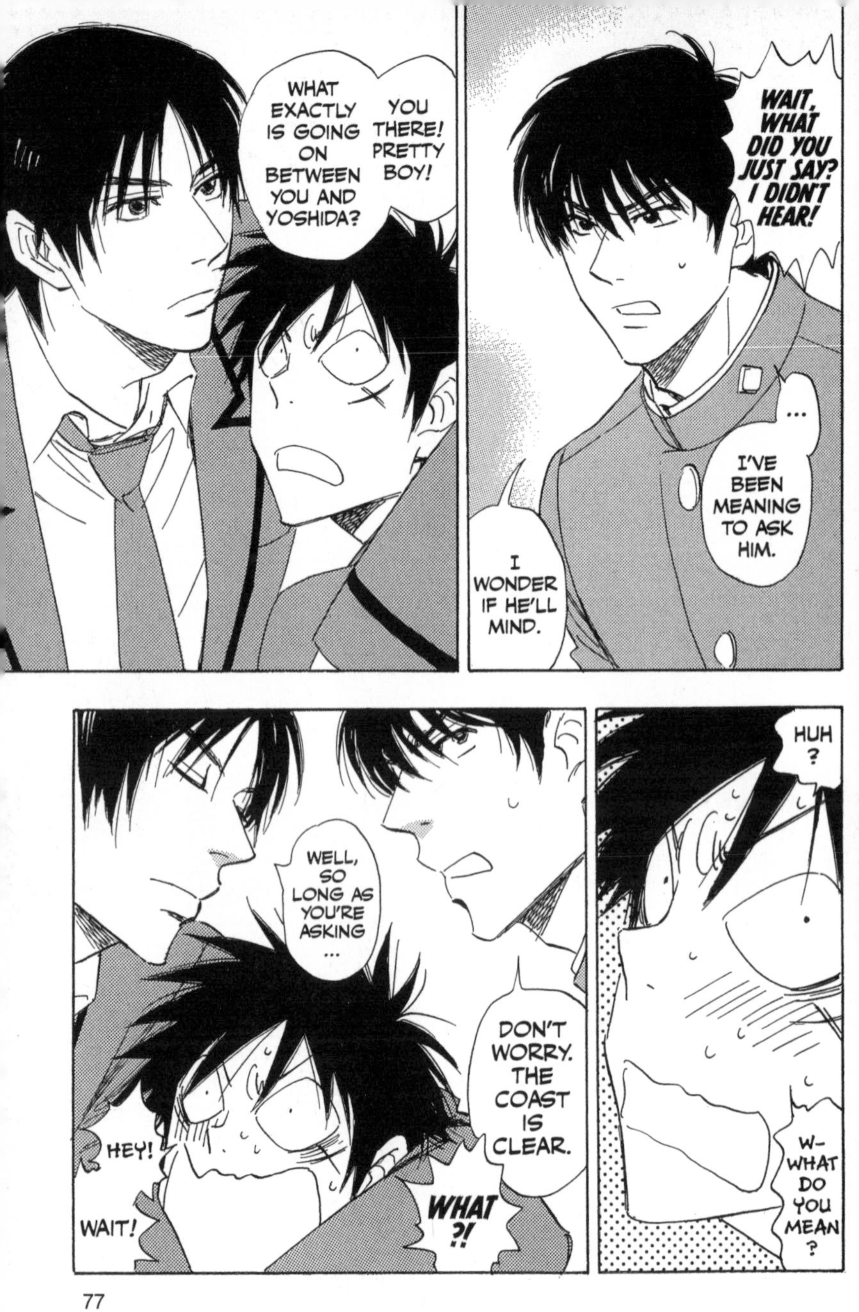
WAIT, WHAT DID YOU JUST SAY? I DIDN'T HEAR!
...
I'VE BEEN MEANING TO ASK HIM.
I WONDER IF HE'LL MIND.
YOU THERE! PRETTY BOY!
WHAT EXACTLY IS GOING ON BETWEEN YOU AND YOSHIDA?
HUH?
W-WHAT DO YOU MEAN?
WELL, SO LONG AS YOU'RE ASKING...
DON'T WORRY. THE COAST IS CLEAR.
WHAT?!
HEY!
WAIT!

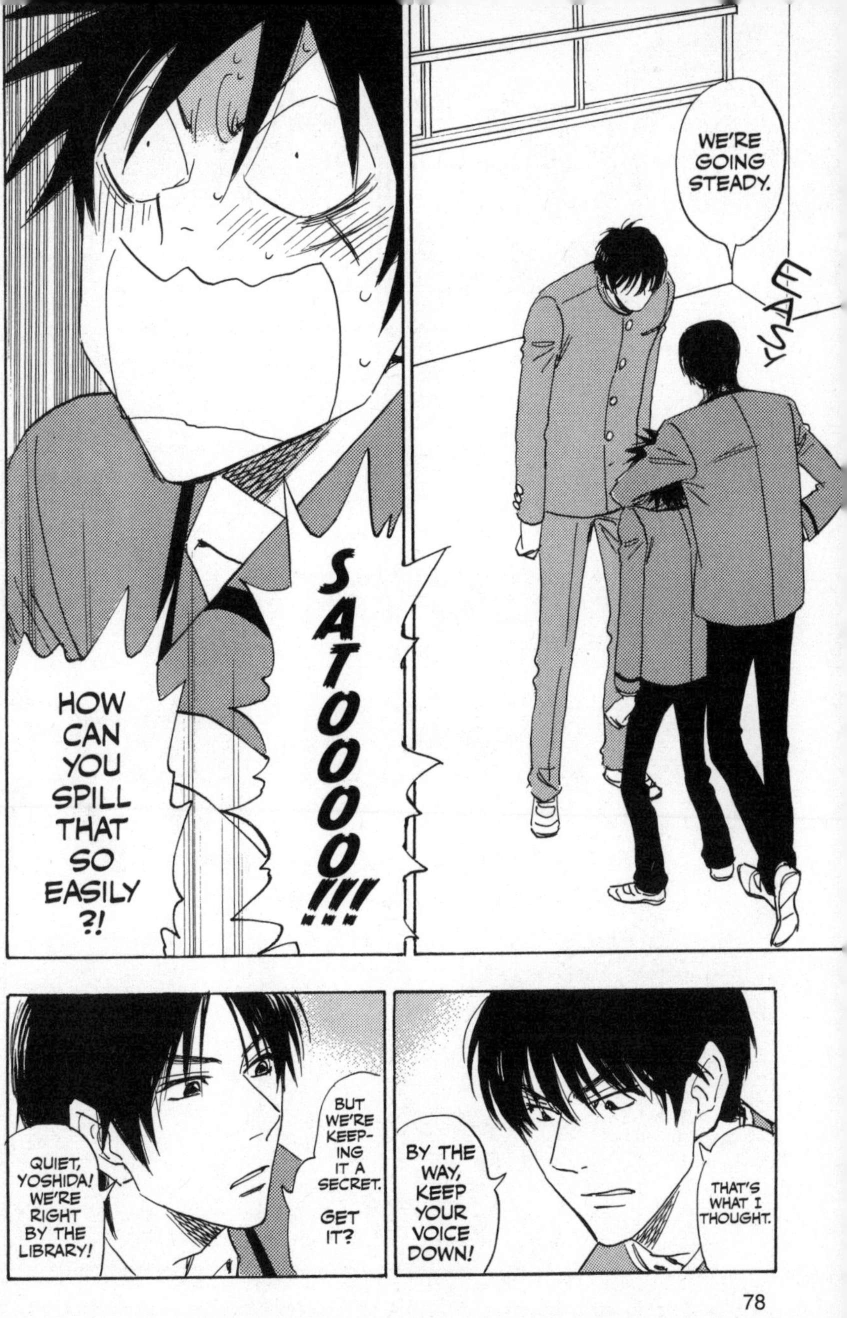
WE'RE GOING STEADY.
EASY
SATOOOOO!!!
HOW CAN YOU SPILL THAT SO EASILY?!
THAT'S WHAT I THOUGHT.
BY THE WAY, KEEP YOUR VOICE DOWN!
BUT WE'RE KEEPING IT A SECRET.
GET IT?
QUIET, YOSHIDA! WE'RE RIGHT BY THE LIBRARY!

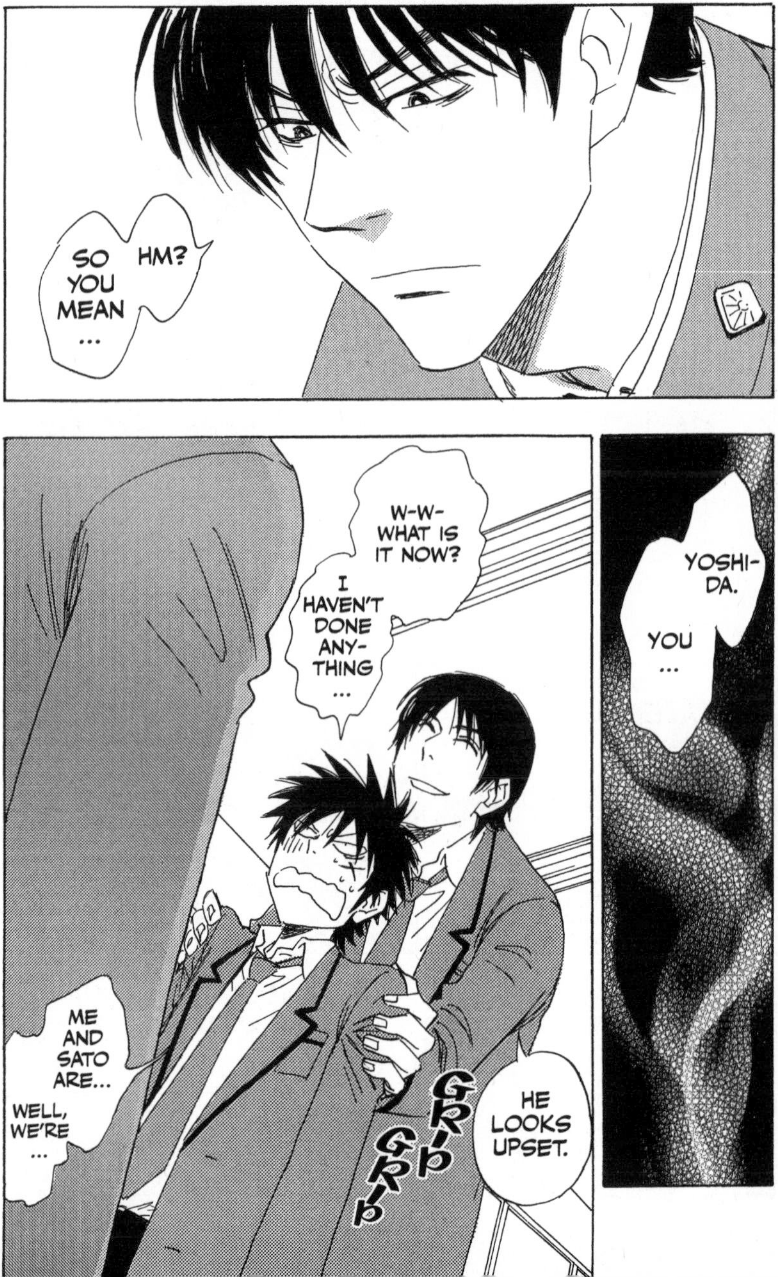
HM?
SO YOU MEAN ...
YOSHIDA.
YOU ...
W-W-WHAT IS IT NOW?
I HAVEN'T DONE ANYTHING ...
HE LOOKS UPSET.
GRIP GRIP
ME AND SATO ARE...
WELL, WE'RE ...

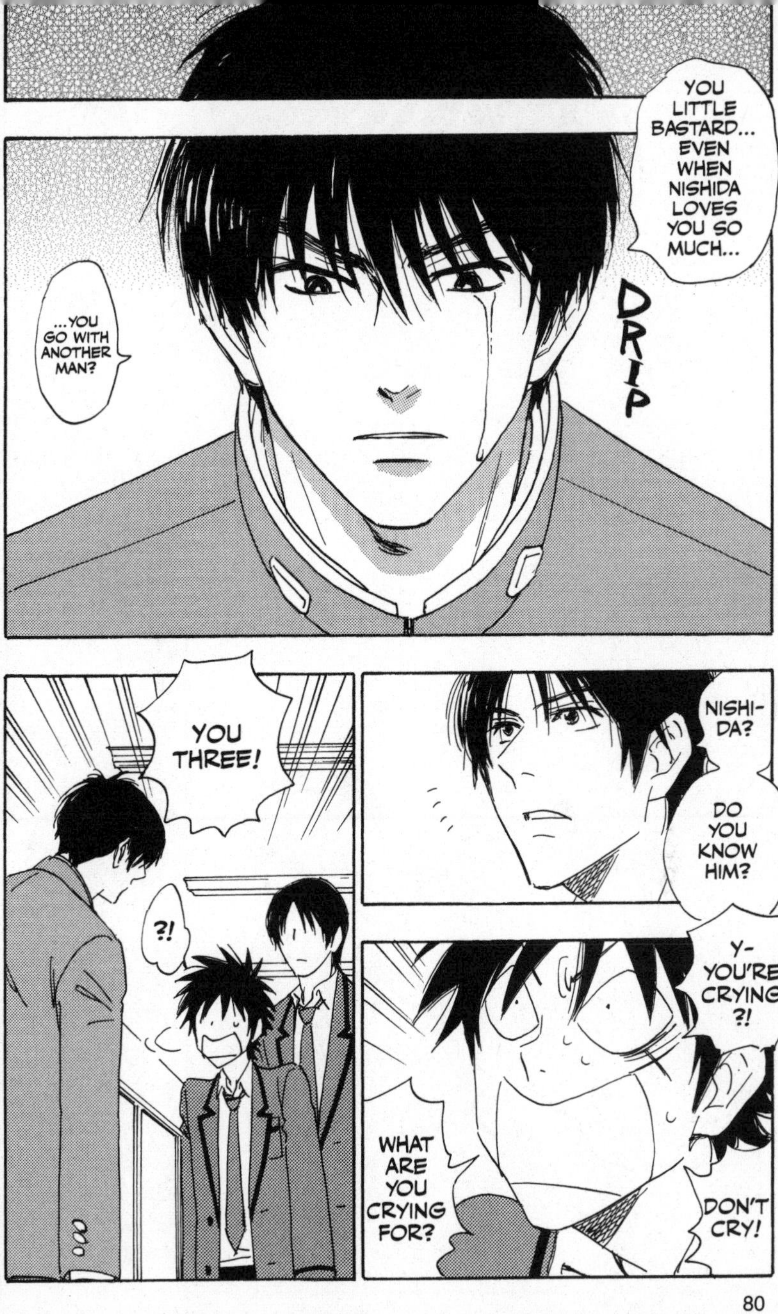
YOU LITTLE BASTARD... EVEN WHEN NISHIDA LOVES YOU SO MUCH...
DRIP
...YOU GO WITH ANOTHER MAN?
NISHI-DA?
DO YOU KNOW HIM?
Y-YOU'RE CRYING?!
DON'T CRY!
WHAT ARE YOU CRYING FOR?
YOU THREE!
?!

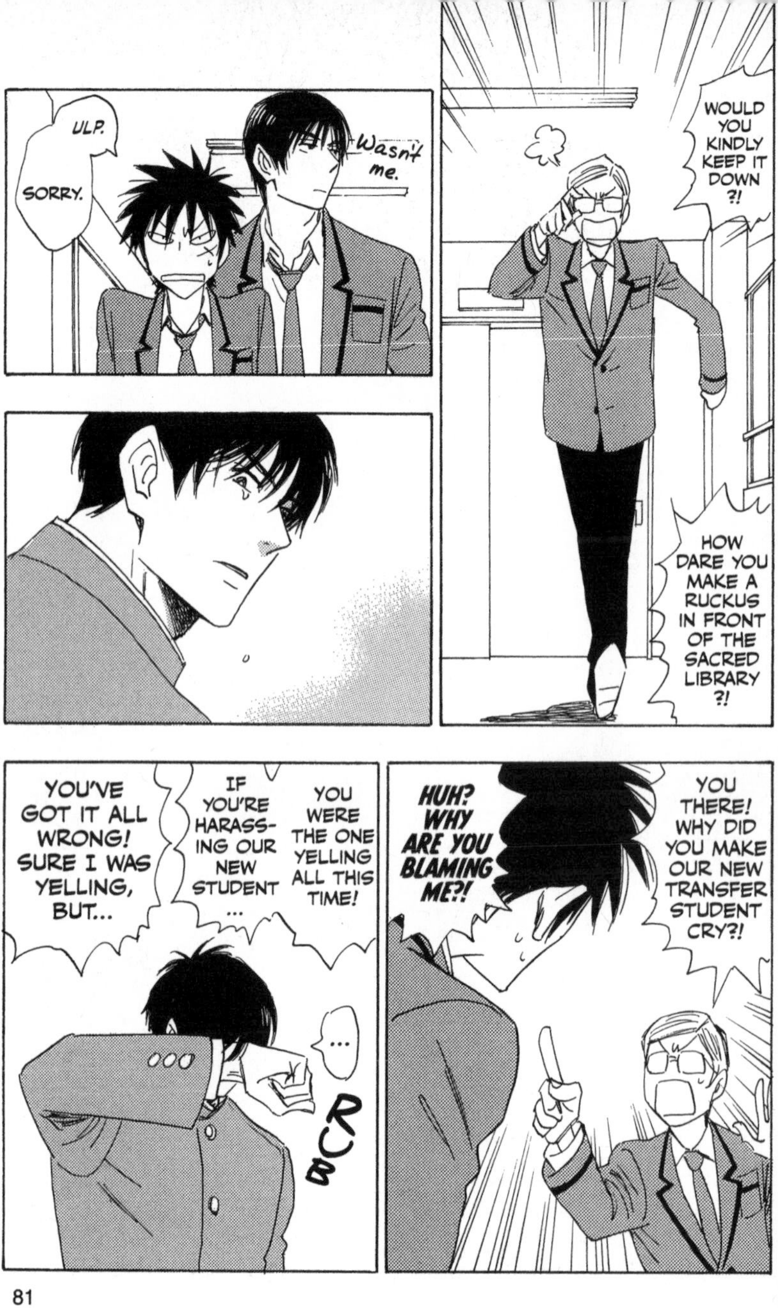
WOULD YOU KINDLY KEEP IT DOWN ?!
HOW DARE YOU MAKE A RUCKUS IN FRONT OF THE SACRED LIBRARY ?!
ULP.
SORRY.
Wasn't me.
YOU THERE! WHY DID YOU MAKE OUR NEW TRANSFER STUDENT CRY?!
HUH? WHY ARE YOU BLAMING ME?!
YOU WERE THE ONE YELLING ALL THIS TIME!
IF YOU'RE HARASS-ING OUR NEW STUDENT ...
YOU'VE GOT IT ALL WRONG! SURE I WAS YELLING, BUT...
...
RUB

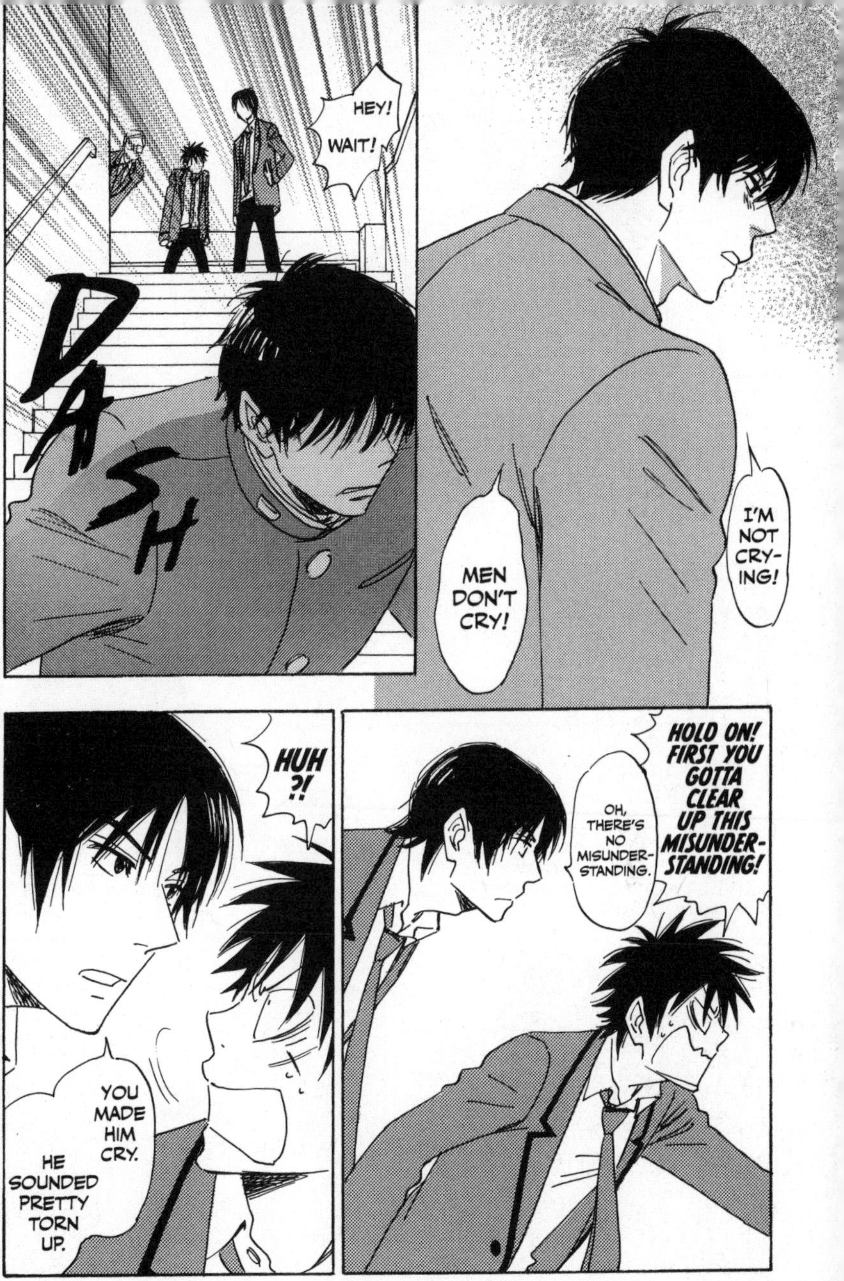
I'M NOT CRYING!
MEN DON'T CRY!
HEY! WAIT!
DASH
HOLD ON! FIRST YOU GOTTA CLEAR UP THIS MISUNDERSTANDING!
OH, THERE'S NO MISUNDERSTANDING.
HUH?!
YOU MADE HIM CRY.
HE SOUNDED PRETTY TORN UP.

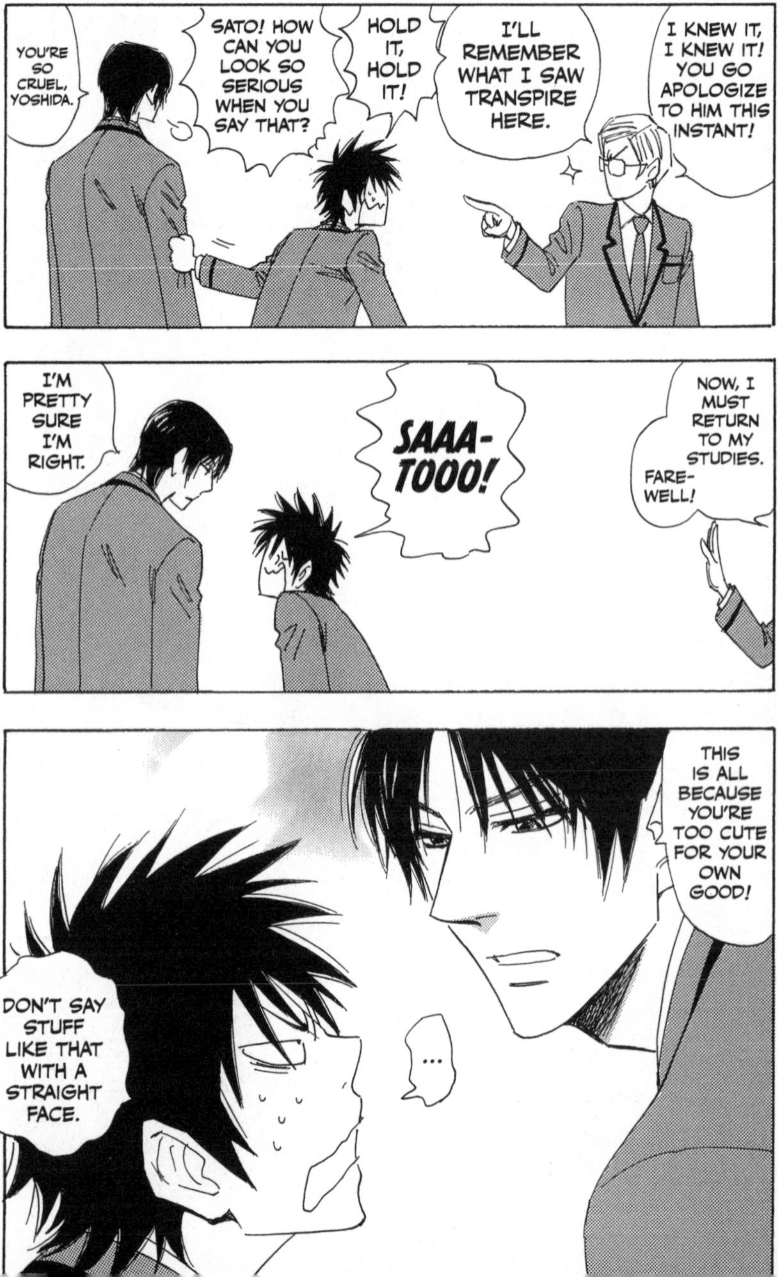
I KNEW IT, I KNEW IT! YOU GO APOLOGIZE TO HIM THIS INSTANT!
I'LL REMEMBER WHAT I SAW TRANSPIRE HERE.
HOLD IT, HOLD IT!
SATO! HOW CAN YOU LOOK SO SERIOUS WHEN YOU SAY THAT?
YOU'RE SO CRUEL, YOSHIDA.
NOW, I MUST RETURN TO MY STUDIES.
FAREWELL!
SAAA-TOOO!
I'M PRETTY SURE I'M RIGHT.
THIS IS ALL BECAUSE YOU'RE TOO CUTE FOR YOUR OWN GOOD!
...
DON'T SAY STUFF LIKE THAT WITH A STRAIGHT FACE.

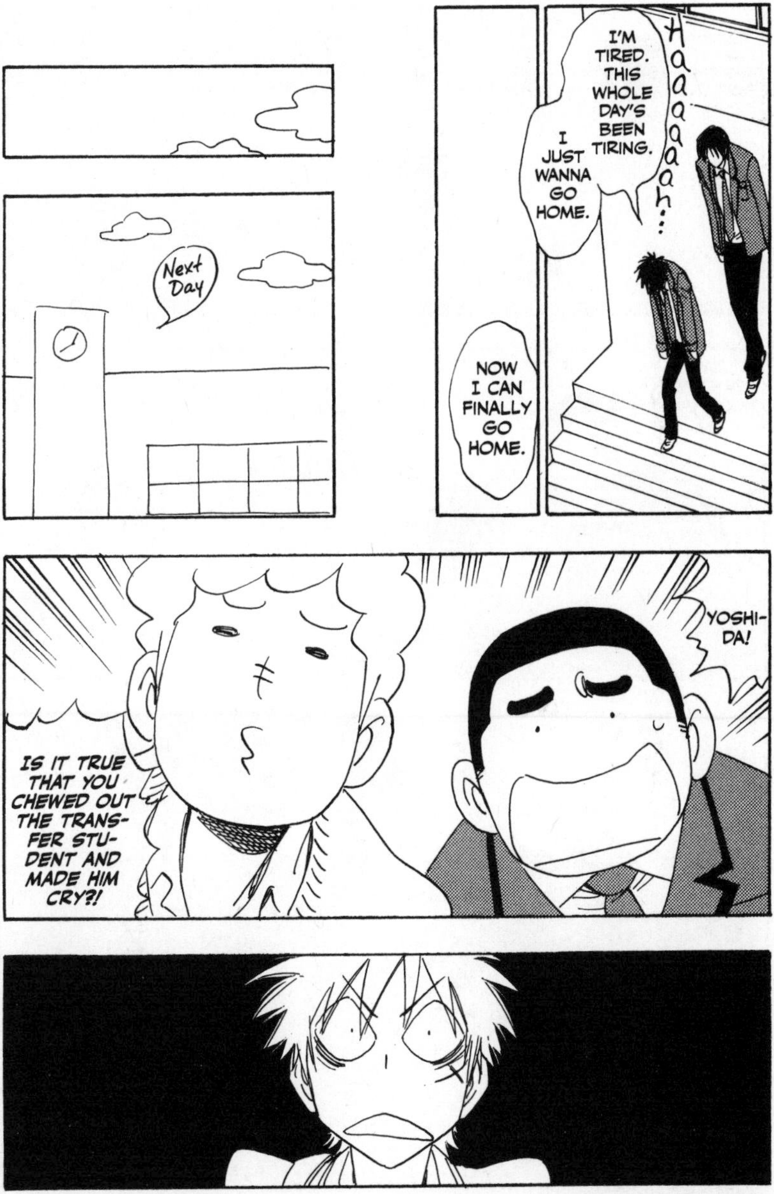
Haaaaaah...
I'M TIRED. THIS WHOLE DAY'S BEEN TIRING.
I JUST WANNA GO HOME.
NOW I CAN FINALLY GO HOME.
Next Day
YOSHIDA!
IS IT TRUE THAT YOU CHEWED OUT THE TRANSFER STUDENT AND MADE HIM CRY?!

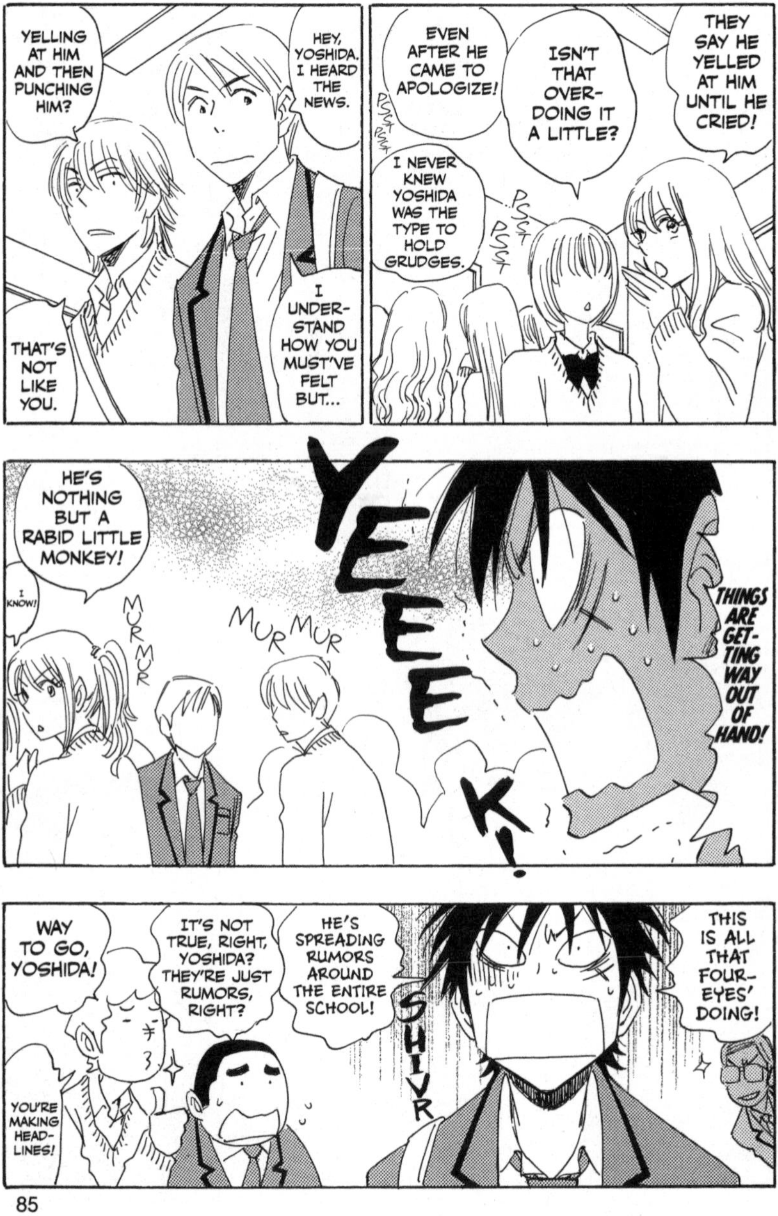
THEY SAY HE YELLED AT HIM UNTIL HE CRIED!
ISN'T THAT OVER-DOING IT A LITTLE?
EVEN AFTER HE CAME TO APOLOGIZE!
PSST PSST
I NEVER KNEW YOSHIDA WAS THE TYPE TO HOLD GRUDGES.
PSST PSST
HEY, YOSHIDA. I HEARD THE NEWS.
YELLING AT HIM AND THEN PUNCHING HIM?
I UNDER-STAND HOW YOU MUST'VE FELT BUT...
THAT'S NOT LIKE YOU.
THINGS ARE GET-TING WAY OUT OF HAND!
YEEEK!
MUR MUR
MURMUR
HE'S NOTHING BUT A RABID LITTLE MONKEY!
I KNOW!
THIS IS ALL THAT FOUR-EYES' DOING!
SHIVR
HE'S SPREADING RUMORS AROUND THE ENTIRE SCHOOL!
IT'S NOT TRUE, RIGHT, YOSHIDA? THEY'RE JUST RUMORS, RIGHT?
WAY TO GO, YOSHIDA!
YOU'RE MAKING HEAD-LINES!

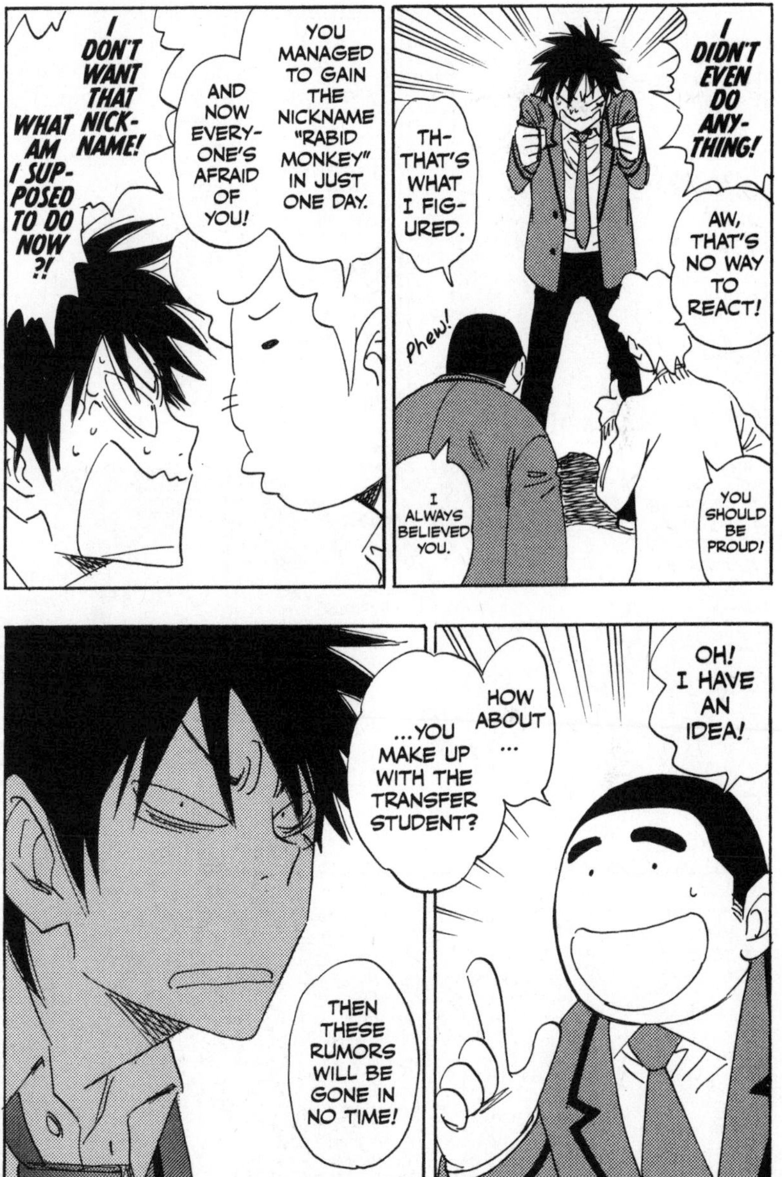
I DIDN'T EVEN DO ANYTHING!
TH-THAT'S WHAT I FIGURED.
AW, THAT'S NO WAY TO REACT!
Phew!
YOU SHOULD BE PROUD!
I ALWAYS BELIEVED YOU.
YOU MANAGED TO GAIN THE NICKNAME "RABID MONKEY" IN JUST ONE DAY.
AND NOW EVERYONE'S AFRAID OF YOU!
I DON'T WANT THAT NICKNAME!
WHAT AM I SUPPOSED TO DO NOW?!
OH! I HAVE AN IDEA!
HOW ABOUT...
...YOU MAKE UP WITH THE TRANSFER STUDENT?
THEN THESE RUMORS WILL BE GONE IN NO TIME!

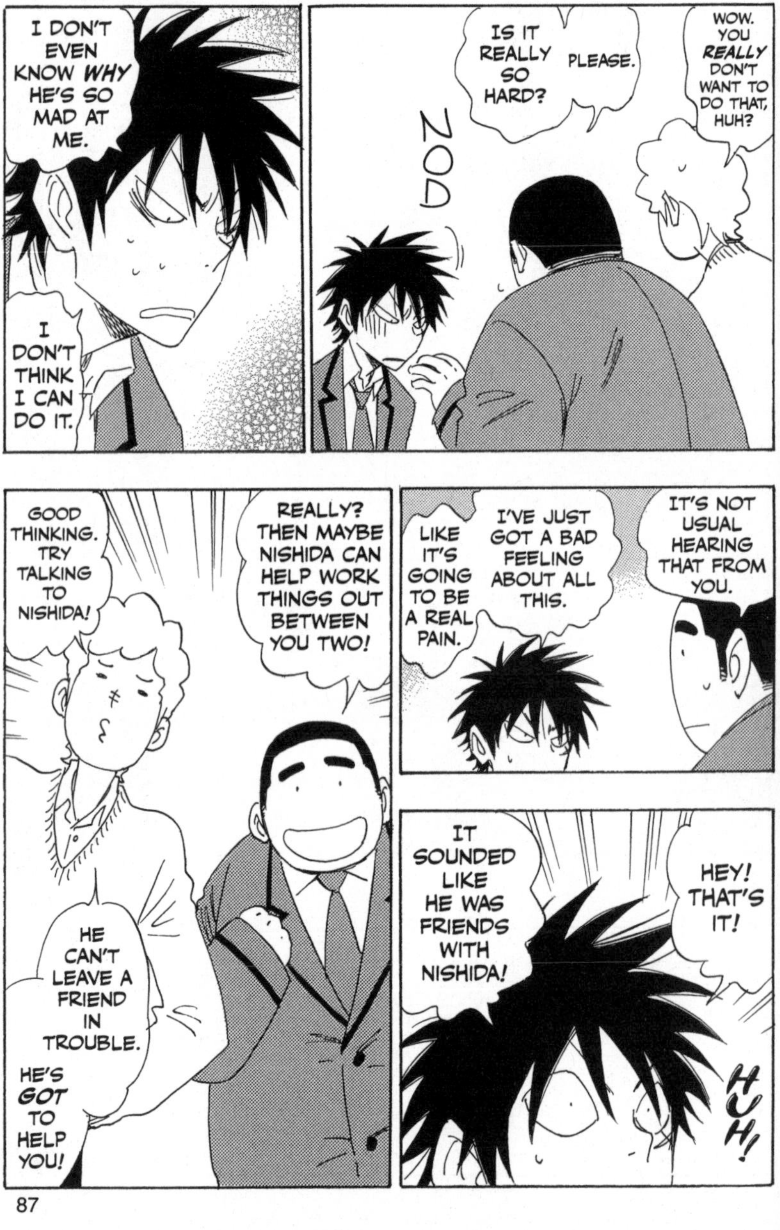
WOW. YOU REALLY DON'T WANT TO DO THAT, HUH?
PLEASE.
IS IT REALLY SO HARD?
NOD
I DON'T EVEN KNOW WHY HE'S SO MAD AT ME.
I DON'T THINK I CAN DO IT.
IT'S NOT USUAL HEARING THAT FROM YOU.
I'VE JUST GOT A BAD FEELING ABOUT ALL THIS.
LIKE IT'S GOING TO BE A REAL PAIN.
HEY! THAT'S IT!
IT SOUNDED LIKE HE WAS FRIENDS WITH NISHIDA!
HUH!
REALLY? THEN MAYBE NISHIDA CAN HELP WORK THINGS OUT BETWEEN YOU TWO!
GOOD THINKING. TRY TALKING TO NISHIDA!
HE CAN'T LEAVE A FRIEND IN TROUBLE.
HE'S GOT TO HELP YOU!

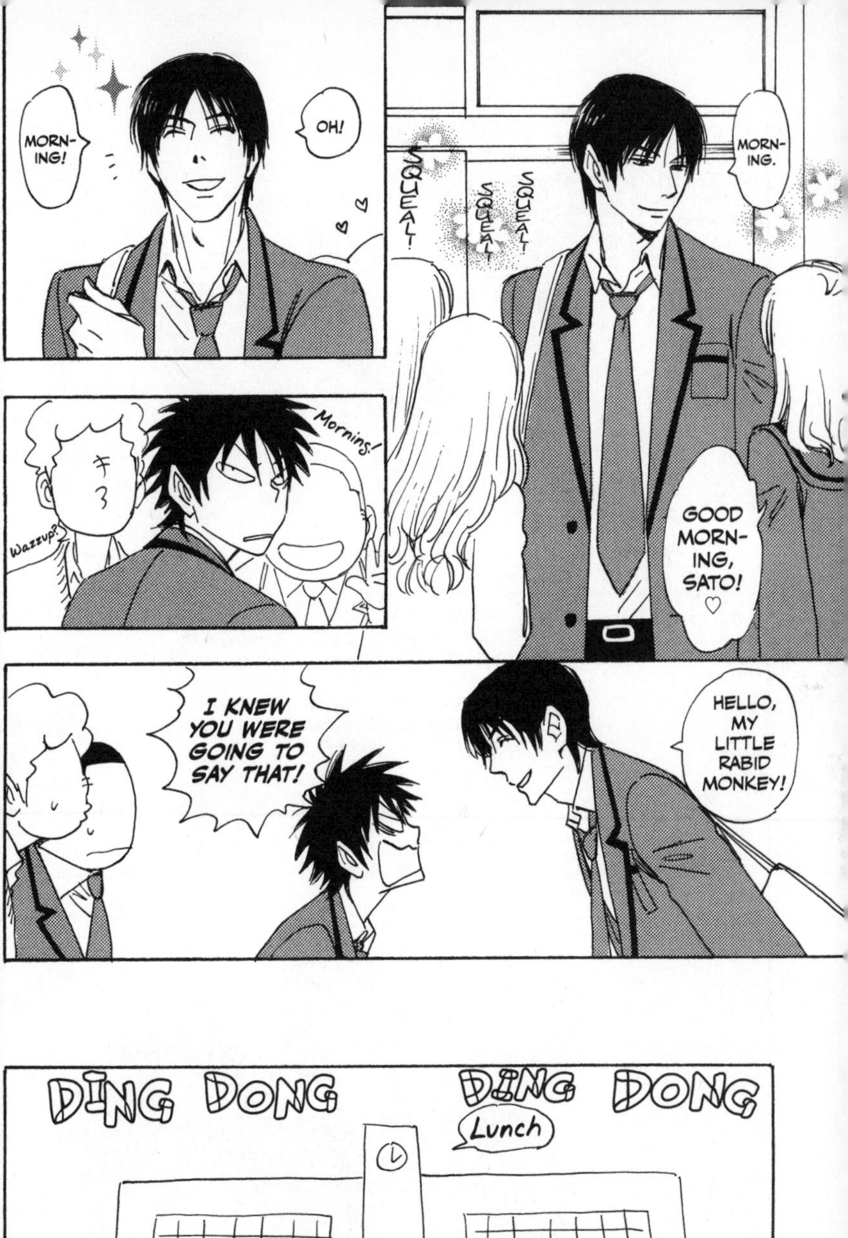
MORN-ING.
SQUEAL!
SQUEAL!
SQUEAL!
GOOD MORN-ING, SATO! ♡
OH!
MORN-ING!
Mornings!
Wazzup?
HELLO, MY LITTLE RABID MONKEY!
I KNEW YOU WERE GOING TO SAY THAT!
DING DONG
DING DONG
Lunch

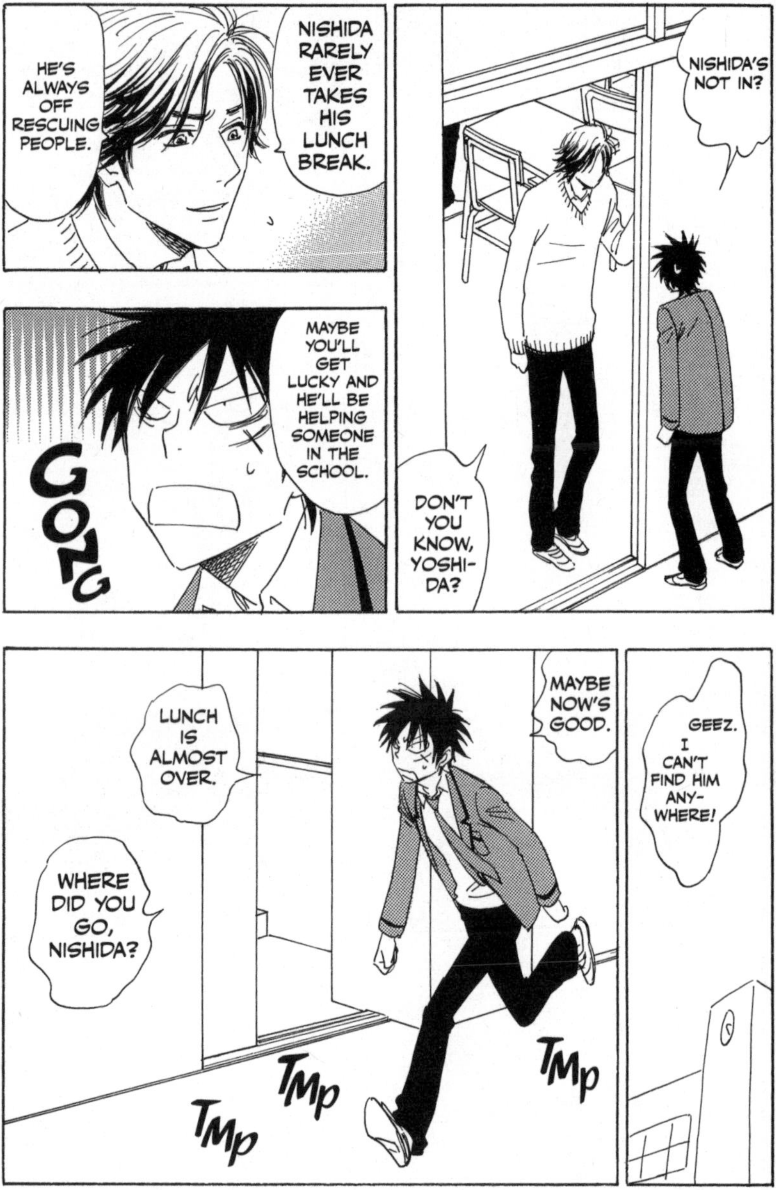
NISHIDA'S NOT IN?
DON'T YOU KNOW, YOSHIDA?
NISHIDA RARELY EVER TAKES HIS LUNCH BREAK.
HE'S ALWAYS OFF RESCUING PEOPLE.
MAYBE YOU'LL GET LUCKY AND HE'LL BE HELPING SOMEONE IN THE SCHOOL.
GOZU
GEEZ. I CAN'T FIND HIM ANYWHERE!
MAYBE NOW'S GOOD.
LUNCH IS ALMOST OVER.
WHERE DID YOU GO, NISHIDA?
TMP
TMP
TMP

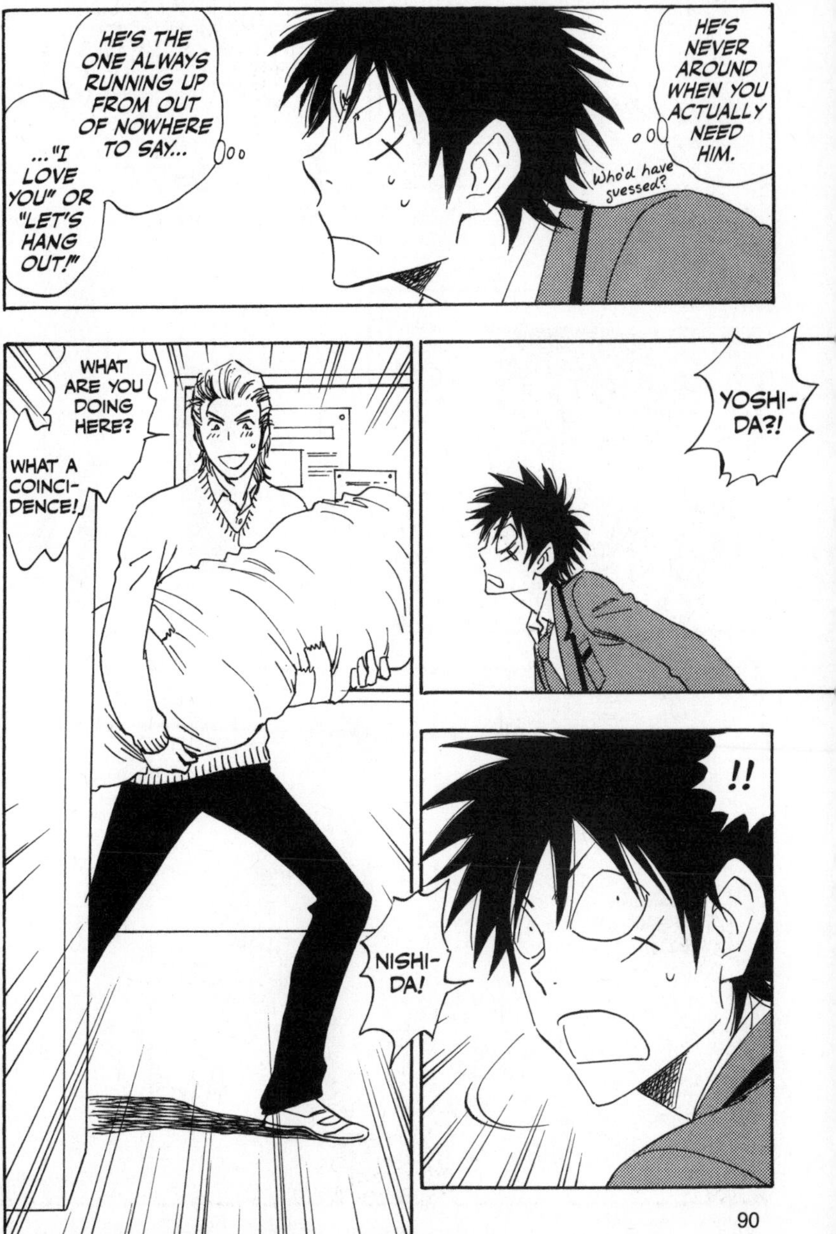
HE'S NEVER AROUND WHEN YOU ACTUALLY NEED HIM.
Who'd have guessed?
HE'S THE ONE ALWAYS RUNNING UP FROM OUT OF NOWHERE TO SAY...
..."I LOVE YOU" OR "LET'S HANG OUT!"
YOSHI-DA?!
!!
NISHI-DA!
WHAT ARE YOU DOING HERE?
WHAT A COINCI-DENCE!

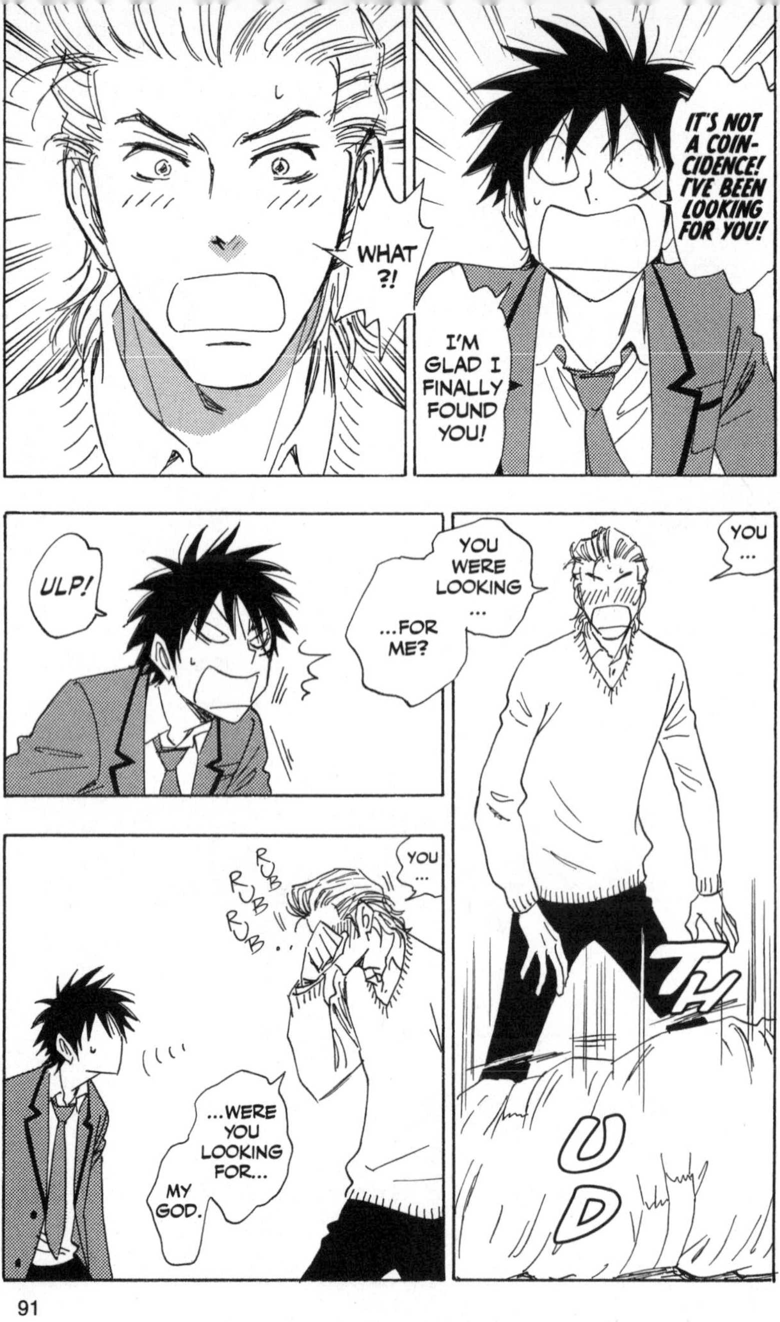
IT'S NOT A COINCIDENCE! I'VE BEEN LOOKING FOR YOU!
I'M GLAD I FINALLY FOUND YOU!
WHAT ?!
YOU ...
THUD
YOU WERE LOOKING ...
...FOR ME?
ULP!
YOU ...
RUB RUB RUB ..
...WERE YOU LOOKING FOR...
MY GOD.

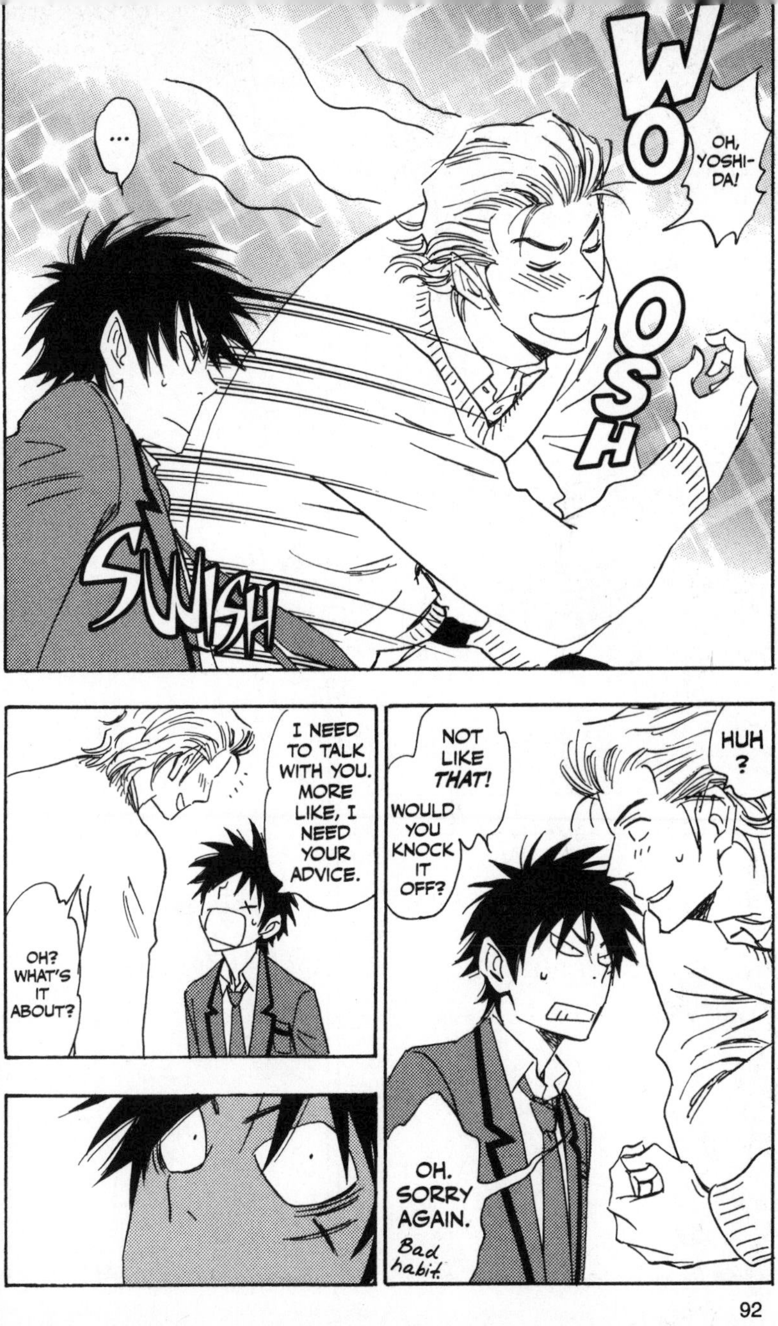
WOOSH
OH, YOSHI-DA!
...
SWISH
HUH?
NOT LIKE *THAT!*
WOULD YOU KNOCK IT OFF?
OH. SORRY AGAIN.
Bad habit.
I NEED TO TALK WITH YOU. MORE LIKE, I NEED YOUR ADVICE.
OH? WHAT'S IT ABOUT?

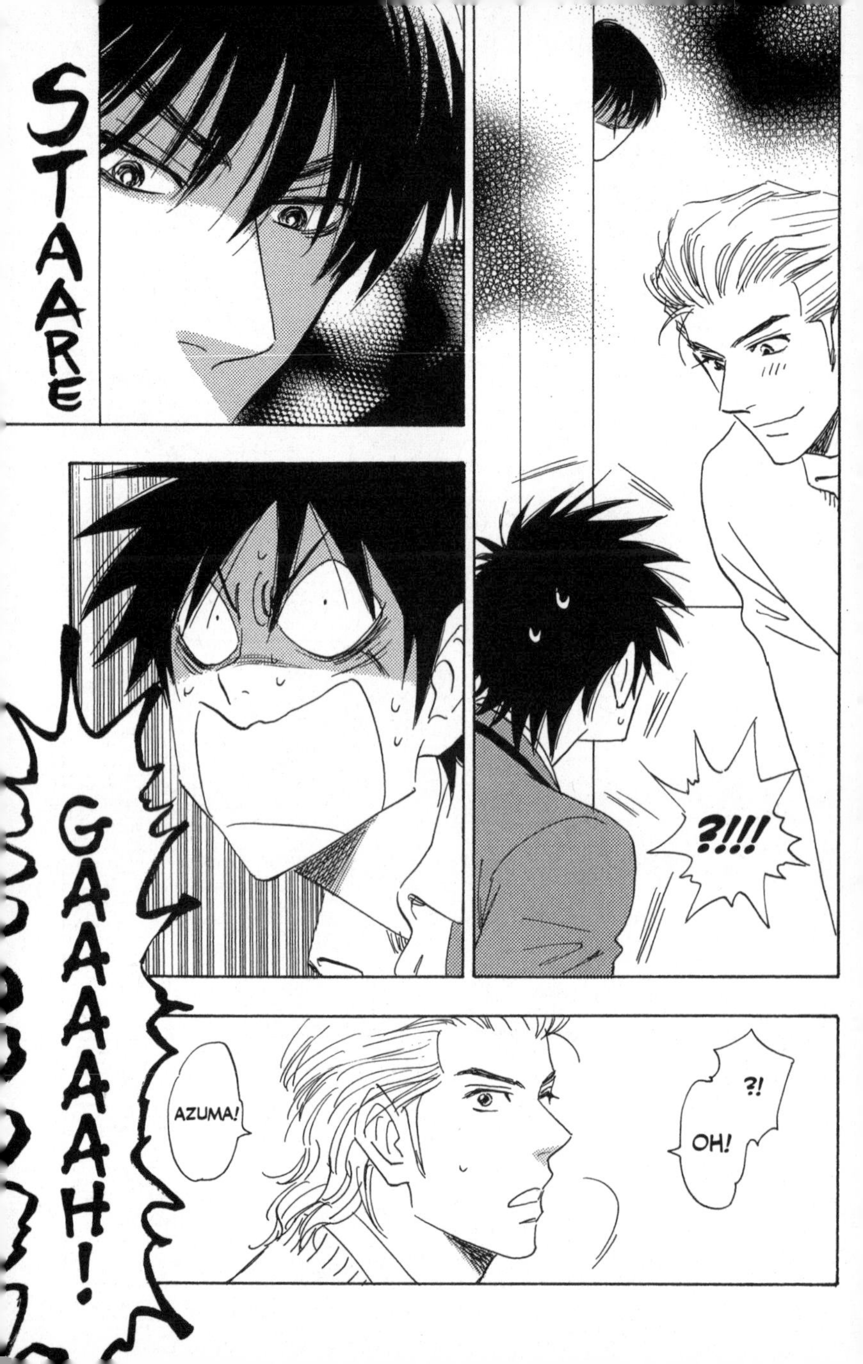
STAARE
?!!!
GAAAAAH!
?!
OH!
AZUMA!

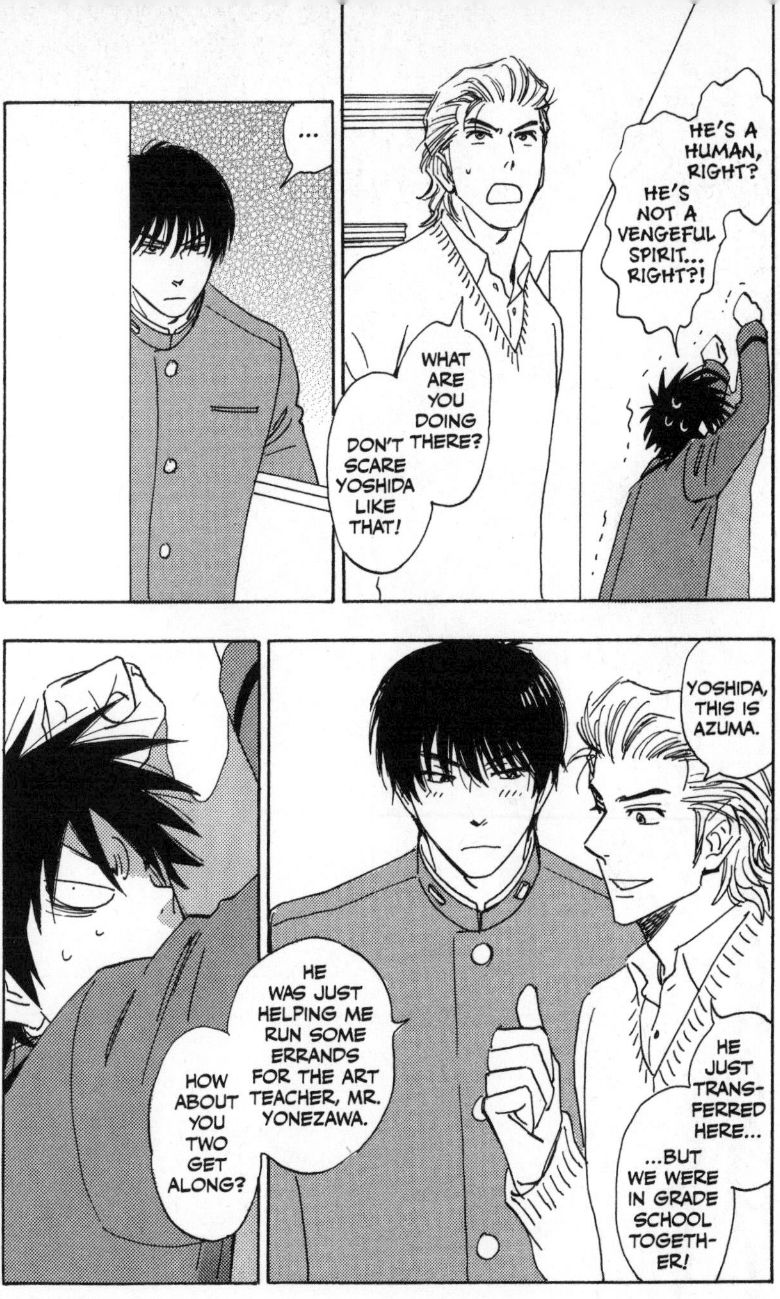
HE'S A HUMAN, RIGHT?
HE'S NOT A VENGEFUL SPIRIT... RIGHT?!
WHAT ARE YOU DOING THERE?
DON'T SCARE YOSHIDA LIKE THAT!
...
YOSHIDA, THIS IS AZUMA.
HE JUST TRANS-FERRED HERE...
...BUT WE WERE IN GRADE SCHOOL TOGETH-ER!
HE WAS JUST HELPING ME RUN SOME ERRANDS FOR THE ART TEACHER, MR. YONEZAWA.
HOW ABOUT YOU TWO GET ALONG?

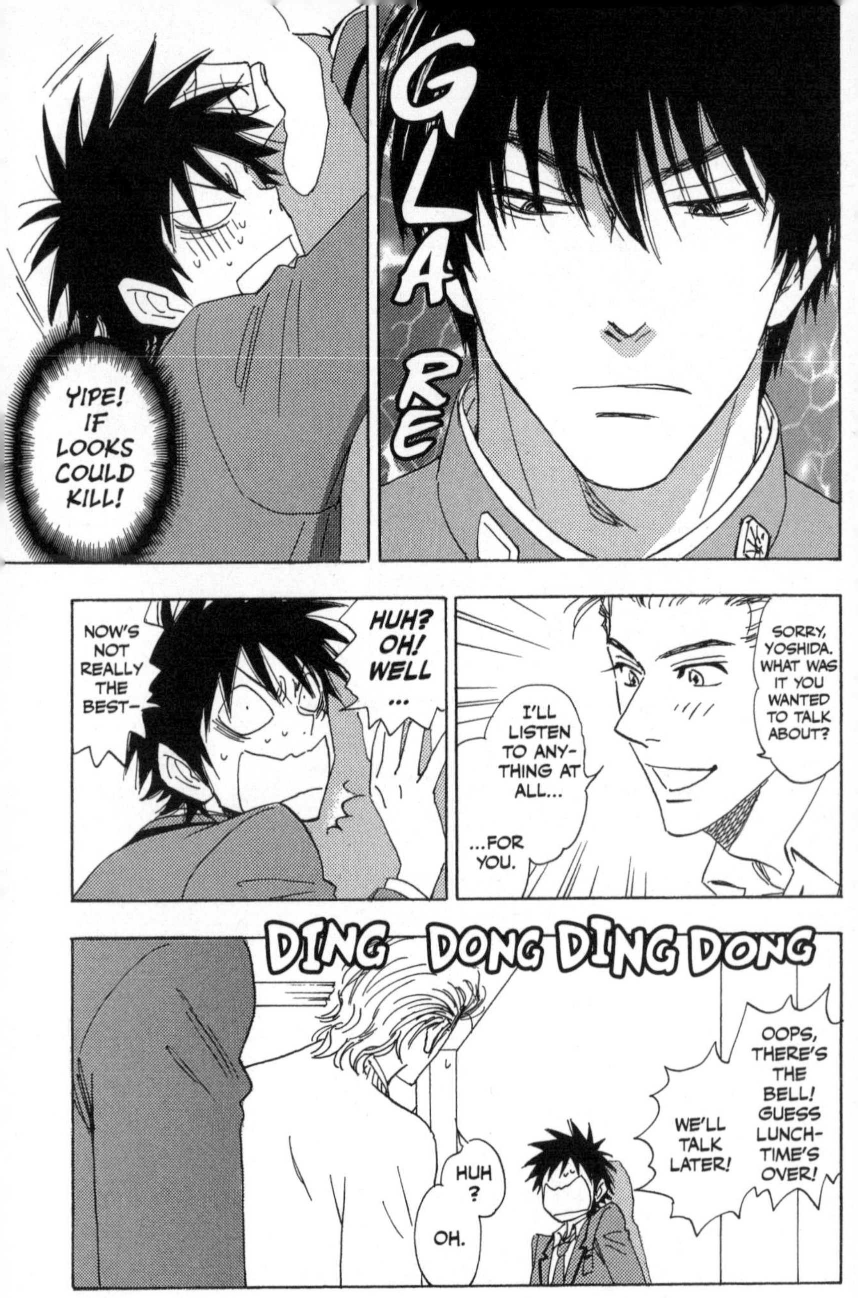
GLARE
YIPE! IF LOOKS COULD KILL!
SORRY, YOSHIDA. WHAT WAS IT YOU WANTED TO TALK ABOUT?
I'LL LISTEN TO ANYTHING AT ALL...
...FOR YOU.
HUH? OH! WELL...
NOW'S NOT REALLY THE BEST-
DING DONG DING DONG
OOPS, THERE'S THE BELL! GUESS LUNCHTIME'S OVER!
WE'LL TALK LATER!
HUH?
OH.

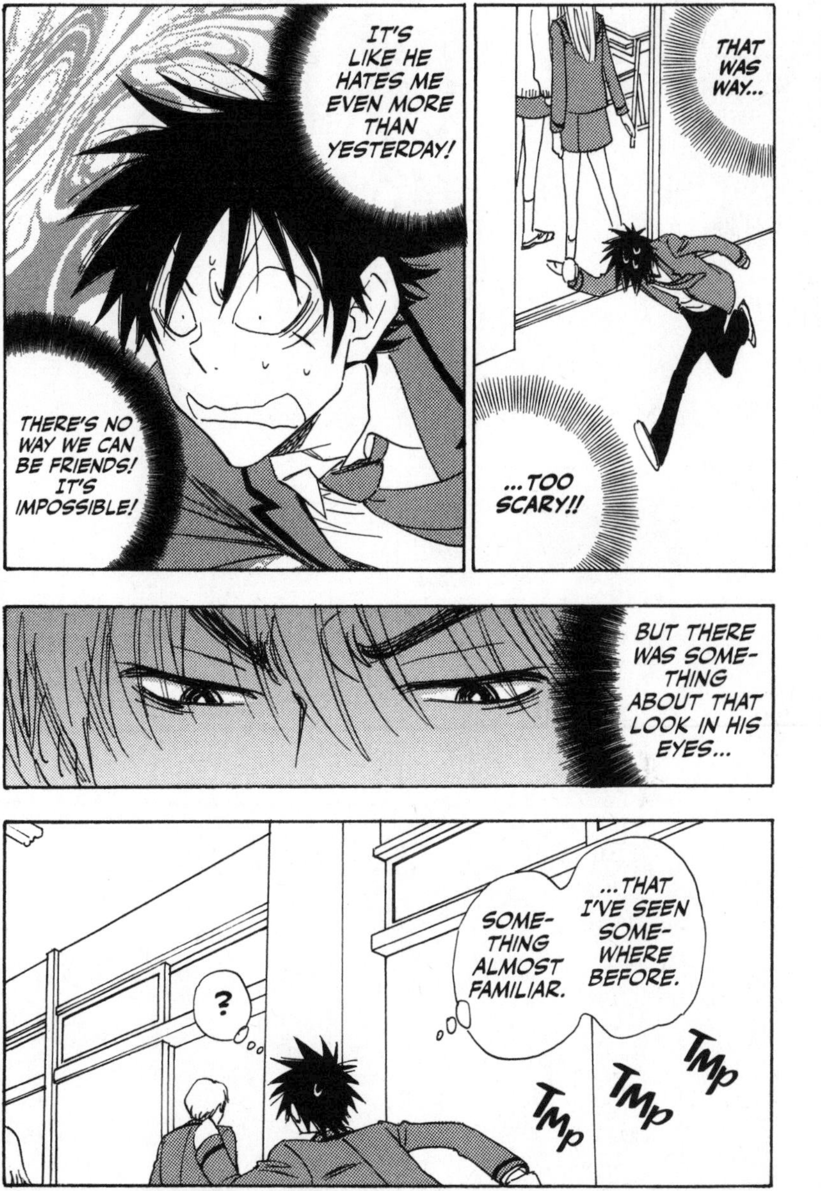
THAT WAS WAY...
...TOO SCARY!!
IT'S LIKE HE HATES ME EVEN MORE THAN YESTERDAY!
THERE'S NO WAY WE CAN BE FRIENDS! IT'S IMPOSSIBLE!
BUT THERE WAS SOME-THING ABOUT THAT LOOK IN HIS EYES...
SOME-THING ALMOST FAMILIAR.
...THAT I'VE SEEN SOME-WHERE BEFORE.
TMP TMP TMP
?

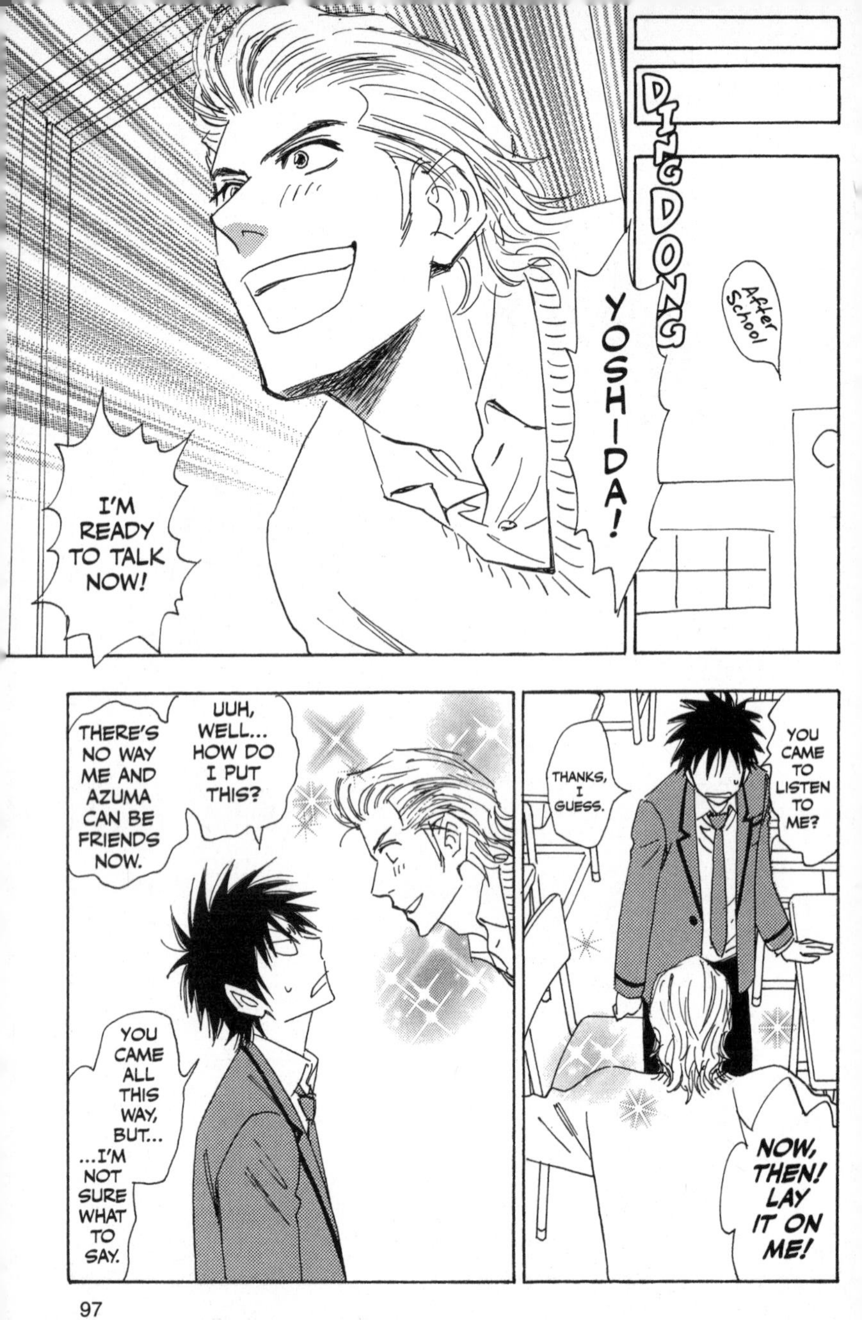
After School
DING DONG
YOSHIDA!
I'M READY TO TALK NOW!
YOU CAME TO LISTEN TO ME?
THANKS, I GUESS.
NOW, THEN! LAY IT ON ME!
UUH, WELL... HOW DO I PUT THIS?
THERE'S NO WAY ME AND AZUMA CAN BE FRIENDS NOW.
YOU CAME ALL THIS WAY, BUT... ...I'M NOT SURE WHAT TO SAY.

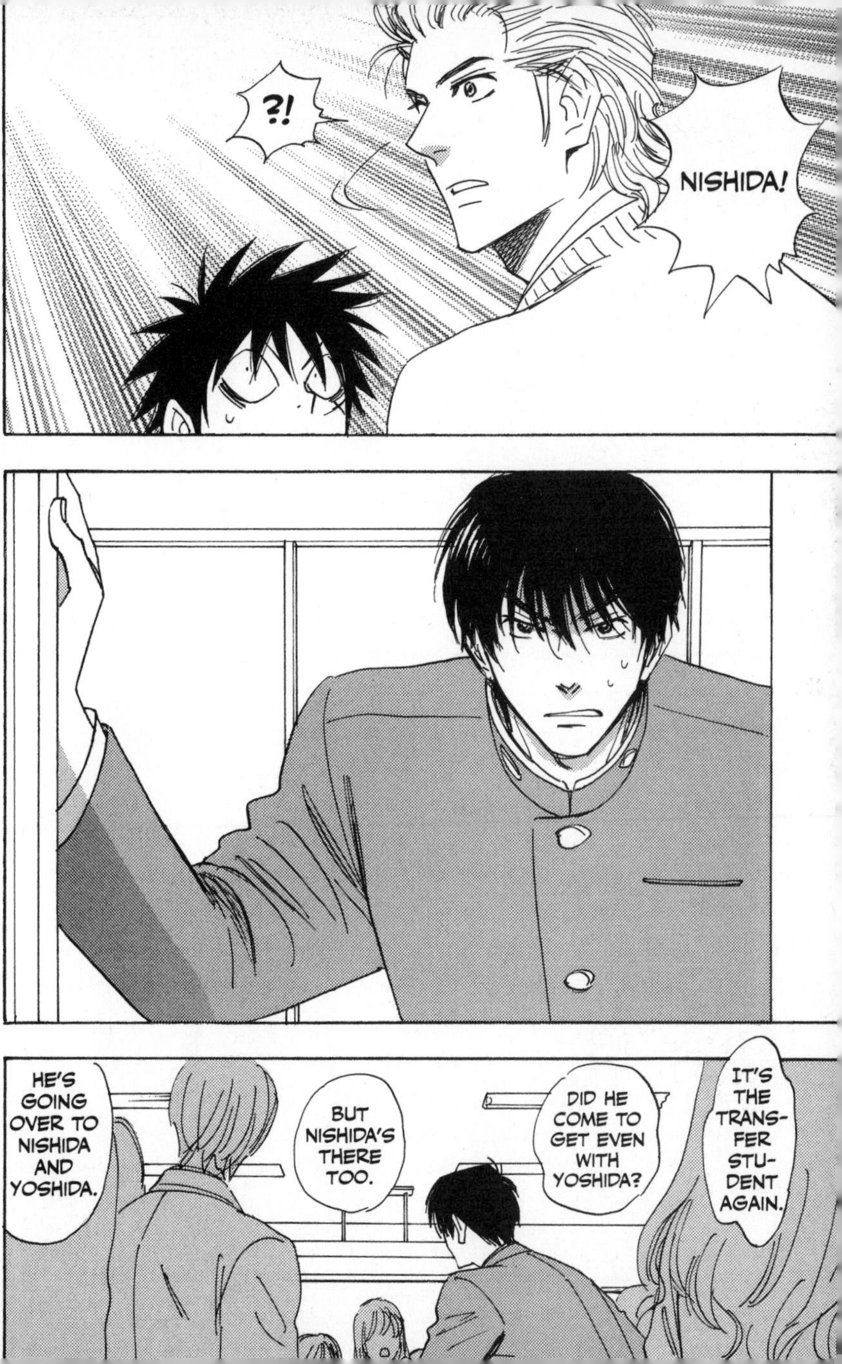
NISHIDA!
?!
IT'S THE TRANS-FER STU-DENT AGAIN.
DID HE COME TO GET EVEN WITH YOSHIDA?
BUT NISHIDA'S THERE TOO.
HE'S GOING OVER TO NISHIDA AND YOSHIDA.

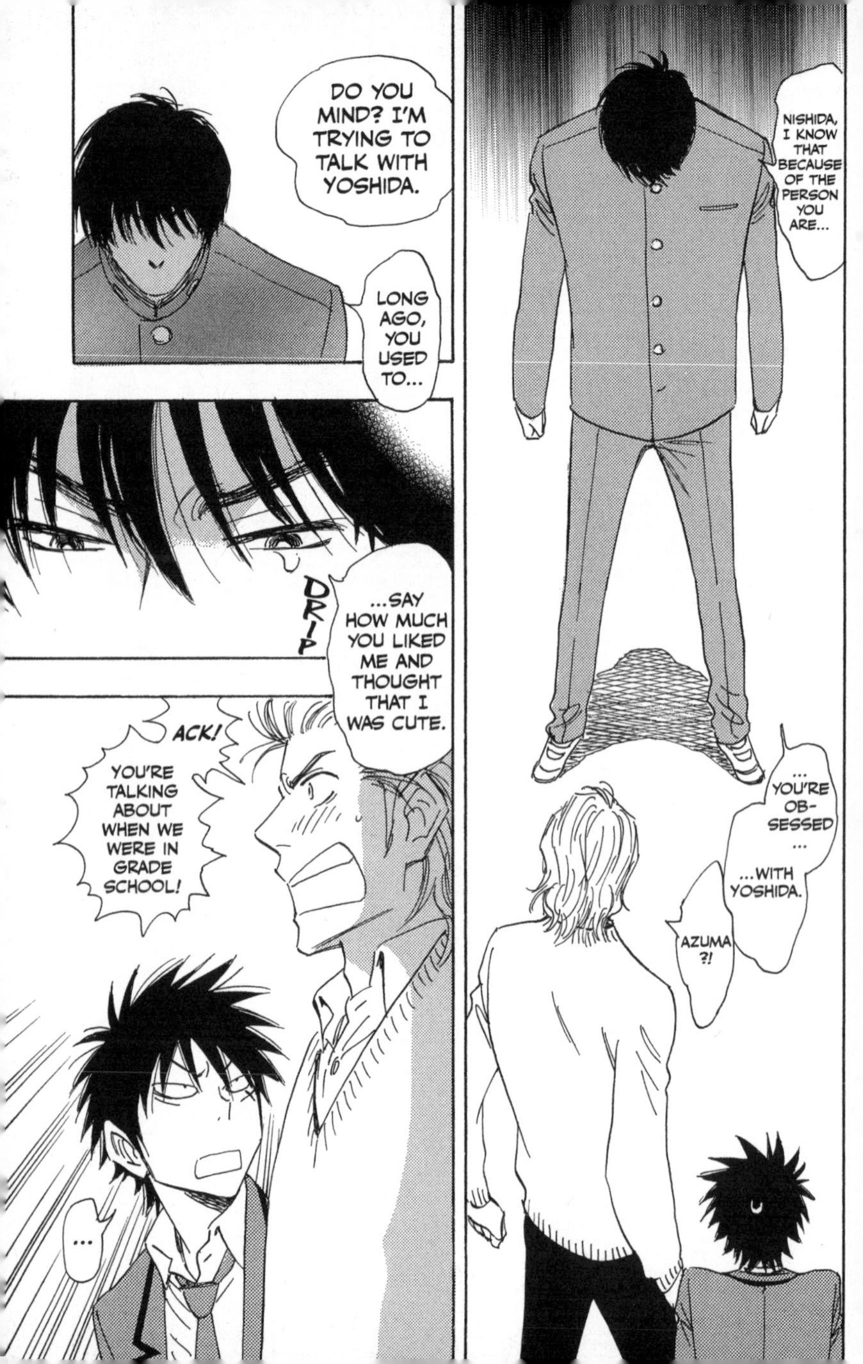
DO YOU MIND? I'M TRYING TO TALK WITH YOSHIDA.
LONG AGO, YOU USED TO...
DRIP
...SAY HOW MUCH YOU LIKED ME AND THOUGHT THAT I WAS CUTE.
ACK!
YOU'RE TALKING ABOUT WHEN WE WERE IN GRADE SCHOOL!
...
NISHIDA, I KNOW THAT BECAUSE OF THE PERSON YOU ARE...
... YOU'RE OBSESSED ...
...WITH YOSHIDA.
AZUMA ?!

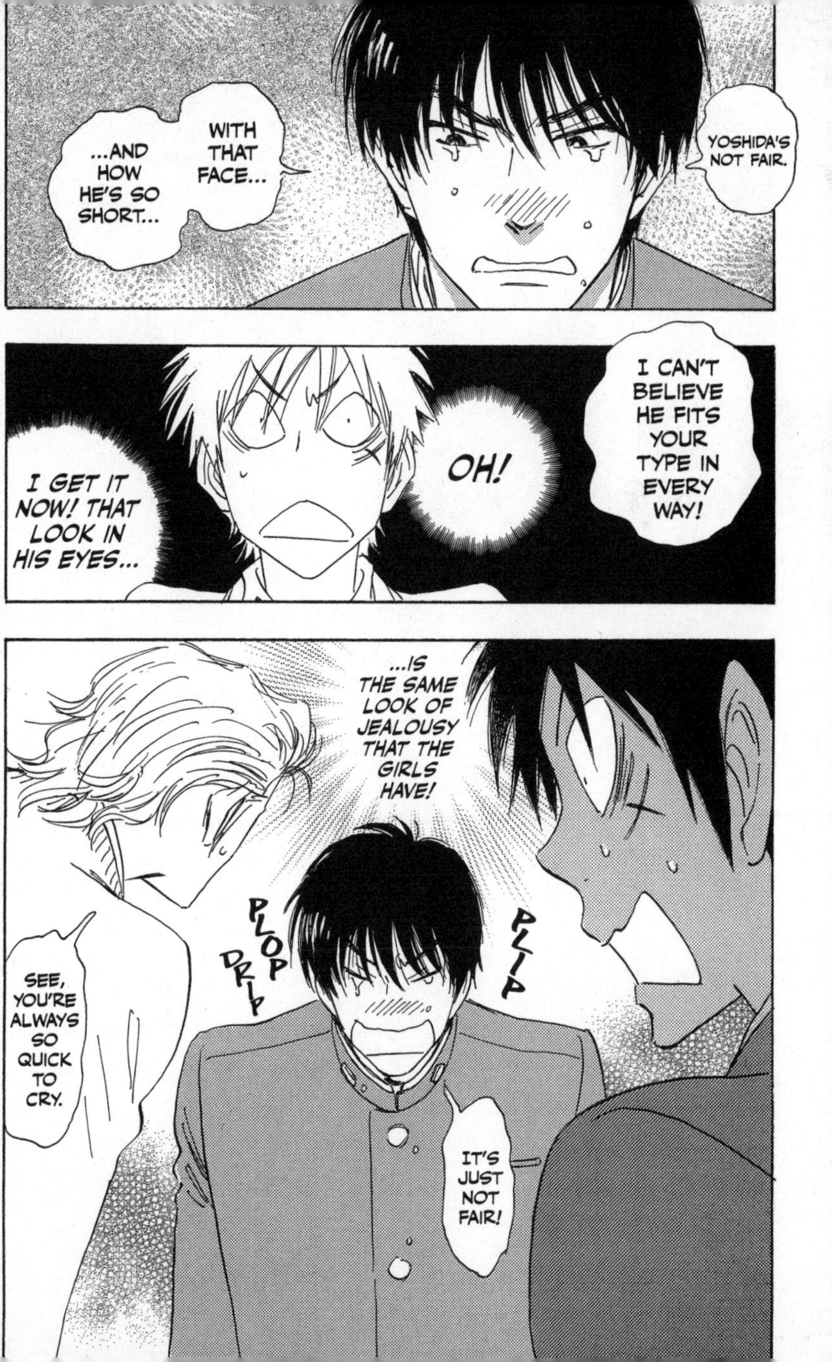
YOSHIDA'S NOT FAIR.
WITH THAT FACE...
...AND HOW HE'S SO SHORT...
I CAN'T BELIEVE HE FITS YOUR TYPE IN EVERY WAY!
OH!
I GET IT NOW! THAT LOOK IN HIS EYES...
...IS THE SAME LOOK OF JEALOUSY THAT THE GIRLS HAVE!
PLIP
PLOP
DRIP
IT'S JUST NOT FAIR!
SEE, YOU'RE ALWAYS SO QUICK TO CRY.

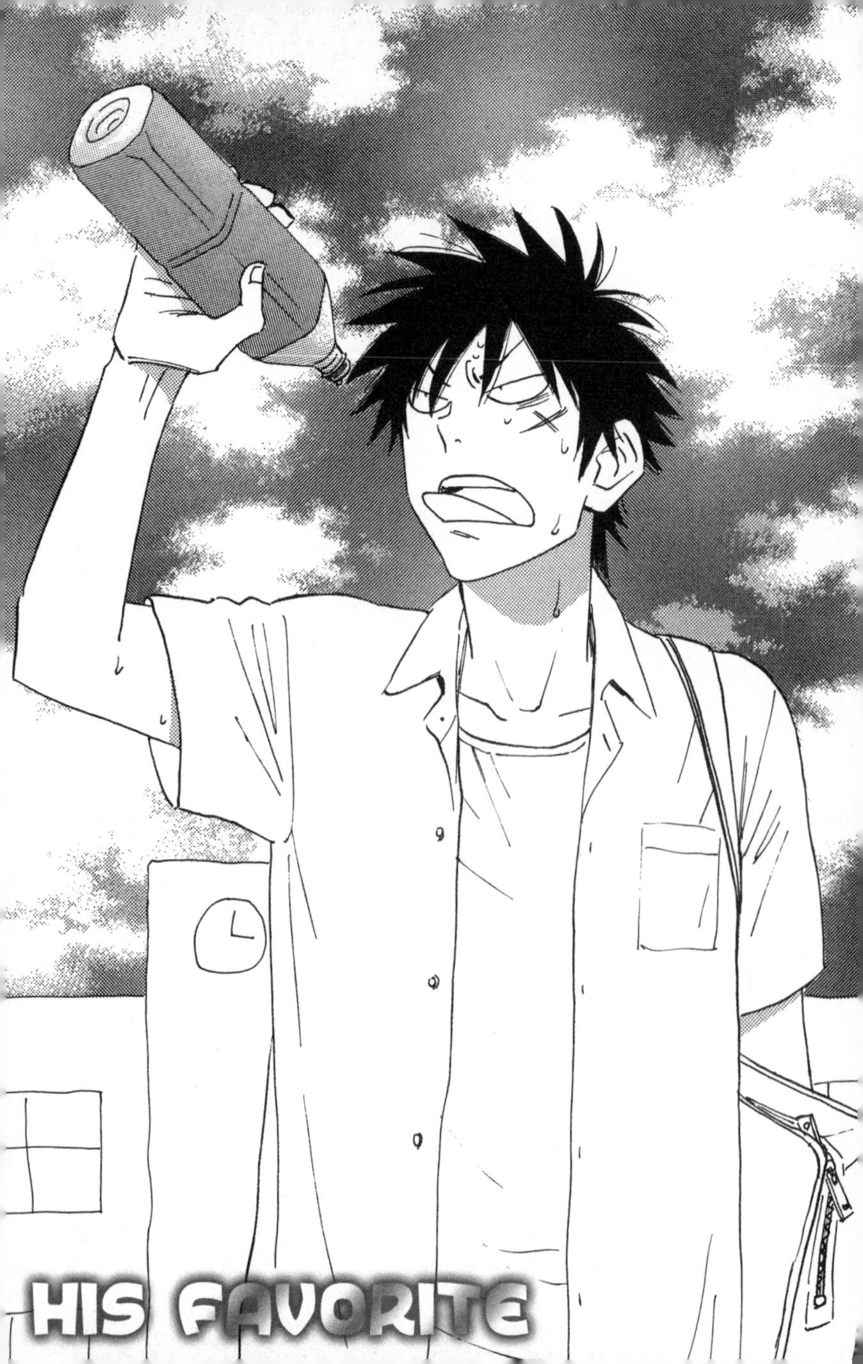
HIS FAVORITE

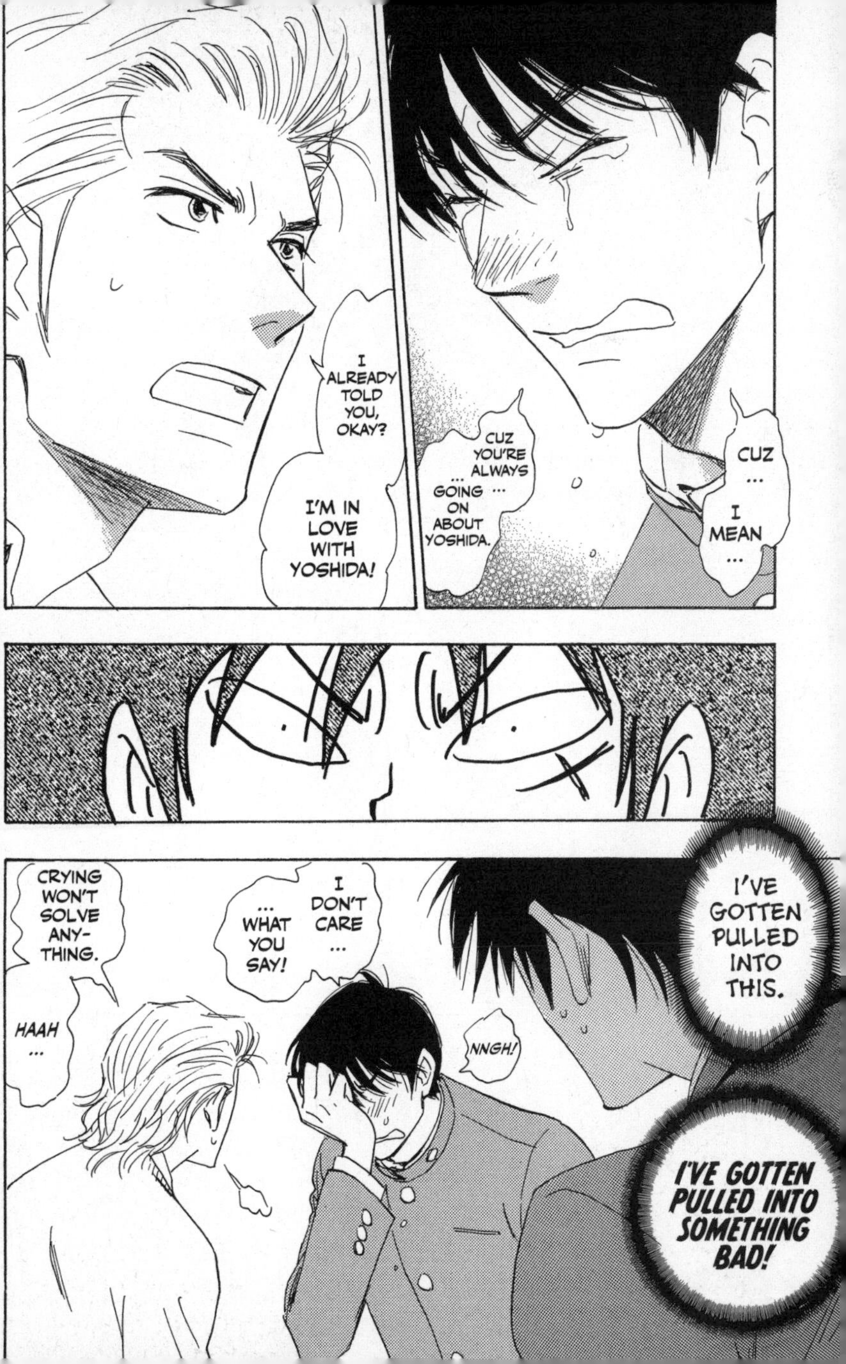

CUZ ... I MEAN ...
CUZ YOU'RE ALWAYS ... GOING ON ABOUT YOSHIDA.
I ALREADY TOLD YOU, OKAY?
I'M IN LOVE WITH YOSHIDA!
I'VE GOTTEN PULLED INTO THIS.
I DON'T CARE ... WHAT YOU SAY!
CRYING WON'T SOLVE ANY-THING.
NNGH!
HAAH ...
I'VE GOTTEN PULLED INTO SOMETHING BAD!

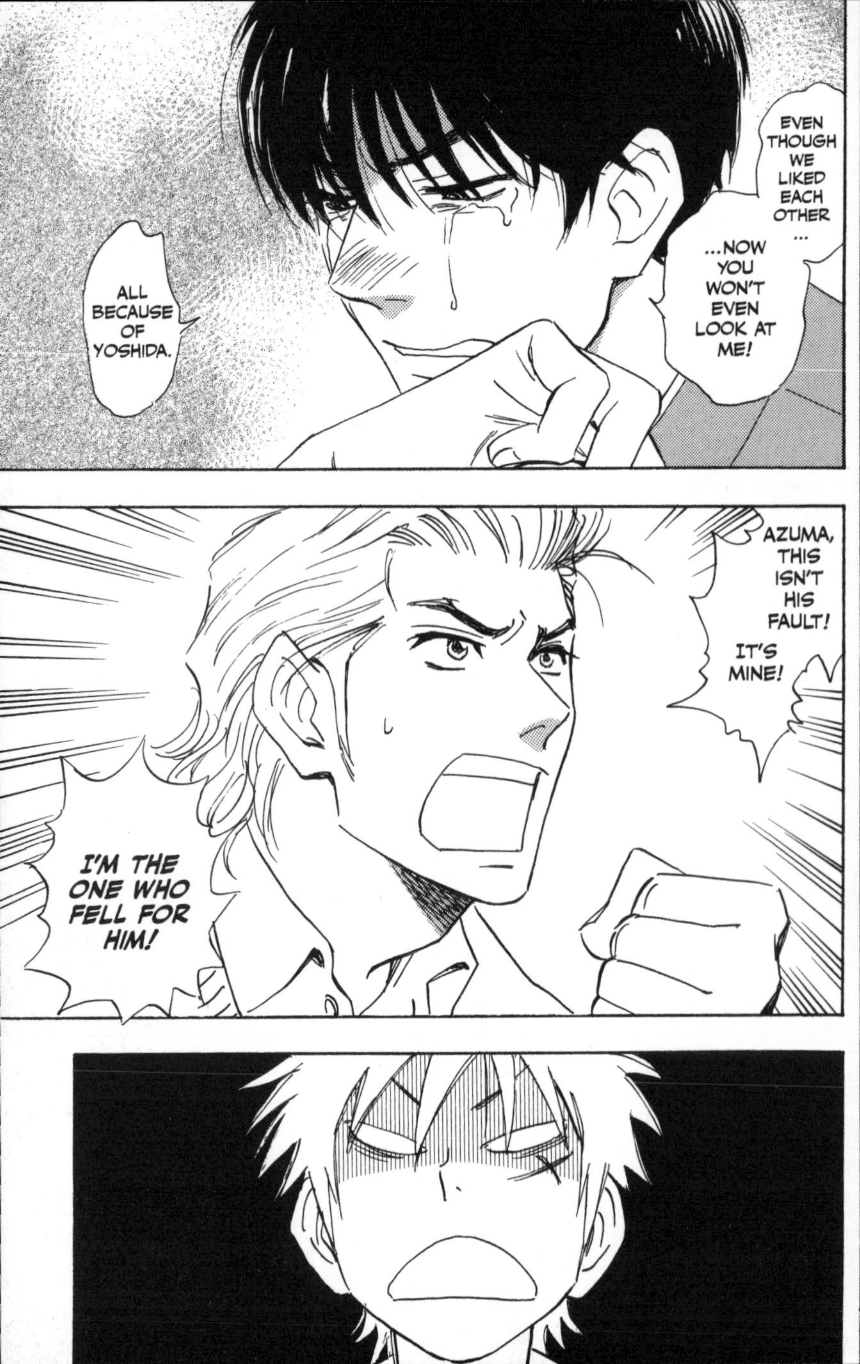
EVEN THOUGH WE LIKED EACH OTHER ...
...NOW YOU WON'T EVEN LOOK AT ME!
ALL BECAUSE OF YOSHIDA.
AZUMA, THIS ISN'T HIS FAULT!
IT'S MINE!
I'M THE ONE WHO FELL FOR HIM!

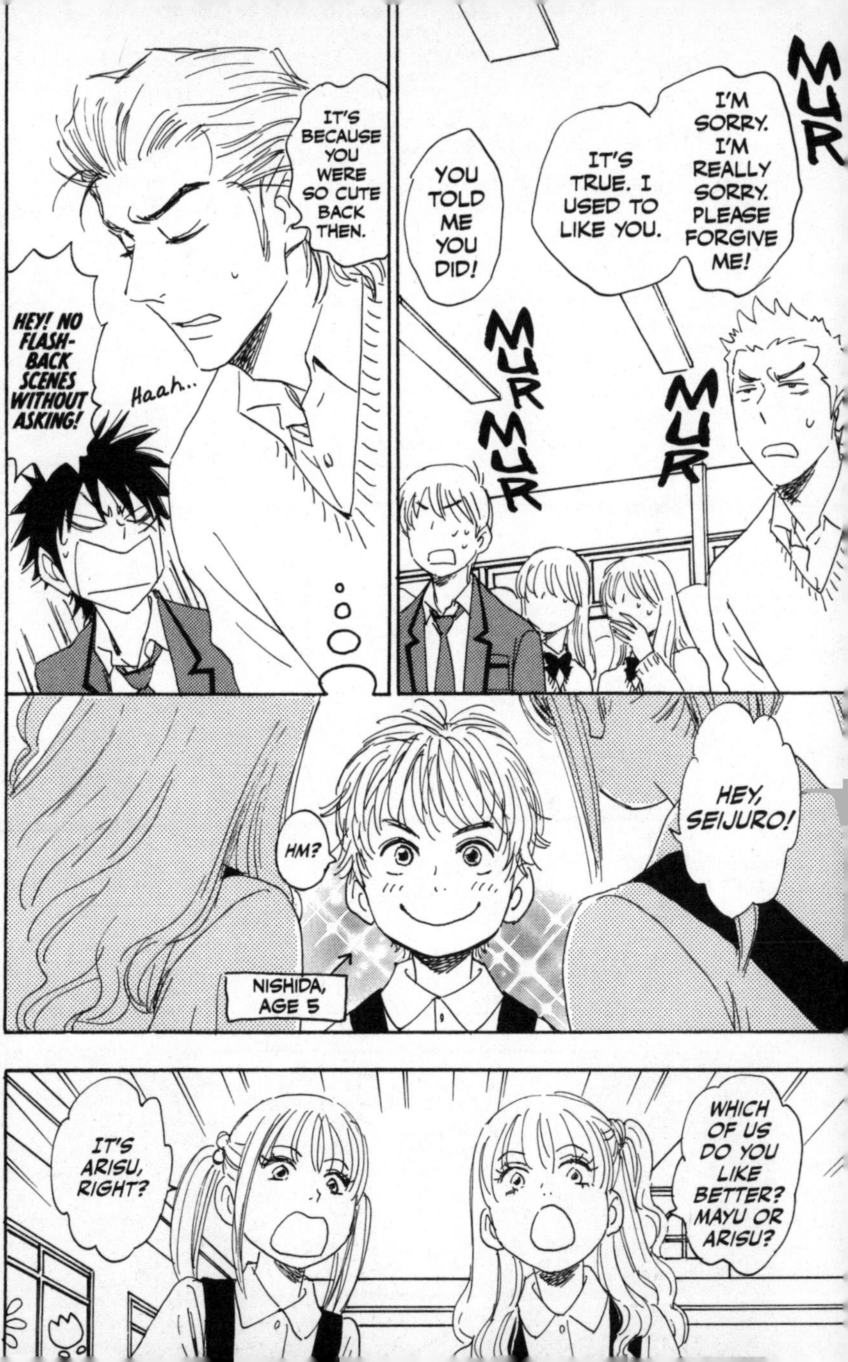

MUR
I'M SORRY. I'M REALLY SORRY. PLEASE FORGIVE ME!
IT'S TRUE. I USED TO LIKE YOU.
YOU TOLD ME YOU DID!
MUR MUR
MUR MUR
MUR
IT'S BECAUSE YOU WERE SO CUTE BACK THEN.
Haah...
HEY! NO FLASH-BACK SCENES WITHOUT ASKING!
HEY, SEIJURO!
HM?
NISHIDA, AGE 5
WHICH OF US DO YOU LIKE BETTER? MAYU OR ARISU?
IT'S ARISU, RIGHT?

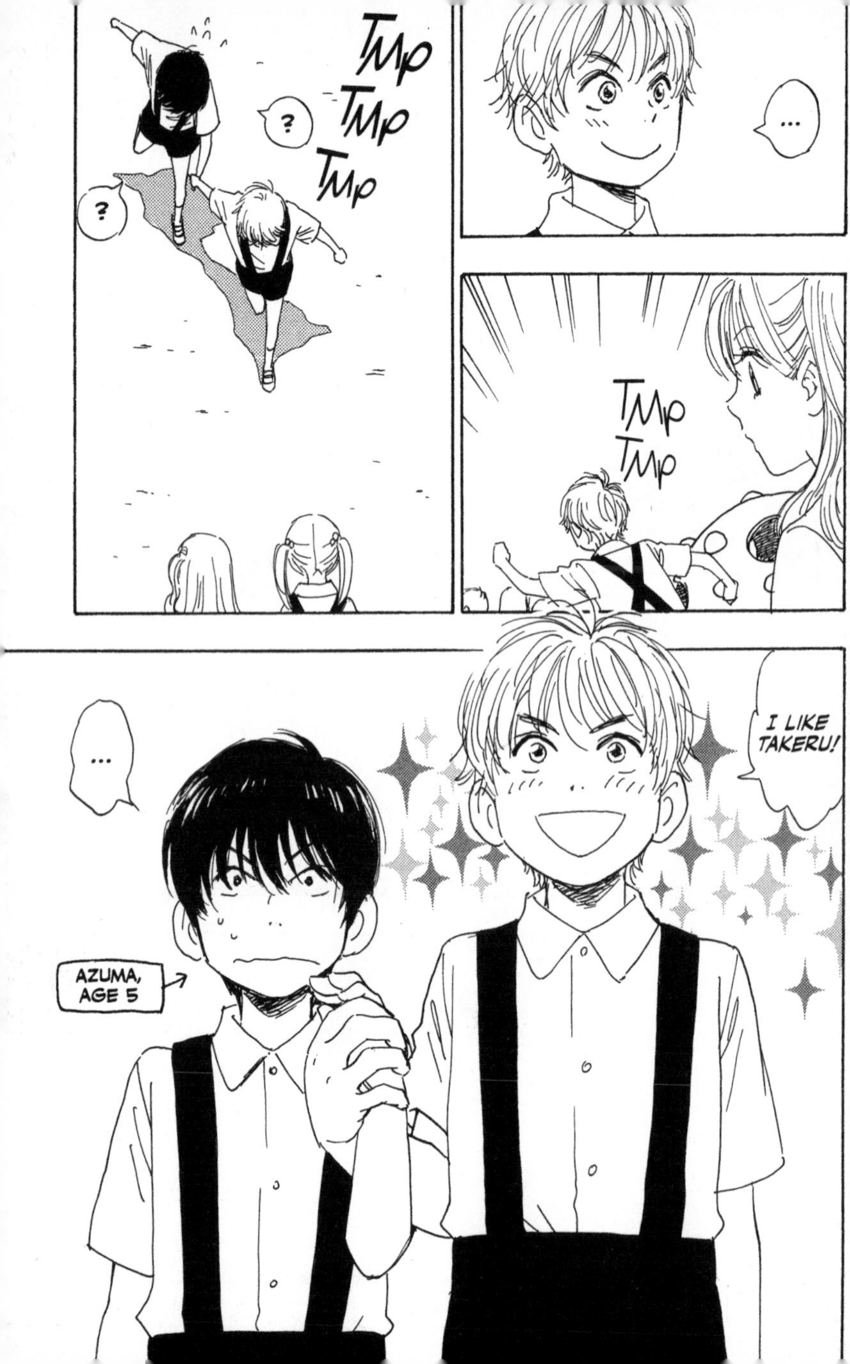
...
TMP
TMP
TMP
TMP
TMP
?
?
I LIKE TAKERU!
...
AZUMA, AGE 5

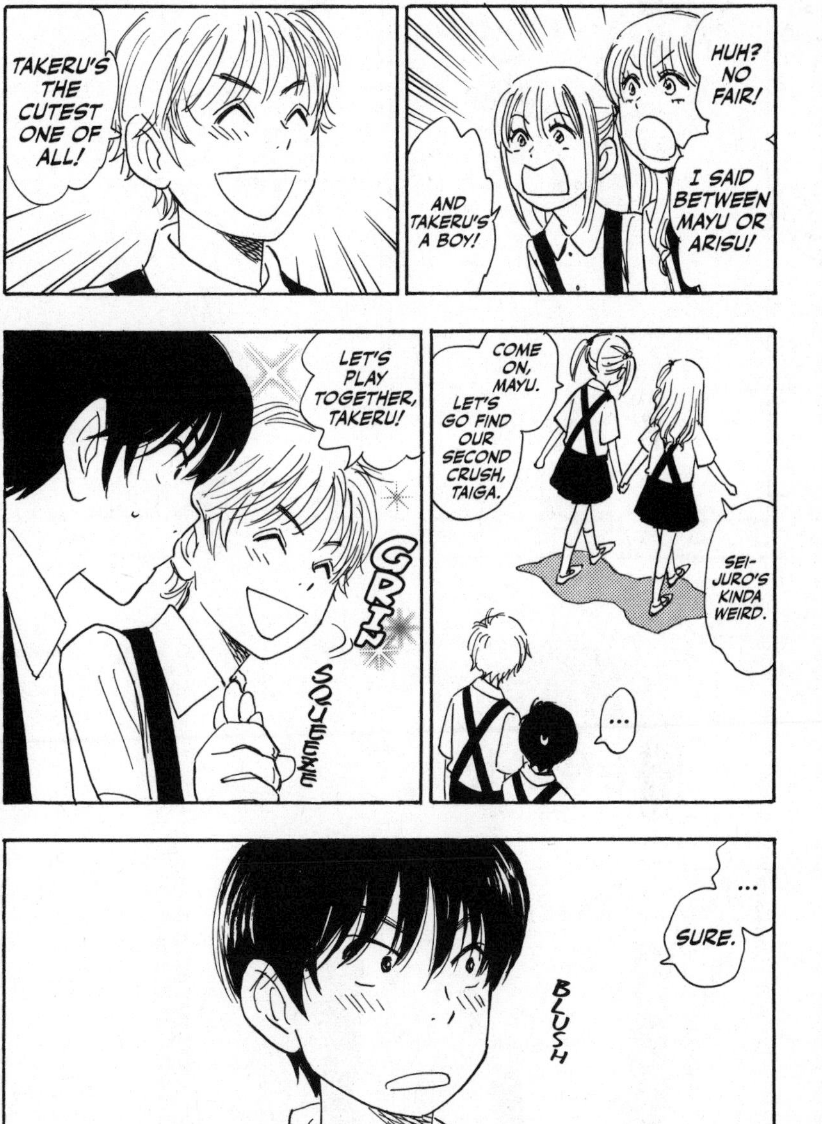
TAKERU'S THE CUTEST ONE OF ALL!
HUH? NO FAIR!
I SAID BETWEEN MAYU OR ARISU!
AND TAKERU'S A BOY!
LET'S PLAY TOGETHER, TAKERU!
GRIN
SQUEEZE
COME ON, MAYU. LET'S GO FIND OUR SECOND CRUSH, TAIGA.
SEI-JURO'S KINDA WEIRD.
...
...
SURE.
BLUSH

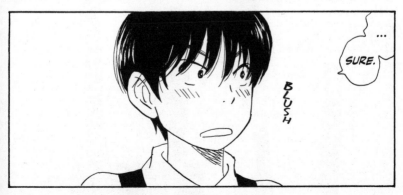

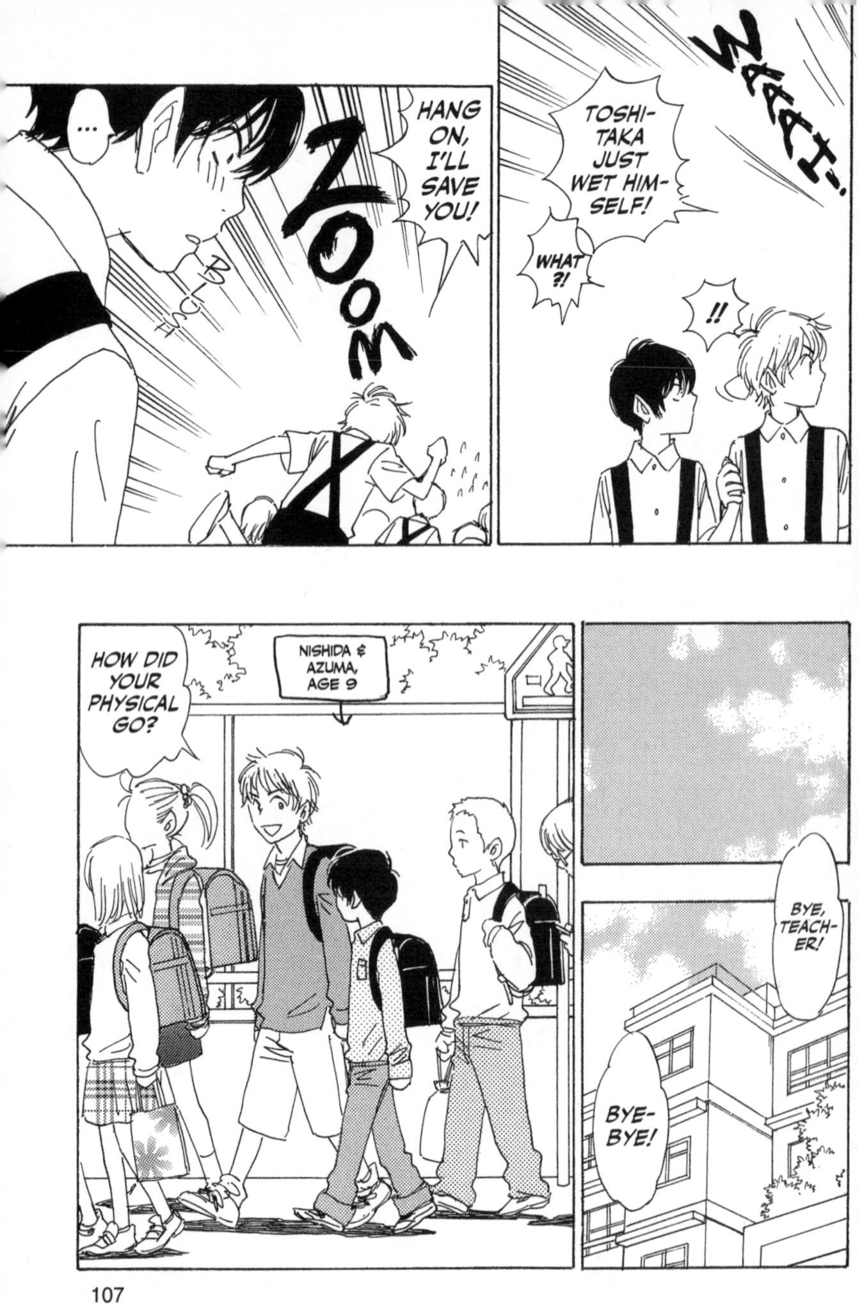
WAAAI-!
TOSHI-TAKA JUST WET HIM-SELF!
WHAT ?!
!!
HANG ON, I'LL SAVE YOU!
ZOOM
...
BLUSH
BYE, TEACH-ER!
BYE-BYE!
NISHIDA & AZUMA, AGE 9
HOW DID YOUR PHYSICAL GO?

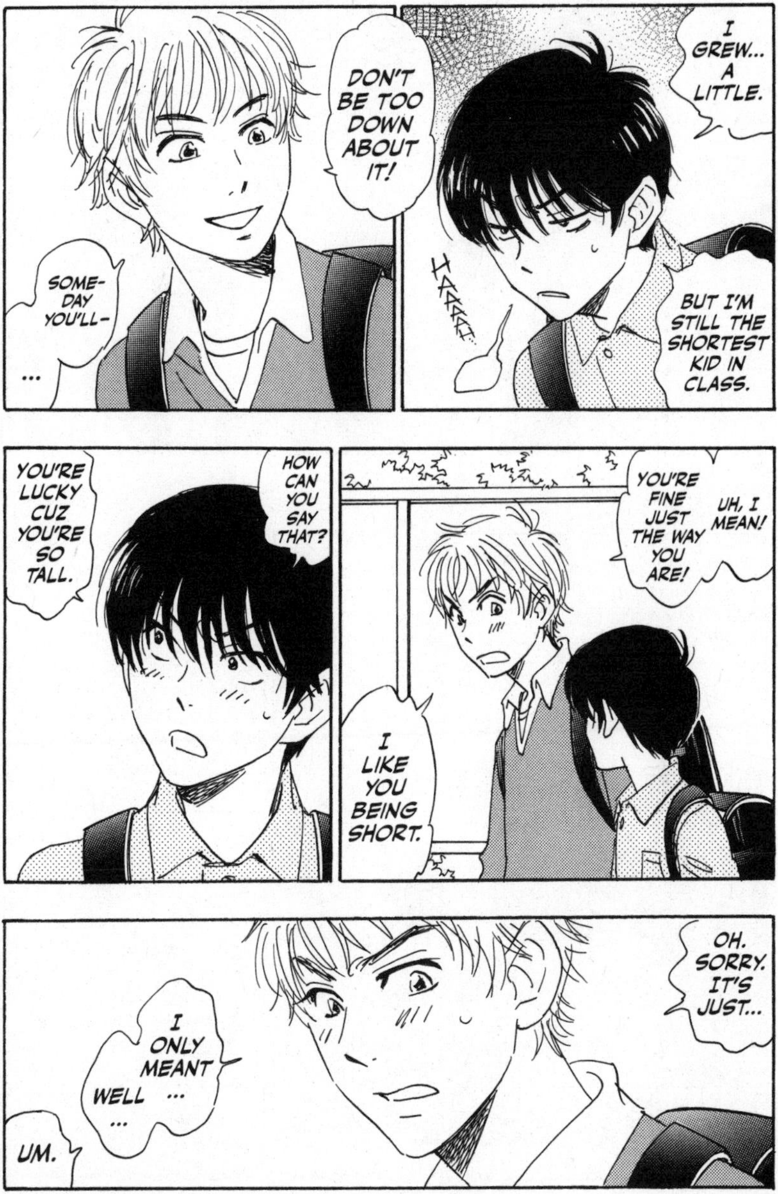
I GREW... A LITTLE.
HAAAAH...
BUT I'M STILL THE SHORTEST KID IN CLASS.
DON'T BE TOO DOWN ABOUT IT!
SOME-DAY YOU'LL-
...
YOU'RE FINE JUST THE WAY YOU ARE!
I LIKE YOU BEING SHORT.
UH, I MEAN!
HOW CAN YOU SAY THAT?
YOU'RE LUCKY CUZ YOU'RE SO TALL.
OH. SORRY. IT'S JUST...
I ONLY MEANT WELL ... ...
UM.

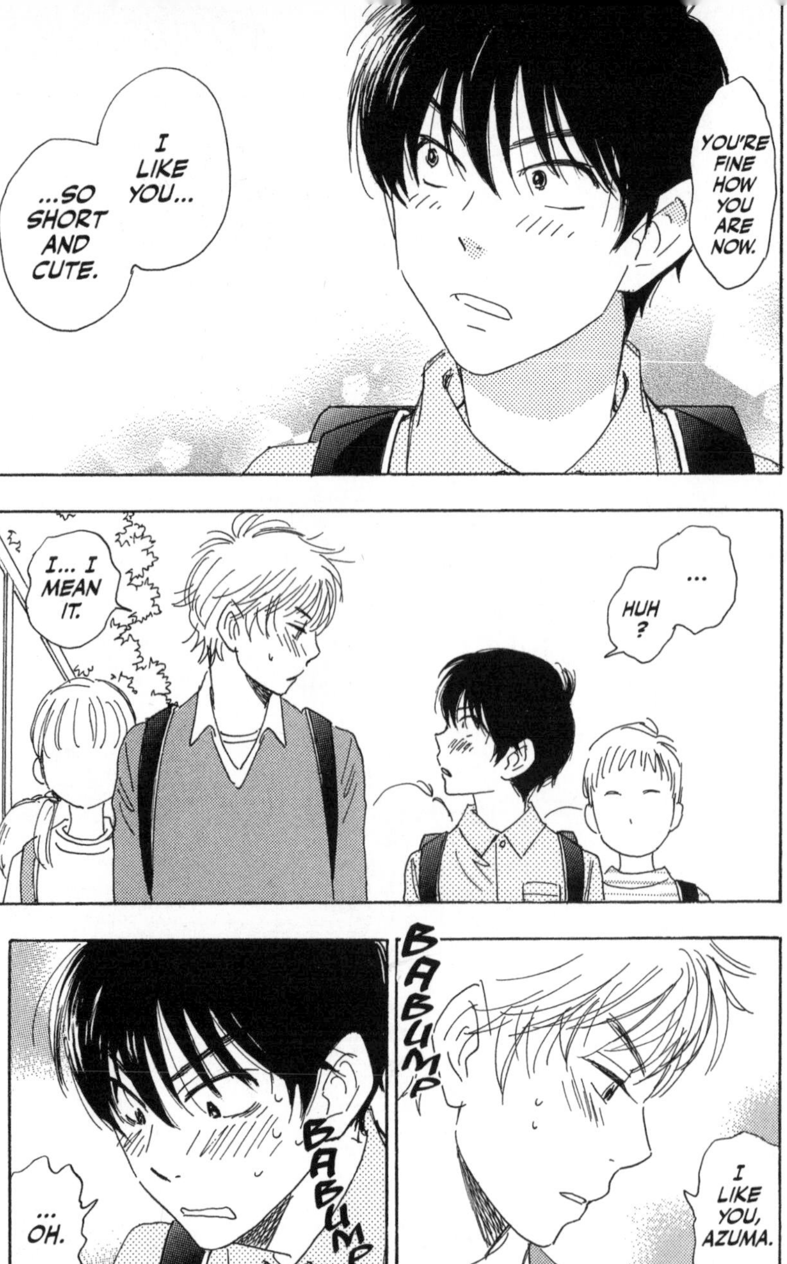
YOU'RE FINE HOW YOU ARE NOW.
I LIKE YOU...
...SO SHORT AND CUTE.
... HUH?
I... I MEAN IT.
BABUMP
I LIKE YOU, AZUMA.
BABUMP
... OH.

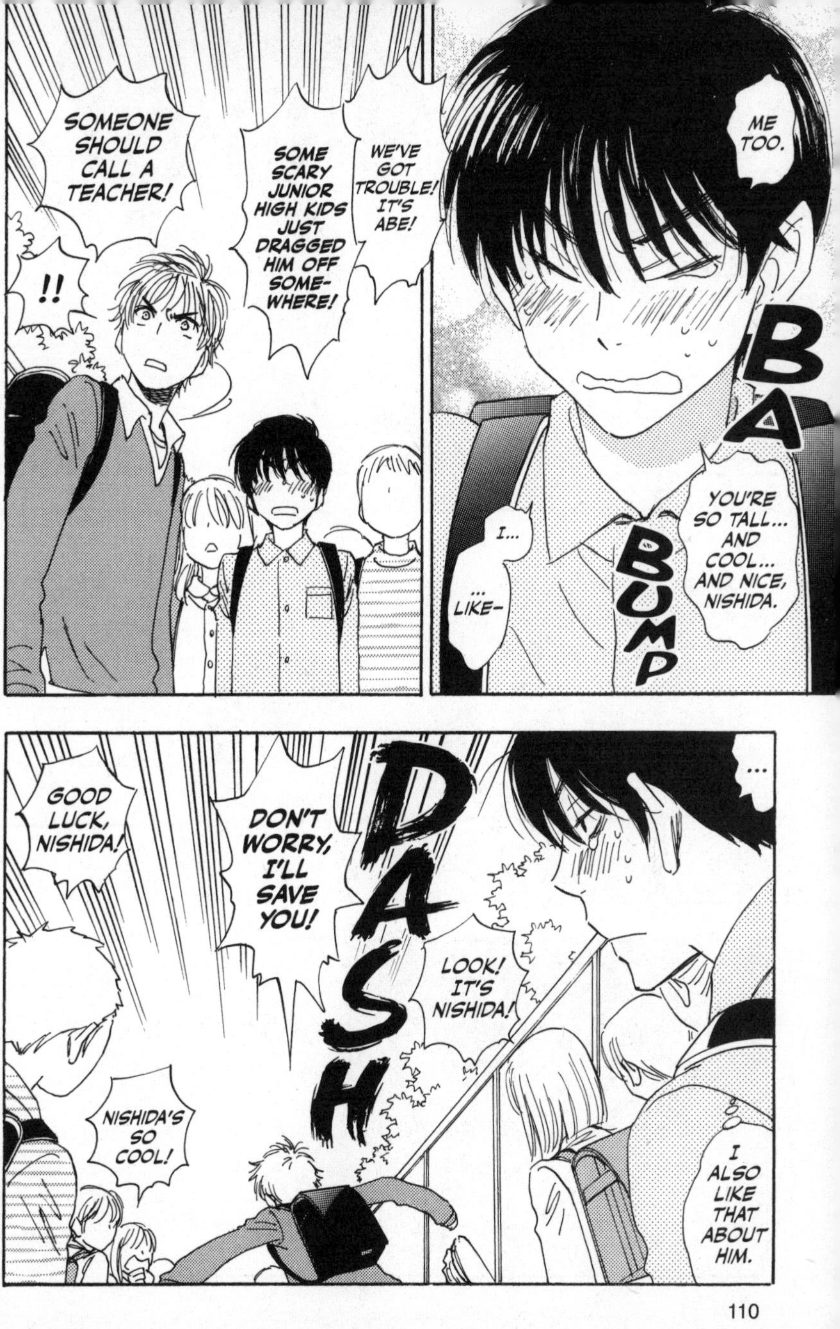
ME TOO.
BA
YOU'RE SO TALL... AND COOL... AND NICE, NISHIDA.
BUMP
I...
... LIKE-
WE'VE GOT TROUBLE! IT'S ABE!
SOME SCARY JUNIOR HIGH KIDS JUST DRAGGED HIM OFF SOME-WHERE!
SOMEONE SHOULD CALL A TEACHER!
!!
...
I ALSO LIKE THAT ABOUT HIM.
LOOK! IT'S NISHIDA!
DASH
DON'T WORRY, I'LL SAVE YOU!
GOOD LUCK, NISHIDA!
NISHIDA'S SO COOL!

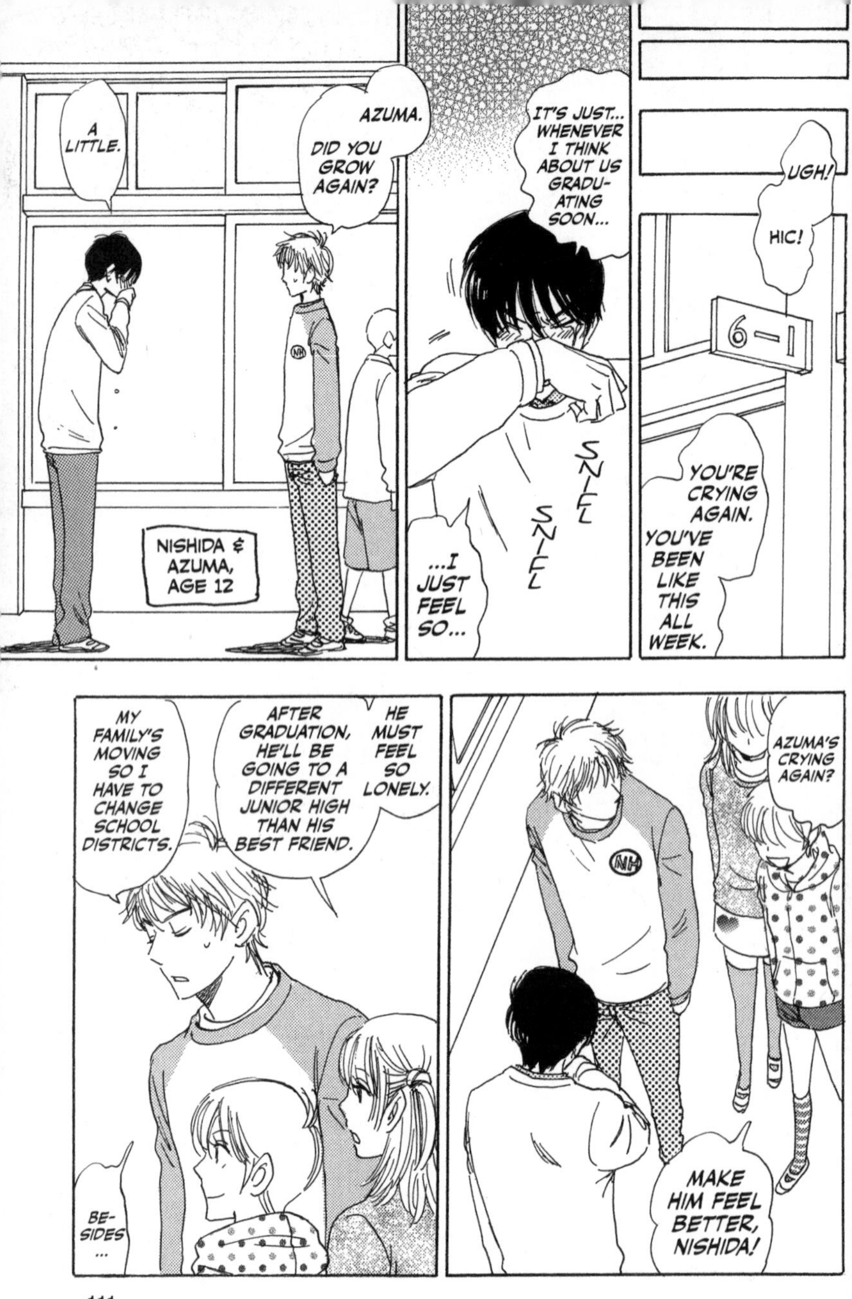
UGH!
HIC!
YOU'RE CRYING AGAIN. YOU'VE BEEN LIKE THIS ALL WEEK.
IT'S JUST... WHENEVER I THINK ABOUT US GRADUATING SOON...
SNIFL
SNIFL
...I JUST FEEL SO...
AZUMA.
DID YOU GROW AGAIN?
A LITTLE.
NISHIDA & AZUMA, AGE 12
AZUMA'S CRYING AGAIN?
MAKE HIM FEEL BETTER, NISHIDA!
HE MUST FEEL SO LONELY.
AFTER GRADUATION, HE'LL BE GOING TO A DIFFERENT JUNIOR HIGH THAN HIS BEST FRIEND.
MY FAMILY'S MOVING SO I HAVE TO CHANGE SCHOOL DISTRICTS.
BESIDES...

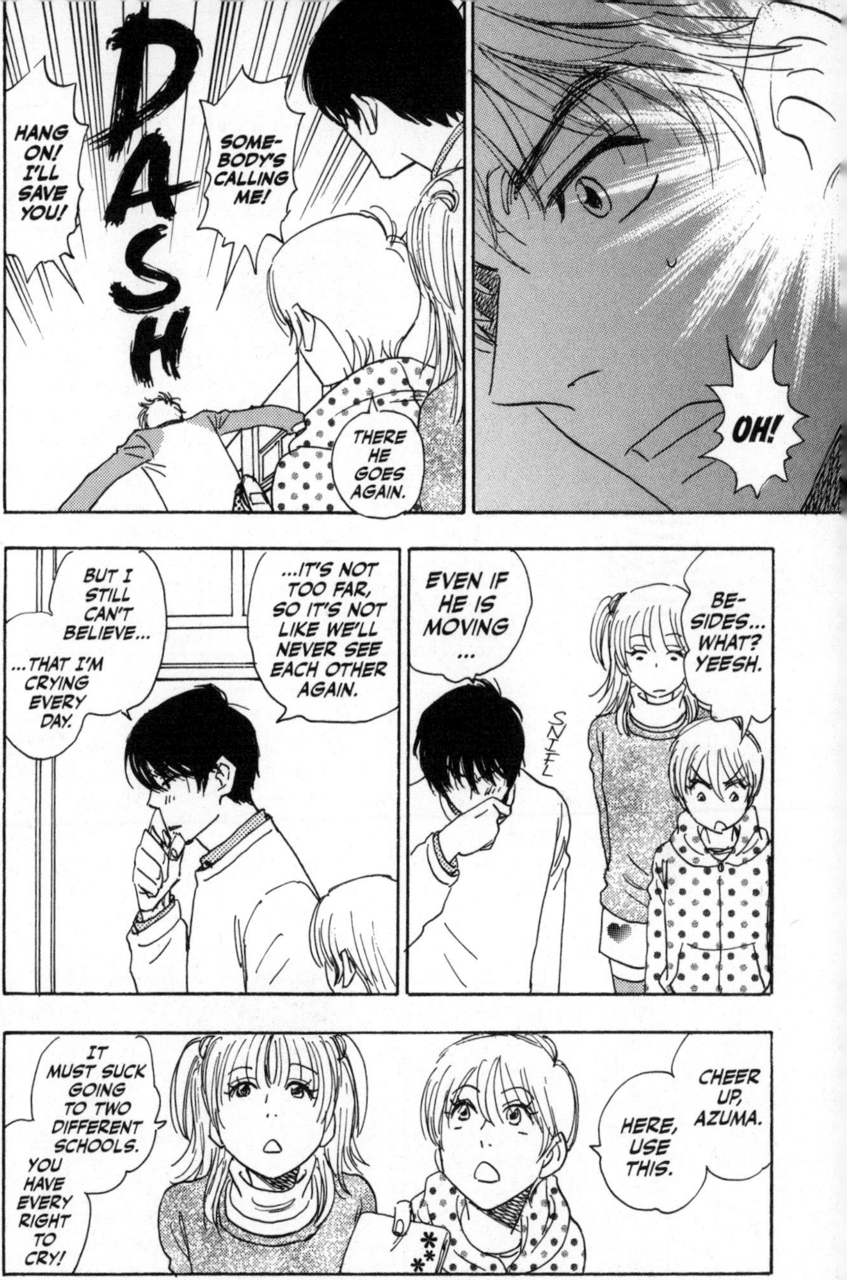
OH!
SOME-BODY'S CALLING ME!
HANG ON! I'LL SAVE YOU!
DASH
THERE HE GOES AGAIN.
BE-SIDES... WHAT? YEESH.
EVEN IF HE IS MOVING ...
SNIFL
...IT'S NOT TOO FAR, SO IT'S NOT LIKE WE'LL NEVER SEE EACH OTHER AGAIN.
BUT I STILL CAN'T BELIEVE...
...THAT I'M CRYING EVERY DAY.
CHEER UP, AZUMA.
HERE, USE THIS.
IT MUST SUCK GOING TO TWO DIFFERENT SCHOOLS.
YOU HAVE EVERY RIGHT TO CRY!

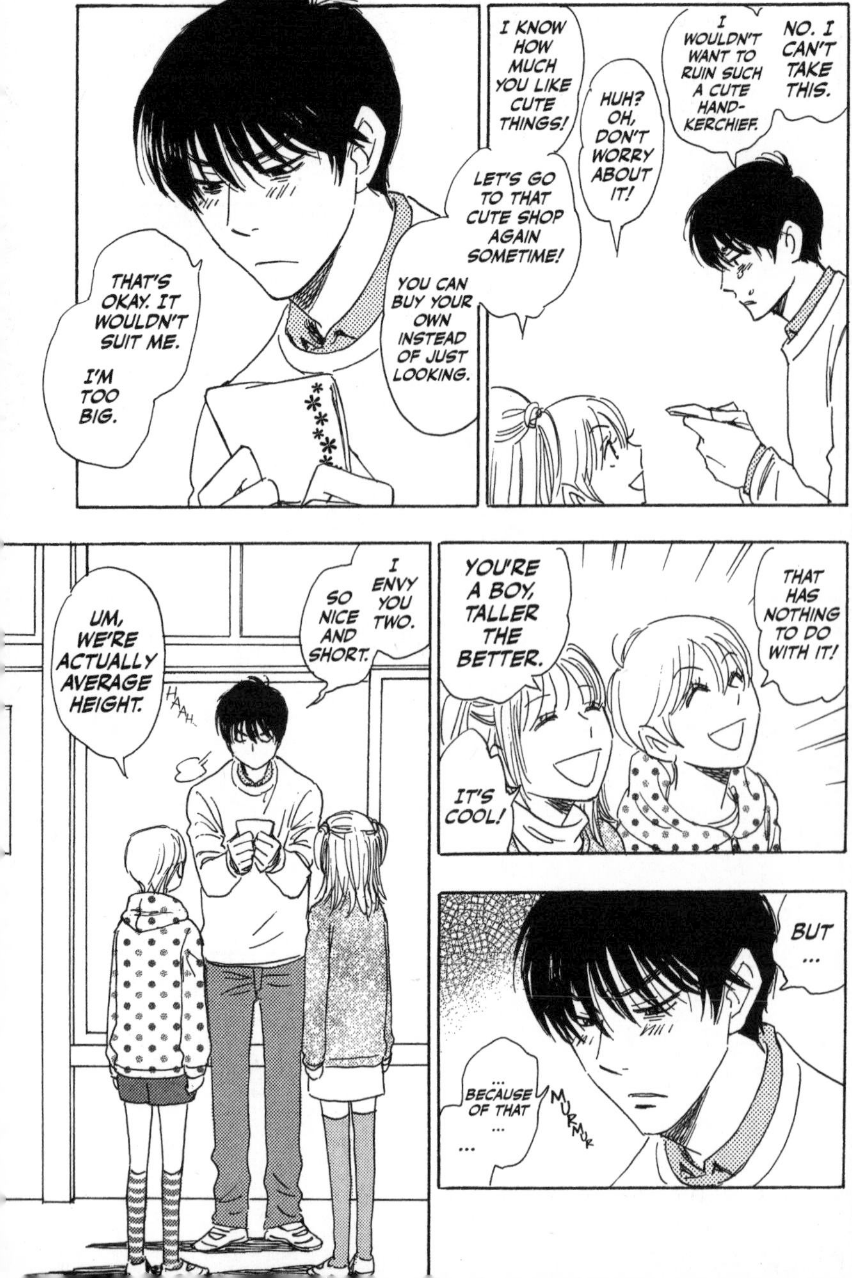
NO. I CAN'T TAKE THIS.
I WOULDN'T WANT TO RUIN SUCH A CUTE HANDKERCHIEF.
HUH? OH, DON'T WORRY ABOUT IT!
I KNOW HOW MUCH YOU LIKE CUTE THINGS!
LET'S GO TO THAT CUTE SHOP AGAIN SOMETIME!
YOU CAN BUY YOUR OWN INSTEAD OF JUST LOOKING.
THAT'S OKAY. IT WOULDN'T SUIT ME.
I'M TOO BIG.
THAT HAS NOTHING TO DO WITH IT!
YOU'RE A BOY, TALLER THE BETTER.
IT'S COOL!
BUT ...
... BECAUSE OF THAT ... ...
MURMUR
I ENVY YOU TWO.
SO NICE AND SHORT.
HAAH
UM, WE'RE ACTUALLY AVERAGE HEIGHT.

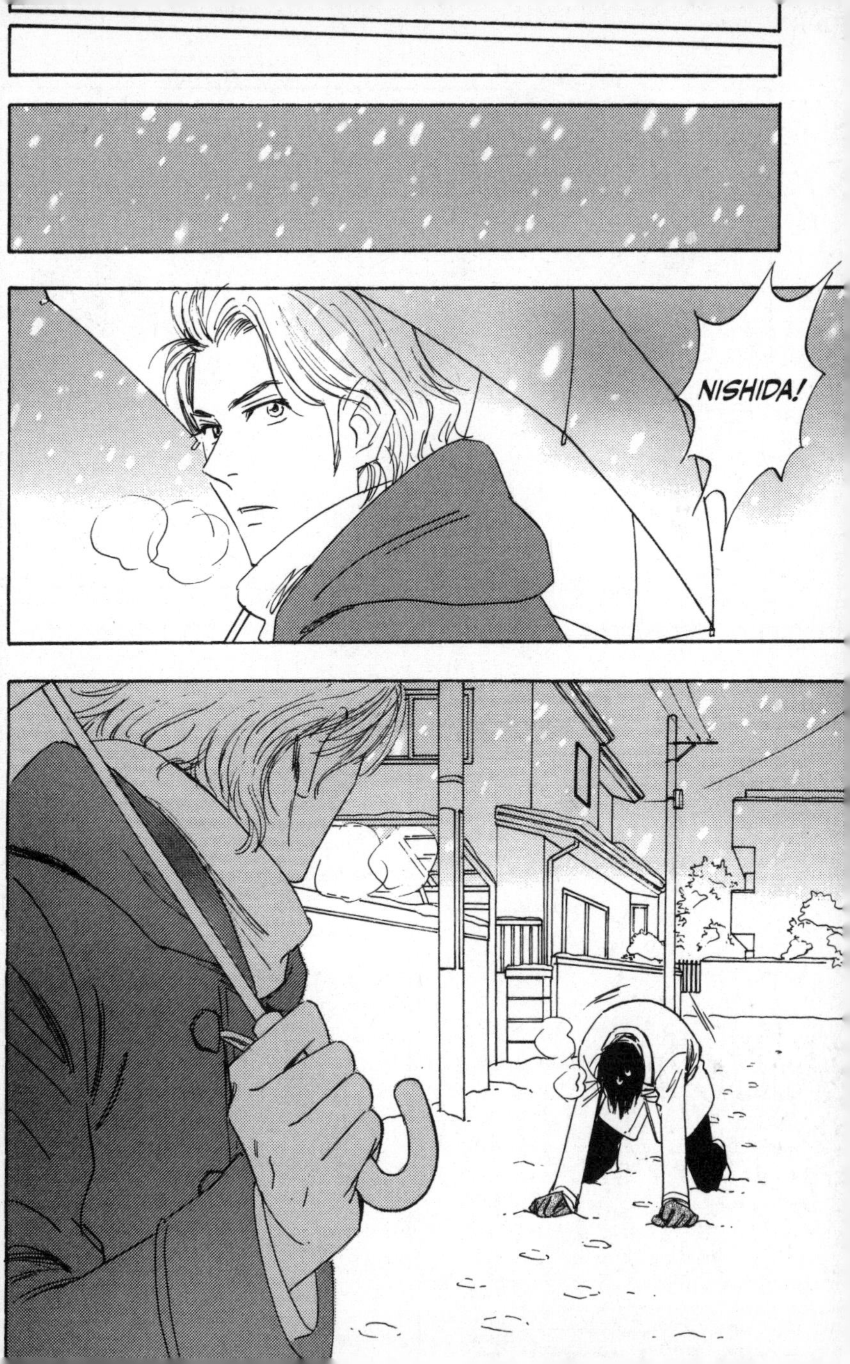
NISHIDA!

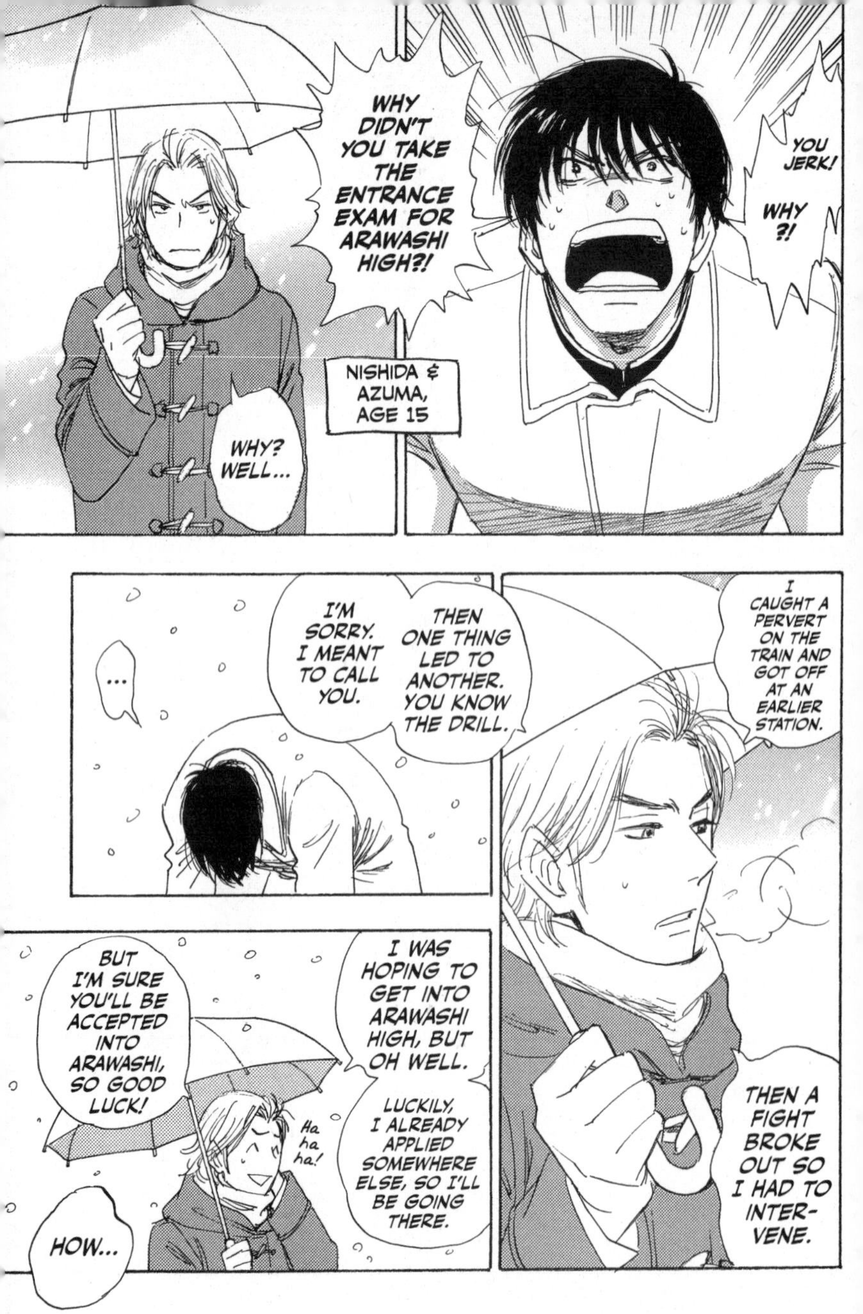
YOU JERK!
WHY ?!
WHY DIDN'T YOU TAKE THE ENTRANCE EXAM FOR ARAWASHI HIGH?!
NISHIDA & AZUMA, AGE 15
WHY? WELL...
I CAUGHT A PERVERT ON THE TRAIN AND GOT OFF AT AN EARLIER STATION.
THEN A FIGHT BROKE OUT SO I HAD TO INTER- VENE.
THEN ONE THING LED TO ANOTHER. YOU KNOW THE DRILL.
I'M SORRY. I MEANT TO CALL YOU.
...
I WAS HOPING TO GET INTO ARAWASHI HIGH, BUT OH WELL.
LUCKILY, I ALREADY APPLIED SOMEWHERE ELSE, SO I'LL BE GOING THERE.
Ha ha ha!
BUT I'M SURE YOU'LL BE ACCEPTED INTO ARAWASHI, SO GOOD LUCK!
HOW...

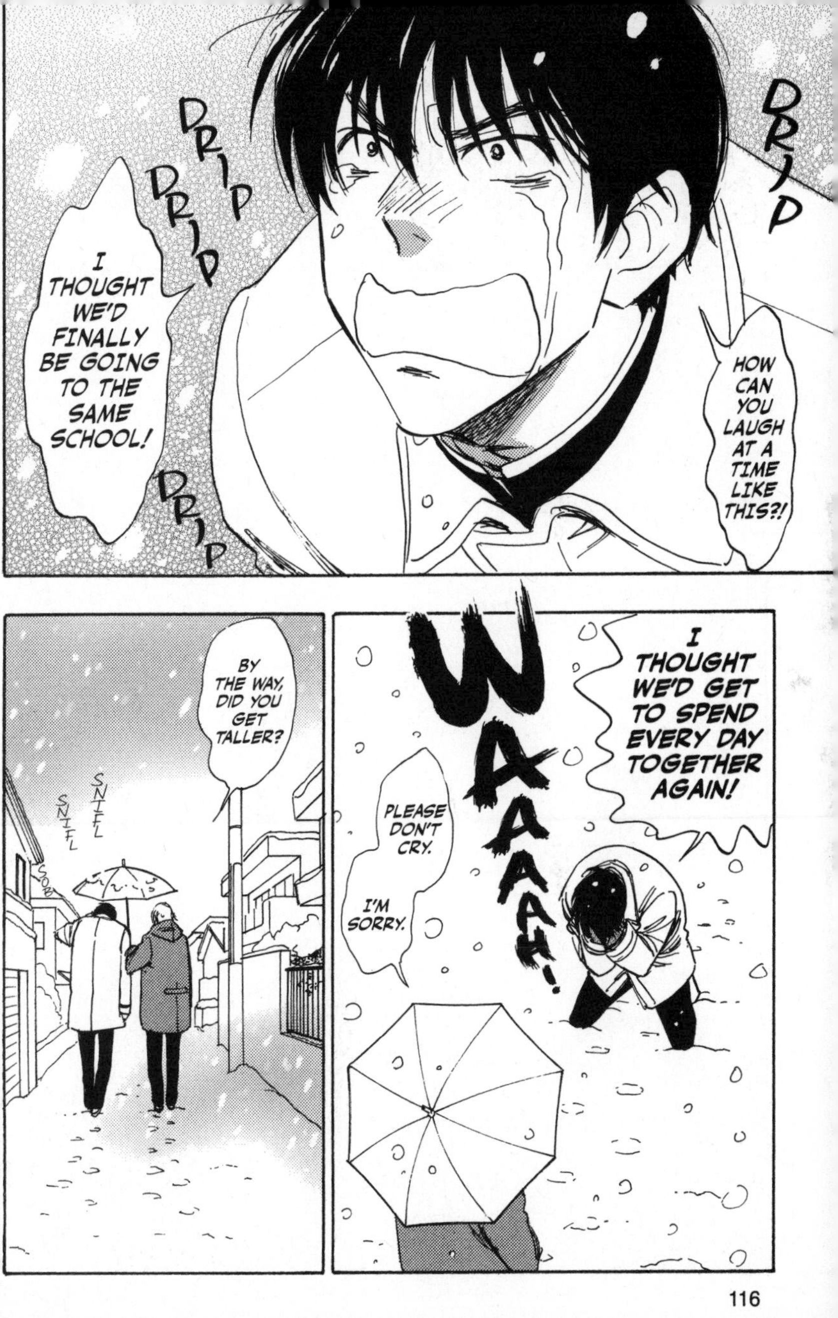
DRIP
DRIP
HOW CAN YOU LAUGH AT A TIME LIKE THIS?!
DRIP
I THOUGHT WE'D FINALLY BE GOING TO THE SAME SCHOOL!
DRIP
I THOUGHT WE'D GET TO SPEND EVERY DAY TOGETHER AGAIN!
WAAAAH!
PLEASE DON'T CRY.
I'M SORRY.
BY THE WAY, DID YOU GET TALLER?
SNIFFL
SNIFFL
SOB

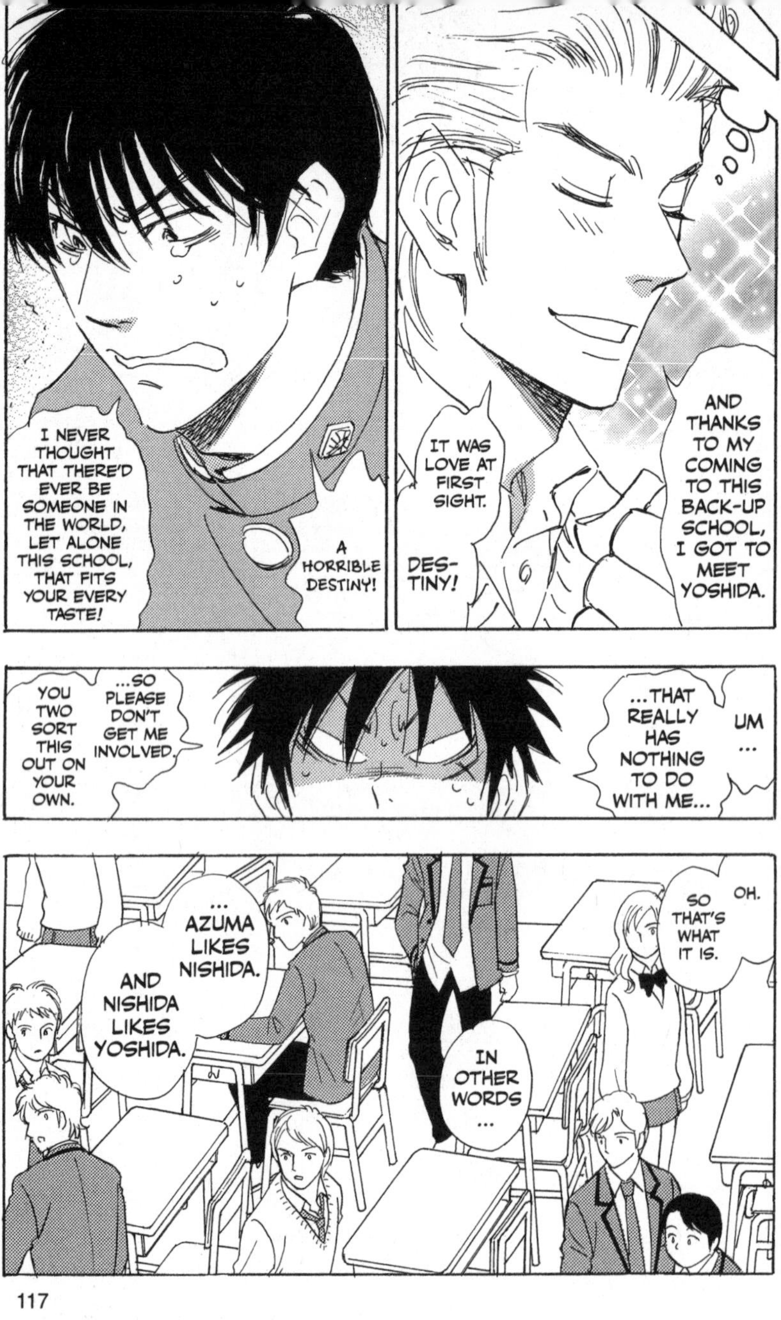
AND THANKS TO MY COMING TO THIS BACK-UP SCHOOL, I GOT TO MEET YOSHIDA.
IT WAS LOVE AT FIRST SIGHT.
DES-TINY!
A HORRIBLE DESTINY!
I NEVER THOUGHT THAT THERE'D EVER BE SOMEONE IN THE WORLD, LET ALONE THIS SCHOOL, THAT FITS YOUR EVERY TASTE!
UM ...
...THAT REALLY HAS NOTHING TO DO WITH ME...
...SO PLEASE DON'T GET ME INVOLVED.
YOU TWO SORT THIS OUT ON YOUR OWN.
OH.
SO THAT'S WHAT IT IS.
IN OTHER WORDS ...
... AZUMA LIKES NISHIDA.
AND NISHIDA LIKES YOSHIDA.

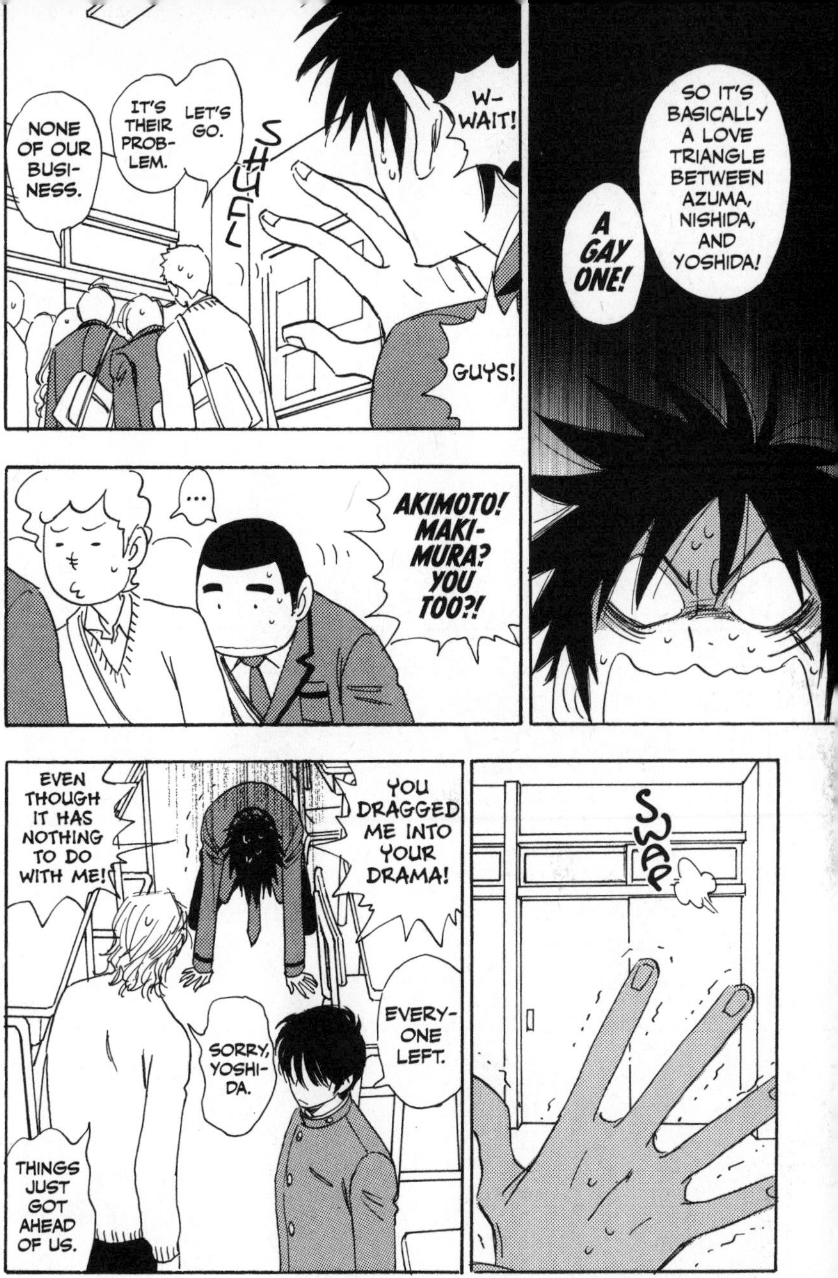
SO IT'S BASICALLY A LOVE TRIANGLE BETWEEN AZUMA, NISHIDA, AND YOSHIDA!
A GAY ONE!
W-WAIT!
SHUFL
LET'S GO.
IT'S THEIR PROB-LEM.
NONE OF OUR BUSI-NESS.
GUYS!
AKIMOTO! MAKI-MURA? YOU TOO?!
...
SWAP
YOU DRAGGED ME INTO YOUR DRAMA!
EVEN THOUGH IT HAS NOTHING TO DO WITH ME!
EVERY-ONE LEFT.
SORRY, YOSHI-DA.
THINGS JUST GOT AHEAD OF US.

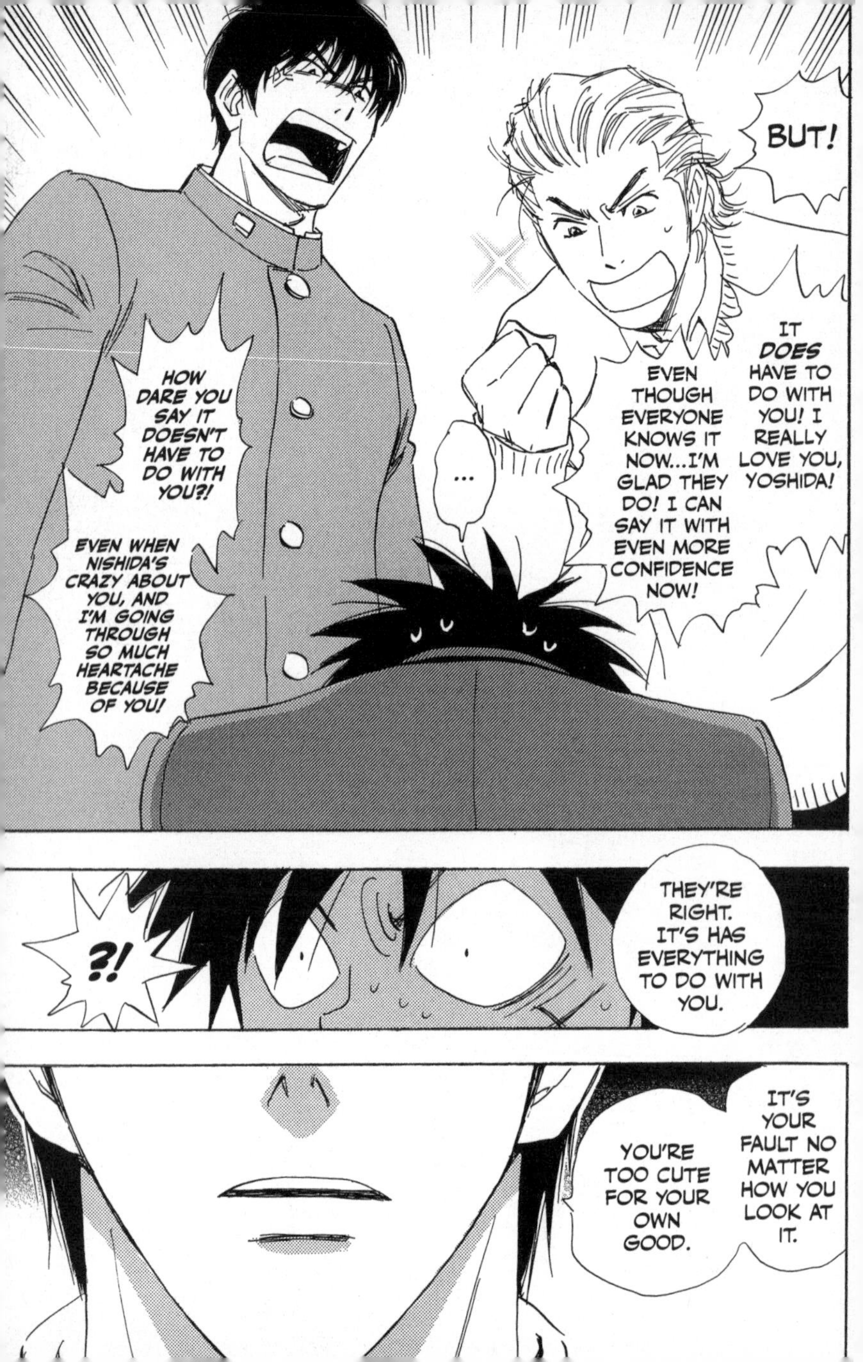
BUT!
IT *DOES* HAVE TO DO WITH YOU! I REALLY LOVE YOU, YOSHIDA!
EVEN THOUGH EVERYONE KNOWS IT NOW...I'M GLAD THEY DO! I CAN SAY IT WITH EVEN MORE CONFIDENCE NOW!
...
HOW DARE YOU SAY IT DOESN'T HAVE TO DO WITH YOU?!
EVEN WHEN NISHIDA'S CRAZY ABOUT YOU, AND I'M GOING THROUGH SO MUCH HEARTACHE BECAUSE OF YOU!
THEY'RE RIGHT. IT'S HAS EVERYTHING TO DO WITH YOU.
?!
IT'S YOUR FAULT NO MATTER HOW YOU LOOK AT IT.
YOU'RE TOO CUTE FOR YOUR OWN GOOD.

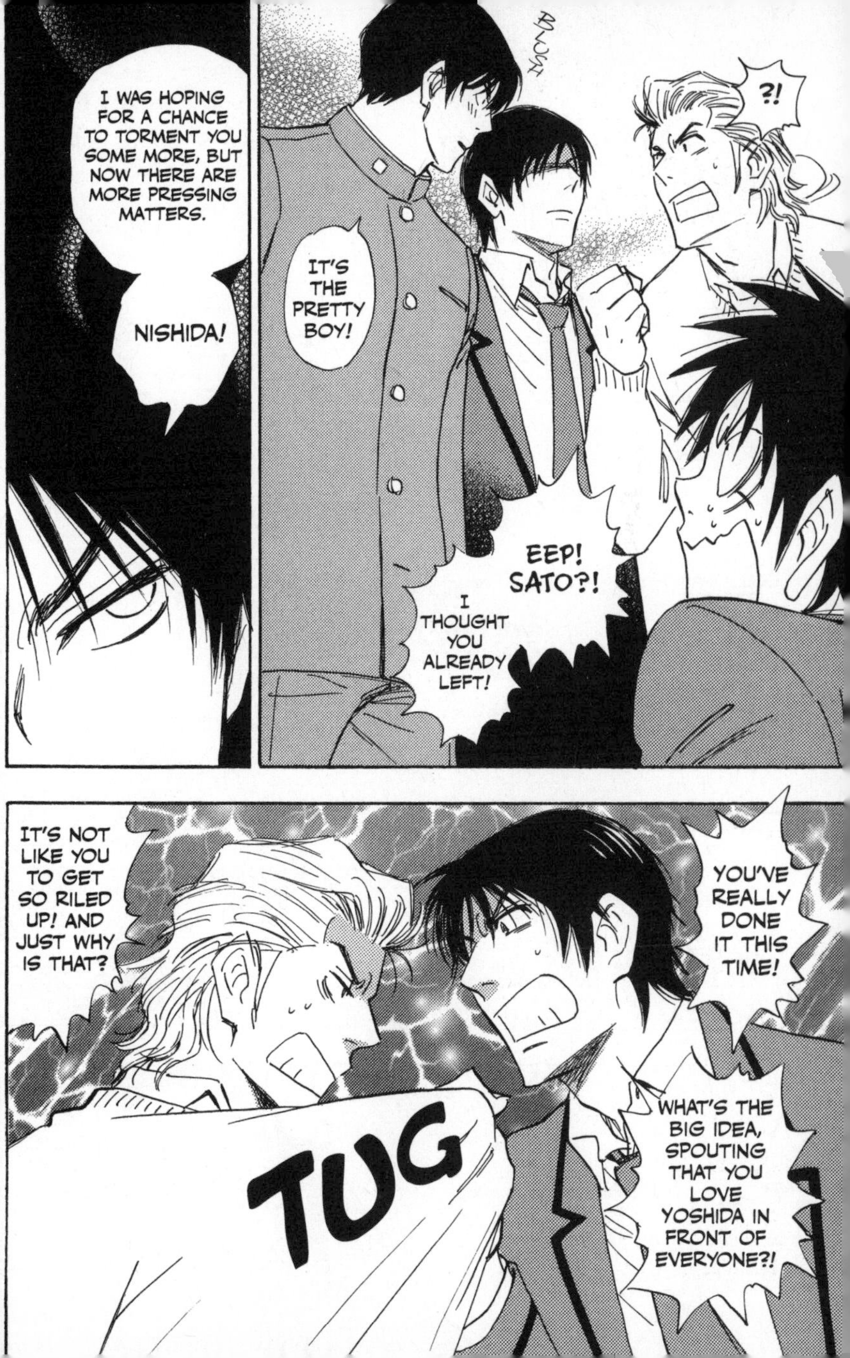
?!
BLUSH
IT'S THE PRETTY BOY!
EEP! SATO?!
I THOUGHT YOU ALREADY LEFT!
I WAS HOPING FOR A CHANCE TO TORMENT YOU SOME MORE, BUT NOW THERE ARE MORE PRESSING MATTERS.
NISHIDA!
YOU'VE REALLY DONE IT THIS TIME!
WHAT'S THE BIG IDEA, SPOUTING THAT YOU LOVE YOSHIDA IN FRONT OF EVERYONE?!
IT'S NOT LIKE YOU TO GET SO RILED UP! AND JUST WHY IS THAT?
TUG

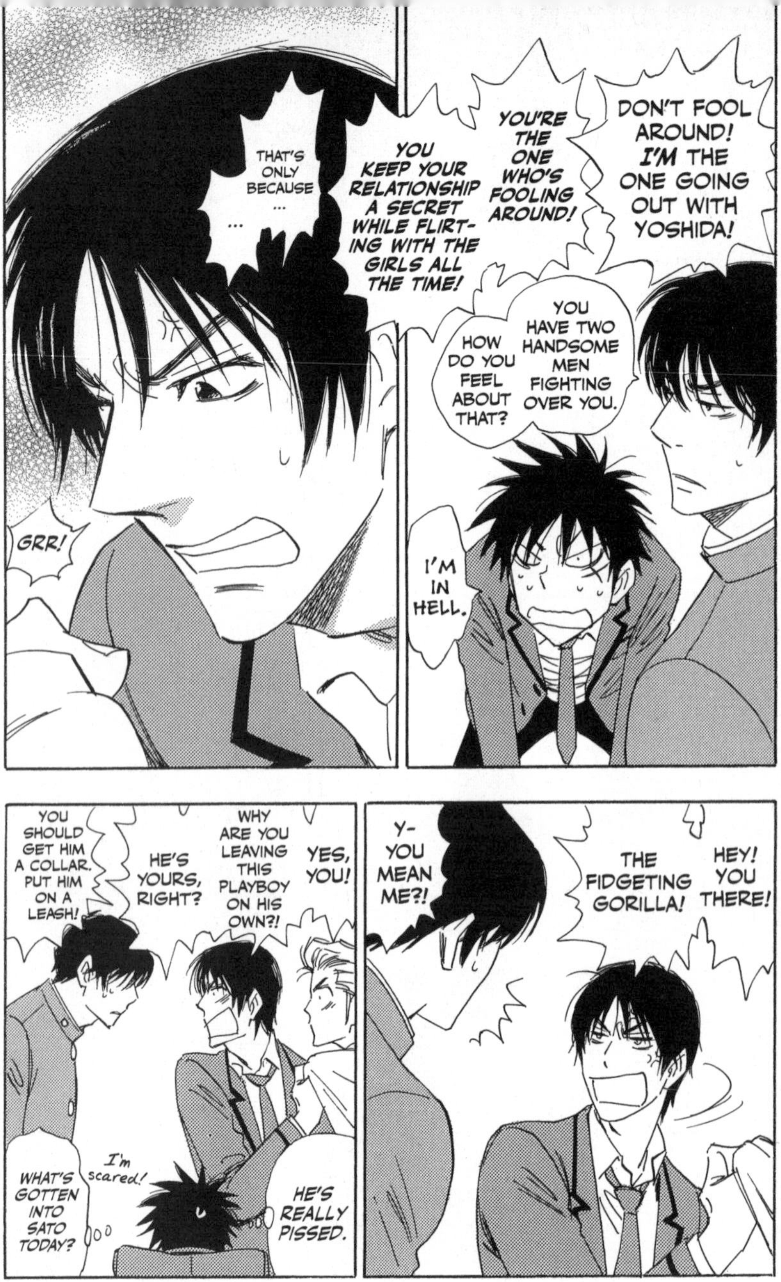
DON'T FOOL AROUND! I'M THE ONE GOING OUT WITH YOSHIDA!
YOU'RE THE ONE WHO'S FOOLING AROUND!
YOU KEEP YOUR RELATIONSHIP A SECRET WHILE FLIRT-ING WITH THE GIRLS ALL THE TIME!
YOU HAVE TWO HANDSOME MEN FIGHTING OVER YOU.
HOW DO YOU FEEL ABOUT THAT?
I'M IN HELL.
THAT'S ONLY BECAUSE ... ...
GRR!
HEY! YOU THERE!
THE FIDGETING GORILLA!
Y- YOU MEAN ME?!
YES, YOU!
WHY ARE YOU LEAVING THIS PLAYBOY ON HIS OWN?!
HE'S YOURS, RIGHT?
YOU SHOULD GET HIM A COLLAR. PUT HIM ON A LEASH!
HE'S REALLY PISSED.
I'm scared!
WHAT'S GOTTEN INTO SATO TODAY?

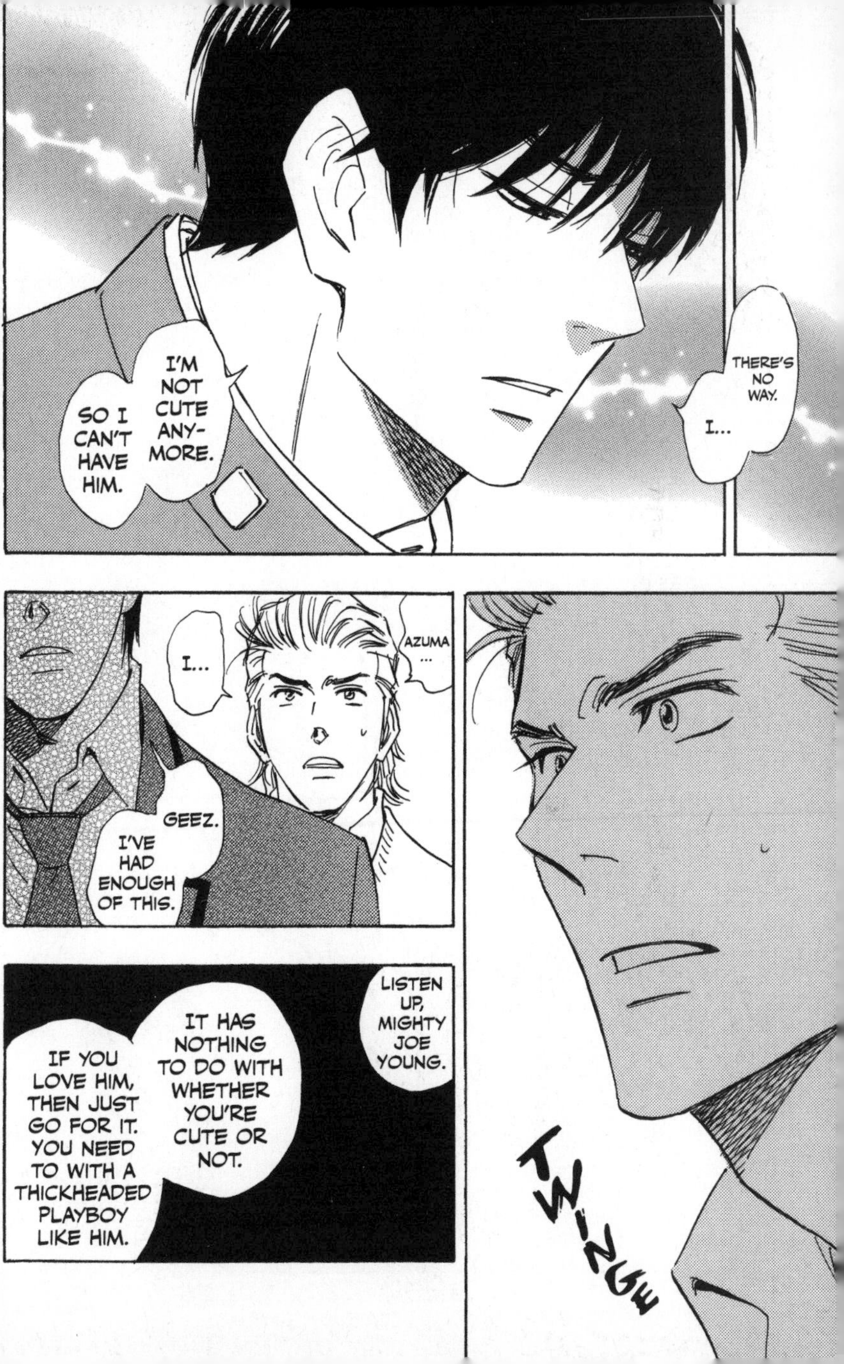
THERE'S NO WAY.
I...
I'M NOT CUTE ANYMORE.
SO I CAN'T HAVE HIM.
AZUMA ...
I...
GEEZ. I'VE HAD ENOUGH OF THIS.
LISTEN UP, MIGHTY JOE YOUNG.
IT HAS NOTHING TO DO WITH WHETHER YOU'RE CUTE OR NOT.
IF YOU LOVE HIM, THEN JUST GO FOR IT. YOU NEED TO WITH A THICKHEADED PLAYBOY LIKE HIM.
TWINGE

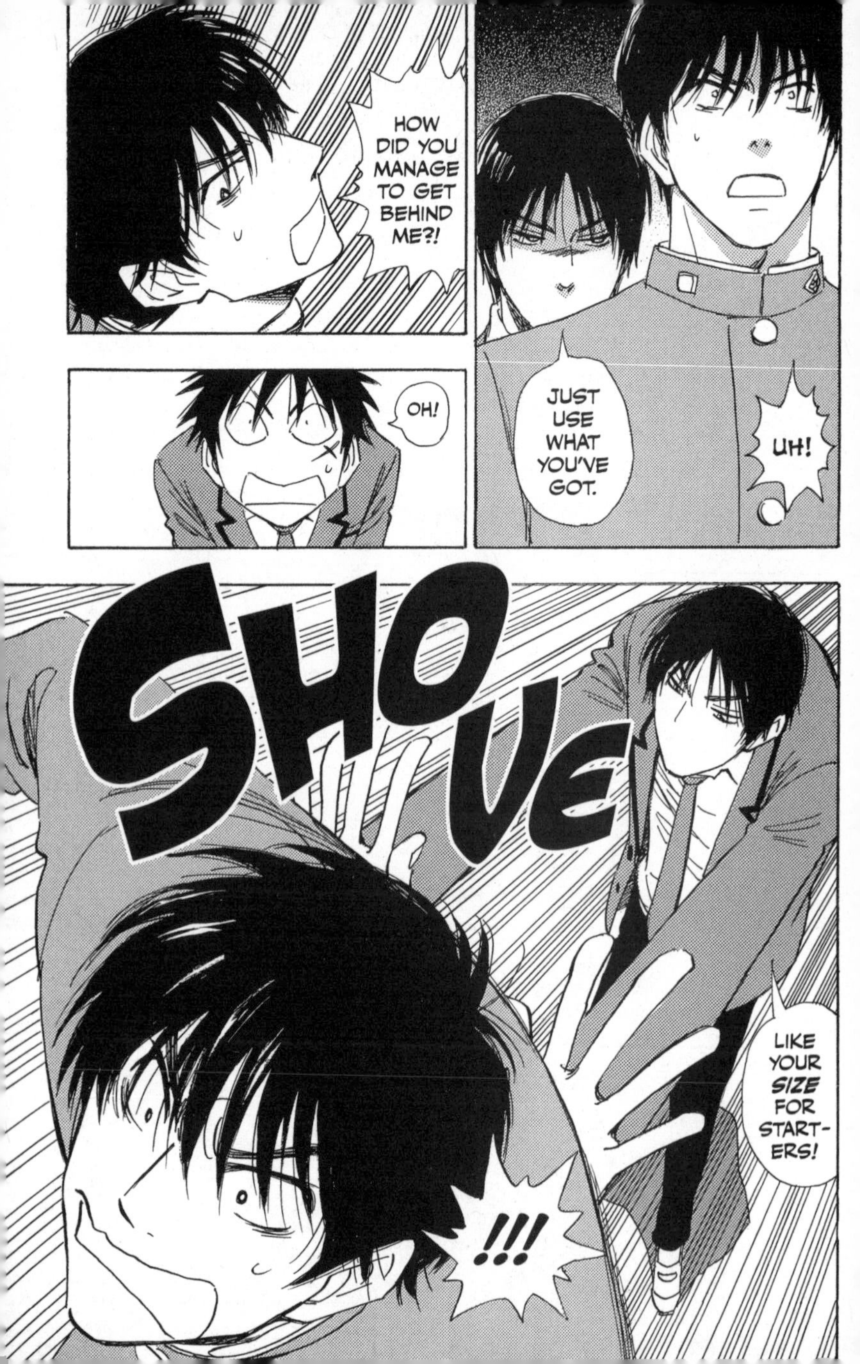
HOW DID YOU MANAGE TO GET BEHIND ME?!
JUST USE WHAT YOU'VE GOT.
UH!
OH!
SHOVE
LIKE YOUR *SIZE* FOR STARTERS!
!!!

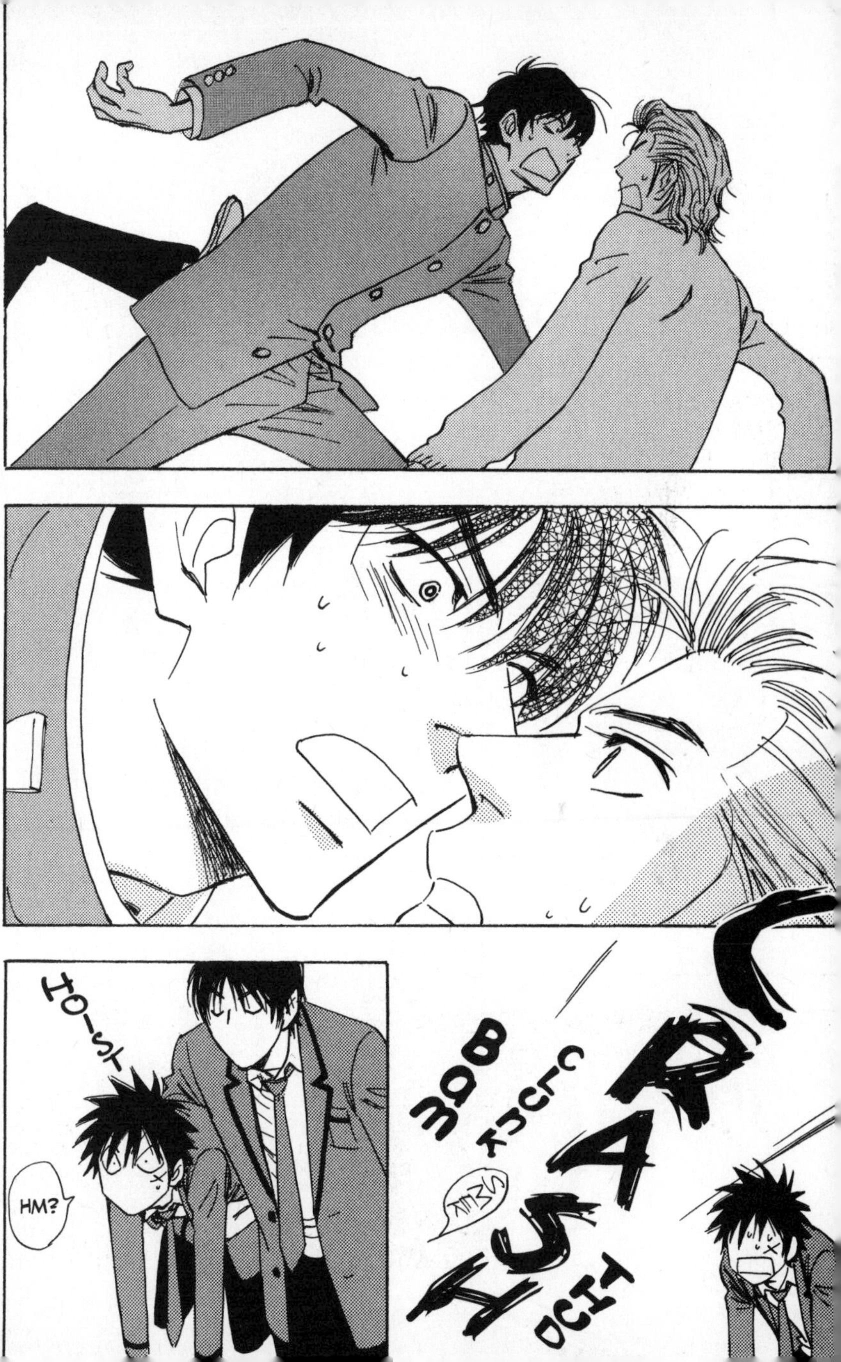
CRASH
BAM
CLICK
HOIST
HM?

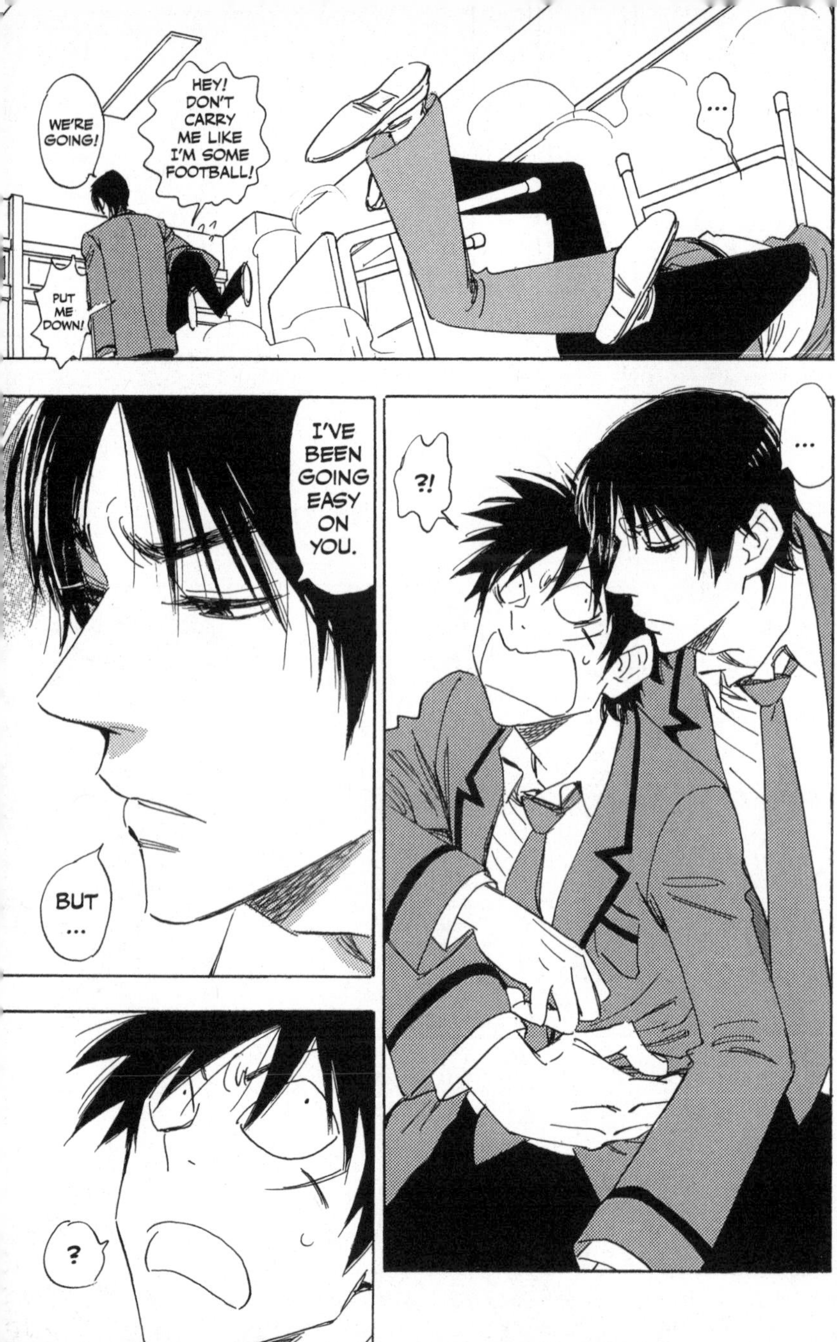
...
HEY! DON'T CARRY ME LIKE I'M SOME FOOTBALL!
WE'RE GOING!
PUT ME DOWN!
...
?!
I'VE BEEN GOING EASY ON YOU.
BUT ...
?

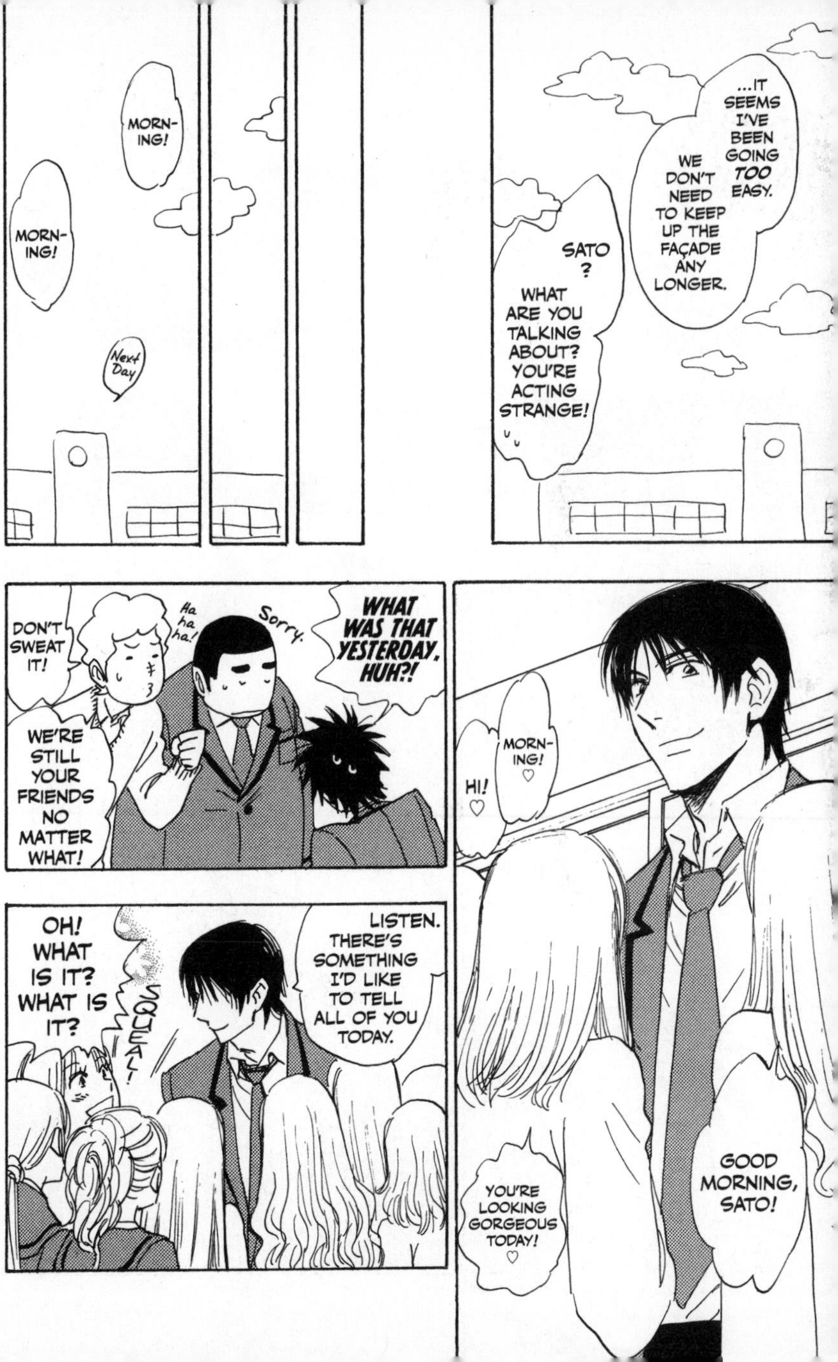
...IT SEEMS I'VE BEEN GOING *TOO* EASY.
WE DON'T NEED TO KEEP UP THE FAÇADE ANY LONGER.
SATO? WHAT ARE YOU TALKING ABOUT? YOU'RE ACTING STRANGE!
MORNING!
MORNING!
Next Day
MORNING! ♡
HI! ♡
GOOD MORNING, SATO!
YOU'RE LOOKING GORGEOUS TODAY! ♡
WHAT WAS THAT YESTERDAY, HUH?!
Sorry.
Ha ha ha!
DON'T SWEAT IT!
WE'RE STILL YOUR FRIENDS NO MATTER WHAT!
LISTEN. THERE'S SOMETHING I'D LIKE TO TELL ALL OF YOU TODAY.
SQUEAL!
OH! WHAT IS IT? WHAT IS IT?

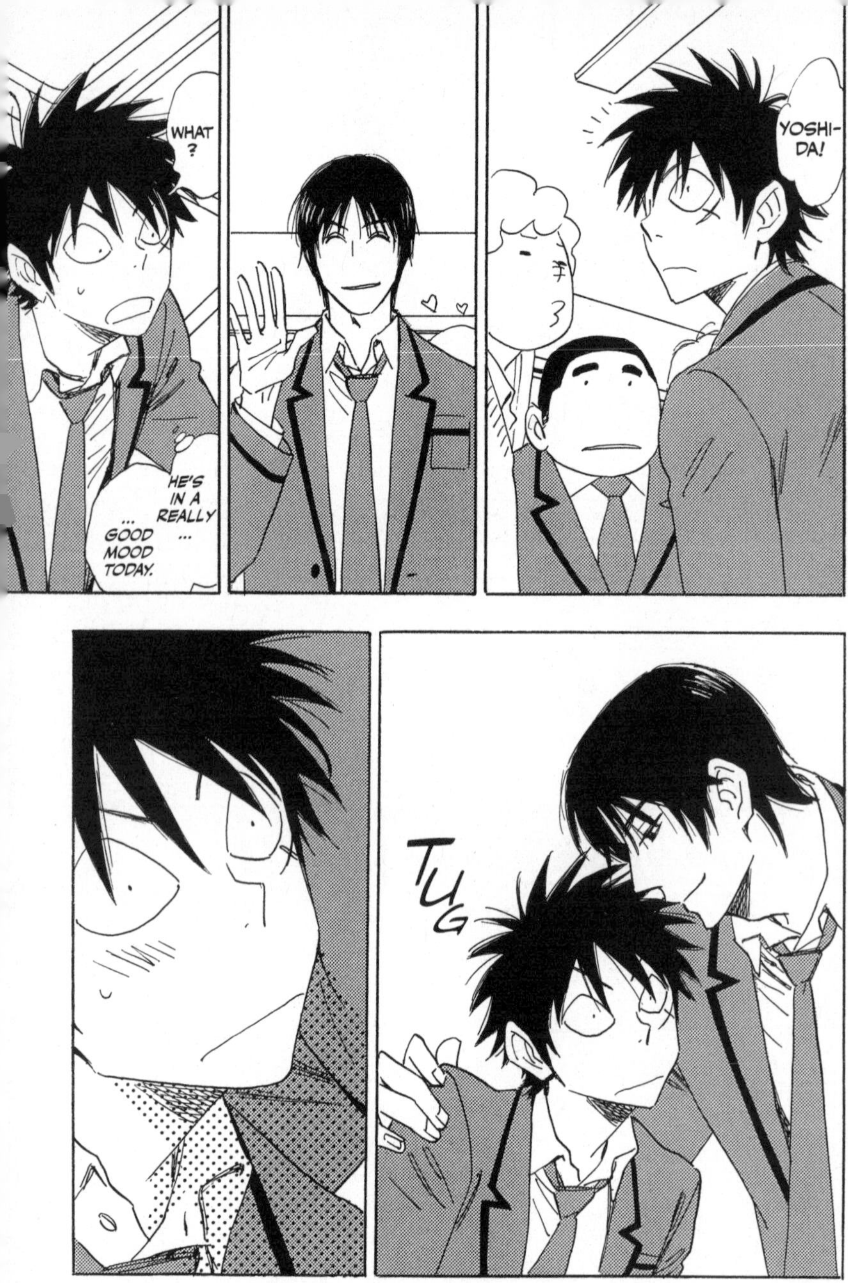
YOSHI-DA!
WHAT?
HE'S IN A REALLY ...
... GOOD MOOD TODAY.
TUG

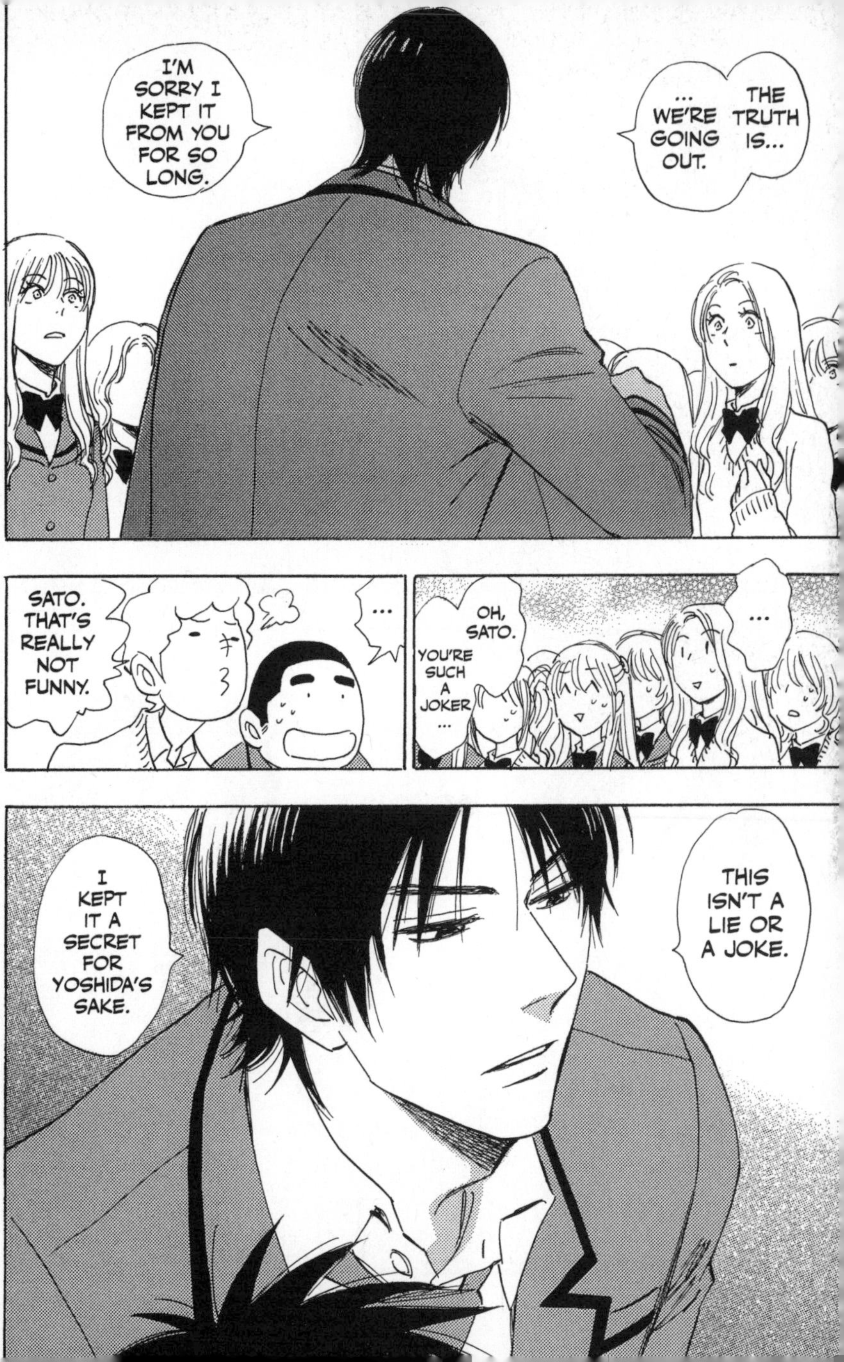
THE TRUTH IS... ...WE'RE GOING OUT.
I'M SORRY I KEPT IT FROM YOU FOR SO LONG.
...
OH, SATO.
YOU'RE SUCH A JOKER ...
...
SATO. THAT'S REALLY NOT FUNNY.
THIS ISN'T A LIE OR A JOKE.
I KEPT IT A SECRET FOR YOSHIDA'S SAKE.

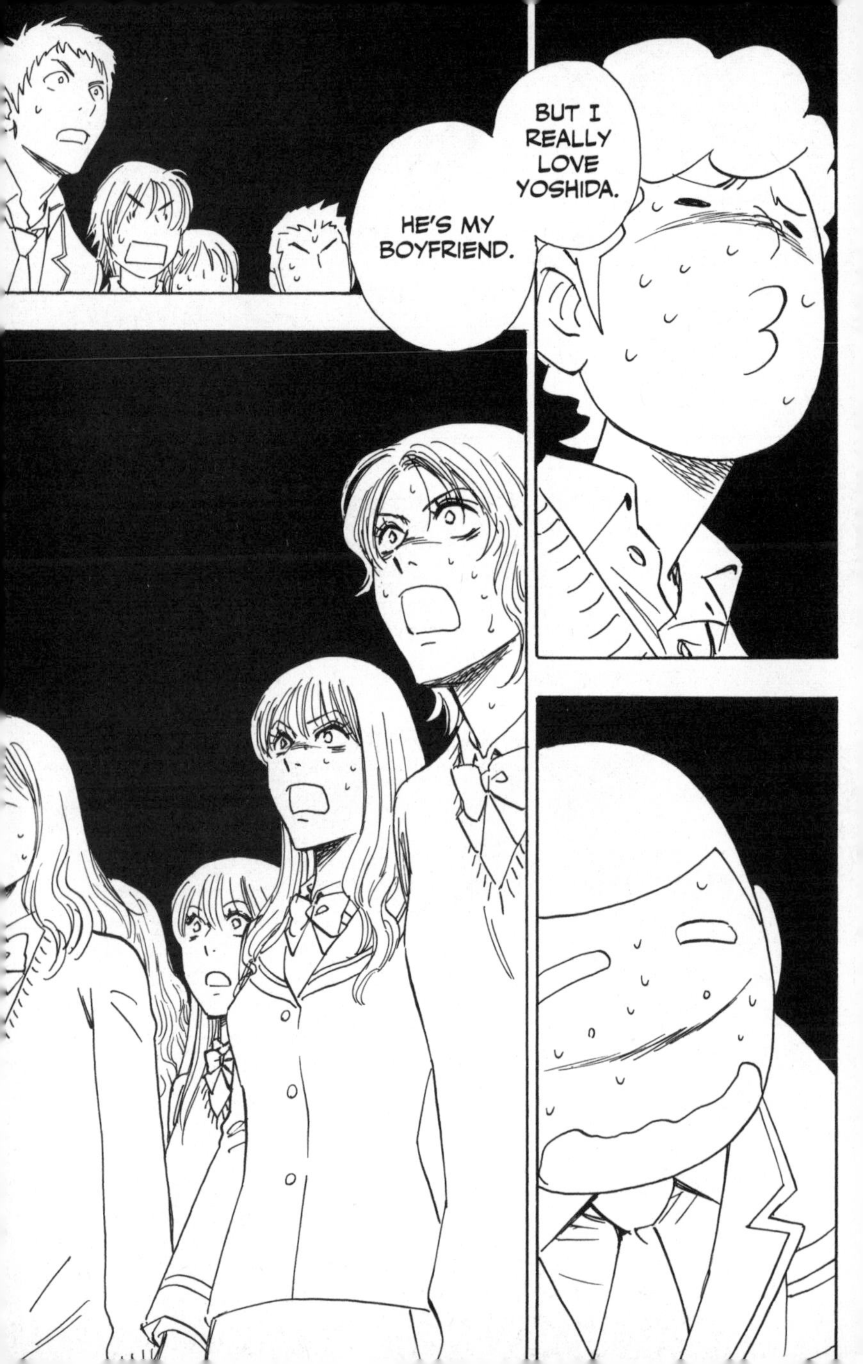
BUT I REALLY LOVE YOSHIDA.
HE'S MY BOYFRIEND.

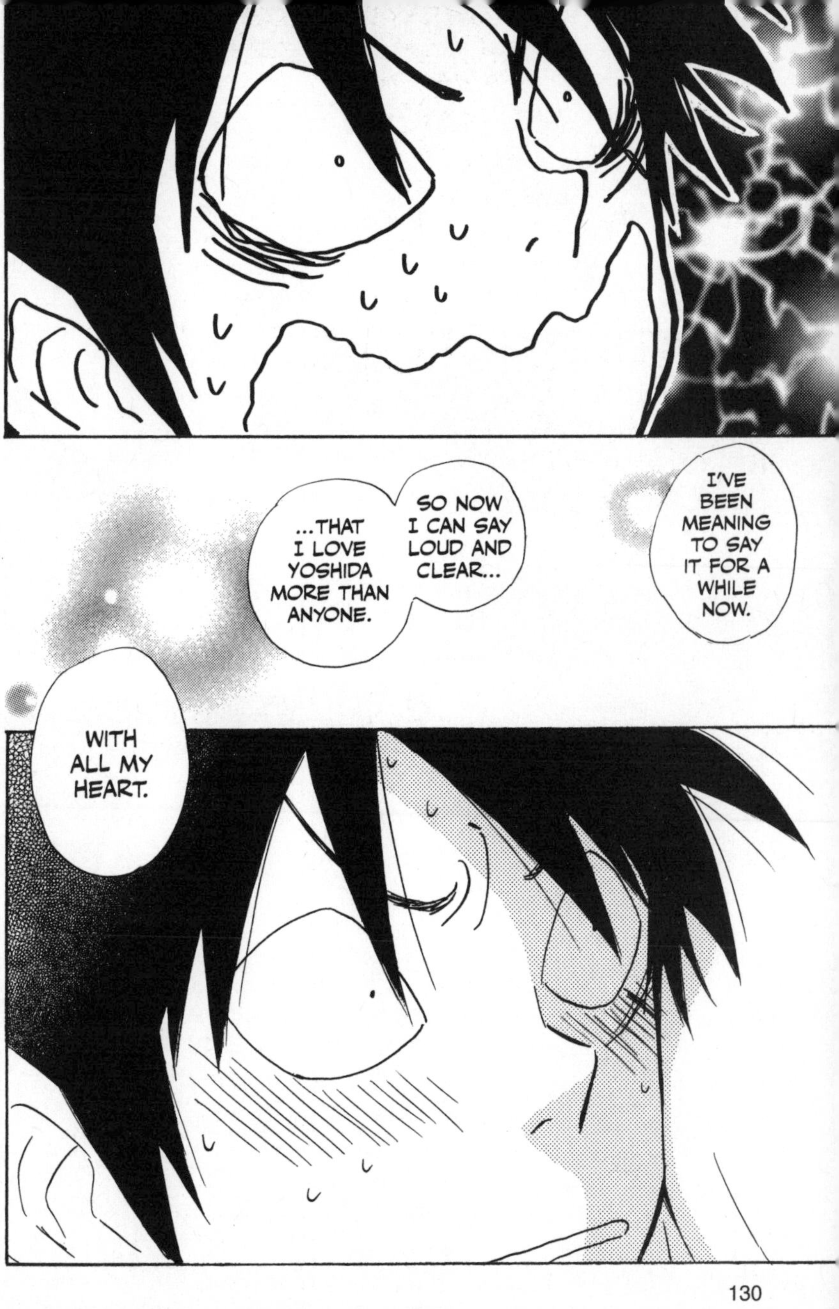
I'VE BEEN MEANING TO SAY IT FOR A WHILE NOW.
SO NOW I CAN SAY LOUD AND CLEAR...
...THAT I LOVE YOSHIDA MORE THAN ANYONE.
WITH ALL MY HEART.

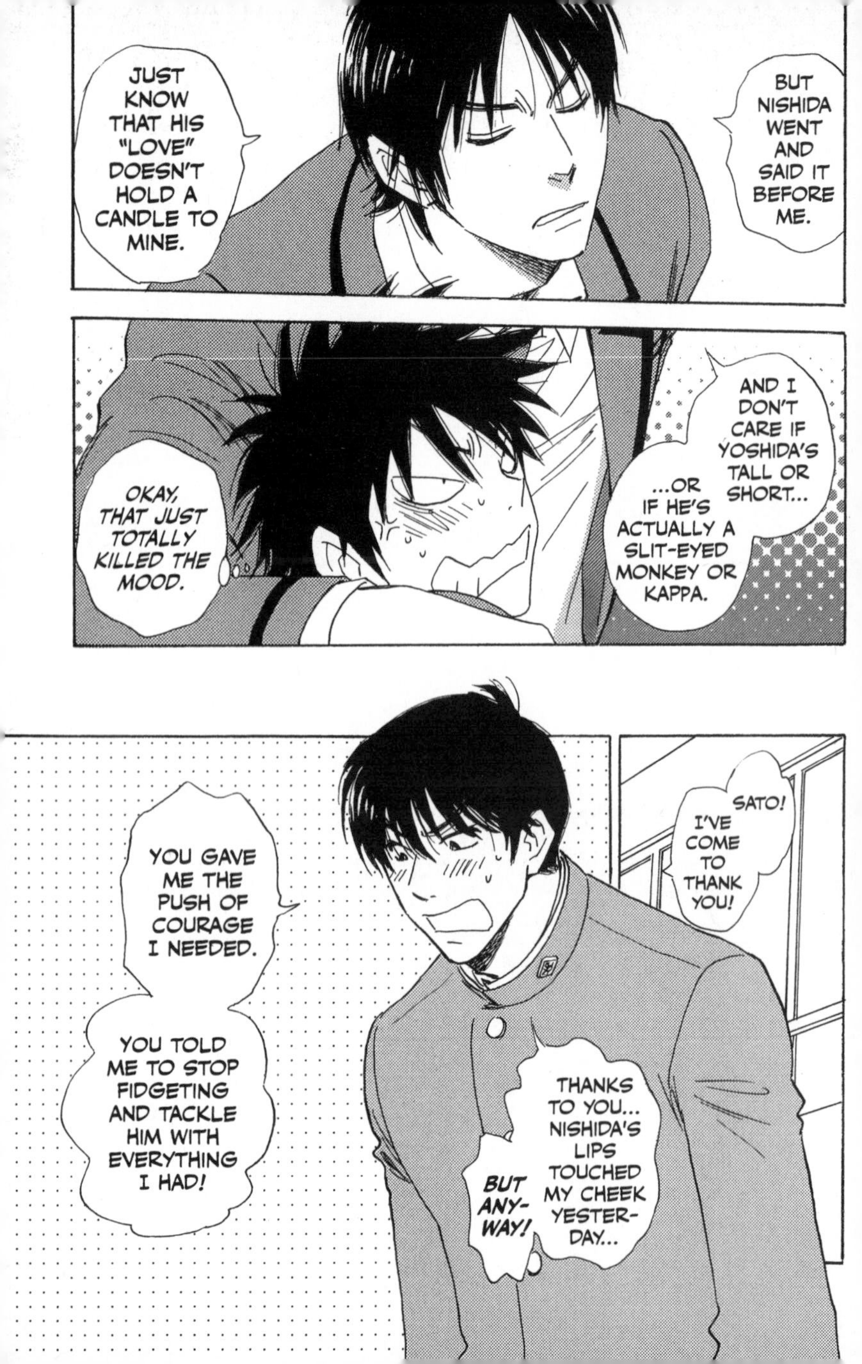
BUT NISHIDA WENT AND SAID IT BEFORE ME.
JUST KNOW THAT HIS "LOVE" DOESN'T HOLD A CANDLE TO MINE.
AND I DON'T CARE IF YOSHIDA'S TALL OR SHORT...
...OR IF HE'S ACTUALLY A SLIT-EYED MONKEY OR KAPPA.
OKAY, THAT JUST TOTALLY KILLED THE MOOD.
SATO! I'VE COME TO THANK YOU!
THANKS TO YOU... NISHIDA'S LIPS TOUCHED MY CHEEK YESTER-DAY...
BUT ANY-WAY!
YOU GAVE ME THE PUSH OF COURAGE I NEEDED.
YOU TOLD ME TO STOP FIDGETING AND TACKLE HIM WITH EVERYTHING I HAD!

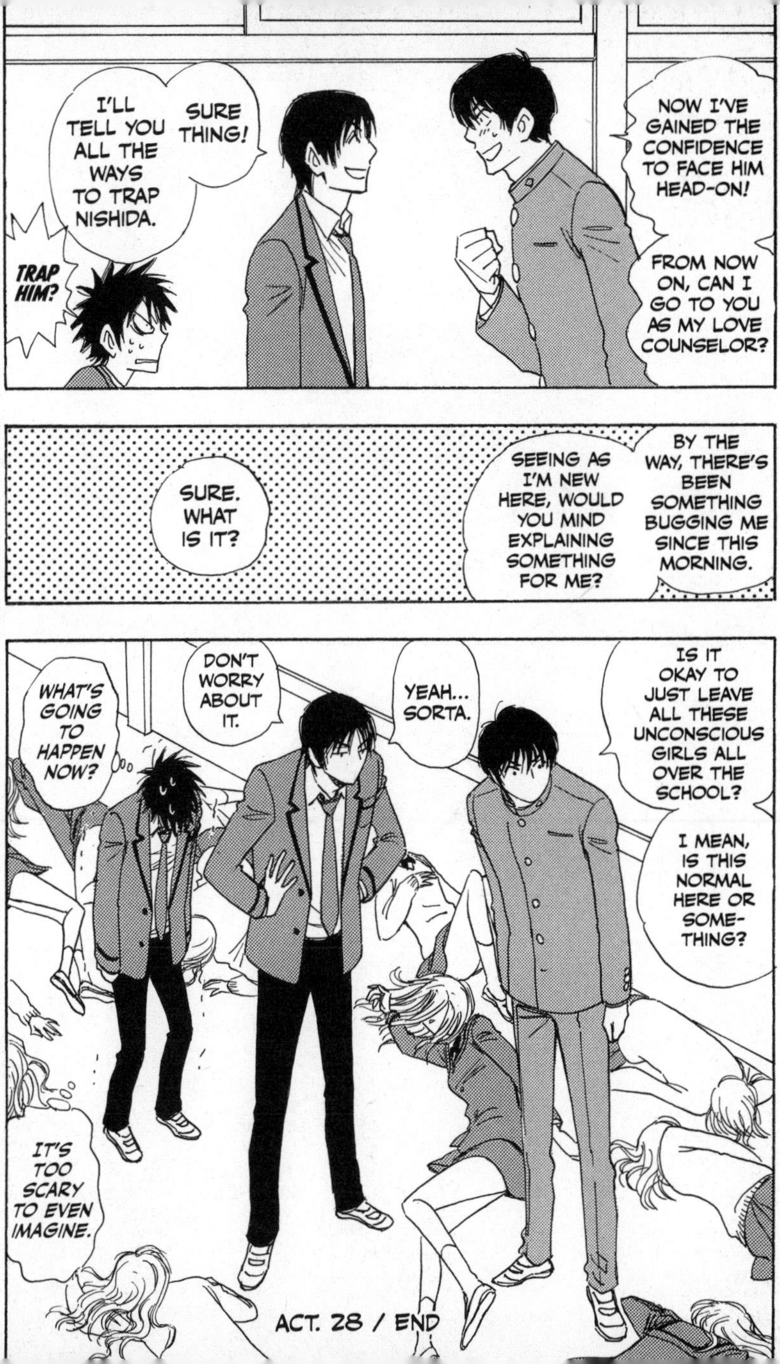
NOW I'VE GAINED THE CONFIDENCE TO FACE HIM HEAD-ON!
FROM NOW ON, CAN I GO TO YOU AS MY LOVE COUNSELOR?
SURE THING!
I'LL TELL YOU ALL THE WAYS TO TRAP NISHIDA.
TRAP HIM?
BY THE WAY, THERE'S BEEN SOMETHING BUGGING ME SINCE THIS MORNING.
SEEING AS I'M NEW HERE, WOULD YOU MIND EXPLAINING SOMETHING FOR ME?
SURE. WHAT IS IT?
IS IT OKAY TO JUST LEAVE ALL THESE UNCONSCIOUS GIRLS ALL OVER THE SCHOOL?
I MEAN, IS THIS NORMAL HERE OR SOME-THING?
YEAH... SORTA.
DON'T WORRY ABOUT IT.
WHAT'S GOING TO HAPPEN NOW?
IT'S TOO SCARY TO EVEN IMAGINE.
ACT. 28 / END

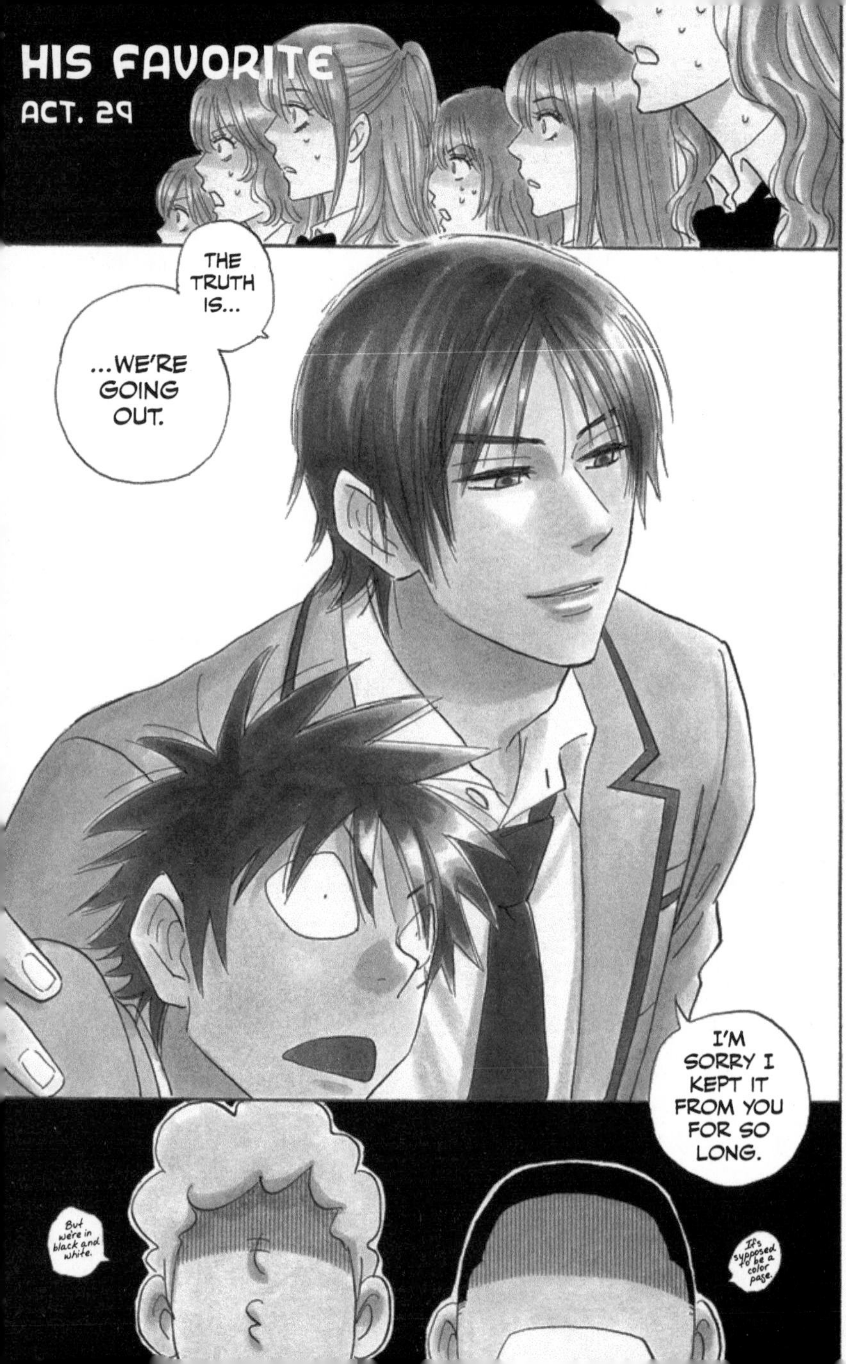
HIS FAVORITE
ACT. 29
THE TRUTH IS...
...WE'RE GOING OUT.
I'M SORRY I KEPT IT FROM YOU FOR SO LONG.
It's supposed to be a color page.
But we're in black and white.

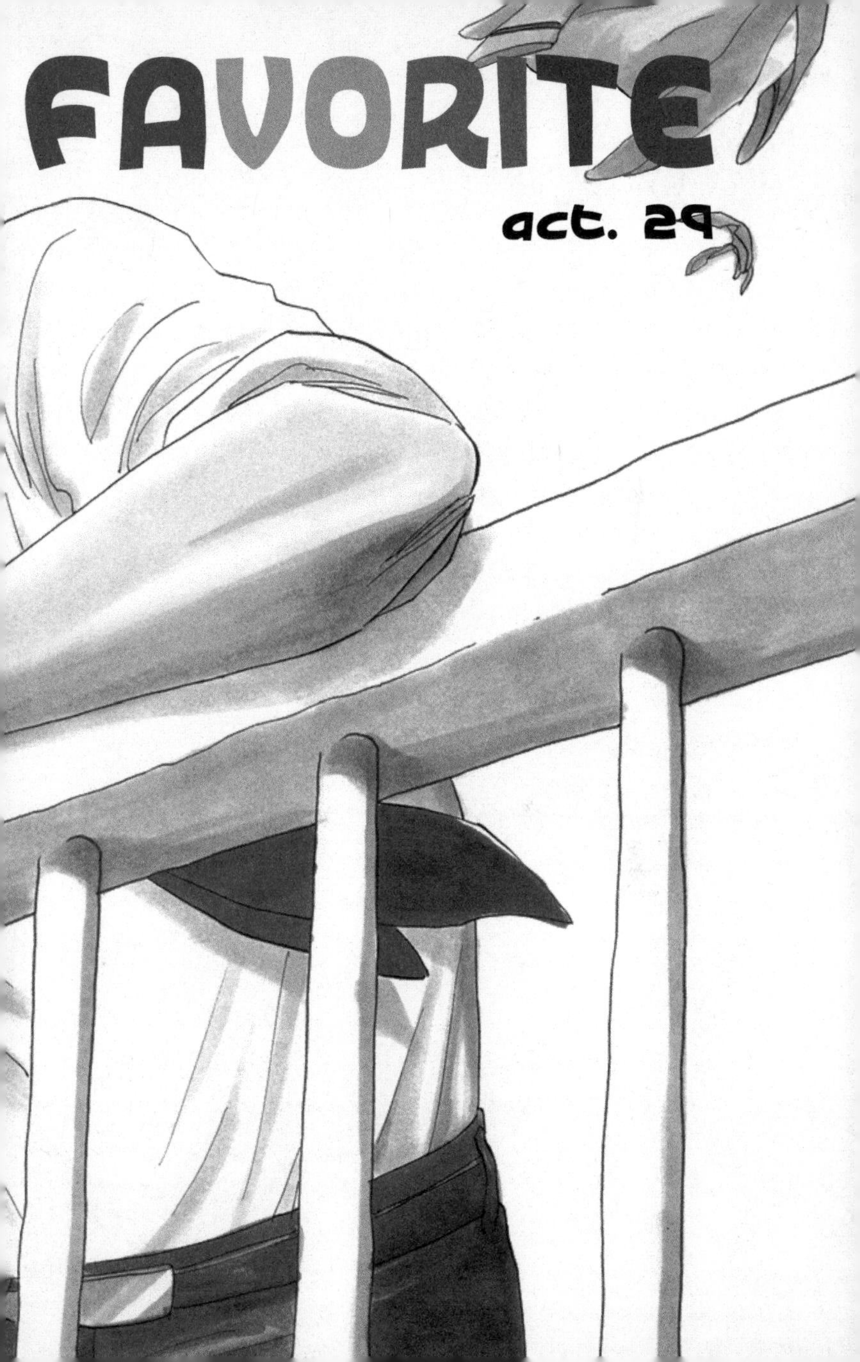
FAVORITE
act. 29

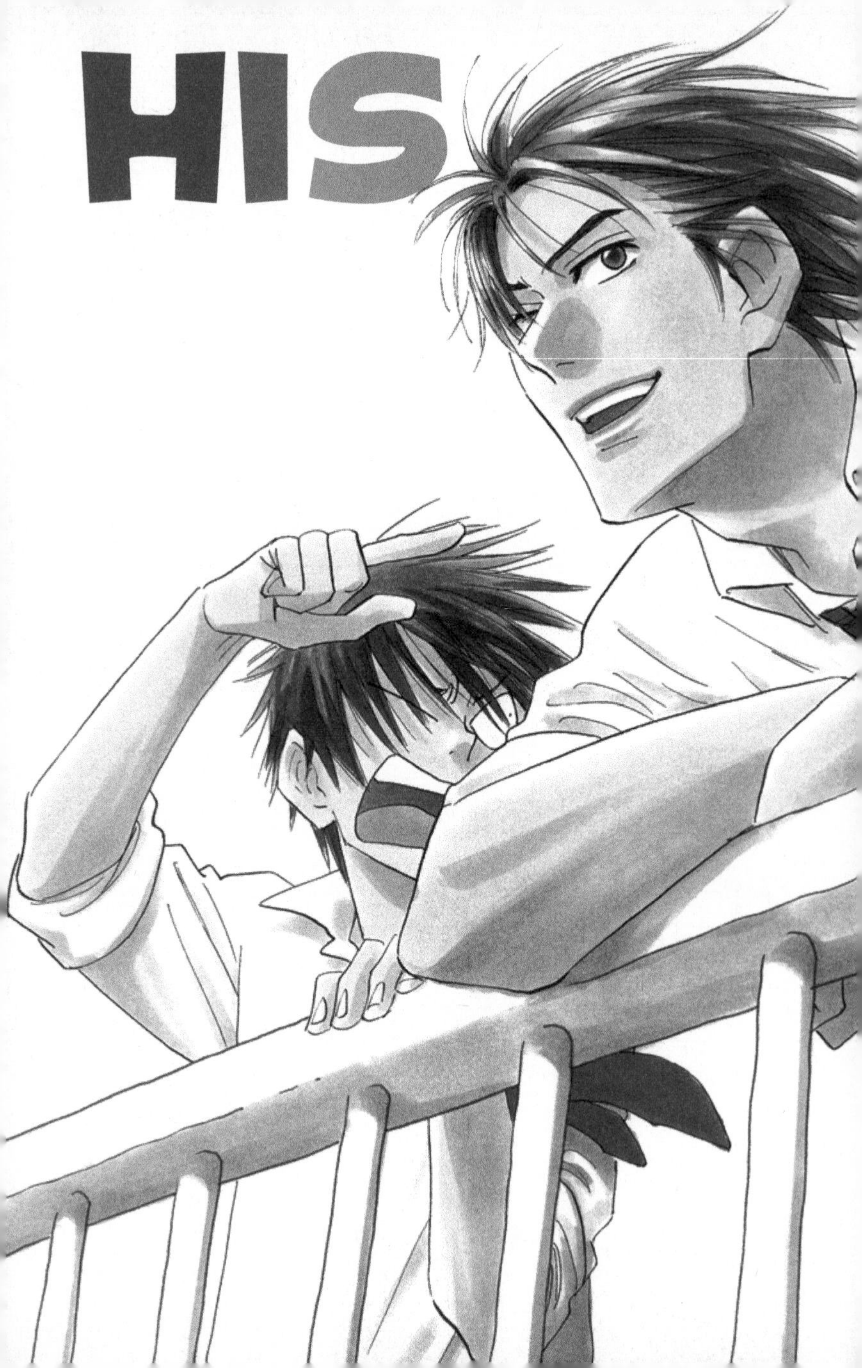
HIS

HIS FAVORITE

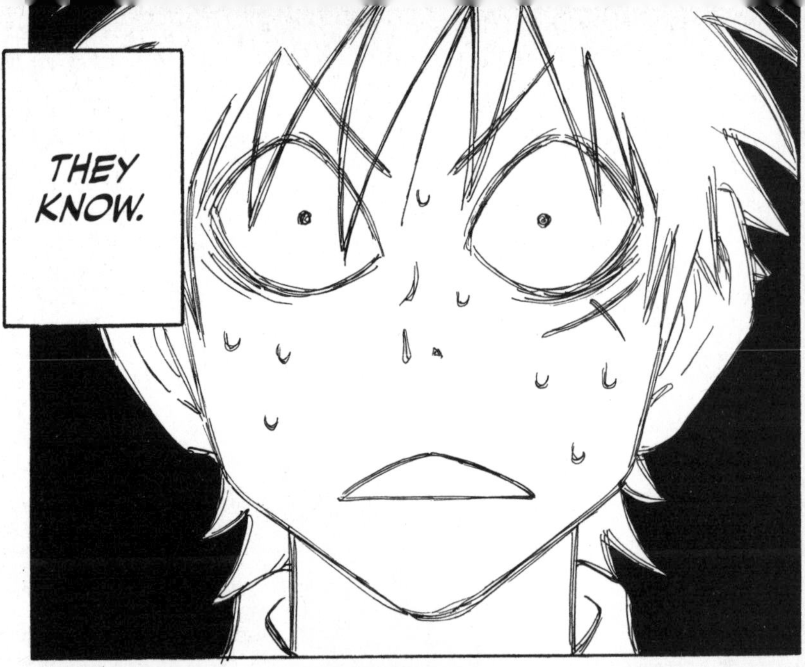
THEY KNOW.
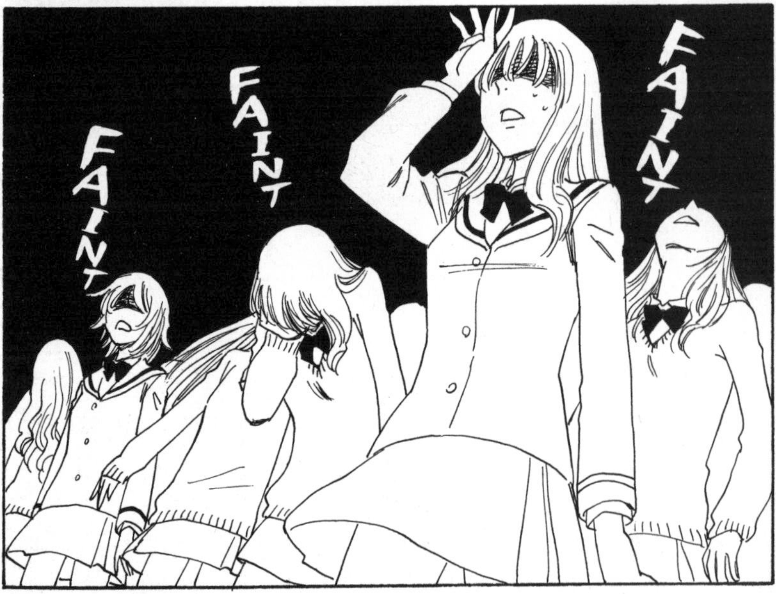
FAINT
FAINT
FAINT

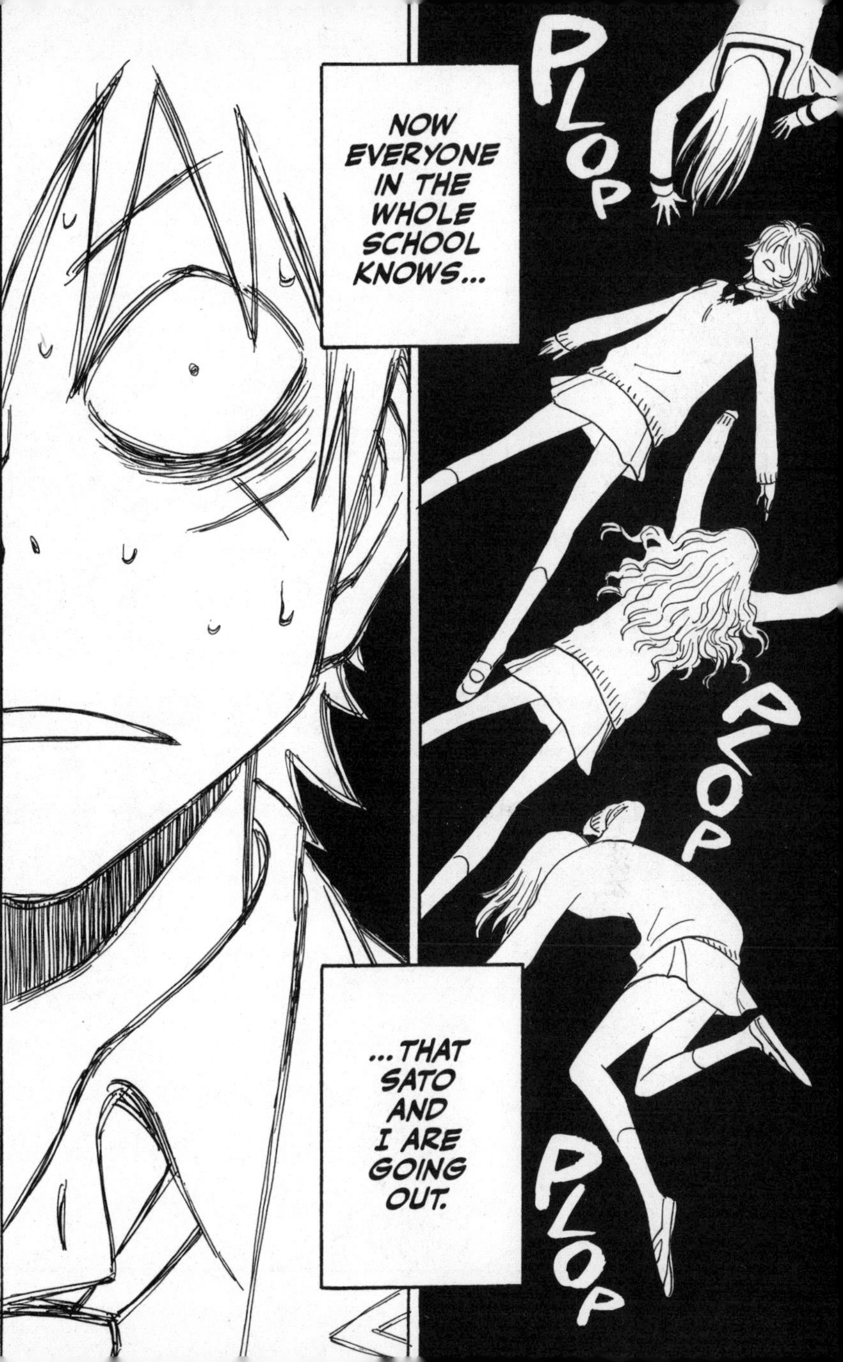
PLOP
NOW EVERYONE IN THE WHOLE SCHOOL KNOWS...
PLOP
...THAT SATO AND I ARE GOING OUT.
PLOP

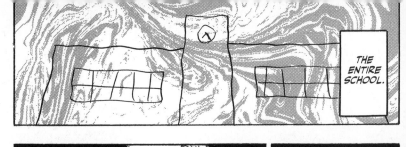

THE ENTIRE SCHOOL.

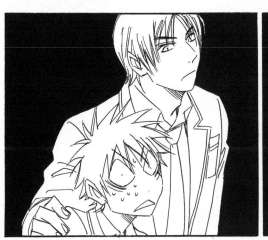

YOSHIDA?

SATO?

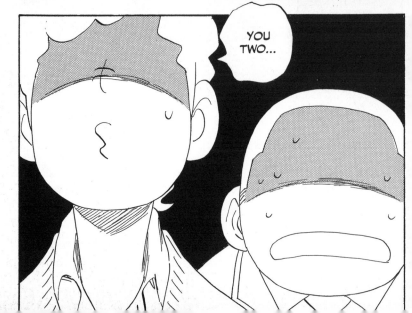

YOU TWO...

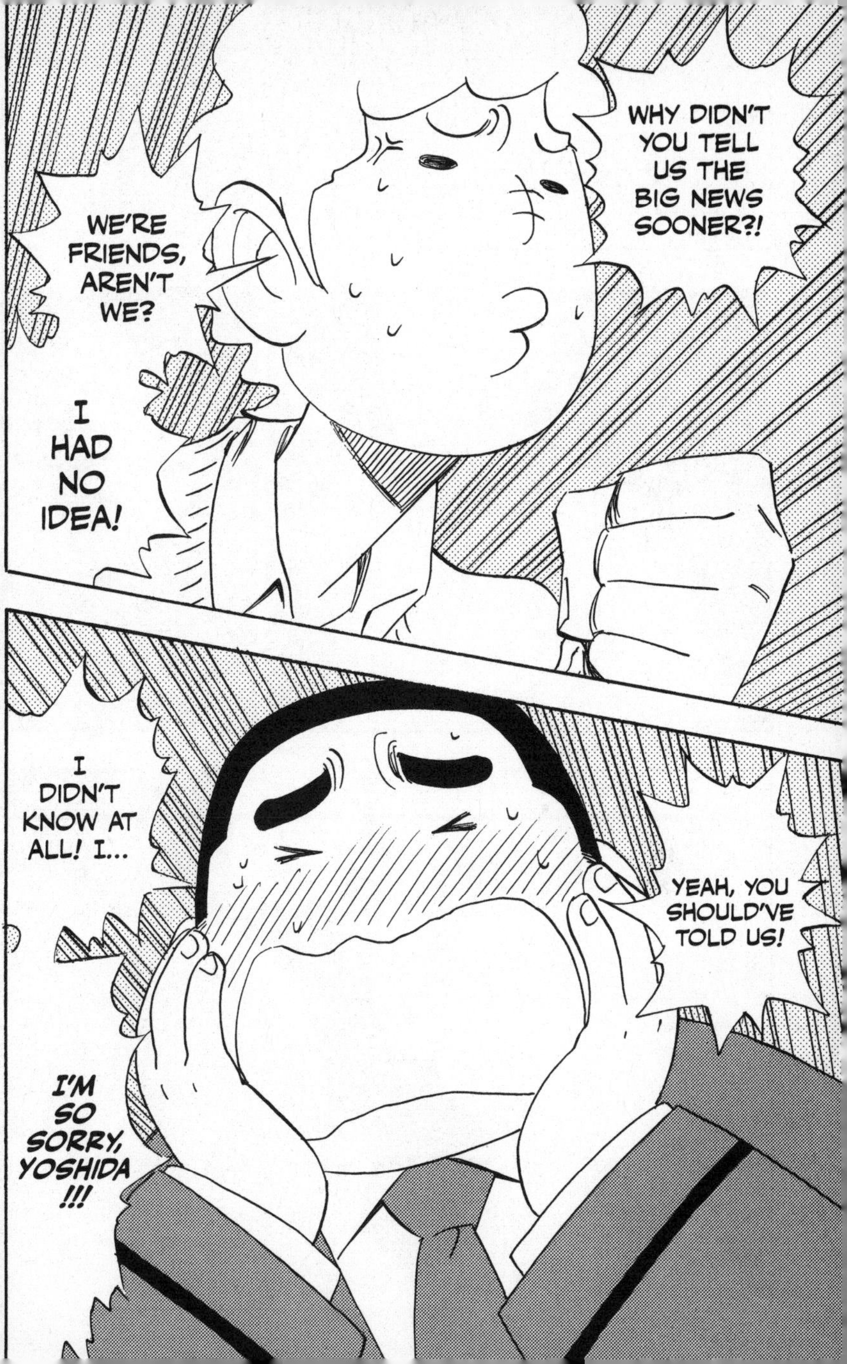
WHY DIDN'T YOU TELL US THE BIG NEWS SOONER?!
WE'RE FRIENDS, AREN'T WE?
I HAD NO IDEA!
YEAH, YOU SHOULD'VE TOLD US!
I DIDN'T KNOW AT ALL! I...
I'M SO SORRY, YOSHIDA!!!

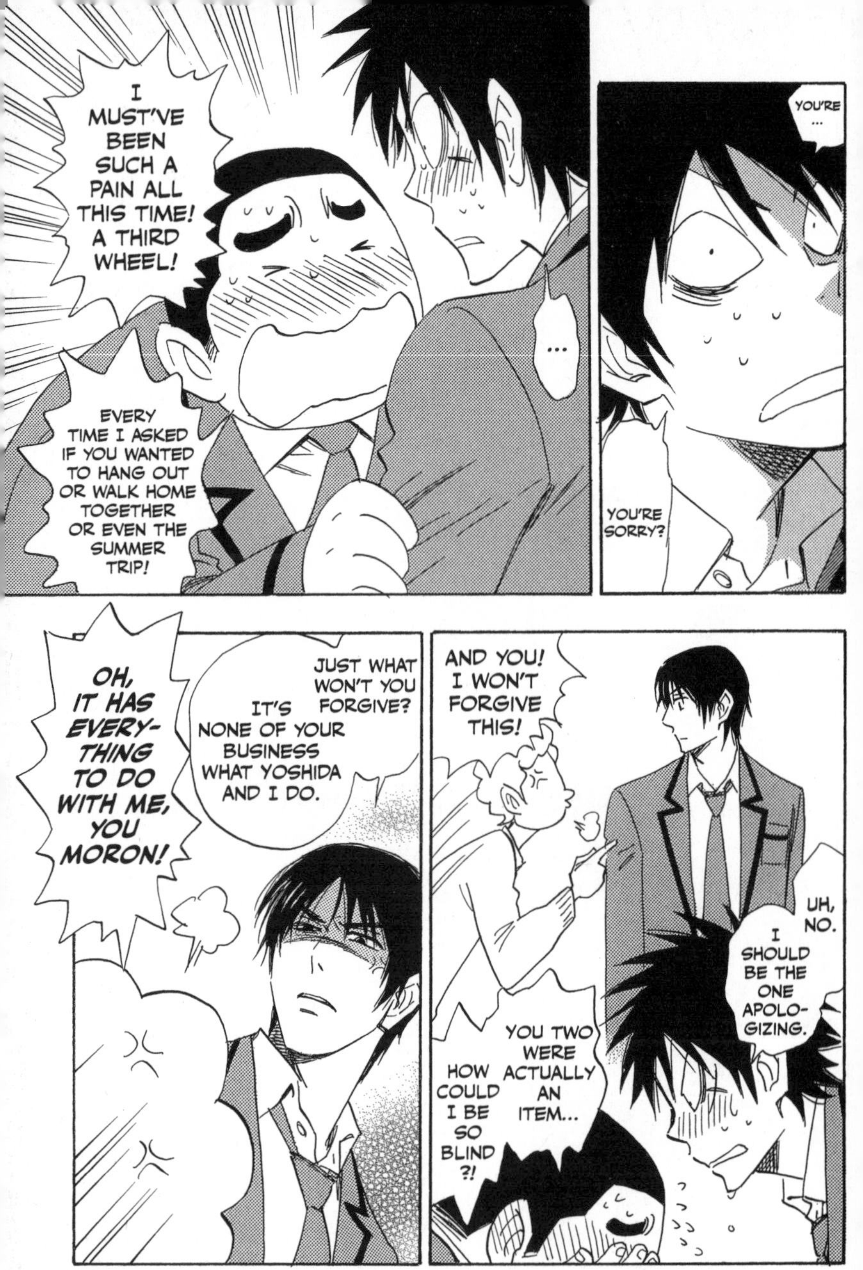
YOU'RE ...
YOU'RE SORRY?
I MUST'VE BEEN SUCH A PAIN ALL THIS TIME! A THIRD WHEEL!
...
EVERY TIME I ASKED IF YOU WANTED TO HANG OUT OR WALK HOME TOGETHER OR EVEN THE SUMMER TRIP!
YOU TWO WERE ACTUALLY AN ITEM...
HOW COULD I BE SO BLIND?!
UH, NO. I SHOULD BE THE ONE APOLOGIZING.
AND YOU! I WON'T FORGIVE THIS!
JUST WHAT WON'T YOU FORGIVE?
IT'S NONE OF YOUR BUSINESS WHAT YOSHIDA AND I DO.
OH, IT HAS EVERYTHING TO DO WITH ME, YOU MORON!

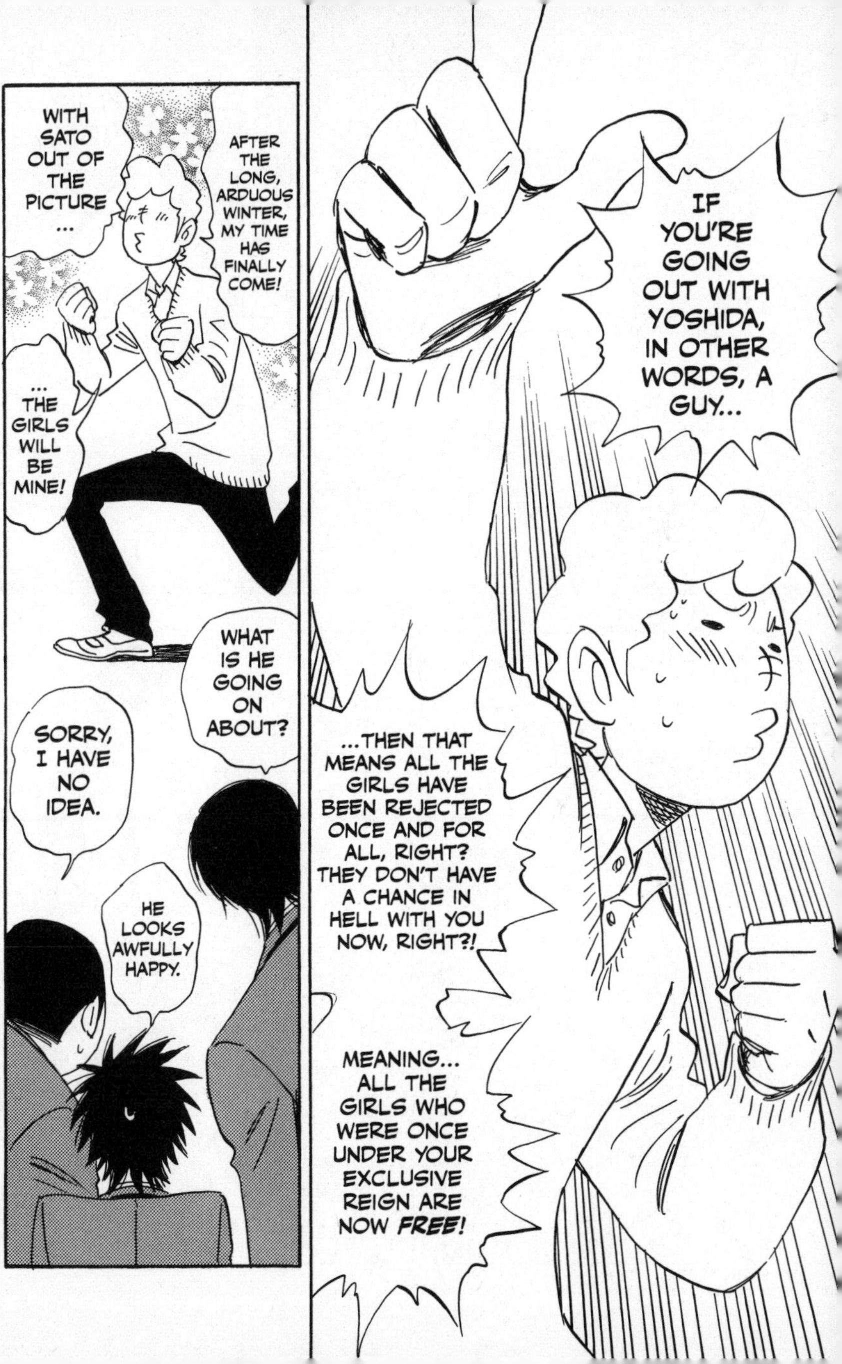
IF YOU'RE GOING OUT WITH YOSHIDA, IN OTHER WORDS, A GUY...
...THEN THAT MEANS ALL THE GIRLS HAVE BEEN REJECTED ONCE AND FOR ALL, RIGHT? THEY DON'T HAVE A CHANCE IN HELL WITH YOU NOW, RIGHT?!
MEANING... ALL THE GIRLS WHO WERE ONCE UNDER YOUR EXCLUSIVE REIGN ARE NOW *FREE*!
AFTER THE LONG, ARDUOUS WINTER, MY TIME HAS FINALLY COME!
WITH SATO OUT OF THE PICTURE ...
... THE GIRLS WILL BE MINE!
WHAT IS HE GOING ON ABOUT?
SORRY, I HAVE NO IDEA.
HE LOOKS AWFULLY HAPPY.

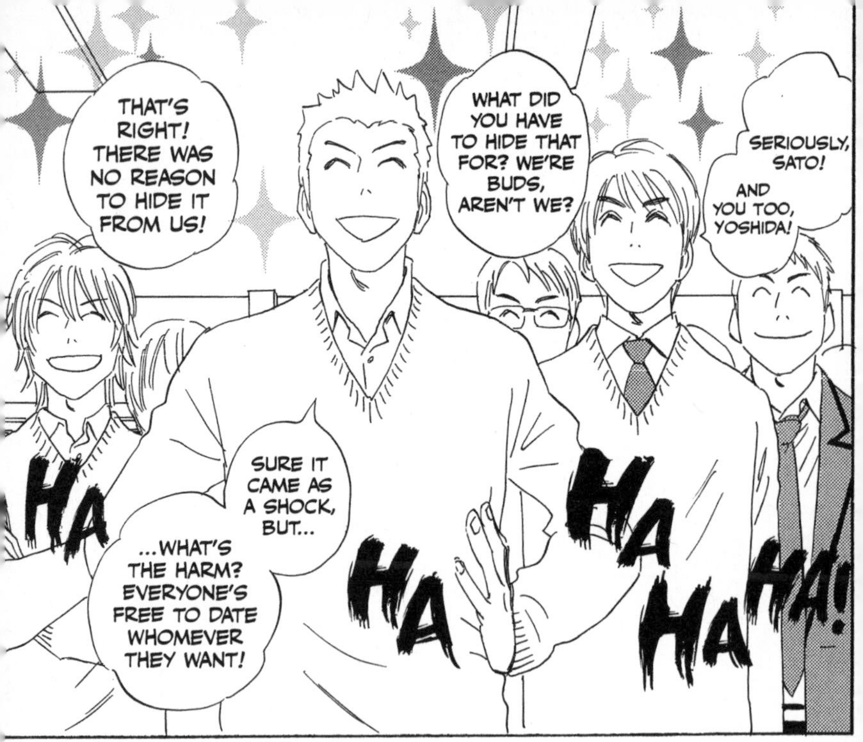
SERIOUSLY, SATO!
AND YOU TOO, YOSHIDA!
WHAT DID YOU HAVE TO HIDE THAT FOR? WE'RE BUDS, AREN'T WE?
THAT'S RIGHT! THERE WAS NO REASON TO HIDE IT FROM US!
SURE IT CAME AS A SHOCK, BUT...
...WHAT'S THE HARM? EVERYONE'S FREE TO DATE WHOMEVER THEY WANT!
HA HA HA HA HA HA!

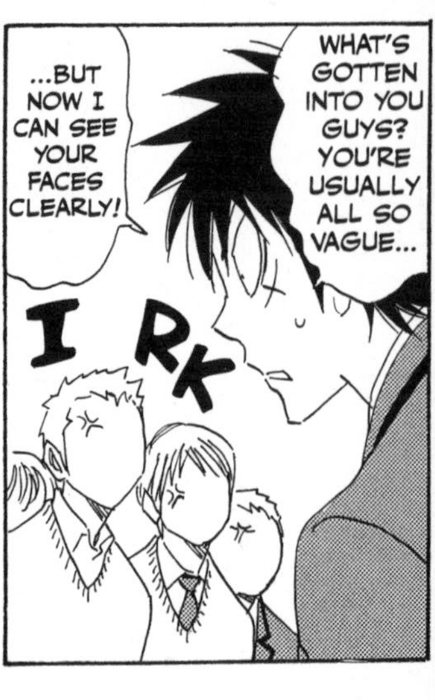
WHAT'S GOTTEN INTO YOU GUYS? YOU'RE USUALLY ALL SO VAGUE...
...BUT NOW I CAN SEE YOUR FACES CLEARLY!
IRK

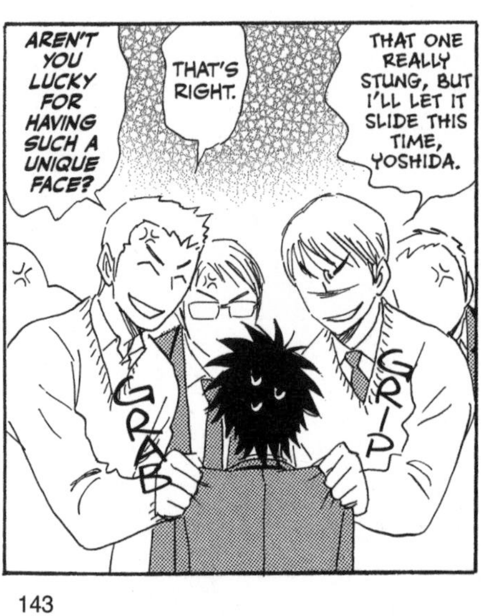
THAT ONE REALLY STUNG, BUT I'LL LET IT SLIDE THIS TIME, YOSHIDA.
THAT'S RIGHT.
AREN'T YOU LUCKY FOR HAVING SUCH A UNIQUE FACE?
GRIP
GRAB

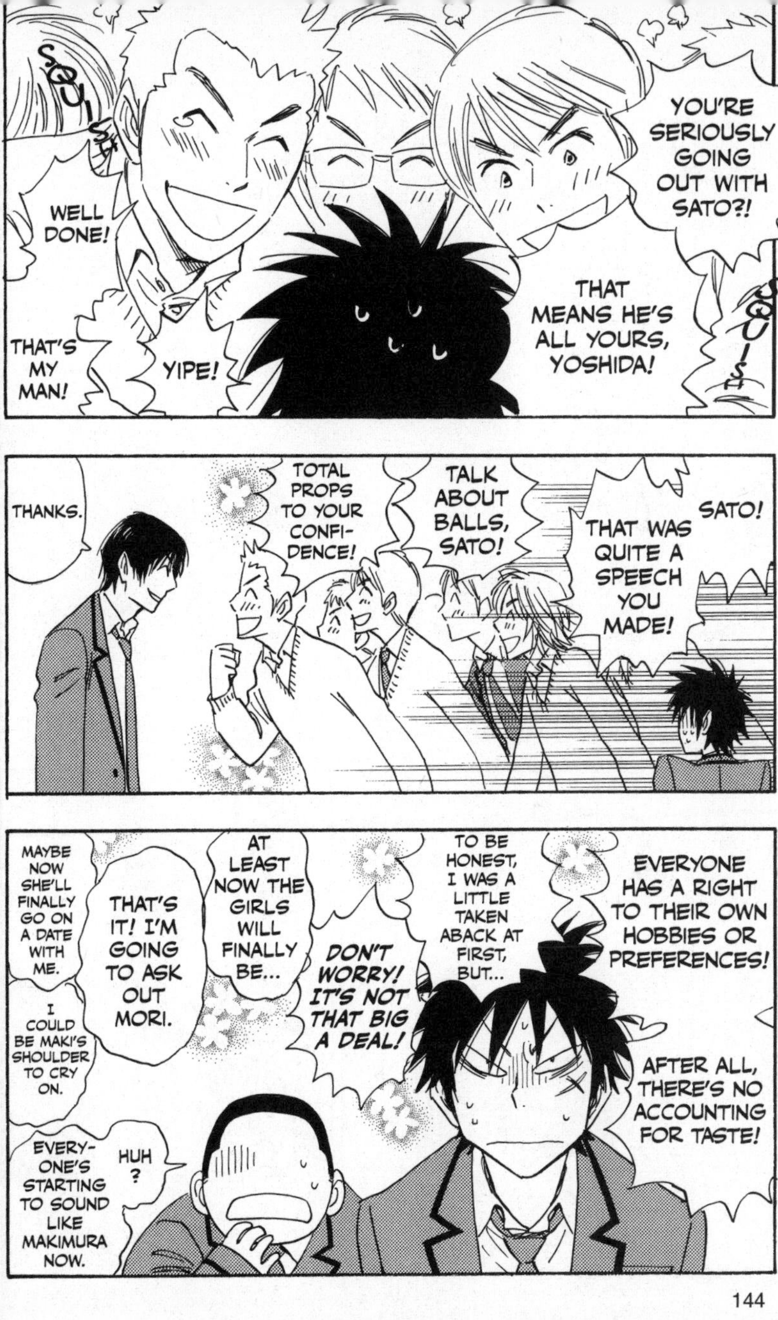
YOU'RE SERIOUSLY GOING OUT WITH SATO?!
SQUISH
THAT MEANS HE'S ALL YOURS, YOSHIDA!
YIPE!
WELL DONE!
SQUISH
THAT'S MY MAN!
SATO!
THAT WAS QUITE A SPEECH YOU MADE!
TALK ABOUT BALLS, SATO!
TOTAL PROPS TO YOUR CONFI-DENCE!
THANKS.
EVERYONE HAS A RIGHT TO THEIR OWN HOBBIES OR PREFERENCES!
AFTER ALL, THERE'S NO ACCOUNTING FOR TASTE!
TO BE HONEST, I WAS A LITTLE TAKEN ABACK AT FIRST, BUT...
DON'T WORRY! IT'S NOT THAT BIG A DEAL!
AT LEAST NOW THE GIRLS WILL FINALLY BE...
THAT'S IT! I'M GOING TO ASK OUT MORI.
MAYBE NOW SHE'LL FINALLY GO ON A DATE WITH ME.
I COULD BE MAKI'S SHOULDER TO CRY ON.
HUH?
EVERY-ONE'S STARTING TO SOUND LIKE MAKIMURA NOW.

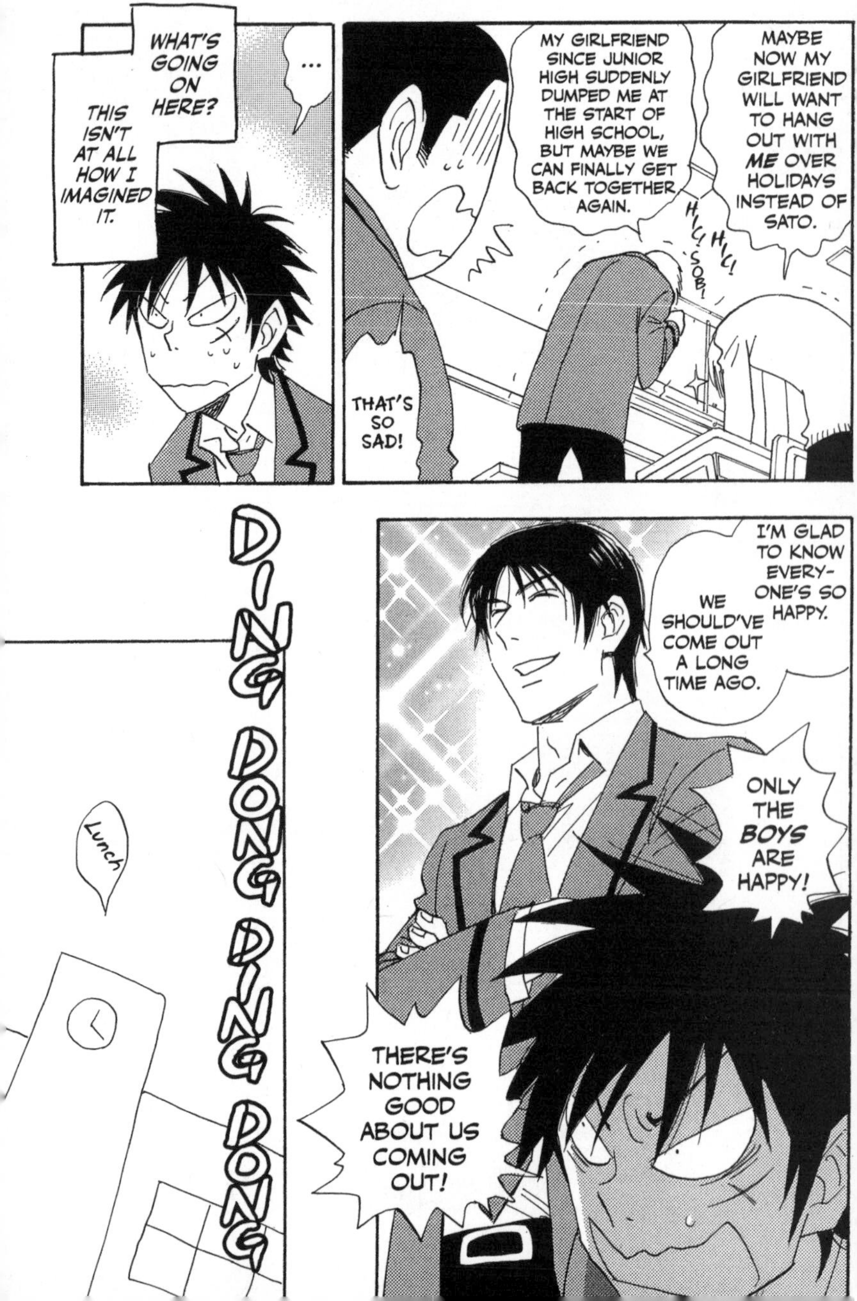
MAYBE NOW MY GIRLFRIEND WILL WANT TO HANG OUT WITH *ME* OVER HOLIDAYS INSTEAD OF SATO.
MY GIRLFRIEND SINCE JUNIOR HIGH SUDDENLY DUMPED ME AT THE START OF HIGH SCHOOL, BUT MAYBE WE CAN FINALLY GET BACK TOGETHER AGAIN.
HIC! HIC! SOB!
THAT'S SO SAD!
...
WHAT'S GOING ON HERE?
THIS ISN'T AT ALL HOW I IMAGINED IT.
I'M GLAD TO KNOW EVERY-ONE'S SO HAPPY.
WE SHOULD'VE COME OUT A LONG TIME AGO.
ONLY THE *BOYS* ARE HAPPY!
THERE'S NOTHING GOOD ABOUT US COMING OUT!
DING DONG DING DONG
Lunch

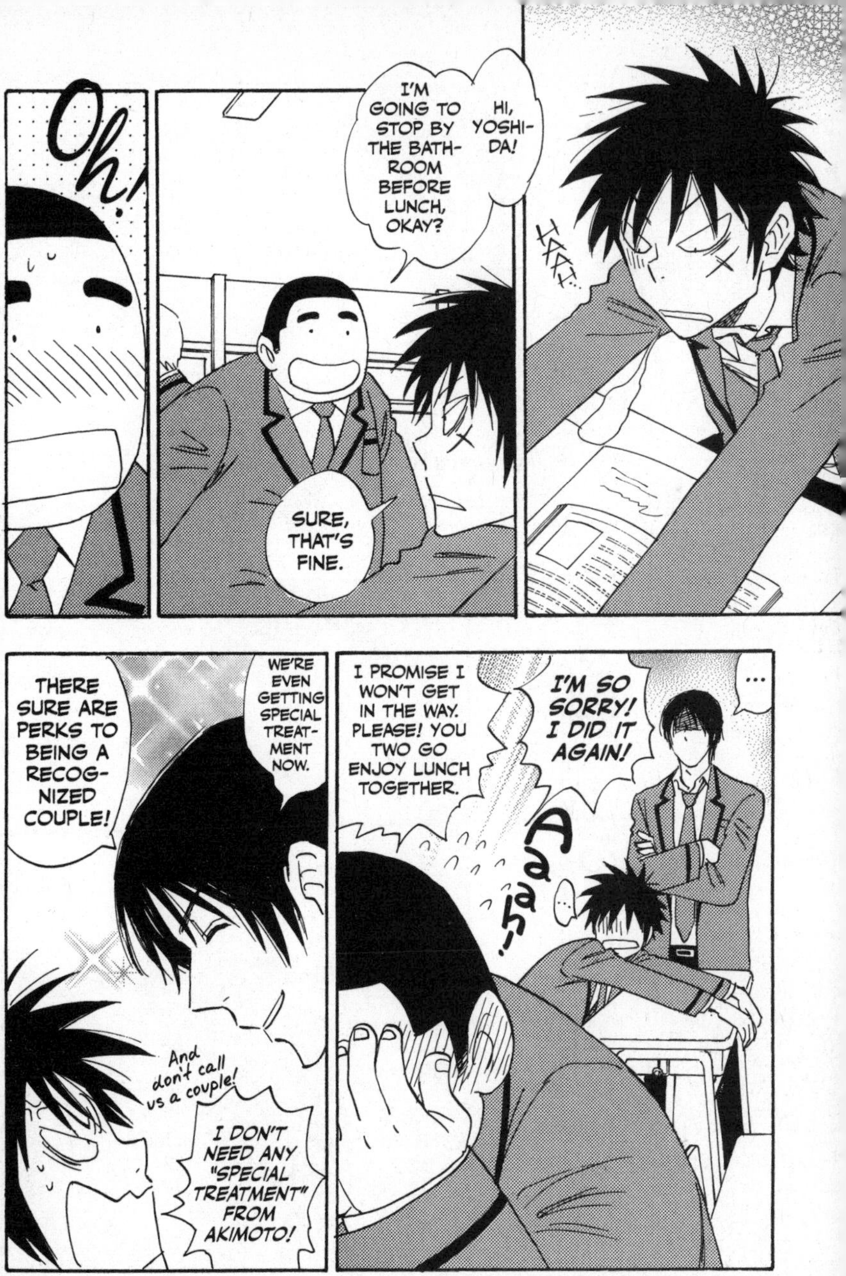
HI, YOSHIDA!
I'M GOING TO STOP BY THE BATHROOM BEFORE LUNCH, OKAY?
SURE, THAT'S FINE.
Oh!
...
I'M SO SORRY! I DID IT AGAIN!
I PROMISE I WON'T GET IN THE WAY. PLEASE! YOU TWO GO ENJOY LUNCH TOGETHER.
Aaah!
...
WE'RE EVEN GETTING SPECIAL TREATMENT NOW.
THERE SURE ARE PERKS TO BEING A RECOGNIZED COUPLE!
I DON'T NEED ANY "SPECIAL TREATMENT" FROM AKIMOTO!
And don't call us a couple!

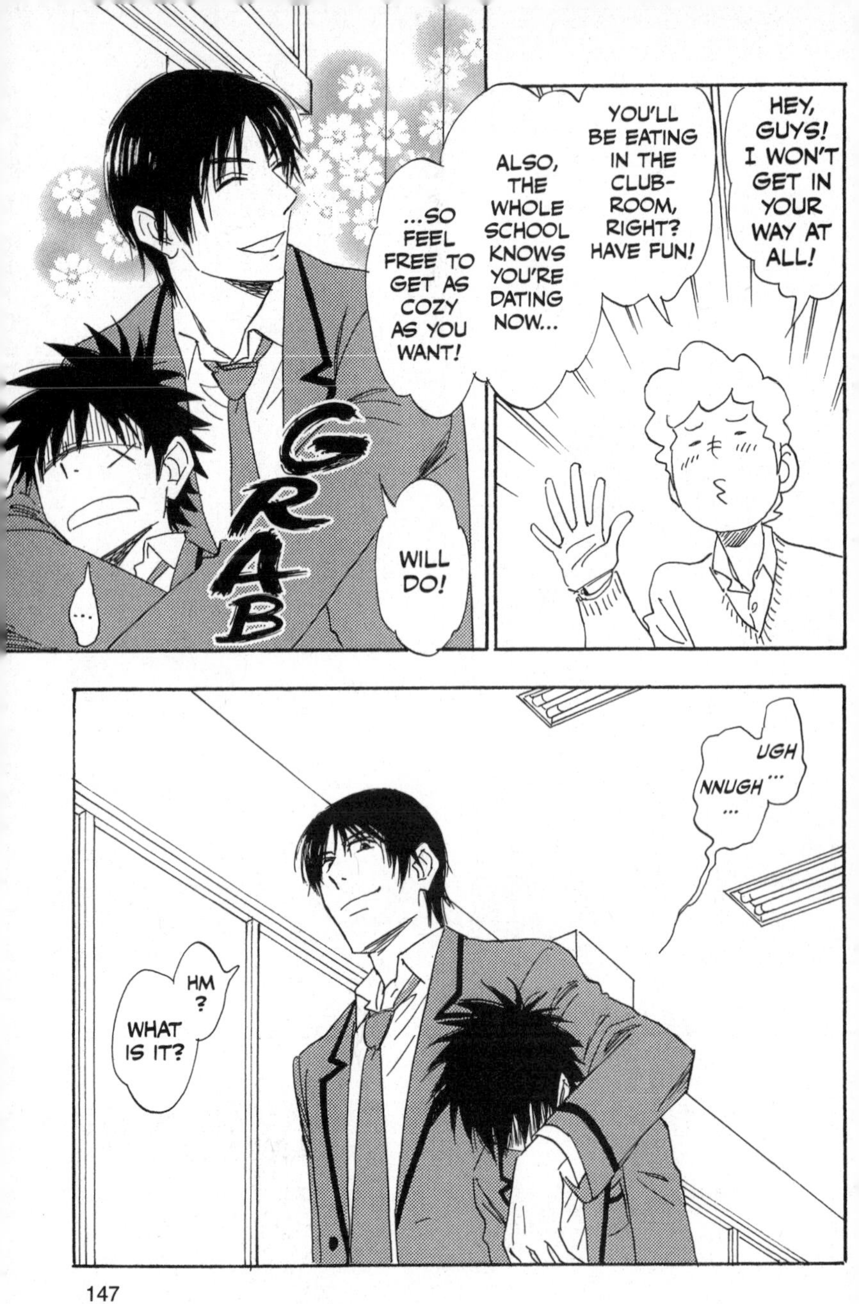
HEY, GUYS! I WON'T GET IN YOUR WAY AT ALL!
YOU'LL BE EATING IN THE CLUB-ROOM, RIGHT? HAVE FUN!
ALSO, THE WHOLE SCHOOL KNOWS YOU'RE DATING NOW...
...SO FEEL FREE TO GET AS COZY AS YOU WANT!
WILL DO!
GRAB
...
UGH... NNUGH...
HM? WHAT IS IT?

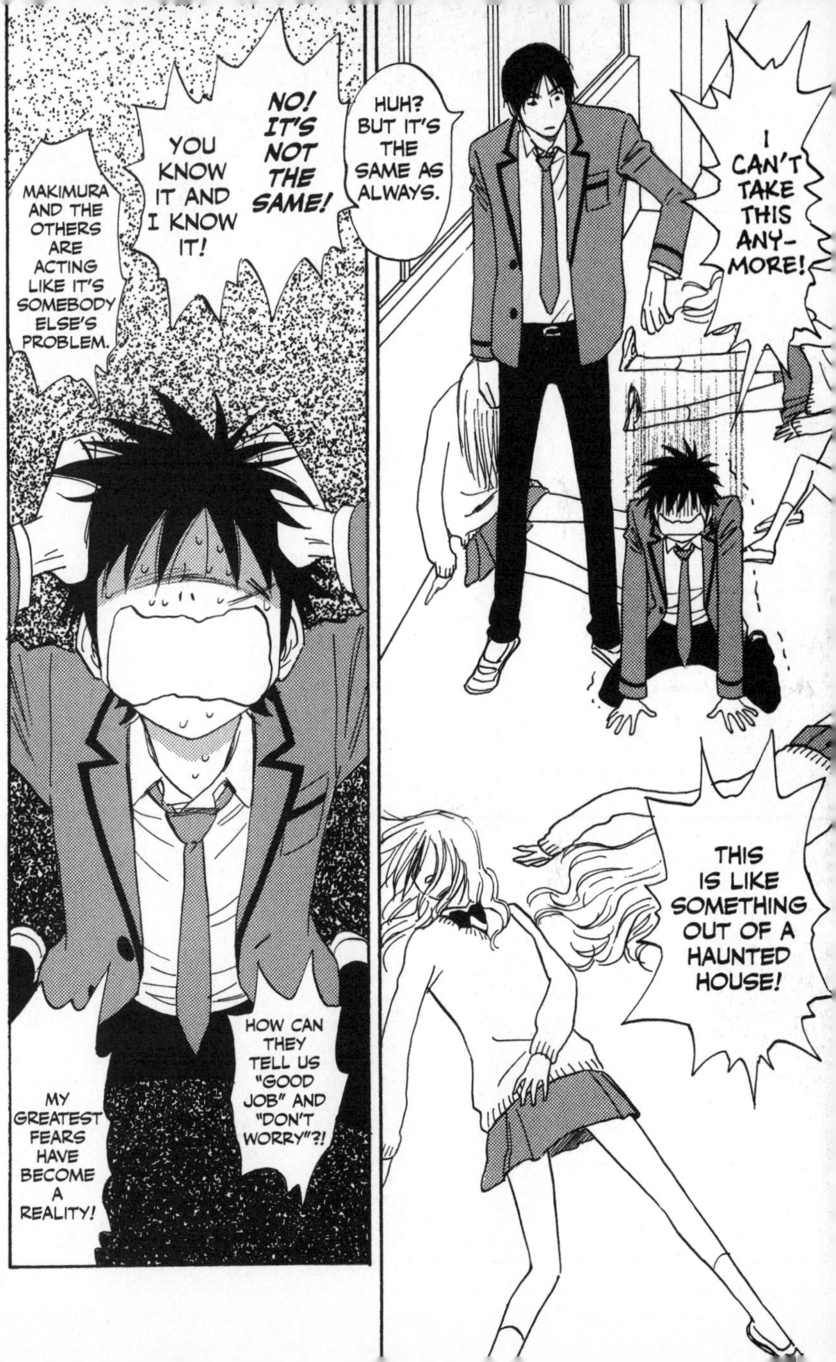
I CAN'T TAKE THIS ANY-MORE!
HUH? BUT IT'S THE SAME AS ALWAYS.
THIS IS LIKE SOMETHING OUT OF A HAUNTED HOUSE!
NO! IT'S NOT THE SAME!
YOU KNOW IT AND I KNOW IT!
MAKIMURA AND THE OTHERS ARE ACTING LIKE IT'S SOMEBODY ELSE'S PROBLEM.
HOW CAN THEY TELL US "GOOD JOB" AND "DON'T WORRY"?!
MY GREATEST FEARS HAVE BECOME A REALITY!

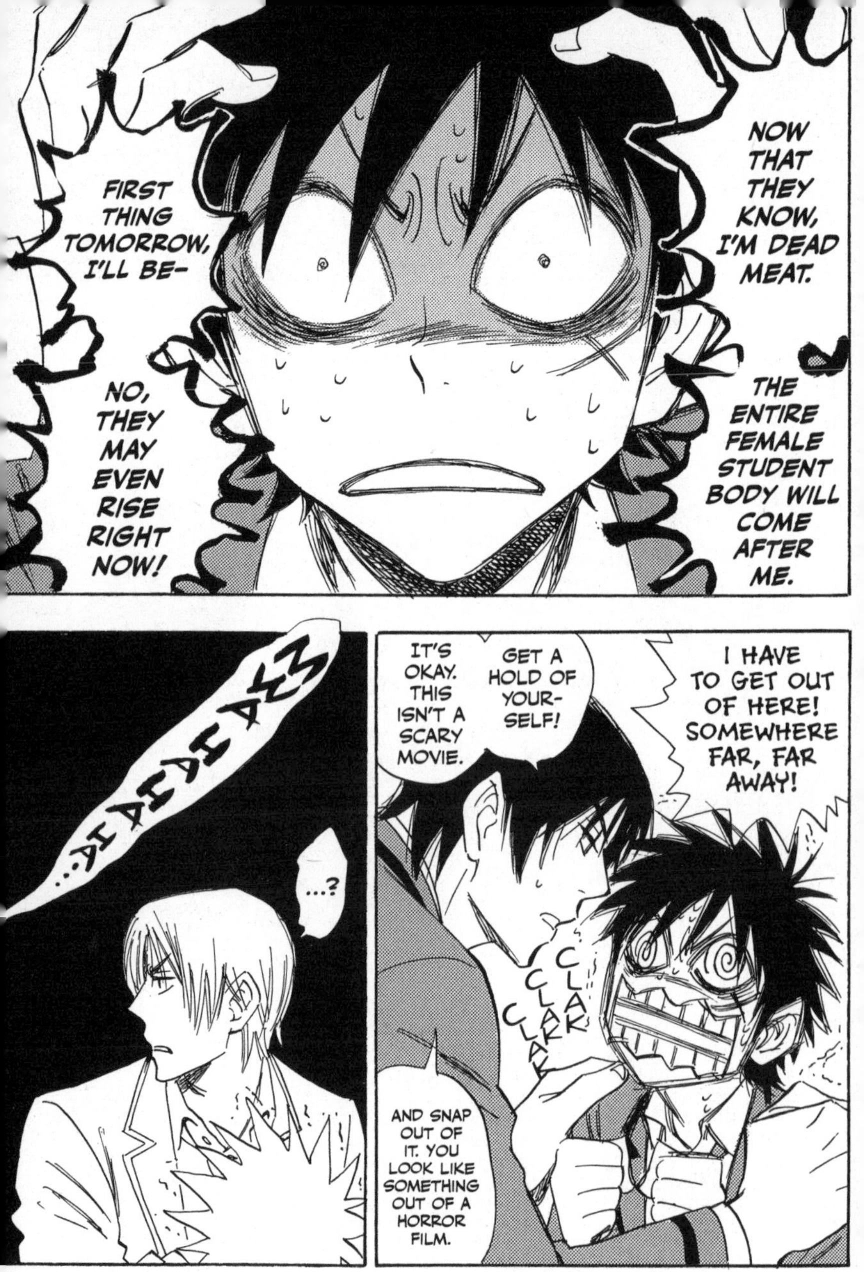
NOW THAT THEY KNOW, I'M DEAD MEAT.
FIRST THING TOMORROW, I'LL BE-
THE ENTIRE FEMALE STUDENT BODY WILL COME AFTER ME.
NO, THEY MAY EVEN RISE RIGHT NOW!
I HAVE TO GET OUT OF HERE! SOMEWHERE FAR, FAR AWAY!
GET A HOLD OF YOURSELF!
IT'S OKAY. THIS ISN'T A SCARY MOVIE.
CLAK CLAK CLAK
AND SNAP OUT OF IT. YOU LOOK LIKE SOMETHING OUT OF A HORROR FILM.
...AIAIAIAEE
...?

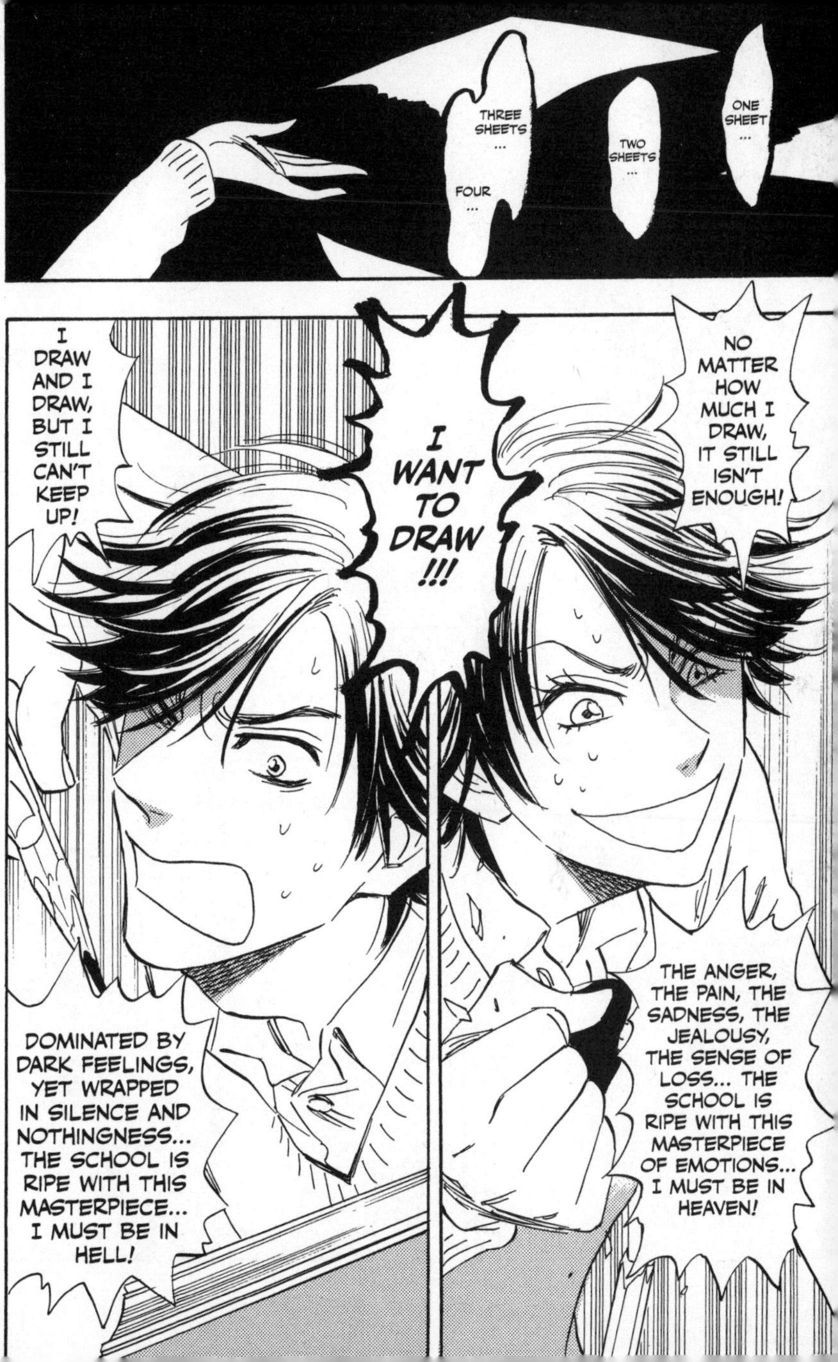
ONE SHEET ...
TWO SHEETS ...
THREE SHEETS ...
FOUR ...
NO MATTER HOW MUCH I DRAW, IT STILL ISN'T ENOUGH!
I WANT TO DRAW !!!
I DRAW AND I DRAW, BUT I STILL CAN'T KEEP UP!
THE ANGER, THE PAIN, THE SADNESS, THE JEALOUSY, THE SENSE OF LOSS... THE SCHOOL IS RIPE WITH THIS MASTERPIECE OF EMOTIONS... I MUST BE IN HEAVEN!
DOMINATED BY DARK FEELINGS, YET WRAPPED IN SILENCE AND NOTHINGNESS... THE SCHOOL IS RIPE WITH THIS MASTERPIECE... I MUST BE IN HELL!

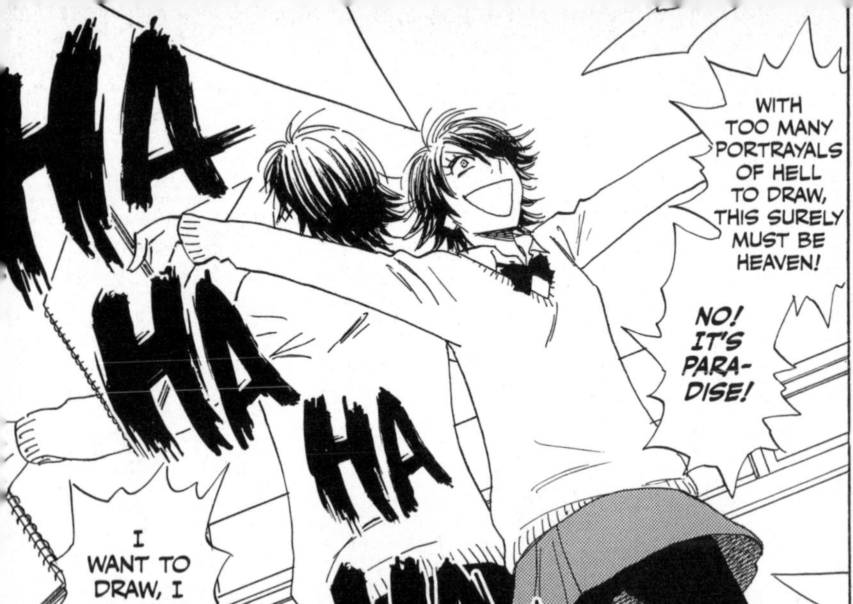
WITH TOO MANY PORTRAYALS OF HELL TO DRAW, THIS SURELY MUST BE HEAVEN!
NO! IT'S PARA-DISE!
HA HA HA HA HA HA HA!
I WANT TO DRAW, I WANT TO DRAW, I WANT TO DRAW!!!

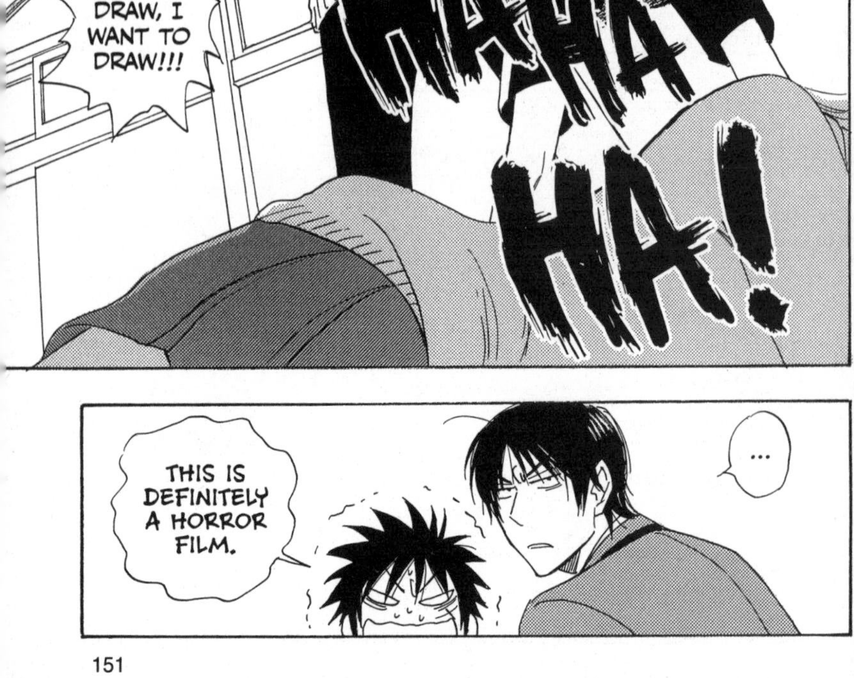
...
THIS IS DEFINITELY A HORROR FILM.

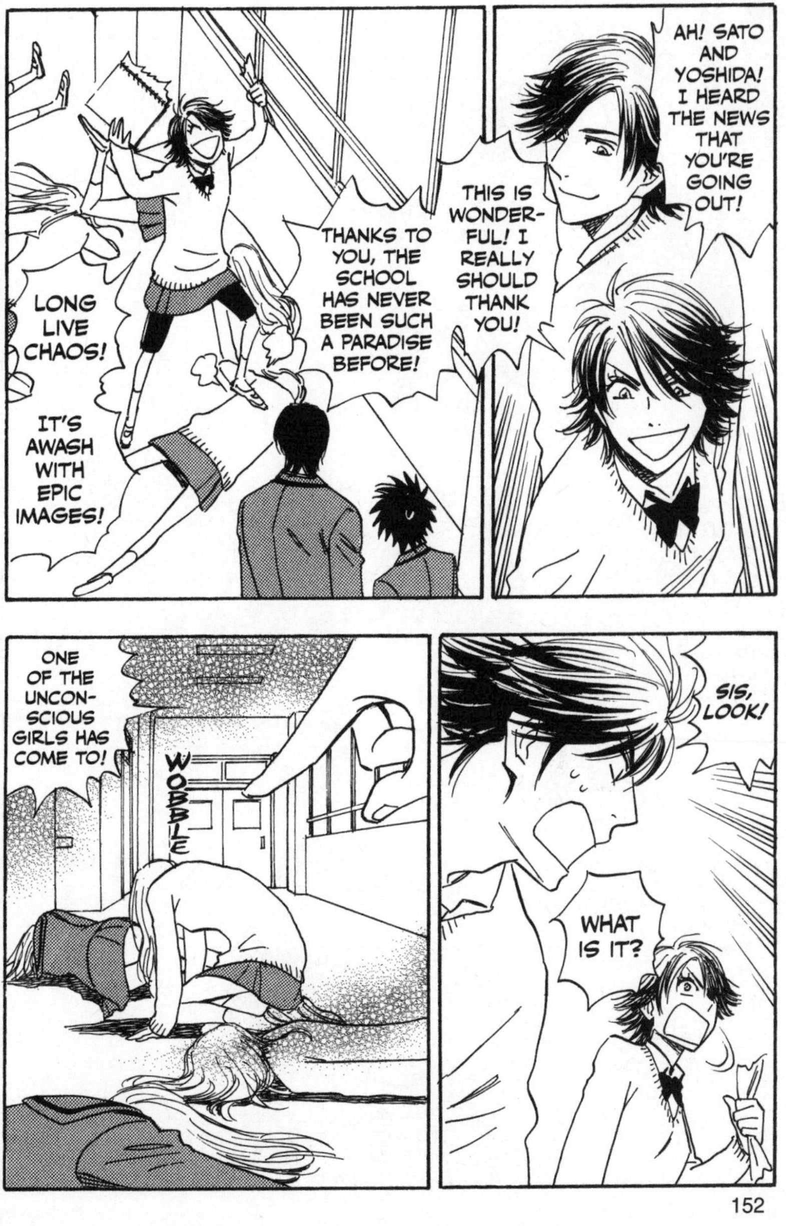
AH! SATO AND YOSHIDA! I HEARD THE NEWS THAT YOU'RE GOING OUT!
THIS IS WONDERFUL! I REALLY SHOULD THANK YOU!
THANKS TO YOU, THE SCHOOL HAS NEVER BEEN SUCH A PARADISE BEFORE!
LONG LIVE CHAOS!
IT'S AWASH WITH EPIC IMAGES!
SIS, LOOK!
WHAT IS IT?
ONE OF THE UNCONSCIOUS GIRLS HAS COME TO!
WOBBLE

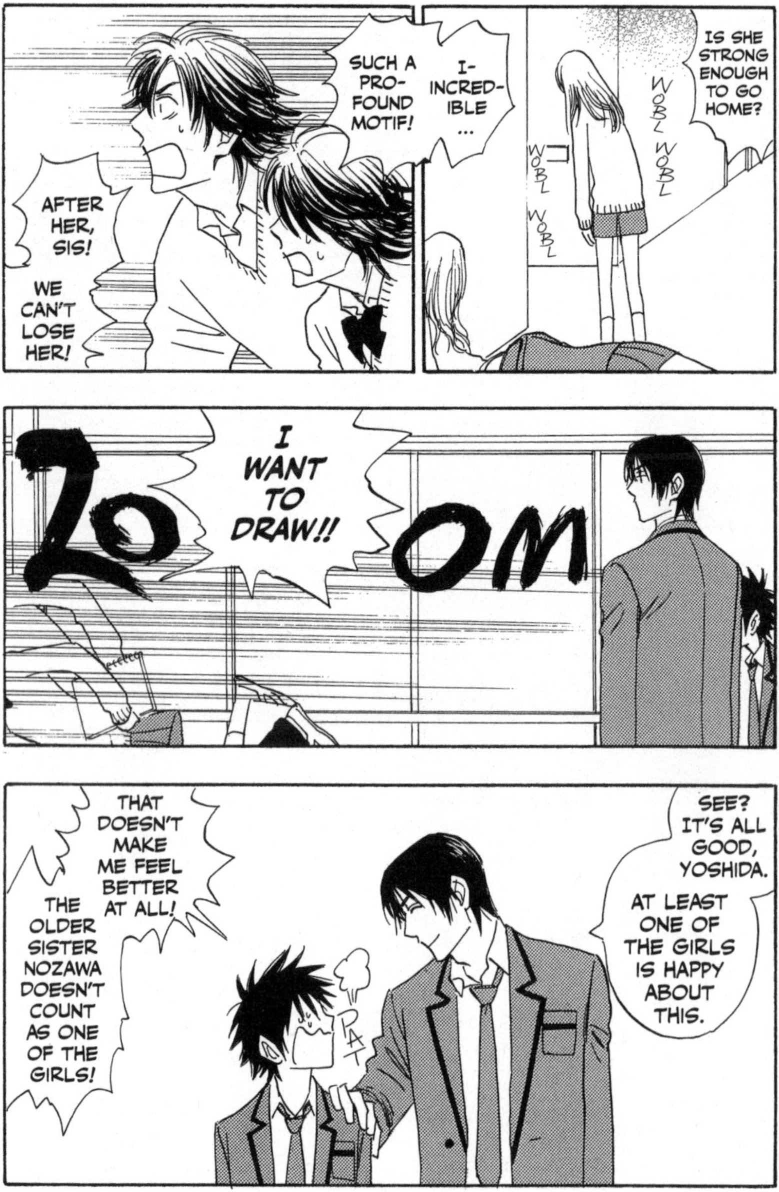
IS SHE STRONG ENOUGH TO GO HOME?
WOBL WOBL
WOBL WOBL
I-INCREDIBLE...
SUCH A PRO-FOUND MOTIF!
AFTER HER, SIS!
WE CAN'T LOSE HER!
I WANT TO DRAW!!
ZOOM
SEE? IT'S ALL GOOD, YOSHIDA.
AT LEAST ONE OF THE GIRLS IS HAPPY ABOUT THIS.
PAT
THAT DOESN'T MAKE ME FEEL BETTER AT ALL!
THE OLDER SISTER NOZAWA DOESN'T COUNT AS ONE OF THE GIRLS!

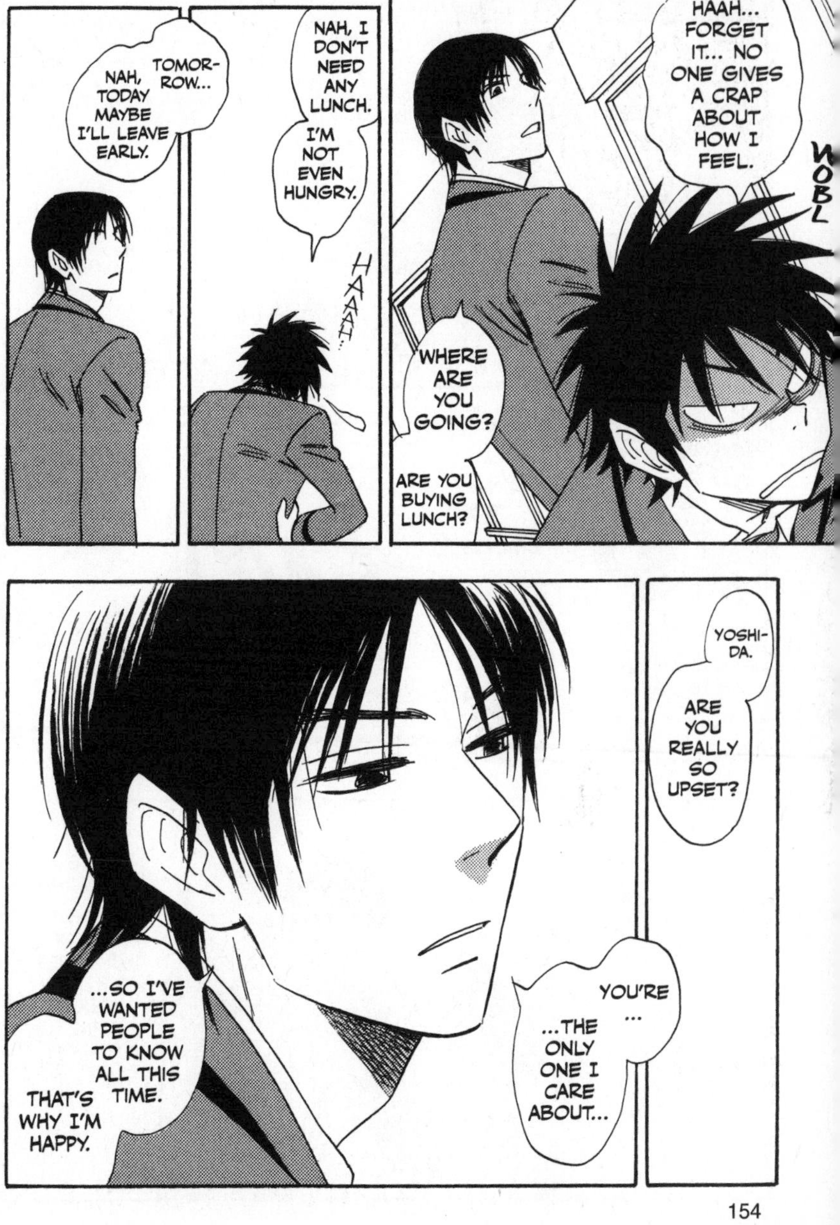
HAAH... FORGET IT... NO ONE GIVES A CRAP ABOUT HOW I FEEL.
WOBL
WHERE ARE YOU GOING?
ARE YOU BUYING LUNCH?
NAH, I DON'T NEED ANY LUNCH.
I'M NOT EVEN HUNGRY.
HAAAH...
TOMORROW...
NAH, TODAY MAYBE I'LL LEAVE EARLY.
YOSHIDA.
ARE YOU REALLY SO UPSET?
YOU'RE ...
...THE ONLY ONE I CARE ABOUT...
...SO I'VE WANTED PEOPLE TO KNOW ALL THIS TIME.
THAT'S WHY I'M HAPPY.

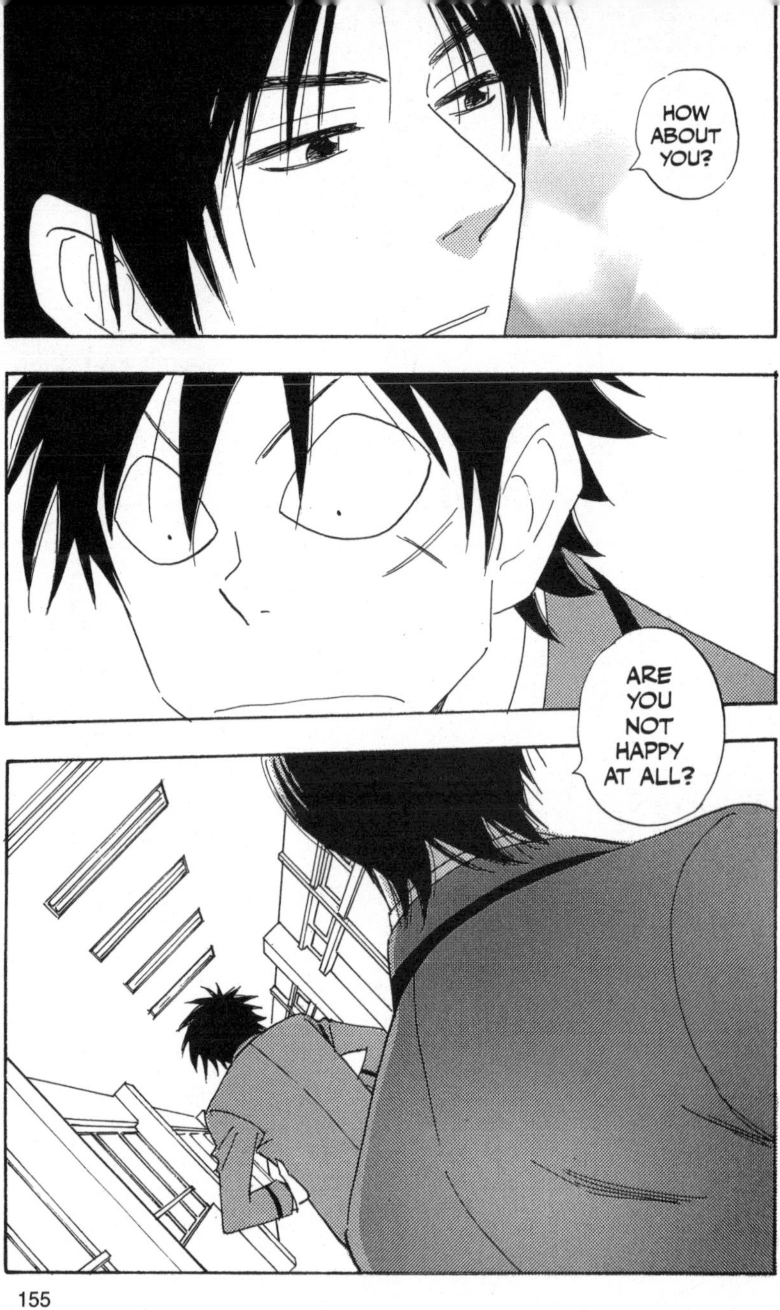
HOW ABOUT YOU?
ARE YOU NOT HAPPY AT ALL?

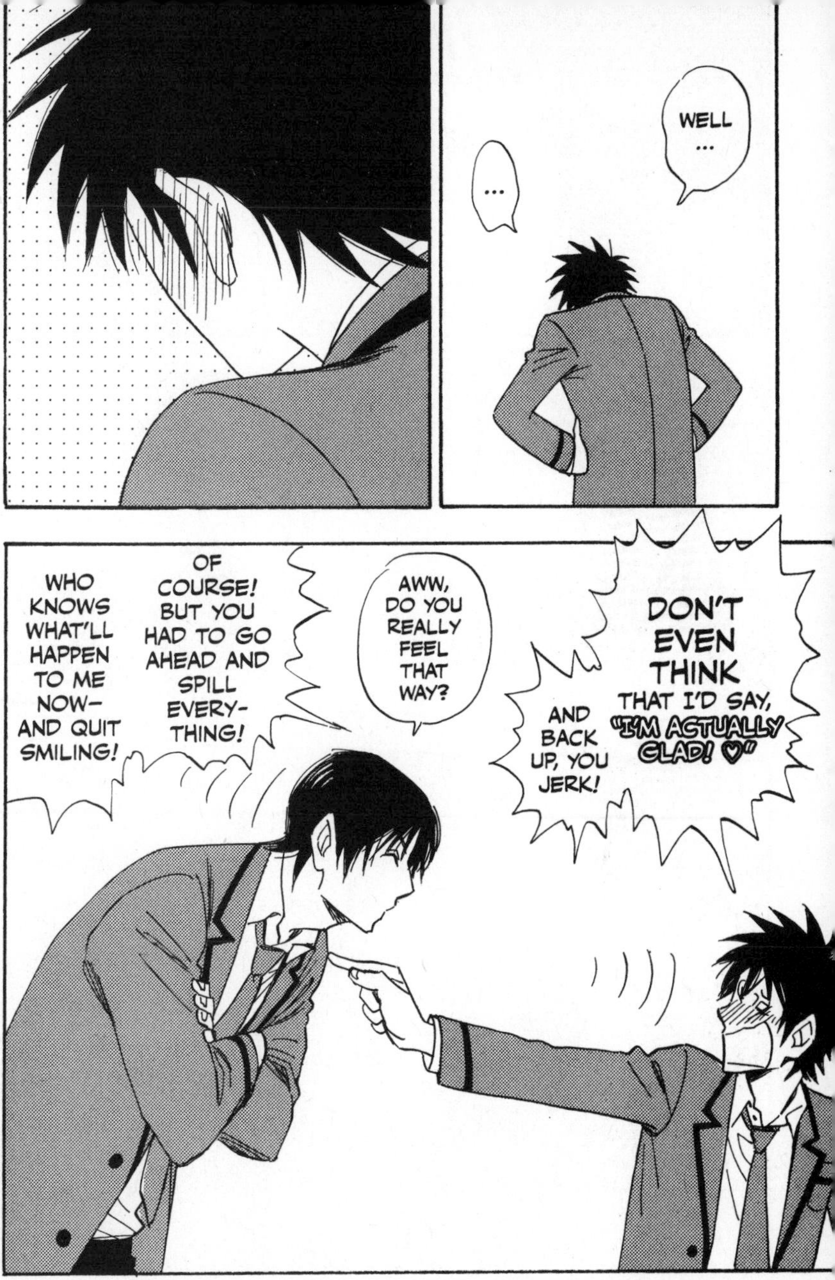
WELL ...
...
DON'T EVEN THINK THAT I'D SAY, "I'M ACTUALLY GLAD! ♡"
AND BACK UP, YOU JERK!
AWW, DO YOU REALLY FEEL THAT WAY?
OF COURSE! BUT YOU HAD TO GO AHEAD AND SPILL EVERY-THING!
WHO KNOWS WHAT'LL HAPPEN TO ME NOW— AND QUIT SMILING!

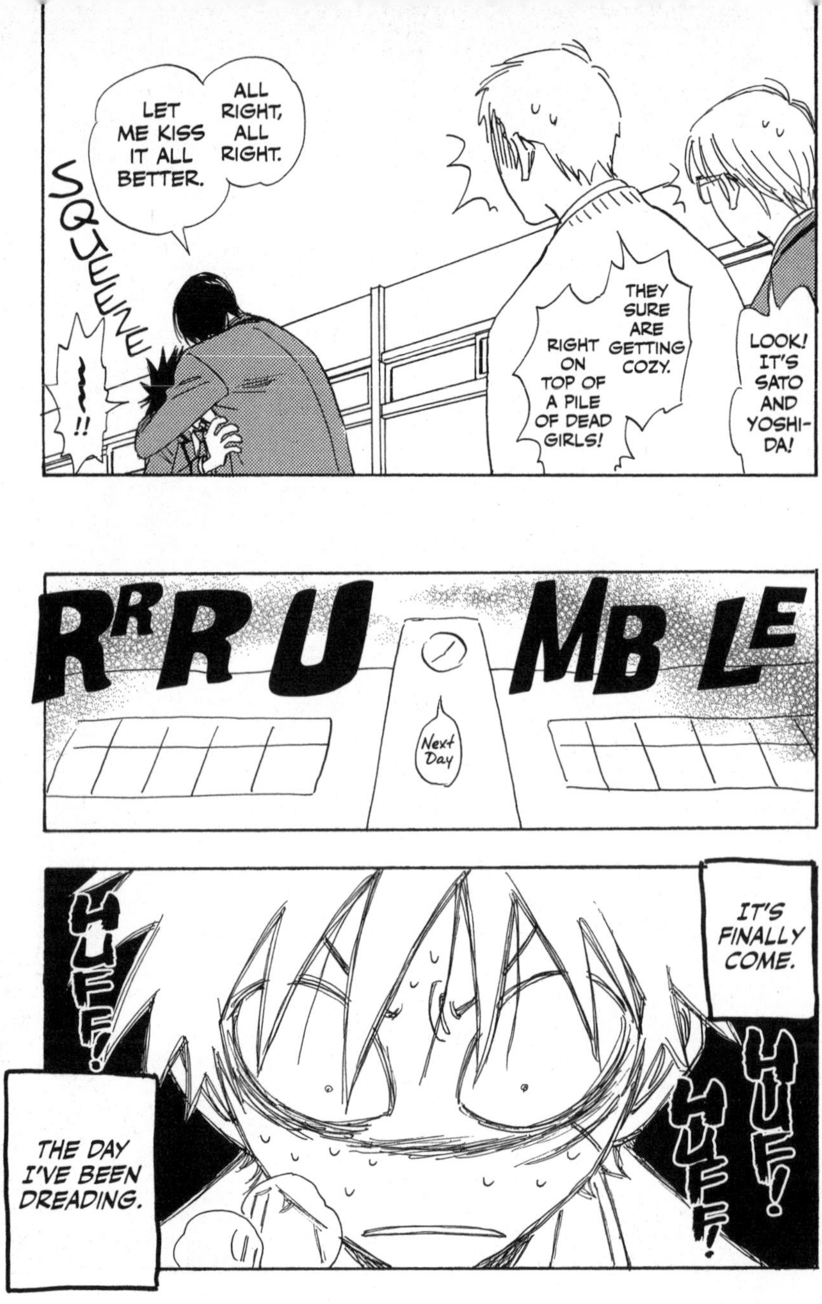
LOOK! IT'S SATO AND YOSHIDA!
THEY SURE ARE GETTING COZY.
RIGHT ON TOP OF A PILE OF DEAD GIRLS!
ALL RIGHT, ALL RIGHT.
LET ME KISS IT ALL BETTER.
SQUEEEEZE
~~!!
RRRUMBLE
Next Day
IT'S FINALLY COME.
HUFF! HUFF!
HUFF!
THE DAY I'VE BEEN DREADING.

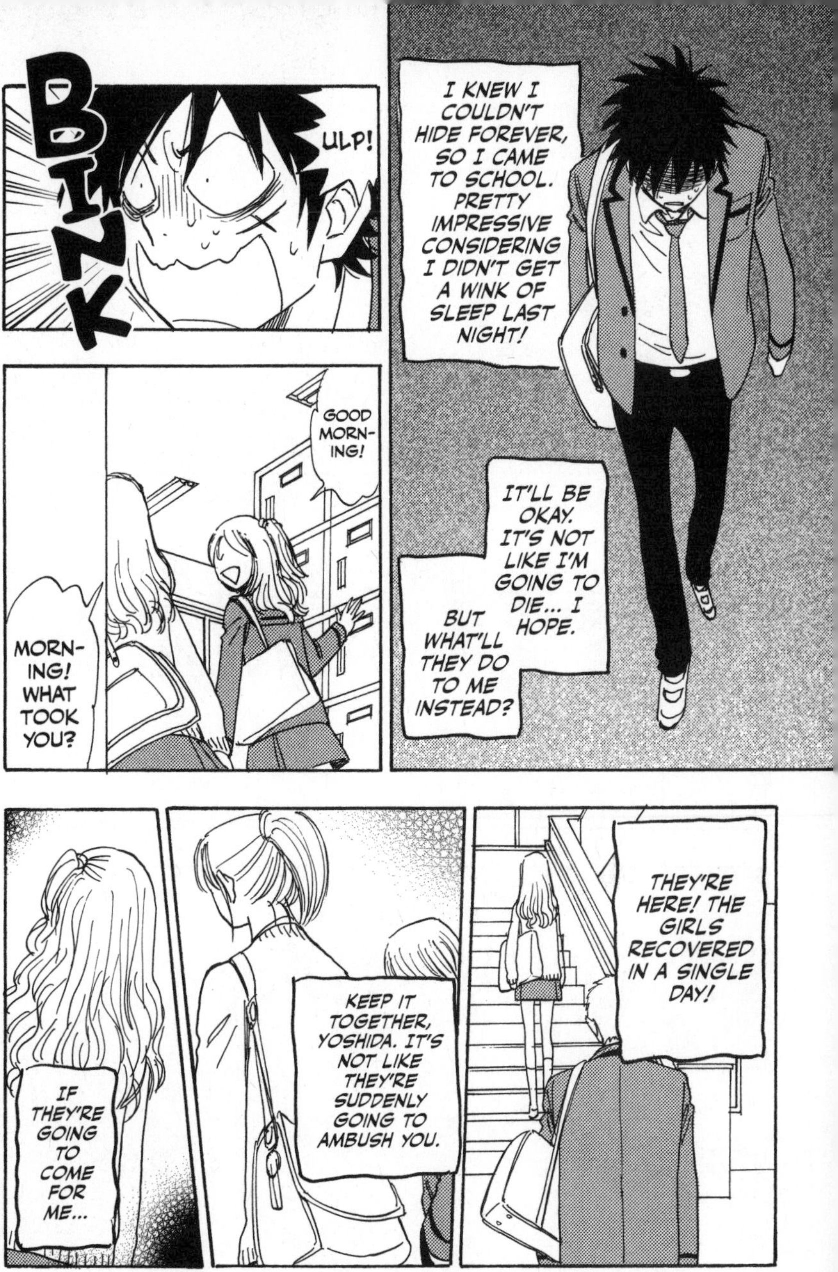
I KNEW I COULDN'T HIDE FOREVER, SO I CAME TO SCHOOL. PRETTY IMPRESSIVE CONSIDERING I DIDN'T GET A WINK OF SLEEP LAST NIGHT!
IT'LL BE OKAY. IT'S NOT LIKE I'M GOING TO DIE... I HOPE.
BUT WHAT'LL THEY DO TO ME INSTEAD?
ULP!
BINK
GOOD MORNING!
MORNING! WHAT TOOK YOU?
THEY'RE HERE! THE GIRLS RECOVERED IN A SINGLE DAY!
KEEP IT TOGETHER, YOSHIDA. IT'S NOT LIKE THEY'RE SUDDENLY GOING TO AMBUSH YOU.
IF THEY'RE GOING TO COME FOR ME...

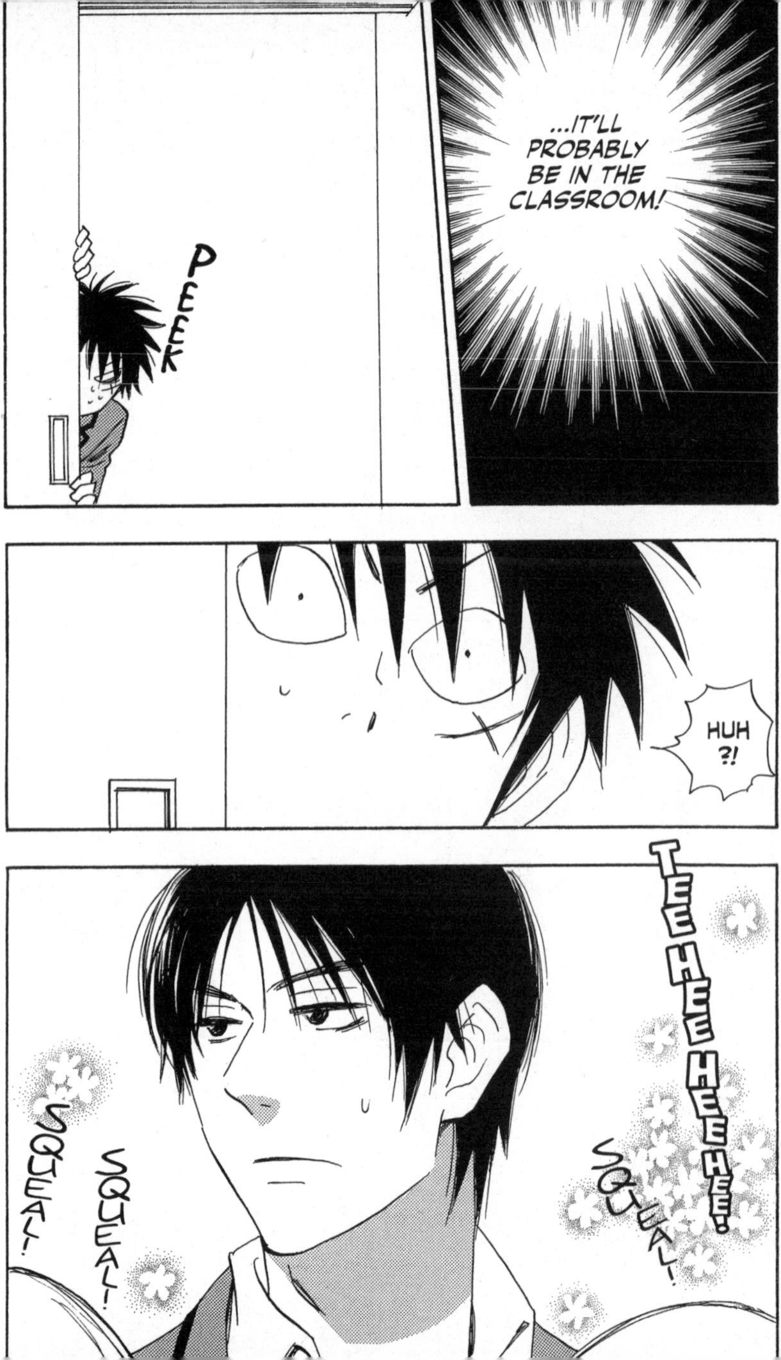
...IT'LL PROBABLY BE IN THE CLASSROOM!
PEEEK
HUH?!
TEE HEE HEE HEE!
SQUEAL!
SQUEAL!
SQUEAL!

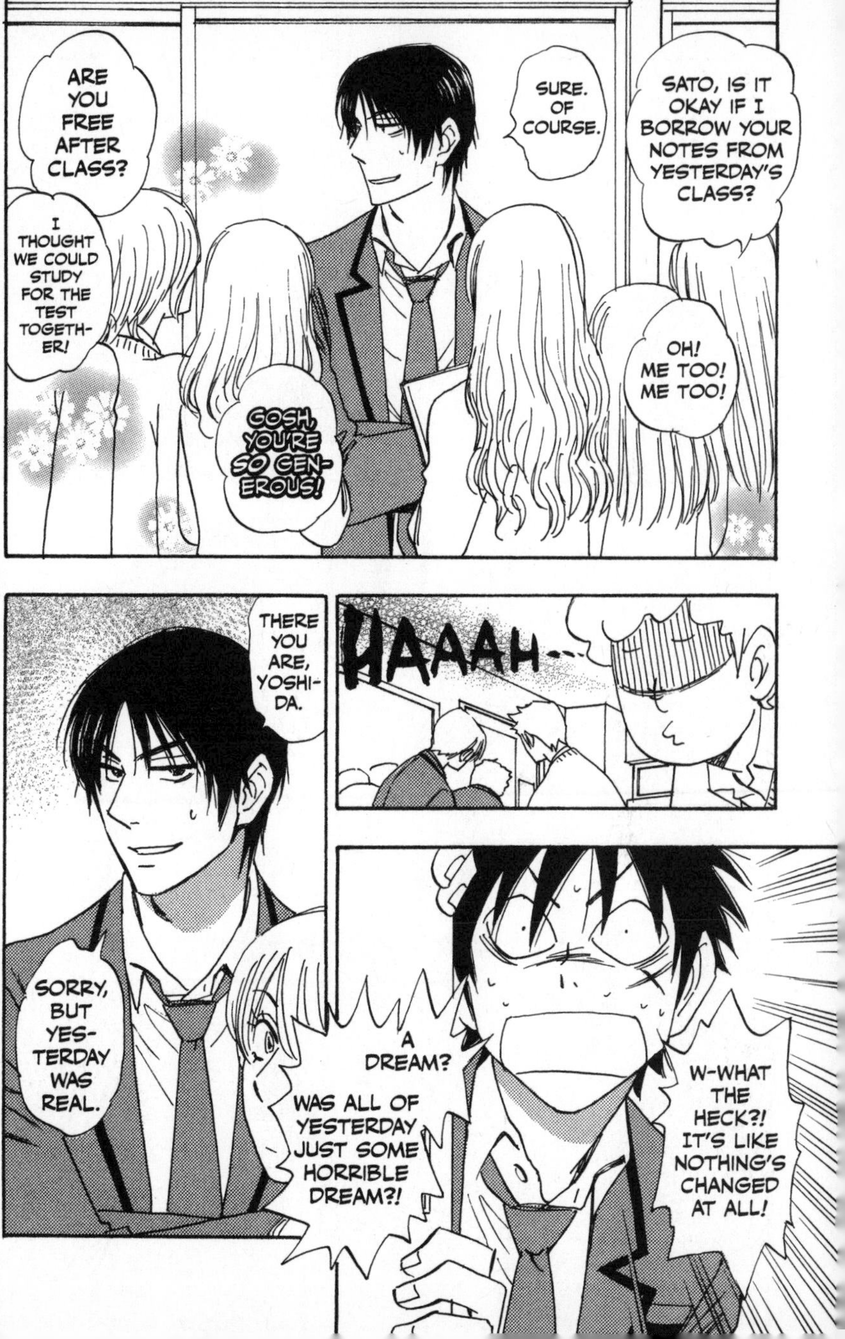
SATO, IS IT OKAY IF I BORROW YOUR NOTES FROM YESTERDAY'S CLASS?
SURE. OF COURSE.
ARE YOU FREE AFTER CLASS?
I THOUGHT WE COULD STUDY FOR THE TEST TOGETHER!
OH! ME TOO! ME TOO!
GOSH, YOU'RE SO GENEROUS!
HAAAH...
W-WHAT THE HECK?! IT'S LIKE NOTHING'S CHANGED AT ALL!
A DREAM?
WAS ALL OF YESTERDAY JUST SOME HORRIBLE DREAM?!
THERE YOU ARE, YOSHIDA.
SORRY, BUT YESTERDAY WAS REAL.

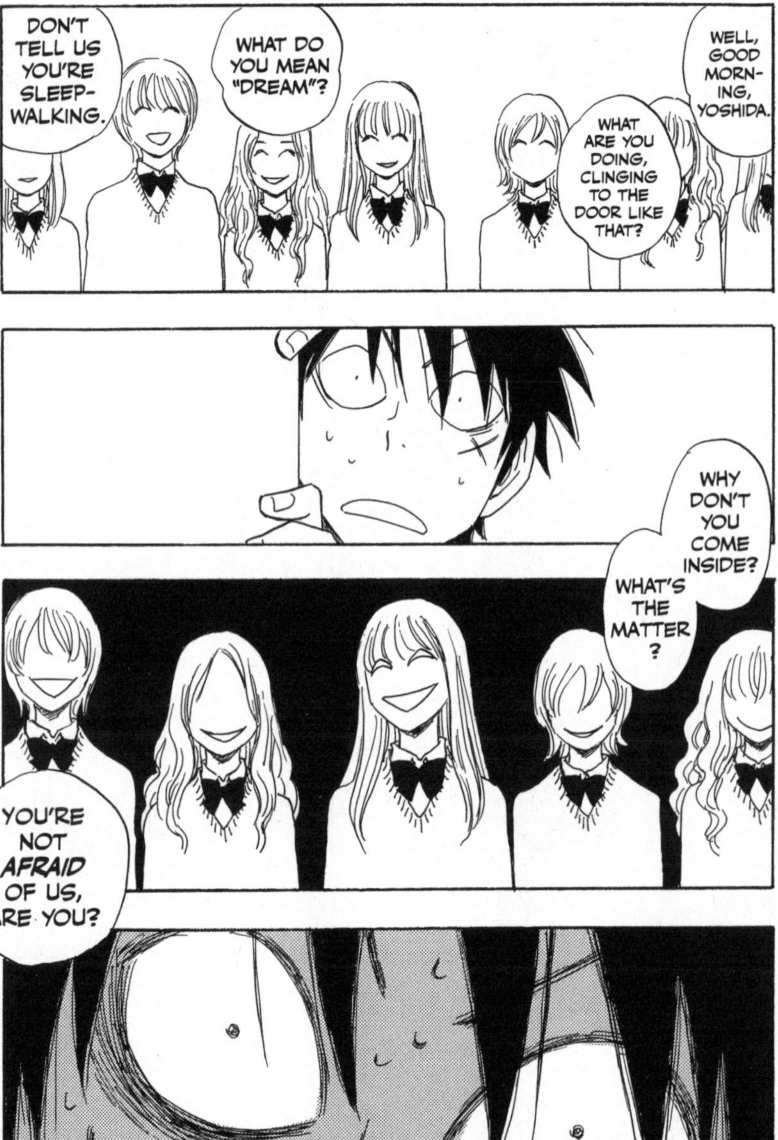
WELL, GOOD MORNING, YOSHIDA.
WHAT ARE YOU DOING, CLINGING TO THE DOOR LIKE THAT?
WHAT DO YOU MEAN "DREAM"?
DON'T TELL US YOU'RE SLEEP-WALKING.
WHY DON'T YOU COME INSIDE?
WHAT'S THE MATTER?
YOU'RE NOT *AFRAID* OF US, ARE YOU?

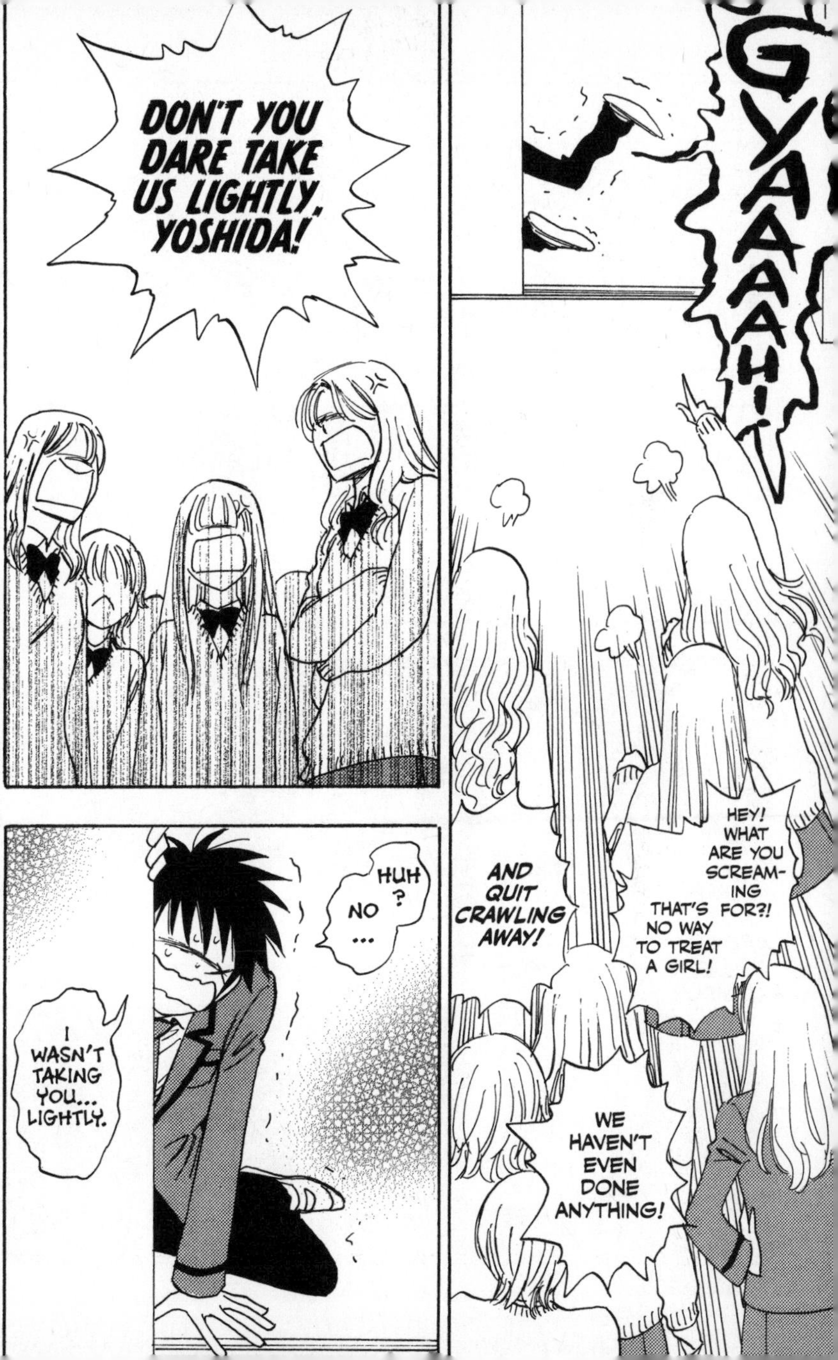
GYAAAAH!
HEY! WHAT ARE YOU SCREAMING FOR?!
THAT'S NO WAY TO TREAT A GIRL!
AND QUIT CRAWLING AWAY!
WE HAVEN'T EVEN DONE ANYTHING!
DON'T YOU DARE TAKE US LIGHTLY, YOSHIDA!
HUH? NO...
I WASN'T TAKING YOU... LIGHTLY.

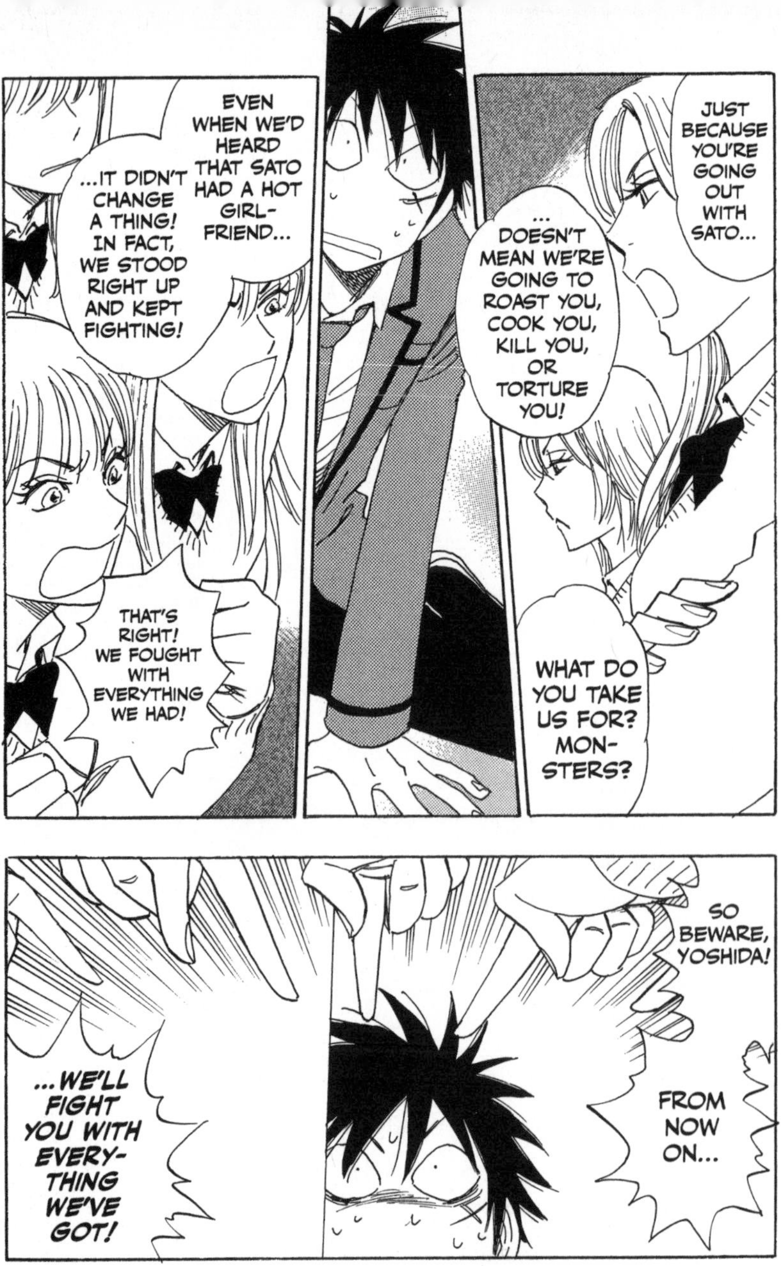
JUST BECAUSE YOU'RE GOING OUT WITH SATO...
...DOESN'T MEAN WE'RE GOING TO ROAST YOU, COOK YOU, KILL YOU, OR TORTURE YOU!
WHAT DO YOU TAKE US FOR? MONSTERS?
EVEN WHEN WE'D HEARD THAT SATO HAD A HOT GIRLFRIEND...
...IT DIDN'T CHANGE A THING! IN FACT, WE STOOD RIGHT UP AND KEPT FIGHTING!
THAT'S RIGHT! WE FOUGHT WITH EVERYTHING WE HAD!
SO BEWARE, YOSHIDA!
FROM NOW ON...
...WE'LL FIGHT YOU WITH EVERYTHING WE'VE GOT!

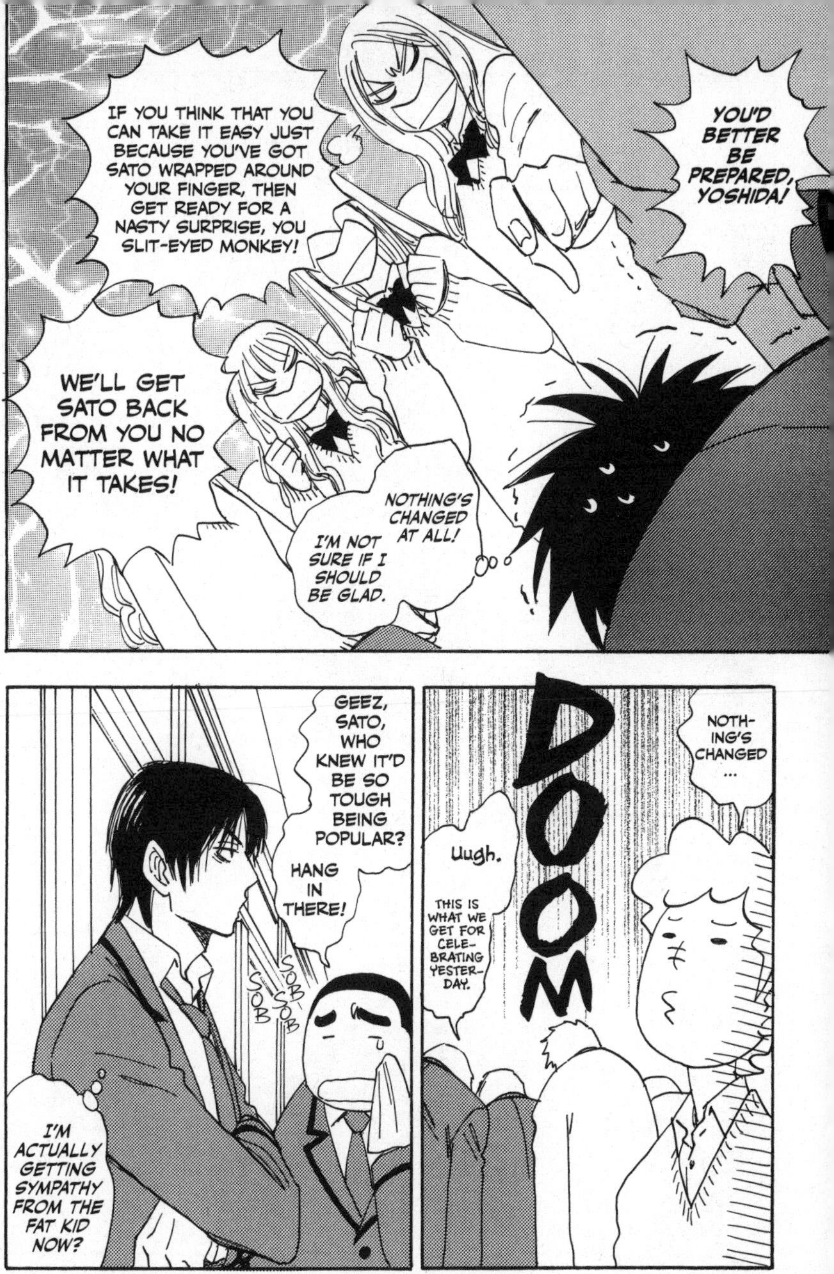
YOU'D BETTER BE PREPARED, YOSHIDA!
IF YOU THINK THAT YOU CAN TAKE IT EASY JUST BECAUSE YOU'VE GOT SATO WRAPPED AROUND YOUR FINGER, THEN GET READY FOR A NASTY SURPRISE, YOU SLIT-EYED MONKEY!
WE'LL GET SATO BACK FROM YOU NO MATTER WHAT IT TAKES!
NOTHING'S CHANGED AT ALL!
I'M NOT SURE IF I SHOULD BE GLAD.
NOTH-ING'S CHANGED ...
DOOM
Uugh.
THIS IS WHAT WE GET FOR CELE-BRATING YESTER-DAY.
GEEZ, SATO, WHO KNEW IT'D BE SO TOUGH BEING POPULAR?
HANG IN THERE!
SOB SOB SOB
I'M ACTUALLY GETTING SYMPATHY FROM THE FAT KID NOW?

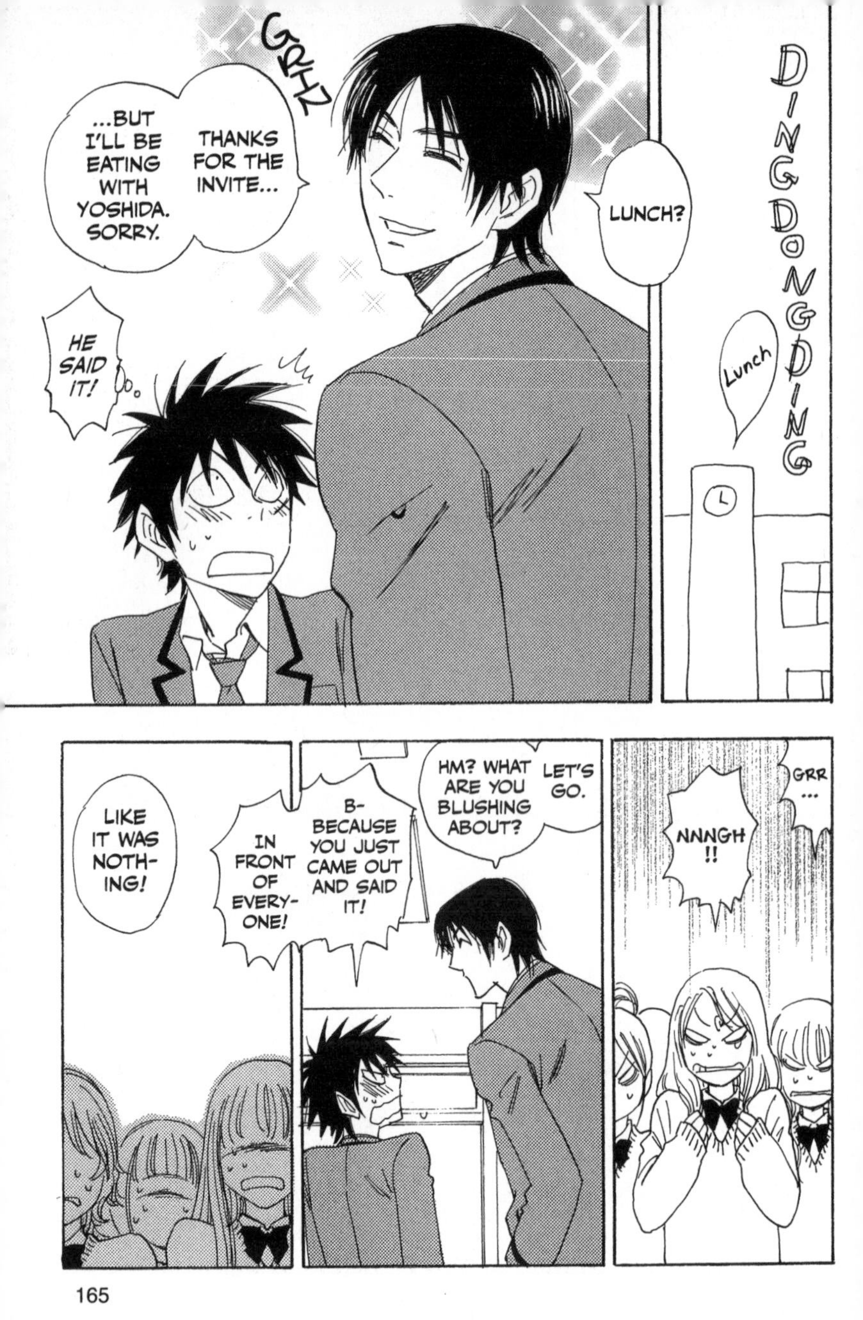
DINGDONGDING
Lunch
LUNCH?
THANKS FOR THE INVITE...
...BUT I'LL BE EATING WITH YOSHIDA. SORRY.
HE SAID IT!
GRR...
NNNGH!!
LET'S GO.
HM? WHAT ARE YOU BLUSHING ABOUT?
B-BECAUSE YOU JUST CAME OUT AND SAID IT!
IN FRONT OF EVERYONE!
LIKE IT WAS NOTHING!

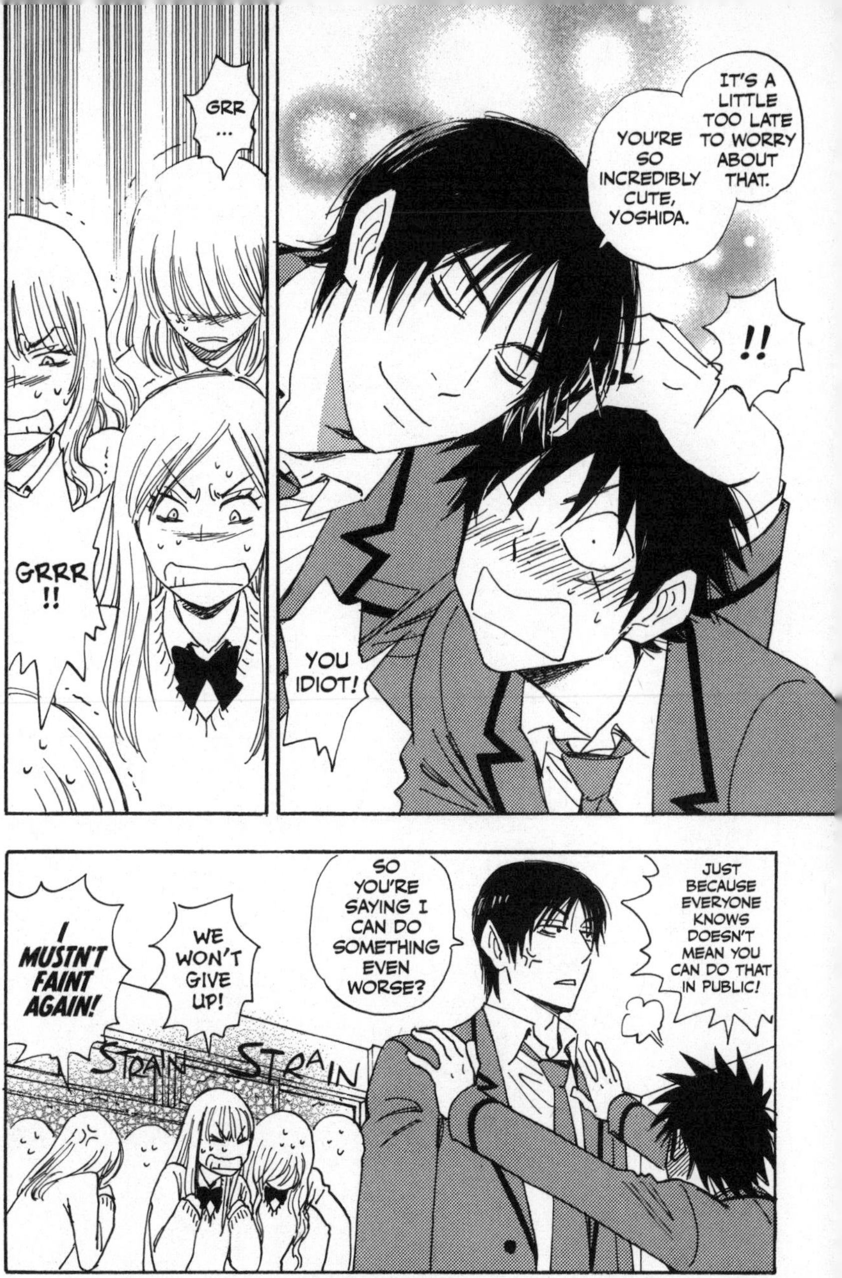
IT'S A LITTLE TOO LATE TO WORRY ABOUT THAT.
YOU'RE SO INCREDIBLY CUTE, YOSHIDA.
!!
YOU IDIOT!
GRR ...
GRRR !!
JUST BECAUSE EVERYONE KNOWS DOESN'T MEAN YOU CAN DO THAT IN PUBLIC!
SO YOU'RE SAYING I CAN DO SOMETHING EVEN WORSE?
WE WON'T GIVE UP!
I MUSTN'T FAINT AGAIN!
STRAIN STRAIN

ACT. 29 / END

??!!

☆

AZUMA & NISHIDA

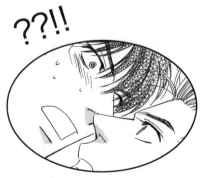

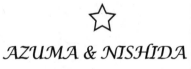

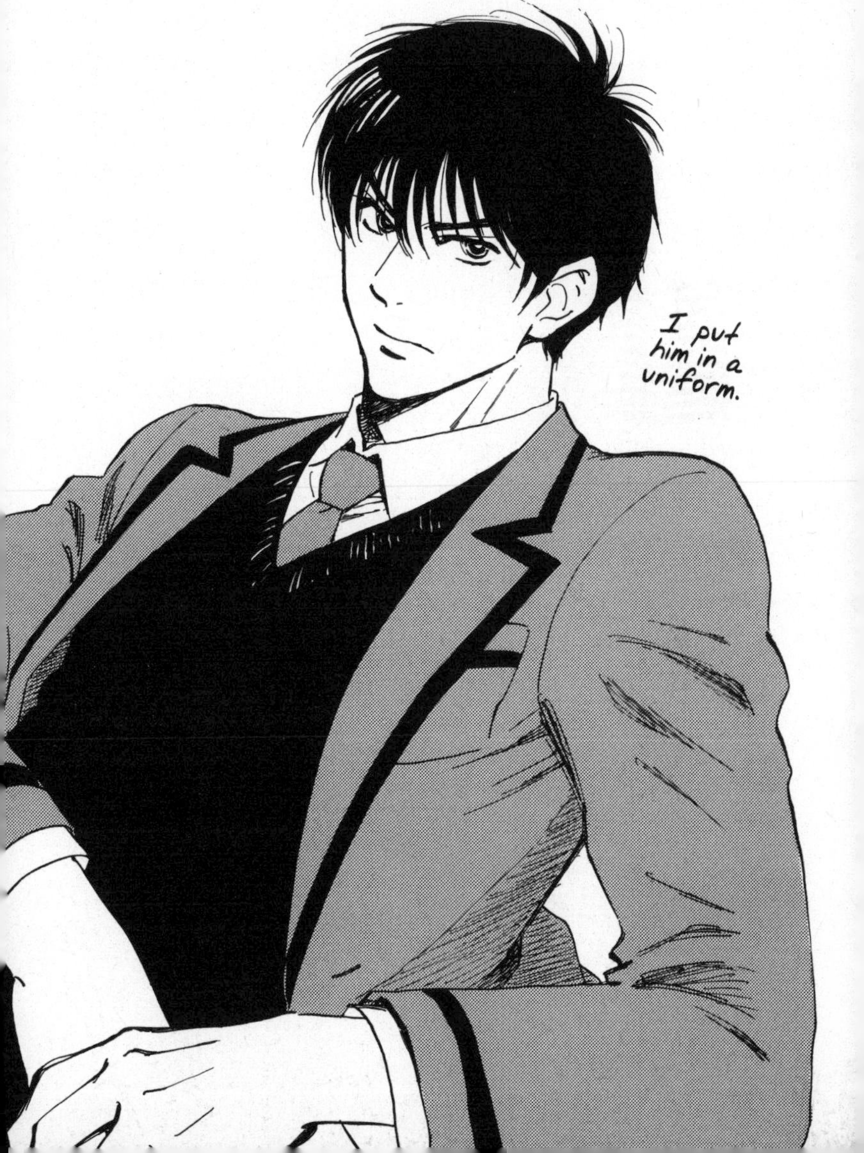
I put him in a uniform.

Another new friend has come to the school. Hope you like him. Then something sorta big but sorta not so big happened... or something. But either way, here we are at Volume 7. Thank you all so very much! I hope you read the next volume, assuming there is one! Until then!

Suzuki Tanaka

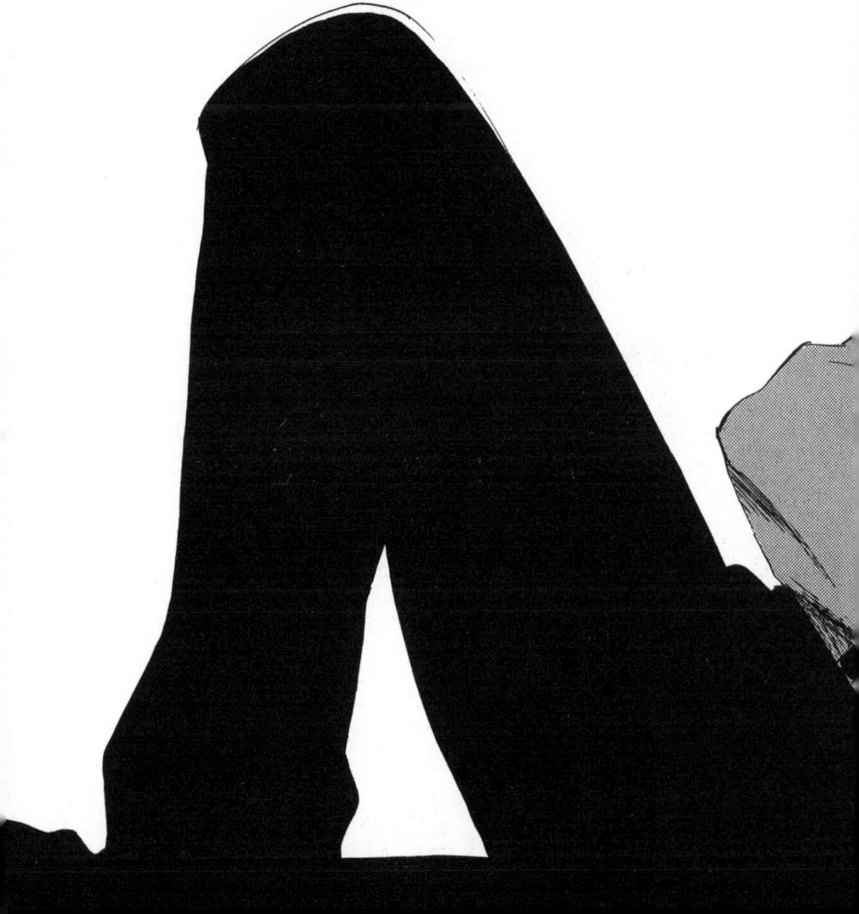

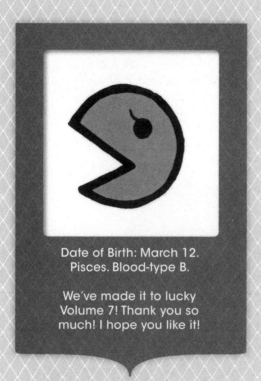

Date of Birth: March 12.
Pisces. Blood-type B.

We've made it to lucky
Volume 7! Thank you so
much! I hope you like it!

About the Author

Known for her engaging stories
and characters drawn with strong
lines, **Suzuki Tanaka** has garnered
plenty of attention for her latest hit,
His Favorite. After taking first place in
the 2009 Boys Love watch list book
Kono BL ga Yabai! 2009, the series
exploded in popularity and led to the
reprint of her earlier work, *Menkui*.

His Favorite
Volume 7
SuBLime Manga Edition

Story and Art by **Suzuki Tanaka**

Translation—**Ivana Bloom**
Touch-up Art and Lettering—**Annaliese Christman**
Cover and Graphic Design—**Fawn Lau**
Editor—**Alexis Kirsch**

Aitsu no Daihonmei ⑦ © 2014 Suzuki Tanaka
Originally published in Japan in 2014 by Libre Publishing Co.,
Ltd. Tokyo.
English translation rights arranged with Libre Publishing Co.,
Ltd. Tokyo.

Printed in the U.S.A.

Published by SuBLime Manga
P.O. Box 77010
San Francisco, CA 94107

10 9 8 7 6 5 4 3 2 1
First printing, September 2014

PARENTAL ADVISORY
HIS FAVORITE is rated T+ for Older Teen and
is recommended for ages 16 and up. This
OLDER TEEN   volume contains suggestive themes.

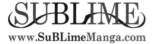
www.SuBLimeManga.com

For more information

on all our products, along with the most up-to-date news on releases, series announcements, and contests, please visit us at:

 SuBLimeManga.com

 twitter.com/**SuBLimeManga**

 facebook.com/**SuBLimeManga**

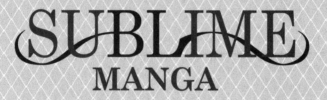

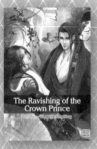
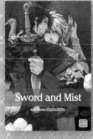
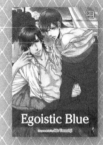
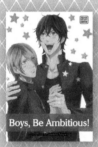
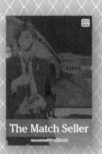
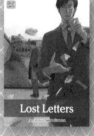

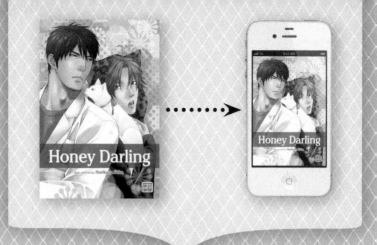

Downloading is as easy as:

1

2

3

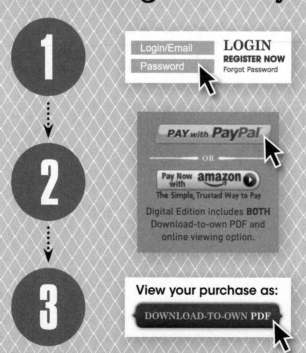

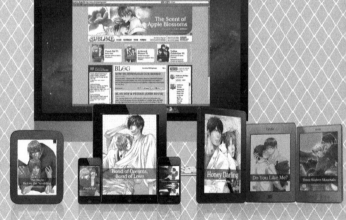
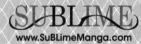

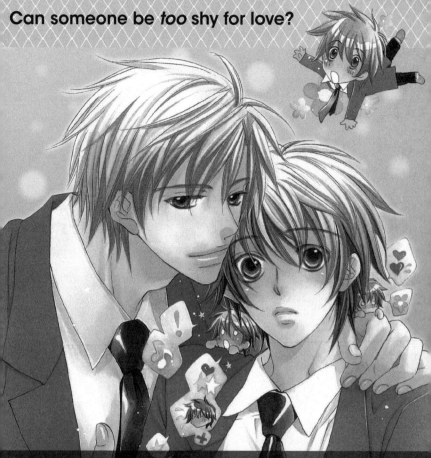

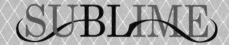

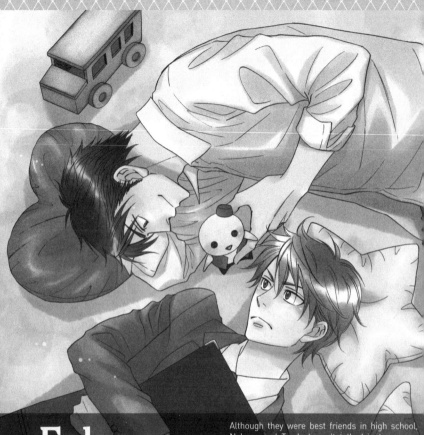

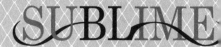

A sweet story of not-so-unrequited love.

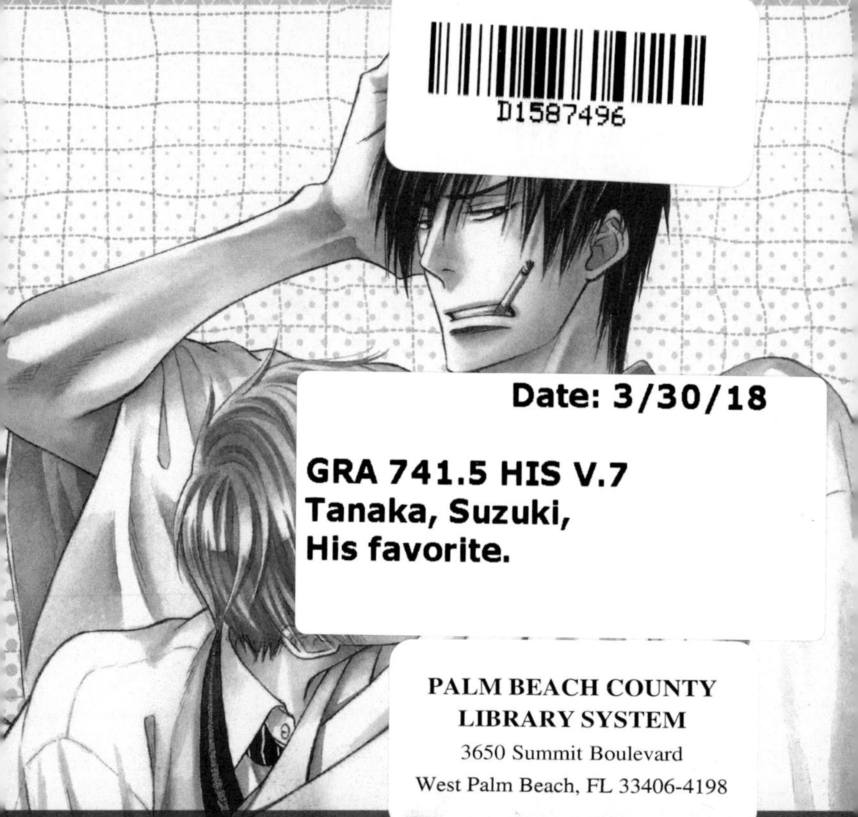

Bond of Dreams, Bond of Love

Story & Art by Yaya SAKURAGI

High school student Ao has been dreaming about his longtime neighbor Ryomei, a priest at the local Shinto shrine. A little freaked out—and a lot excited—at the prospect of having a relationship with Ryomei, Ao gathers up his courage, confesses his feelings...and gets turned down flat. Luckily, Ao's not the kind to give up easily. Thanks to some creative persistence (and Ryomei's weakening resolve), he finally gets a kiss. But one single kiss won't satisfy him for long!

M MATURE

On sale now at
SuBLimeManga.com
Also available at your local bookstore or comic book store.

SUBLIME

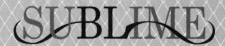